HIDDEN IN HISTORICISM

Hidden in Historicism considers how the nineteenth-century philosophy of historicism depicts three "forgotten time regimes": a time of rise and fall, an ambiguous time of synchronicity of the non-synchronous, and a time in which decisive moments dominate.

Before the eighteenth century, time was past-oriented. This inversed in the Enlightenment, when the future became dominating. Today, this time of progress continues to be embraced as a "time of the modern". Yet, inequality, increasing violence, epidemics, pandemics and climate change lead to doubts over a bright future. In this book, Harry Jansen moves away from the heritage of Reinhart Koselleck and his single time of the modern towards a historicist, threefold temporal approach to history writing. In the time regime of the twenty-first century past, present and future coexist. It is a heterogeneous time that takes on the three forms of historicism. Jansen's study shows how all three times exist together in current historiography and contribute to a better understanding of the world today.

Based on the idea that an incarnated time rules everything that happens in reality, the book offers a fresh perspective on the ongoing discussion about time and time regimes in contemporary philosophy and theory of history for students and scholars, both time specialists and the non-specialist.

Until his retirement, **Harry Jansen** lectured philosophy of history at Radboud University Nijmegen.

HIDDEN IN HISTORICISM

Time Regimes since 1700

Harry Jansen

LONDON AND NEW YORK

First published 2020
by Routledge
2 Park Square, Milton Park, Abingdon, Oxon OX14 4RN

and by Routledge
52 Vanderbilt Avenue, New York, NY 10017

Routledge is an imprint of the Taylor & Francis Group, an informa business

© 2020 Harry Jansen

The right of Harry Jansen to be identified as author of this work has been asserted by him in accordance with sections 77 and 78 of the Copyright, Designs and Patents Act 1988.

All rights reserved. No part of this book may be reprinted or reproduced or utilised in any form or by any electronic, mechanical, or other means, now known or hereafter invented, including photocopying and recording, or in any information storage or retrieval system, without permission in writing from the publishers.

Trademark notice: Product or corporate names may be trademarks or registered trademarks, and are used only for identification and explanation without intent to infringe.

British Library Cataloguing-in-Publication Data
A catalogue record for this book is available from the British Library

Library of Congress Cataloging-in-Publication Data
A catalog record for this book has been requested

ISBN: 978-0-367-42101-4 (hbk)
ISBN: 978-0-367-42100-7 (pbk)
ISBN: 978-0-367-82179-1 (ebk)

Typeset in Bembo
by Apex CoVantage, LLC

The time is out of joint

—William Shakespeare,
Hamlet 1, verse 188–189.

CONTENTS

List of illustrations ix
Preface x

1 Introduction 1

PART 1
In search of new times 25

2 The empty time of the Enlightenment 27

3 The incarnated time of the Counter-Enlightenment 46

PART 2
The romanticist time of politics 65

4 Hegel's time of the state 67

5 Ranke's undulating time of continuing entities 86

PART 3
The ambiguous time of societies 101

6 Tocqueville's time of an aristocratic and democratic society 103

7 Marx's synchronicity of the non-synchronous 126

PART 4
The kairotic time of cultures **149**

8 Nietzsche's *Augenblick* 151

9 Huizinga and the historical sensation 172

PART 5
The time out of joint **193**

10 Historicist times in the twentieth and twenty-first centuries 1: France and the Anglo-Saxon world 195

11 Historicist times in the twentieth and twenty-first centuries 2: the German way 214

12 Epilogue: the benefits of historicist times 225

Bibliography 237
Index 251

ILLUSTRATIONS

2.1	Etienne-Louis Boullée, *Newton Memorial*	28
2.2	Design Etienne-Louis Boullée of the *National Library of Paris*	29
2.3	Jean-Antoine Watteau, *Love in the Italian Theatre*	29
5.1	Caspar David Friedrich, *Strandszene in Wiek*	87
5.2	Jean Charles Pellerin: Images d' Epinal, *Degrees of Ages*	88
6.1	Salvador Dali, *Slave Market with the "Invisible" Bust of Voltaire*	117
7.1	Paris Universal Exposition, 1867	127
9.1	Kairos, Fresco, in the Palazzo Sacchetti in Rome (1552–1554)	172
12.1	The change in the relationship between the human system and the earth system with regard to sources and sinks, respectively, to meet human needs and to get rid of their emissions	227
12.2	Global Income Growth 1988–2008	229

PREFACE

Experiences of time can be found throughout the history of mankind. They run in criss-cross lines from the Indian subcontinent towards the Hawaiians and from Aristotle in the fourth century B.C. to the French philosopher Paul Ricoeur, who passed away in 2005. Man mostly undergoes time without articulating its appearance. The best chance of achieving the latter is in historiography. Therein we have to investigate how the interrelation between past, present and future is presented in consecutive time regimes. Recently Carlo Rovelli in his *Order of Time* investigates time for physics.[1] I will do something similar for the discipline of history.

Until now very specialized articles focus on this issue, without providing a comprehensive view. The French François Hartog and Paul Ricoeur and the German Reinhart Koselleck are the only exceptions. Hartog connects time to its social and cultural context, calling this connection *régime d'historicité*.[2] Ricoeur in his *Temps et Récit* relates historical time to the narrative.[3] Koselleck argues in several books that historical time originates in the eighteenth-century Enlightenment, producing a progressive time of the future that runs into the twentieth century.[4] His works have the great advantage that they present a clear proposition, namely historical time as a "time of the modern". In this book I contradict that statement, assuming that I create a thesis that will in turn be contradicted. New times, new propositions; that's the way it is in the historical discipline. "History is an endless discussion", as the Dutch historian Peter Geyl said long ago.

Koselleck's heritage is cherished by contributions in Chris Lorenz's and Berber Bevernage's *Breaking up Time*.[5] That study shows how especially Aleida Assmann, François Hartog and Lucian Hölscher follow Koselleck's footsteps.[6] Although they put his "time of the modern" into perspective, they maintain his idea that the time of progress continues into the twentieth century. However, in this book I attempt a new comprehensive view, observing that not eighteenth-century Enlightenment but nineteenth-century historicism must be the framework for looking at contemporary historical temporalities. It does not result in a time of the modern but in a time "out of joint" (a term I derive from Assmann).

Ricoeur, in his *Time and Narrative*, states that historical time is created by the plot of the narrative in all forms of historiography and in time novels. He only distinguishes an intrigue of rise and fall. Contrary to his view, I perceive other temporalities than this undulating one. My story runs from a time regime with an empty temporality during the Enlightenment to a gradually evolving, incarnated time in our century.

Exposing the development of thinking about time in history and the philosophy of history, during the eighteenth and nineteenth centuries, four different forms come to the fore. First, an empty time of progress; secondly, an undulating configuration; thirdly, a structure of synchronicity of the non-synchronous; and fourthly, a sudden temporality, called kairotic time, after the Greek god Kairos. To show these four time regimes we need philosophers as their outspoken representatives, because historians mostly are less explicit. That is the reason why I connect for each time regime a historian to a philosopher.

A time out of joint appears to be more fruitful in dealing with contemporary social problems than the relatively simple time of progress. Progress suggests a utopian future, neglecting the past. The three times I focus on, give past, present and future the attention each deserves, albeit in different ways.

This book is not a study only based on sources. I will use texts from the protagonists I research but also texts about them. It is a quest in all kinds of sources to create the time regimes, which are hidden in the Enlightenment, Counter-Enlightenment and most of all in Historicism.

Fragments of this book have been published previously. I want to express my gratitude to the editors of *History and Theory*, who have allowed me to republish parts that have appeared in their journal.

Last but not least, I want to thank those who have helped or encouraged me. First of all, Reinbert Krol, who has followed this project from the hesitant first steps to the bitter but also satisfactory end. In addition, Maria Michielsen, who has gone through most of the text to make it clear and understandable. I discussed several time issues with Frank Ankersmit, and he was kind enough to send me his lecture at the Outo Preto conference in August 2016. An important part of it helped me to understand the transition in conceptions of time from the Counter-Enlightenment to Historicism. Last but not least I thank the members of staff of Routledge and Taylor and Frances, in particular Eve Setch and Zoe Thomson, who were very patient, especially if I wanted to make corrections again to the text.

Harry Jansen
Nijmegen, January 2020

Notes

1 C. Rovelli, *Order of Time* (London: Penguin, 2018).
2 François Hartog, *Regimes of Historicity: Presentism and Experiences of Time* (transl. Saskia Brown; New York: Columbia University Press, 2017³).
3 Paul Ricoeur, *Temps et Récit*, vol. I, II and III (ed. Du Seuil, 1983, 1984, 1985); idem, *Time and Narrative*, vol. I, II and III (Chicago: University of Chicago, 1984, 1985 and 1988).
4 Reinhart Koselleck, *Vergangene Zukunft. Zur Semantik geschichtlicher Zeiten* (Frankfurt a. M.: Suhrkamp, 1989²); idem, *Futures Past: On the Semantics of Historical Time* (New York: Columbia University Press, 2004); idem, *The Practice of Conceptual History: Timing, History, Spacing Concepts* (Stanford: Stanford University Press, 2002).
5 Chris Lorenz and Berber Bevernage (eds.), *Breaking up Time: Negotiating the Borders between Present, Past and Future* (Göttingen: Vandenhoeck & Ruprecht, 2013).
6 Aleida Assmann, "Transformations of the Modern Time Regime", in: Chris Lorenz and Berber Bevernage, *Breaking up Time*, 39–56 and idem, *Ist die Zeit aus den Fugen? Aufstieg und Fall des Zeitregimes der Moderne* (Köln: Carl Hanser Verlag, 2015), 131–208; François Hartog, "The Modern Régime of Historicity in the Face of Two World Wars", in: Lorenz and Bevernage, *Breaking up Time*, 124–133; and idem, *Regimes of Historicity*; Lucian Hölscher, "Mysteries of the Historical Order: Ruptures, Simultaneity and the Relationship of the Past, the Present and the Future", in: Lorenz and Bevernage, *Breaking up Time*, 134–154; Chris Lorenz, "'The Times They Are a-Changin'. On Time, Space and Periodization in History", in: Mario Carretero, Stefan Berger and Maria Grever (eds.), *Palgrave Handbook of Research in Historical Culture and Education* (Houndmills: Palgrave, 2017), 109–133.

1
INTRODUCTION

Siddharta, the protagonist in Hermann Hesse's novel of the same name, becomes a ferryman one day. Listening to the water, he brings clock time into perspective and discovers the synchronicity of past, present and future. Like Hesse's ferryman, the historian needs to uncover the temporalities Clio holds hidden in her hands. But there is a problem. Historians perceive chronology as the most obvious aspect of time; however, other and more important temporalities are concealed in historiography.[1] From a historiographical point of view, chronology, like clock time, is most of all an arithmetic and therefore an almost empty temporality. As such it transcends cultures and traditions.[2] The times this book focuses on are based on experience and reflection, hence they are culture-bound. That is the reason why it researches time in connection to the cultures they are part of. Hence this study investigates time *regimes*. The aim is to make visible other times than chronology in philosophy and historiography. It happens in connection with other cultural utterances. This Introduction presents four initial topics to illuminate that goal: (1) the heritage of Reinhart Koselleck and Paul Ricoeur, (2) the methodology of time regimes, (3) historicism and (4) the two fundamental time regimes of Antiquity and the Middle Ages.

1 The heritage of Koselleck and Ricoeur

Koselleck's heritage of the time of the modern

Usually time is considered a transition from the past into the present and the future. As a result, it is a time to come, characterized by expectation. That brings us to the impressive heritage of the German Koselleck, for whom it is obvious that time can be comprehended in the metaphor of the arrow.[3] Its roots can be found in the Enlightenment. Then, a time of progress arises from the change of the traditional, Christian virtue of "*profectus*" (perfectness) into the general human belief of "*progressus*".[4] This implies a transition from *Historie* in *Geschichte*. *Historie* can be translated in English in "histories" and *Geschichte* in "history", seen by Koselleck as a "collective singular". Before the eighteenth century, history was an "aggregate" of stories, about saints, heroes, events, disputes, battles, wars and so on, whereas during the eighteenth century, it becomes a "system", bringing together all the different historical brooklets and streams into one great flood of History with a capital H. Koselleck's collective singular shows in what way history creates progress during the Enlightenment. Historical time thus becomes a "time of the modern". Moreover, Koselleck considers this time accelerating, which means that the "old-fashioned" past disappears from the present, faster and faster.[5] As a result, the past displays an "otherness" that requires research.[6]

Koselleck has become famous for his definition of time, in which the past is a space of experience and the future a horizon of expectation.[7] In my opinion, he creates in this way a spectrum with, on the one hand, ontological and, on the other, epistemological aspects. He refers by the term "space of experience" to the ontological side consisting of a past that was once believed to be reality. "Horizon of expectation" then forms the epistemological side of the spectrum, because a horizon constantly recedes, which means that the future never can be considered experienced; it can only be presented at the level of information, in the form of prophecies or prognoses.[8]

Koselleck perceives the time of the modern as a movement in which experience diminishes and expectation increases.[9] We will see in Chapter 3 that this interpretation can be substantiated by the role Koselleck attributes to Johann Martin Chladenius (1710–1759). The latter claims that historical knowledge is not substantial but always depends on what he calls a *Sehepunkt*, a point of view. For Kosselleck's definition of time this means that the epistemological side outweighs the ontological. It may be the reason why he views time accelerating, with the past disappearing faster and faster and the horizon of expectation constantly changing.[10] After all, an epistemological time means a lightweight time, which can easily accelerate. This time also entails the fiction that it is possible to begin anew and leads to what Aleida Assmann calls "creative destruction".[11] Hartmut Rosa discusses, in the footsteps of Marx and Engels, its *fortwährende Umwälzung*, which implies a continuous revolution.[12] To me it means that Koselleck's time might be addressed as being empty. In Chapters 2 and 3, I will explain where the emptiness of his time comes from.[13]

At the end of the twentieth century Koselleck's time of progress begins to crack. Historians and philosophers, like Fernando Esposito, François Hartog, Aleida Assmann and Lucian Hölscher, question it. Esposito refers to postmodernism and what he calls the *posthistoire*, entailing new forms of conservatism.[14] Hartog in his *Regimes of Historicity* maintains Koselleck's forward-looking temporality until 1989, after which he rather suddenly sees the emergence of a time of the present. The past returns as a part of it, but in a negative form, in particular because of what he calls the heritage industry.[15]

Approximately at the same moment, Assmann also perceives a discontinuity, but less abruptly. According to her, historians like Hermann Lübbe and Odo Marquardt introduce a compensation theory around 1990. They do not leave Koselleck's time of the modern but become sceptical about its rosy aspects. Marquardt launches pithy *Zukunft braucht Herkunft* ("the future needs origin"), but he finds it a shame that identity thinkers use the past as a repository for recognition and identification.[16] According to him a return to the past must therefore be done carefully. Assmann rejects the compensation theory and wants to give the past much more weight than Lübbe and Marquardt have done. She points to a temporality in which the boundaries between past, present and future are removed.[17] She calls this time "out of joint" and considers it an opportunity to balance the past and the future. She does not judge it and gives neither the past nor the future priority.

In summary I distinguish in the works of Hartog and Assmann two temporalities: (1) Koselleck's future-oriented time of the modern and (2) a time of the present, in which past and future have a certain presence. In the latter case the past is something that deserves attention for its democratic achievements but also for its crimes and traumas. The future needs consideration as a source of fantasy and perspective.[18] In my view Assmann's "time out of joint" differs fundamentally from Koselleck's "time of the modern". It is not an empty but an embodied time, not rooted in the Enlightenment but in nineteenth-century historicism. In the penultimate chapter of this book, I shall discuss Assmann's views.

Hölscher observes, in the footsteps of Koselleck, a third temporality "the non-simultaneity of the simultaneous", also finding its origins in the eighteenth century.[19] He believes that in the twentieth century this idea is taken up by philosophers and historians like Ernst Bloch, Fernand Braudel and Ullrich Wehler. I want to discuss this observation, because I think that their temporalities are based on the synchronicity of the non-synchronous, which is a fundamental break with the homogeneous time of the eighteenth century. Koselleck's and Hölscher's non-simultaneity of the simultaneous, as it is put into words in the Enlightenment, is not the same as the synchronicity of the non-synchronous of the twentieth century. The former points to nations and cultures that exist in the same time but are not in the same stage of progress in their development. "'Civilised' societies in [then, the eighteenth century] present day Europe could be represented as the future of 'primitive' societies elsewhere".[20] It is the result of synchronizing, done by philosophers and historians like the French Denis Diderot, Jean le Rond d'Alembert and the German Johann Gatterer.[21] They want to know what nations and cultures are close to or stay far behind West-European civilizations. It is a *diachronical* and *non-related* approach in which the most modern is the measure for those who lag behind.[22] This is important because it connects the time of the non-simultaneity of the simultaneous to states, nations, cities, trade-unions and so on, being continuing entities, without ruptures or revolutions.[23]

The synchronicity of the non-synchronous of the twentieth century implies that past, present and future coexist *synchronically* and that they are more or less *dialectically related*. Then the past can go hand in hand with the present and the future, or even can be a brake on both. The framework here is not only progress, but also criticism or retardation.[24] It is about whether or not to achieve a more egalitarian society or a more modern economy in the future. It is an embodied time in which progress can be criticized or delayed, which does not happen in the non-simultaneous time of the Enlightenment. It makes societal entities discontinuous.

Synchronicity of the non-synchronous is one of the three forms of an embodied time, which play a significant role in nineteenth-century historicism. The others are the aforementioned time of the present, about which Hartog and Assmann speak and a third one that I will discuss in the next section about Paul Ricoeur. These three temporalities are embodied and should be mentioned here, because it is one of the propositions of this book that embodied and arduous times evolve in nineteenth century historicism, alongside the progressive, accelerating and forward-looking time of Koselleck.

In his "The Modern *Régime* of Historicity in the Face of Two World Wars", Hartog defends the proposition that futurism survives the crisis of two World Wars.[25] He even holds that only at the end of the twentieth century, the future-oriented time of the modern is replaced by a present-oriented one. Hölscher, however, does not agree and sees a break in the time of the modern after the First World War. In his "Mysteries of Historical Order" he argues that since this war, time is no longer experienced as homogeneous.[26] For Hölscher, the time of the modern does not end around 1990, as for Hartog and Assmann, but around 1920. In my view, its end already starts at the beginning of the nineteenth century.

Ricoeur and narrativism

Ricoeur makes us aware of the relationship between narrativism and temporality. That is not so obvious, because Louis Mink and Frank Ankersmit argue that time is obliterated in the historical narrative.[27] Ricoeur's *Time and Narrative* claims the opposite. According to him, the narrative articulates time. Ricoeur considers experiences of time as disordered and discordant. Only the narrative, and especially the intrigue of it, can make temporality consistent and homogeneous. In my view Ricoeur elaborates on two historicist times. In the first volume of his *Time and Narrative*, he creates a romanticist time of rise and fall, as an alternative for Koselleck's time of the modern, whereas in the last volume of it he develops a Heideggerian "kairotic" time. The latter concerns a "now" as a dwelling place for a future that is "moving toward itself" and a past that is "coming back to itself". In this way he grants, in the footsteps of Husserl, a "certain thickness to the lived-through present that distinguishes it from the point-like instant" which is implicit in the accelerating time of Koselleck.[28] This kairotic time I will discuss in Chapters 8 and 9.

An example of the way Ricoeur constitutes a time of rise and fall is his analysis of Fernand Braudel's *The Mediterranean and the Mediterranean World in the Age of*

Philip II.[29] Therein Braudel displays a synchronicity of the non-synchronous of three different times: the *longue durée*, a conjunctural time and a vibrating time of politics. Ricoeur presses all three in the paradigm of a homogeneous, intriguing time of rise and decline.[30]

A second problem with Ricoeur's view is his phenomenological hermeneutics, giving an *a priori* view on the relationship between narrative and time. He does so by choosing a specific temporality, the one of the patriarch Augustine, which I will discuss below. He connects Augustine's temporality with Aristotle's theory of the narrative, as the latter elaborates in his *Poetica*.[31] The time of Ricoeur reveals a connection between a specific temporality and a specific form of the narrative, resulting in stories with a time of rise and fall. In his narrativism, he neglects Heidegger's kairotic time and thereby gives time a certain one-sidedness. In contrast to the phenomenological hermeneutism of Ricoeur, I prefer a more historicist-pragmatic approach (see the section "Time regimes"), through which other times can be revealed.

There still is a third problem. Ricoeur's approach implies that time manifests itself only in the intrigue or plot of the narrative. In my view time can manifest itself also in other ways, for instance in pictures or periodizations (see below). Moreover, in Ricoeur's view time experiences are unformed and opaque until the narrative, by emplotment, has done its shaping work. I consider the inverse plausible too: time experiences can also create all kinds of emplotment and representation.[32] Is Ricoeur's vision embedded in narrativism, mine is post-narrative in nature. In post-narrativism time can be the co-creator of the narrative. Temporality and narration are, so to speak, reciprocally working elements.[33] Ricoeur's views will be discussed in Chapter 10 of this book.

2 Time regimes

Regimes of historicity and time regimes

Although Assmann uses the term *Zeitregimes* and Hartog the concept of *Régimes d'historicité*, they do not develop a methodology of time regimes. That is the reason why they observe a continuation of the time of the modern until the end of the twentieth century. Besides this empty time of the Enlightenment, I perceive an embodied time which forms, since the end of the eighteenth century, the base of three historicist time regimes, continuing until now. Apart from this, I also will introduce a time regime method.

Hartog departs from Reinhart Koselleck's time, consisting of a distance and a tension between the space of experience and the horizon of expectation.[34] However, he adds a difference in prominence, whereby past, present and future vary according to historical periods and geographical regions. Before the French Revolution time is past-oriented and the same is true for time perceptions of people outside Europe. Hartog investigates the Greek and Pacific cultures of time to contrast them with the modern European time perceptions in the nineteenth and twentieth centuries.[35] In the nineteenth century a time perception arises in which the future dominates the past and the present. According to Hartog, "progress" and "revolution" are the keywords here.[36] The only exception is François de Chateaubriand, who displays an almost obsessive focus on the past.[37] Since approximately the 1990s of the twentieth century, when the so-called postmodern order of time develops, Hartog perceives futurism overruled by presentism. Then "there seems to be nothing but the present, like an immense stretch of water restlessly rippling".[38] As a consequence, Hartog comprehends *régimes d'historicité* as different experiences of time, articulating either the past, the present or the future. As such it demolishes a presupposed formal equivalence between past, present and future. Therefore, Terence Holden sees Hartog's disbalanced time as a pathological crisis of the present. According to Holden it is a present with a fragile identity and a relation to a past that does not pass.[39]

In contrast to Hartog, I do not see a domination of past, present or future during a certain period but different patterns of connections between all three. Like me, Assmann does not see a domination of one of them either.[40] During the nineteenth century historians, philosophers and others utter the want to take all of them together. Alexis de Tocqueville wrote in 1840: "When the past no longer illuminates the future, the spirit walks in darkness" (a quote from Hartog himself).[41] In my opinion, Tocqueville's statement can be interpreted only as a specific combination of past and future and not just as part of a future-oriented regime of historicity. Unlike Hartog, I consider a time regime as being characterized by a specific connection between past, present and future in a certain period. This option allows for multiple time regimes, which Hartog also takes into account but does not elaborate on.[42]

Hartog's idea of a modern time regime, focusing on the future and a postmodern time regime of the present, seems too homogeneous to me. I agree with Helge Jordheim that "the regime of temporality identified as 'modern', has been challenged by other times, other temporalities, slower, faster, with other rhythms, other successions of events, other narratives, and so on".[43] The difference between Jordheim's approach and mine is that he talks about a multiplicity of times, whereas I am talking about a multiplicity of time regimes.

Koselleck's connection between social history and historical time

Time regimes presuppose a close connection between time and its social context. In his "Historical Time and Social History", Koselleck relates modern temporality to modern social history.[44] He observes that since the Industrial Revolution and the French Revolution, "structures changed more rapidly than they did before".[45] The same happens with historical time. Koselleck connects social history and time by linguistic reflection, researching social and political *concepts* in their historical development.[46] In the eighteenth century this development accelerates, which has consequences for the perception of time. He gives as an example the concept of *res publica*. Before the Enlightenment this term only collects past experiences, exploring them theoretically in the form of monarchy, aristocracy or democracy.[47] This will change in the Enlightenment. Then, "all types of constitution are forced into an alternative choice. There was only the Republic, everything else was despotism".[48] Since the Enlightenment, all notions of "republic" are future-oriented. *Res publica* becomes *republicanism*, followed by democratism, liberalism, socialism, communism and fascism. Koselleck makes two important remarks: first, "at the time when these concepts were created, they had no content in terms of experience", and second, "political and social concepts become the navigational instruments of the changing movement of history".[49]

This corroborates my idea that Koselleck first reduces historical time to the accelerating time of the Enlightenment and second, that he perceives the then developing social concepts as ontologically empty.[50] After all, in the Enlightenment concepts become stripped from experience and thus from the past, because of their future orientation. This implies four important differences with my approach. First, Koselleck's historical time itself is empty, whereas I consider the possibility of embodied temporalities. Second, he uses concepts in which form and content have become distinct elements. In, for instance, *res publica* the content changes in republicanism, liberalism, socialism and so on, whereas its form, *res publica* as referring to public affairs in general, remains the same. I will show hereafter, in the footsteps of Brandom, that form and content are one and therefore change together. Third, as a consequence, Koselleck identifies the time of the Enlightenment – "the time of the modern" – as the only regime of time and ignores the possibility of a plurality of time regimes. For me the latter is the case. Last but not least, Koselleck does not distinguish objective and subjective time, which is a very old, but indeed still important distinction.

Time regimes and pragmatism

Time can be considered objectively and subjectively. We must investigate objective time as part of a time regime, which requires a conceptual approach. Subjective time can vary from person to person, although a time experience cannot do without a social context.[51] Its wording needs metaphors, images or representations, such as an arrow, a plot of rise and fall, a continuous flow or a discontinuous staccato. We will see in the following that these subjective and objective aspects already are taken into account in Antiquity and the early Middle Ages. Time in its subjective aspect will be discussed in the next section, mainly as a social experience. Here I will explain objective time by conceptualizing time regimes. Robert Brandom and Jonathan Gorman are my guides in these conceptual investigations.

Brandom's pragmatism is crucial for the concept of time, because he rejects our ordinary views on concepts. To him, they originate from Immanuel Kant and his predecessors, who distinguish concepts from perceptions or intuitions.

According to Brandom, Kant's interpretation of this distinction concerns three aspects: first, a concept is a *form* that differs from *matter*; second, a concept is something *general*, differing from the *particular*, and third, a concept is the result of a *spontaneous activity*, whereas perceptions and others are something being only the product of *receptivity*.[52] Brandom summarizes Kant's view, by stating: "The concepts are supposed to be the source of *structure*, while something else provides the *content* or matter".[53]

Brandom's pragmatism differs from Kant's philosophy in assigning to concepts a *material* inferential role in all kinds of expressions (factual statements, judgements, beliefs etc.). In inferential correct expressions Kant's contrasts disappear, because the correctness of an inference *includes* the *particular contents* of the concepts, invoked by their premises and conclusions and not only by their *form*.[54] Brandom gives as example "Pittsburg is to the West of Philadelphia" and "Philadelphia is to the East of Pittsburg" and explains that the correctness of these inferences is part of the content of the concepts of *East* and *West*.[55] There is no contrast between concepts as *form* and something else as *matter*. The inferential role, which is the conceptual role, *is* the content.[56] In the frame of this reasoning Brandom states: "Facts are just true claims. Facts, like other claims, are conceptually articulated by their inferences and incompatible relations to other claims".[57] Concerning judgements Brandom stipulates: "What a judgement expresses or makes explicit, its content, is conceptual all the way down".[58] With regard to temporality it means that time as a concept, practiced in a certain tradition, order, culture or regime, is also its content. It implies that time's content is co-determined by its use in the culture it is part of.[59] It means that time should not only be conceptualized on an epistemological level; its – assumed – ontological aspects must be included. Because time is the central concept here, I follow Brandom's approach to inferences, taking them as parts of a more comprehensive whole. He sees as wholes: judgements, speech acts, expressions and assertions. Expressions are part of assertions. Of an assertion, it can be said that it "comes into being only when its relationship to another assertion is at issue".[60]

This means that we can call a conglomeration of assertions a culture, regime or order, and when such a conglomeration concerns time, it can be called a *time regime*.[61] Instead of "regime", Brandom uses the term "tradition", which includes the articulation of inferential relationships among assertions of various individuals. They can thus constitute a tradition of inquiry, "making assertions about the same evolving logical object".[62] The historicist times I aim at deserve a non-Kantian, inferential approach to discover four different time regimes, one in the eighteenth and three in the nineteenth centuries.[63] Two of them are homogeneous and the other two heterogeneous. By Brandom's inferential approach, method and content are closely connected.[64]

With regard to a more sophisticated description of a regime, we need, besides Brandom's inferential approach also Jonathan Gorman's pragmatist views. According to me, the latter gives a magnificent definition of regime when he speaks of language (which can be spoken in words as well as in images) as "a successfully shared social institution", embodying "decisions how to sort the world".[65] Gorman's ideas centre on his so-called "rolling web of reality sorting beliefs and expressions".[66] It is the "web of beliefs, what expresses reality as a whole".[67] The web implies a view on reality, being something we organize through the classifications of our language. As Brandom, Gorman does not separate concepts from content, because "organising reality through the classifications of our language happens not in terms of fixed categories but in something human beings can consciously *do* by choice".[68]

Gorman perceives the web as continually changing, and as such, it should be understood diachronically rather than synchronically.[69] However, the term "web" points already in the direction of synchronicity. Gorman borrows his web-idea from Willard Van Orman Quine, who speaks of changes in the web in terms of "sufficient adjustment".[70] This means that the web is a configuration of assertions maintaining an equilibrium, which in case of changes can be restored. Following Brandom (see previous discussion) and Quine, I would like to say that the web contains two aspects: first, a synchronic *perceived* web of assertions about reality as a whole, and second, a continually changing web. It suggests some coherence, which means that assertions as parts of it have inferential relationships. Change in synchronicity entails that we have to look for sufficient adjustments in those relationships.[71] The rolling aspect of the web clarifies that it can be revised, partly by the necessity to adjust, partly by choice. Gorman rightly claims with regard to choice:

> How we do this is not a timeless question for philosophers but a factual question appropriate for historical recovery, so making the history of historiography important for the philosophy of history.[72]

That is why I want to investigate historiography in the form of a consecutive series of different webs, which are referred to in this study as time regimes. I distinguish for the last three centuries consecutively the Enlightenment, the Counter-Enlightenment and the webs of a romanticist, an ambiguous and a kairotic time. The conventions of a time regime often remain implicit in the *practice* of history writing. They become explicit when they are, expressed in Brandom's words, *rules for reasoning*.[73] See for instance hereafter Leopold von Ranke's statement:

> To history has been assigned the office of judging the past, of instructing the present for the benefit of future ages. To such high offices this work does not aspire: It wants only to show what actually happened.[74]

Ranke displays here a commitment to a form of history writing that differs fundamentally from the one of his forerunners during the Enlightenment. Here he introduces a new rule of reasoning with regard to time. Nonetheless, the awareness and utterance of such a rule does not make the whole time regime explicit.

All Ranke's assertions do not have to be compatible with his new perception of time. Investigation is required here. Complete new and *interrelated* utterances about time can make implicit endorsement of existing time assertions explicit. Here we see the configurational aspects of the time regimes, which I want to research.

Time regimes as a social experience

Brandom's and Gorman's inferential approach to temporality ask for a study of time experiences in a social context. Earlier we defined "regime" in Gorman's words as "a successfully shared social institution", embodying "decisions how to sort the world". The regime therefore responds to the question of how we make decisions with regard to the sorting of reality. As a result, we constitute a reality. We do so in the form of cultural developments or periods, which end with the emergence of new ones. This happens, as Hans Kellner states, "[when] a generation fails to find any figures adequate to their legitimate needs and desires in the models that the existing culture offers it, they will turn away from their historical culture and create another by choosing a different past".[75]

Choosing a different past does not mean that a new generation makes choices *ex nihilo*. It uses different pasts, taking representations of predecessors. As a consequence, regimes have an active, performing side, but also a receptive one. Here comes Brandom's view in sight, stating that a regime can be "a synchronic perception of a conglomeration of assertions".[76] It is not about the whole of reality (how could this be done?) but about aspects of it. A whole series of assertions about some aspects of reality can be called a representation.[77]

Time regimes, as discussed in this study, are representations of time, experienced in a certain period.[78] In Antiquity and the Middle Ages, they are put into words by Aristotle and the patriarch Augustine. Due to Koselleck's research, we know that more modern forms come about after 1700, the reason why I start my research in the eighteenth century. In my opinion, a time regime is not only a phenomenon in historiography and is not only felt by historians, it shows itself in a fairly broad spectrum of the cultural elite in a certain period.[79] Philosophers and representatives of literature, science and visual arts display similar patterns of temporal experiences. Therefore, I investigate the perception of time patterns in historiography in relation to other cultural utterances. Next to historiography, philosophy is a main field of research. Smaller references are, in a less systematic way, possible to other cultural fields, like literature and painting.

I intend to present an intellectual history of European time regimes and their reflection in historiography, displaying how they form a correction on thinking in terms of progress and modernization.[80] Progressive thinking can lead to ethnocentric assumptions, accepting only those cultures that are "modern" (and white and male).[81] I expect to discover different time periods in the philosophy of history and historiography as a result of those different regimes of time.

Revealing them is important because of the apparent ignorance of historians with regard to the role that time plays in their writings.[82]

As I argued before, I bring Ricoeur's refiguration of time experience by narrative into perspective, because his approach implies that time manifests itself only in the *intrigue* or plot of the narrative. His method suggests that experience comes first and is unformed until the narrative has done its shaping work. Language thus seems to be the necessary and sufficient condition for the existence of time, but in my view, experience of time and language come as one. Hans-Georg Gadamer, being Martin Heidegger's pupil, perceives language and understanding (*Verstehen*) as belonging to the basic structure of being.[83] In Heidegger's *Time and Being*, being and time come together in care (*Sorge*). Hence we can say that time also belongs to the basic structure of being. According to Heidegger, the experience of being and time are even interchangeable. Being, language, experience and time are aspects of a world exploring totality. None of these comes first.[84]

However, it is different with their articulation.[85] In the life of human beings it starts with language; the articulation of time comes later.[86] This does not mean that language is the only necessary and sufficient condition of thinking in terms of time. Time experience is articulated by the fact that the individual human life is embedded in a historical and societal context.[87] For time the same is true as what Maurice Halbwachs has shown on the issue of memory.[88] They both are social experiences.[89] This means that we find marks of historical-social contexts in every time regime. In the nineteenth century, these contexts are characterized by three crises, which we will retrace in the then time regimes.

At the beginning of the nineteenth century, there exists a crisis concerning the disintegration of society by the French Revolution and the conquests of Napoleon. The Industrial Revolution in England and France, since approximately 1830, is seen as a source of social problems that require societal solutions. Allan Megill regards the last quarter of the nineteenth and the first part of the twentieth centuries as an era of cultural crisis.[90]

In a note in his *Meaning, Truth and Reference*, Ankersmit enumerates all the Germans, who in my view react on the three crises of the nineteenth century.[91] Hegel, Ranke, Marx and Nietzsche are chosen from this list. Tocqueville and Huizinga have been added to it. They are the most striking representatives to me of an embodied time.

Hegel and Ranke react on the political, Tocqueville and Marx on the industrial and Nietzsche and Huizinga on the cultural crisis of their time. Despite their similarity in crisis-thinking, they all have very different perceptions of it. Hegel's reaction on the political crisis is predominantly directed by his craving for freedom, whereas that of Ranke is conservative, seeing that one has to move along with reality. Tocqueville's response on the industrializing society is moderate and prudent, rejecting the atomization of society. Marx assumes atomization inevitable and reacts in a revolutionary way. Nietzsche responds to the cultural revolution with a radical and mythical perception of the past, whereas Huizinga's reaction is anti-mythical and nostalgic. Even with a divergence inside the pairs, each pair still represents a specific time regime. With Hegel and Ranke, it is the regime of Romanticism, characterized by homogeneity and integration. Tocqueville and Marx display an ambiguous regime of the industrial crisis and Nietzsche and Huizinga a regime of time, which I have called "kairotic" (see Chapters 8 and 9). This is important because the three time regimes show a close relationship between its representatives, despite differences.

3 Historicism

Central to my study are the three time regimes of the nineteenth century. This century is the age of historicism, and I want to show that it is still important for the twenty-first century. I think that a historicist attitude to time is more important than the historical-anthropological approach that Koselleck chooses.[92] Such an approach invites to see the present as a crisis, as an ever-widening gap in-between past and future, instead of perceiving it as a dwelling place in which we can reflect on the past to take better choices for the future.[93] As I have shown earlier there is a relationship between Koselleck's style of reasoning and the empty time in which it results. The same is true for perceiving the present as being in a continuing crisis. When every present continues to be in crisis, then past and future are always in crisis either, which means that the term "crisis" loses its content and becomes an empty form.

My views on historicism agree with Ankersmit's defence of it, especially with his observation that "historicism . . . is the view that the nature of a thing lies in its history".[94] Ankersmit refers to Maurice Mandelbaum, who perceives historicism as

> the belief that an adequate understanding of the nature of any phenomenon and an adequate assessment of its value are to be gained through considering it in terms of the place it occupied and the role it played within a process of development.[95]

The same reference can be found with the Indian author of *Provincializing Europe*, Dipesh Chakrabarty.[96] I refer to him to demonstrate that historicism also exists outside Europe and subsists into the twenty-first century. It seems not to be incommensurable with non-European cultures.[97]

The most extensive and the most inclusive definition of historicism comes from the German-Hungarian sociologist Karl Mannheim.[98] He considers it a *Weltanschauung*, a term without a right equivalent in English:

> Historicism is therefore neither a mere fad nor a fashion; it is not even an intellectual current, but the very basis on which we construct our observations of the socio-cultural reality. It is not something artificially contrived, something like a program[me], but an organically developed basic pattern,

the *Weltanschauung* itself, which came into being after the religiously determined medieval picture of the world had disintegrated and when the subsequent Enlightenment, with its dominant idea of a supra-temporal Reason, had destroyed itself. Those present-day romantics who deplore the lack of a contemporary *Weltanschauung*, who have the slogan "organically developed" constantly on their lips and who miss this "organically developed" in present-day life, these romantics fail to notice that it is just historicism, and historicism alone, which today provides us with a world view of the same universality as that of the religious world view of the past, and that historicism alone could have developed "organically" out of the preceding historical intellectual roots. . . . All this does not mean that we should accept historicism as something given, as a fate which we cannot alter, as a higher and hostile power: historicism is indeed itself a *Weltanschauung* and hence is going through a dynamic process of development and systematization. It requires the philosophical labours of generations to help it mature and reach its final pattern. One would show little understanding if one were to accept any of its preliminary formulations as a final one.[99]

We can learn from Mannheim that, although he sees the origins of historicism in the Counter-Enlightenment and Romanticism, he certainly does not want to limit it to the formulation used at the time of its creation. Certainly, he uses the term "organically" quite often, but this does not imply that the historicist *Weltanschauung* itself requires a form of organicist thinking. As Mannheim rightly perceives, historicism is not "something given, . . . which cannot alter". Thus, a whole range of historians and philosophers can be considered historicists, despite their neglect or even rejection of an organicist worldview.

In his explanation of the definition of Mandelbaum, Ankersmit remains in the footsteps of Ranke and ends up in an "idea- and identity-oriented" historicism, in which a dynamic conception of society is crucial.[100] According to Ranke and Ankersmit, society is constantly changing. In other studies, Ankersmit maintains a historicism in which Huizinga plays an important role, although it is known that Huizinga denies developmental thinking as important for historiography.[101] For Huizinga, history writing means building images related to historical eras. His historicism is based on Ranke's *Jede Epoche is unmittelbar zu Gott*. This is probably the reason why Ankersmit formulates his historicism in Rankean terms. He therefore articulates it in a dynamic evolutionary but also in a structural, "epochal" way.[102] In both cases, a different view of time is at stake. For me, historicism does not need to be associated with an organic social structure. However, it is certainly connected to an *embodied* historical time. In the nineteenth century, various forms developed from this, all loaded with mostly burdensome events. That is one of the main threads from which historicism is woven in this book.

In summary, we can say that historicism is the *Weltanschauung* in which the nature of a phenomenon is considered to be situated in its history, where history can be understood both in a dynamic and in a structural sense. In both senses, past, present and future are interrelated. According to this definition all authors of the nineteenth-century time regimes, which I will discuss in this study, belong to historicism. They are the testators to whom we must pay attention to understand the current forms of historicism. The same applies to time regimes. In my opinion, stereotypical thinking in terms of progress is too simple. Even the sophisticated way in which Koselleck deals with modernity, and especially with the historical time that goes with it, is too straightforward in my view. As we will see in the penultimate chapter of this book, his insights are still hardly followed.

My book defends a historicism in which the present, the past and the future belong together, although this coherence can occur in different constellations. Historicism is a *Weltanschauung* that is averse to a belief in the past, the present or the future as separate parts of time. It is neither reactionary nor presentish, nor is it focused solely on the future. It does not believe in a statement like "there is only the now". An empty form of progress is also not in its creed. The most important common aspect of historicist time is the supposition that time incarnates in reality, resulting in an embodied time.

4 Early time regimes, a definition of time and the structure of this book

Early time regimes

To get a first impression of what a time regime entails, I will discuss the "time regimes" of Antiquity and early medieval Christianity. This is only an impression because I do not intend to investigate these regimes extensively. I only think that Aristotle (384–322 BC) and the Patriarch Augustine (354–430 AD) are the most obvious thinkers to briefly illustrate these time regimes. Their contributions are also crucial for the question of what time is. Aristotle conceives time as more or less objective, cosmological and eternal, having neither a beginning nor an end. Augustine's time shows both: it is created and ends with the Last Judgement. Both regimes go into questions like: is there time and, if so, how should it be defined; is time something in the mind or in reality; is it an objective or a subjective phenomenon; and is time not just a now? I think that these issues cannot be completely and adequately answered, but at the end of the section about Augustine, I will refer to a statement by Collingwood in which time is defined in the best possible way. It covers to a large extent the temporalities that are at stake in the regimes of this book. Collingwood's definition can prevent us from getting lost in the wacky wood of temporal pitfalls.[103]

Aristotle and Augustine rack their brains about the question whether time exists. They experience that the three elements of time, namely past, present and future, are fleeting.[104] They realize, too, that the past no longer exists, the future is not yet there and the present is slipping by so quickly that it is hardly impossible to grasp. Nevertheless, both conclude that time is real.

The question how time needs to be defined brings even more confusion and hesitation. Augustine puts that into words by his famous quote: "If no one asks me, I know what it is. If I wish to explain it to him who asks me, I do not know".[105] In the end Aristotle and Augustine yet give an answer to this question, and both start with the quickly flowing away of the present. They cling to the "now" as a reference point for the existence of time. But the connotations with regard to the "now" are completely different.

Aristotle and the time regime of antiquity

In his *Physics*, Aristotle defines time as "the number of movement in respect to the before and after".[106] This definition originates in a cosmological orientation, because Aristotle's time is related to the movement of heavenly bodies like the sun and the moon. The "present", the "now", is for the Greek philosopher an arbitrary point in this movement. By that "now-point" we can determine what comes before and after it, and thus we can perceive time as a succession. We also can collect now-points and unite them in minutes, hours, days, weeks, months and so on. Points and collections of it can be counted; therefore, Aristotle speaks in his definition of the *number* of movement. The cosmological view of time, in which the "now" serves as a starting point and in which movement is pivotal, makes Aristotle's time objective, spatial, perceptible and measurable. Especially its spatiality is important, as we will see in the next sections. Moreover, his time is homogeneous because each point in the succession of time is a corresponding now-point. Time is also absolute, because it has no beginning or end.

The cosmological movement from one point to another has been interrupted, and as such, Aristotle's view of time is discontinuous. Although there are no hourglasses during his life, the discontinuity of Aristotle's time conception can be understood if we realize that ultimately each grain falls individually. Around 1916 an electric clock is invented in which the hands move continuously and smoothly along the dial. Before this time, the hands jump from minute to minute and from hour to hour, as Aristotle would expect, if he had known the pendulum.

The definition of Aristotle, which emphasizes a discontinuous movement, differs from other definitions of time, such as the one of Augustine. The latter does not associate time with a cosmological movement, but with an aesthetic practice. He refers to an involvement in music, which is an experience not of the senses but of the soul. He exhibits a subjective, inner, continuous time, opposite to the objective, cosmological temporality of the ancient Greeks. The contrast between Aristotle and Augustine must not be overestimated. Aristotle points out that time is not equal to the movement of the celestial bodies but to the number of this movement. It implies the existence of a soul capable of numbering, which brings Aristotle close to Augustine, who also presupposes a soul for his own perception of time.

Some wonder whether a numbering soul really alludes to an experience. Is temporal numbering an experience of time? According to Ricoeur, time experience implies "a time that envelops us", while a quantity makes time more or less an object in front of us.[107] We can therefore doubt whether the time of Aristotle is an experienced time, although his time can be deduced from the experience of a change of day and night. This conclusion and his reference to a numbering soul brings Aristotle's time not far from an experienced time. Yet the conclusion must be that the time of Aristotle is above all an objective, cosmological, linear and spatial time of succession.

The early Christian time regime, represented by Augustine

The patriarch Augustine defines, in his *Confessions*, time completely distinct from Aristotle, although he starts with the now as well.[108] His "now" is the presence of attention as an enduring act of the human "mind".[109] To explain his definition, the patriarch refers to a psalm.[110] He thus introduces a Christian time regime. Listening to music requires a continuous attention to the notes being played. However, we do not listen to each note individually, apart from the preceding and the next, but we listen to the current notes with a reminder of the notes we have already heard and anticipating the notes that are coming. With regard to an aesthetic experience, "mind" may be not the right term; "soul" is more adequate. It includes someone's whole person. This is surely true for a Christian believer like Augustine, just when he is listening to a psalm. But as we know, Aristotle also speaks of "soul" when numbering is the essential aspect of time.

There is another, more important difference between Augustine's and Aristotle's temporality. Augustine does not perceive time only in the context of a before and an after the now, but the now is a presence of attention, remembrance and expectation.[111] Opposite to Aristotle, Augustine does not see time as a succession of distant-apart points, but as a *distentio animi*, a distention of the soul. It is a distance in which remembrance, attention and expectation can emerge. As such, remembrance refers to the past, attention to the present and expectation to the future. The now is for Augustine not only distance but also succession. Time has a diachronic move. Listening to a psalm corroborates this. As a piece of music, it is not accidently chosen. Next to time as a *distentio animi*, it also is an *intentio animi*. Time has a direction; it has the intention to find God and eternity. A psalm is the adequate instrument for this arrow-like movement. Notice here that Koselleck's time of the Enlightenment has the same direction.

This movement of time to eternity has the connotation to juxtapose the perfectness of God and eternity to the imperfectness of all earthly things. In eternity "time" is a complete whole, while on earth, it is split in past, present and future.[112] Although time is to Augustine foremost an inner, a subjective aspect of life, it also has an analytical and thus an objective aspect. The imperfectness of time, compared to eternity and thus its disunity and sequence, refers to an earthly phenomenon. As such, time is also something of God's creation and hence objective.[113]

A preliminary definition of time

As mentioned earlier, the views of Aristotle and Augustine are still current. Questions like the objectivity or subjectivity of time, its distinction from eternity, the dilemma of being absolute or created and so on continue to haunt our thoughts to this day. Jonathan Gorman, questioned about this by the editors of "Breaking up time", gives in his answer an extensive quote from Robin Collingwood, which can act as a preliminary paraphrase of what is at stake in this study:[114]

> The real is the present, conceived not as a mathematical point between the present and the past, but as the union of present and past in a duration or permanence that is at the same time change. Thus the past as past and the future as future do not exist at all, but purely ideal; the past as living in the present and the future as germinating in the present are wholly real and indeed are just the present itself. It is because of the presence of these two elements in the present . . . that the present is a concrete and changing reality and not an empty mathematical point.[115]

The perception "The past as past and the future as future do not exist at all" does not only come from Collingwood. We find it in Augustine's *Confessions*, but also in Koselleck's crisis between the space of experience and horizon of expectation. This leads to the idea that past and future are synchronous in the present, so that the distinction between past, present and future seems superfluous.[116] The differences between all three, however, are based on changing experiences and as such very real. Related to the past, we see it in loss, regret and nostalgia, expressed by Nietzsche in his "That time does not run backward, that is its wrath".[117] The present may be experienced in the knowledge of being born, ageing and being destined to die. But it is also the place where we can reflect on the living past and await a future, which is already there. It consists of anticipating disasters, dystopias, biblical prophecies, progress, utopias or, more neutrally, in all types of care (Heidegger's *Sorge* amongst others) and expectations. These experiences can be tough, but also enlightening and even creative.[118] Collingwood's quote makes different perceptions of time possible, which is important for the distinction between time regimes. It also means that past, present and future must be taken together when we discuss them. From that perspective, neither the past nor the present or the future are autonomous or primordial.[119]

The book's structure

The outcome of my study is a story line, running from a culture with an empty temporality during the Enlightenment into a gradually developing incarnated time from the last part of the eighteenth century until Nietzsche and Huizinga in the beginning of the twentieth century. As I stated before, its incarnation takes three different forms: (1) an undulating configuration, (2) a structure of synchronicity of the non-synchronous and (3) a kairotic temporality. Historians are usually less explicit in the use of time constructions, the reason why I connect for historicism a historian with a philosopher in every time regime.

In Chapter 2, I deal with the time regime of the Enlightenment. This linear and universal temporality comprehends history as consisting of different stages. Time itself is characterized by chronology, progress and a certain emptiness. In contrast to the empty time of the Enlightenment, Chapter 3 deals with the incarnated or embodied temporality of the Counter-Enlightenment, which makes the historical time a "collective singular", to use a term of Koselleck. It lays the foundation of the time regimes of the nineteenth century.

In the second, third and fourth part of my book I will discuss the historicist nineteenth-century time regimes. In Part 2, consisting of the Chapters 4 and 5, I elaborate on the romanticist pattern of time. Therein the present is understood as part of developments, beginning in the past and continuously progressing into the future. Although the romanticist time perception remains linear and homogeneous, it is not straightforward and upward going, but undulating. It also partly loses its universal nature. Each culture, nation, state or other "continuing entity" has its own temporal development, based as it is on its own destination and individual tendency.

Pivotal in my retrospective representation of time regimes is, as stated previously, the period after 1830. This starts with the emergence of two new temporalities, which must be called heterogeneous. They are more or less purposively constructed in opposition to the homogeneity of the two foregoing time regimes. First we see a regime with a temporality that is called the synchronicity of the non-synchronous (Part 3), in which Tocqueville (Chapter 6) and Marx (Chapter 7) are the protagonists. This time is also referred to as coevalness of the non-coeval or as simultaneity of the non-simultaneous. It must be distinguished from the non-simultaneity of the simultaneous, because that is the dis-simultaneous time of the Enlightenment. The latter is a non-ambiguous, but an empty and homogeneous time, different from the embodied synchronicity of the non-synchronous, originating in the ambiguous time regime, beginning after 1830. After 1880 a new time order arises of which the temporality can be labelled by the name of the Greek god "Kairos". The culture of kairotic time will be discussed in Part 4, in the Chapters 8 and 9. In that regime the "right moment" is crucial. Chapters 10 and 11 are about the time regime of the twentieth and of the first part of the twenty-first centuries. In this period is harvested what the nineteenth century has sown. Historicism wins once again from superficial progress thinking. This book ends with the advantages of a historicist, threefold temporal approach to history writing, above Koselleck's single time of the modern.

Notes

1 A. Landwehr, "Die vielen, die anwesenden und abwesenden Zeiten", in: Fernando Esposito (ed.), *Zeitenwandel. Transformationen geschichtlicher Zeitlichkeit nach dem Boom* (Göttingen and Bristol: Vandenhoeck & Ruprecht, 2017), 227–253, esp. 229. *"Während sich in zahlreichen anderen wissenschaftliche Disziplinen (. . .) eine umfangreiche und seit Langem etablierte Diskussion zum Thema 'Zeit' entwickelt hat, halten sich die Geschichtswissenschaften in diesem Feld eher vornehm zurück".*
2 Although the calendar is an arithmetic and cosmological instrument, it has some culture-bound aspects. See: Landwehr, "Die vielen, die anwesenden und abwesenden Zeiten"; Vanessa Ogle, *The Global Transformation of Time 1870–1950* (Cambridge, MA and London: Harvard University Press, 2015) and William M. Reddy, "The Eurasian Origins of Empty Time and Space", *History and Theory* 55, 3 (October 2016), 325–356. For the Christian calendar see: M. Van Dyck, "Tijdmeting en tijdservaring in de Middeleeuwen", *Hermes* 64, 22 (September 2018), 6–12. Compared to the temporalities, I focus on, clock- and calendar-time remain empty.
3 Koselleck's views have been very influential: See for instance: Ricoeur, *Time and Narrative*, esp. vol. III; Hartog, *Regimes of Historicity*; Assmann, *Ist die Zeit aus den Fugen*; Lorenz and Bevernage, *Breaking up Time*; Christopher Clark, *Time and Power: Visions of History in German Politics, from the Thirty Years' War to the Third Reich* (Princeton and Oxford: Princeton University Press, 2019); Helge Jordheim, "Against Periodization. Koselleck's Theory of Multiple Temporalities", *History and Theory* 51, 2 (2012), 151–172; Alexander Geppert and Till Kössler (Hg), *Obsession der Gegenwart. Zeit im 20. Jahrhundert* (Göttingen and Bristol: Vandenhoeck & Ruprecht, 2015); Fernando Esposito (ed.), *Zeitenwandel. Transformationen geschichtlicher Zeitlichkeit nach dem Boom* (Göttingen and Bristol: Vandenhoeck & Ruprecht, 2017); Chris Lorenz, "Der letzte Fetisch des Stamms der Historiker. Zeit, Raum und Periodisierung in der Geschichtswissenschaft", in: Esposito, *Zeitenwandel*, 63–92.
4 Koselleck, *Futures Past*, 265.
5 Acceleration has since become an important topic in Koselleckian time thinking. See: Koselleck, "Historia Magistra Vitae. The Dissolution of the Topos into the Perspective of a Modernized Historical Process", in: idem, *Futures Past*, 26–42, esp. 40–41; Koselleck, "Time and History", in: idem, *The Practice of Conceptual History*, 112–113 and Koselleck, "Gibt es eine Beschleunigung der Geschichte?", in: idem, *Zeitschichten. Studien zur Historik* (Frankfurt a. M., 2000), 150–176. See also: Hartmut Rosa, *Beschleunigung. Die Veränderung der Zeitstruktur der Moderne* (Frankfurt a. M.: Suhrkamp, 2005); Geppert and Kössler, *Obsession der Gegenwart. Zeit im 20. Jahrhundert*, 7–36, esp. 26–31; Alexandre Escudier, "Das Gefühl der Beschleunigung der Moderne Geschichte: Bausteine für eine Geschichte", *Esprit* (Juni 2008), 165–191; Lorenz, "Der letzte Fetisch des Stamms des Historiker", 68–75 and Lucian Hölscher, "Von leeren und gefüllten Zeiten. Zum Wandel historische Zeitkonzepte seit dem 18. Jahrhundert", in: Geppert and Kössler, *Obsession der Gegenwart*, 63–64; Juri Auderset, Philip Müller and Andreas Behr, "Einleitung: Beschleunigung und plurale Temporalitäten = Introduction: Accélération et temporalités plurielles", *Traverse: Zeitschrift für Geschichte = Revue d'histoire* 23, 3 (2016). See herein the contributions of Theo Jung, Stefan Hanss, Wolfgang Kruse, Carolin Matjeka, Sabine Mischner, Nanina Egli and Rüdiger Graf. They all see, besides the time of progress and acceleration, more past-oriented times in the historiography of the nineteenth and twentieth centuries.
6 Koselleck, "The Eighteenth Century as the Beginning of Modernity", in: idem, *The Practice of Conceptual History*, 154–169, esp. 165–169.
7 Koselleck, "'Space of Experience' and 'Horizon of Expectation'. Two Historical Categories", in: idem, *Futures Past*, 259–275. Perhaps its origins lie in a Heideggerian "being" (*Sein*) and a Gadamerian "fusion of horizons" (*Horizontverschmelzung*). They both have a personal connotation; therefore, Koselleck makes them into super-personal, historical categories.

20 Introduction

8 Koselleck, "Modernity and the Planes of Historicity", in: idem, *Futures Past*, 9–25, esp. 22–25. Koselleck, "'Space of Experience' and 'Horizon of Expectation'", 265–275.
9 "The lesser the experience, the greater the expectation: this is a formula for the temporal structure of the modern, to the degree that it is rendered a concept by 'progress'". Koselleck, "'Space of 'Experience' and 'Horizon of Expectation'", 274.
10 Koselleck, "Gibt es eine Beschleunigung der Geschichte?", 150–176; Koselleck, "Time and History", 112–113; see also: Geppert and Kössler, "Zeit-Geschichte als Aufgabe", in: idem, *Obsession der Gegenwart*, 7–36, esp. 26–31.
11 Assmann, *Ist die Zeit aus den Fugen?*, 45–47.
12 Rosa, *Beschleunigung*, 16; Esposito, "Transformationen geschichtliche Zeitlichkeit nach dem Boom", 23, n. 61.
13 Lucian Hölscher has rightfully perceived that an empty time originates in the eighteenth century. Lucian Hölscher, *Semantik der Leere. Grenzfragen der Geschichtswissenschaft* (Göttingen: Wallstein Verlag, 2009). See also: Lorenz, "Der letzte Fetisch des Stamms der Historiker", 83.
14 Esposito, "Transformationen geschichtlicher Zeitlichkeit nach dem Boom", in: Esposito, *Zeitenwandel*, 28–29.
15 Hartog, *Regimes of Historicity*, 107–127.
16 Assmann, *Ist die Zeit aus den Fugen?*, 226–238.
17 Ibid., 201–203.
18 Ibid., 321–324.
19 Koselleck, "History, Histories and Formal Time Structures", in: idem, *Futures Past*, 93–104, esp. 95–96; See also: "Geschichte, Geschichten und formale Zeitstrukturen", in: idem, *Vergangene Zukunft*, 130–143, esp. 132–133; Hölscher, "Mysteries of Historical Order", in: Lorenz and Bevernage, *Breaking up Time*, 134–154, esp. 142–144. Also: Hölscher, "Von leeren und gefüllten Zeiten", 66–67.
20 Lorenz and Bevernage, "Introduction", in: Lorenz and Bevernage, *Breaking up Time*, 32 and 142–144.
21 Helge Jordheim, "Introduction: Multiple Times and the Work of Synchronization", *History and Theory* 53, 4 (2014), 498–518, esp. 515. See also: Harry Jansen, "In Search of New Times: Temporality in the Enlightenment and Counter-Enlightenment", *History and Theory* 55, 1 (2016), 66–90, esp. 72.
22 That Koselleck has a diachronic perception of the "*Gleichzeitigkeit des Ungleichzeitigen*" is also apparent from his view on German history as a "Sonderweg". Therein Germany lags behind Western democracy till 1945. See: Lorenz, "Der letzte Fetisch des Stamms der Historiker", 80.
23 See Chapter 3.
24 Ernst Bloch, "Ungleichzeitigkeit, nicht nur Rückständigkeit", in: idem, *Philosophische Aufsätze zur objektiven Phantasie* (Frankfurt a. M.: Suhrkamp Verlag, 1969), 41–49, esp. 44–45.
25 Hartog, "The Modern *Régime* of Historicity in the Face of Two World Wars", in: Lorenz and Bevernage, *Breaking up Time*, 124–134. See also Hartog, *Regimes of Historicity*, 108.
26 Hölscher, "Mysteries of Historical Order", 145–146.
27 Louis Mink, "History and Fiction as Modes of Comprehension", *New Literary History* 1, 3 (1970), 541–558, esp. 557–558 and idem, *Historical Understanding* (ed. Brian Fay, Eugene Golob and Richard Vann; Ithaca: Cornell University Press, 1987); Frank Ankersmit, *Meaning, Truth and Reference in Historical Explanation* (Cornell: Leuven University Press, 2012), chapter 2, esp. 39.
28 Ricoeur, *Time and Narrative*, vol. III, 133.
29 Fernand Braudel, *The Mediterranean and the Mediterranean World in the Age of Philip II* (transl. Siân Reynolds; Berkeley and Los Angeles: University of California Press, 1999).
30 Ricoeur, *Time and Narrative*, vol. I, 209–217. See also Chapter 10 of this book.
31 Ibid., vol. 1, 5–51.

32 See also: Harry Jansen, "Time, Narrative, and Fiction: The Uneasy Relationship between Ricoeur and a Heterogeneous Temporality", *History and Theory* 54, 1 (February 2015), 1–24.
33 This book is not the place to elaborate on this issue. I have done so in Harry Jansen, "Research, Narrative and Representation. A Post-narrative Approach", *History and Theory* 58, 1 (2019), 67–88.
34 Hartog, *Regimes of Historicity*, 17 and 73.
35 Ibid., 23–40. See also: Abdelmajid Hannoum, "What Is an Order of Time?", *History and Theory* 47, 3 (2008), 465. Are the Greeks and the Hawaiians representative for all the experiences of time in traditionalist societies?
36 Hartog, "The Modern *Régime* of Historicity in the Face of Two World Wars", 126.
37 Abdelmajid Hannoum, "What Is an Order of Time?", 465.
38 Hartog, *Regimes of Historicity*, 18.
39 Terence Holden, "Hartog, Koselleck and Ricoeur: Historical Anthropology and the Crisis of the Present", *History and Theory* 58, 3 (2019), 385–405, esp. 394–396 and 398–400.
40 See also: Assmann, *Ist die Zeit aus den Fugen?*, 323. She states: *Das Verhältnis zwischen Vergangenheit, Geggenwart und Zukunft ist ein dreistelige Relation, bei der nicht dauerhaft – wie Hartog dies nachgezeignet hat – nur eine Zeitdimension auf Kosten der anderen existieren kann.*
41 Hartog, "The Modern *Régime* of Historicity in the Face of Two World Wars", 125.
42 Hartog states: "the dispersion or simply a multiplicity of different regimes of temporality could be a constitutive or distinctive feature of the present" in: Hartog, *Régimes d'historicité*, 208. In his "Multiple Times and the Work of Synchronization", Helge Jordheim refers to this phrase of Hartog and he also detects that he "leaves this idea by the wayside". Jordheim, "Multiple Times and the Work of Synchronization", 501. I must add to this, that Hartog is talking about "a multiplicity of time regimes" and not of a multiplicity of times, about which Jordheim is talking.
43 Jordheim, "Multiple Times and the Work of Synchronization", 502. With Jordheim, I endorse the phenomenon of pluri-temporality, which implies that time is not a given but a human construction. See also: Achim Landwehr, "Die vielen, anwesenden und abwesenden Zeiten", in: Esposito, *Zeitenwandel*, 227–253, esp. 237 and 241–243.
44 Koselleck, "Historical Time and Social History", in: idem, *The Practice of Social History*, 115–130.
45 Ibid., 126.
46 Next to temporality is the history of concepts, another field of interest for him.
47 Koselleck, "Historical Time and Social History", 128.
48 Ibid.
49 Ibid., 129.
50 See also: Holden, "Hartog, Koselleck and Ricoeur", 386–387.
51 For the relationship between research and social experience, see: Harry Jansen, "Research, Narrative and Representation", 67–88.
52 Robert Brandom, *Making It Explicit: Reasoning, Representing and Discursive Commitment* (Cambridge, MA and London: Harvard University Press 1998[2]), 616.
53 Ibid., 616.
54 Ibid., 618. It must be noticed here that Kant in his *Critique of Judgement* also thinks the particular in the context of the general. Brandom thus turns the Kant of the *Third Critique* against the Kant from the *First Critique of Reason*.
55 Brandom, *Making It Explicit*, 97–98 and 618.
56 Ibid., 618.
57 Ibid., 622.
58 Ibid., 616.
59 Hereafter we will see that time's content can be "empty" or "embodied".
60 David L. Marshall, "The Implications of Robert Brandom's Inferentialism for Intellectual History", *History and Theory* 52 (February 2013), 1–31, esp. 7.

22 Introduction

61 Ibid., 17. Actually, I endorse Pocock's idea, that tradition stands for a "continuity of the languages in which a debate was conducted" and for "connexions between the speech acts by whose performance [that debate] was conducted." Marshall, "The Implications of Robert Brandom's Inferentialism for Intellectual History", 18.
62 Ibid., 17.
63 Despite Brandom's view, Kant remains important for the conception of time in the Enlightenment. It results in a homogeneous and empty time. In the next chapter I will pay extensive attention to it, because Koselleck distils from it his homogeneous "time of the modern".
64 Inferences, which have both form and content, are, as a result, based on both epistemic and ontological assumptions. Following Brandom's vision, Koselleck's conclusion that conceptual history can be without ontological presuppositions must be rejected. Social history and conceptual history both have epistemic and ontological presuppositions, although as forms of knowledge they are of course merely epistemic. See: Koselleck, "Social History and Conceptual History", in: idem, *The Practice of Conceptual History*, 20–37, esp. 35–36.
65 Jonathan Gorman, "The Limits of Historiographical Choice in Temporal Distinctions", in: Lorenz and Bevernage, *Breaking up Time*, 163. Maybe it is better to speak of "means of communication", instead of "institution", because the latter has the connotation of a belonging together according to rules and aims.
66 Gorman, "The Limits of Historiographical Choice in Temporal Distinctions", 162.
67 Ibid.
68 Ibid. Brandom and Gorman derive their inferential relationships between concept and content from Quine's rejection of the radical distinction between analytic and synthetic propositions.
69 Gorman, "The Limits of Historiographical Choice in Temporal Distinctions", 163.
70 Ibid., 162.
71 Compare Gorman's features of the web with those Robert Brandom proposes: "To treat states or performances as intentionally contentful in the sense of being conceptually articulated involves treating them as situated in a web of proprieties of inferential transitions from one content to the other". Brandom, *Making It Explicit*, 90.
72 Gorman, "The Limits of Historiographical Choice in Temporal Distinctions", 163.
73 See Brandom, *Making It Explicit*, 20.
74 Leopold von Ranke, *Geschichten der romanischen und germanischen Völker von 1494 bis 1535* (Leipzig: Reimer, 1824), v–vi. Transl.: Gertrud Himmelfarb, *The New History and the Old: Critical Essays and Reappraisals* (Cambridge, MA and London: Harvard University Press, 2004), 17. See also: Felix Gilbert, *History: Politics or Culture. Reflections on Ranke and Burckhardt* (Princeton: Princeton University Press, 1990), 15–31.
75 Hans Kellner, "Introduction", in: F. Ankersmit, E. Domanska and H. Kellner (eds.), *Re-figuring Hayden White* (Stanford: Stanford University Press, 2009), 4. Although I presume that the change of time regimes is related to change of generations, I do not want to develop a theory of generation phases as is done by Dilthey in his "Pantheismus nach seinem geschichtlichen Zusammenhang mit den älteren Pantheistischen Systemen", in: Wilhelm Dilthey, *Gesammelte Schriften*, vol. II (Stuttgart: B.G. Teubner, 1957) or by Ortega y Gassett in his, "Die Aufgabe unserer Zeit (1923)", in: *Gesammelte Werke* (transl. Helene Weyl and Ulrich Weber, 4 Vols.; Stuttgart: Deutsche Verlags-Anstalt, 1950), 455–466.
76 Marshall, "The Implications of Robert Brandom's Inferentialism for Intellectual History", 7 and 17.
77 See for the relation between representations and aspects: Ankersmit, *Meaning, Truth and Reference*, 84.
78 This happens along the line I set out in: Jansen, "Research, Narrative and Representation", 78 and 84–87.
79 Time regimes are representations of cultural phenomena, constructed by the historian. My investigation is historical, not philosophical or sociological.

80 Intellectual history of time needs to be distinguished from a cultural or anthropological history of time. A cultural history would include European popular culture, and an anthropological history would include time perceptions of cultures outside Europe. My history of time regimes is predominantly European, though some attention is paid to postcolonial history. See: Hannoum, "What Is an Order of Time?", 463.
81 See the ultimate chapter of this study.
82 In this context a remark must be made: I do not make any distinction between "time" and "temporality". Both terms refer to an experienced time as it is epitomized in the writings of philosophers and historians in the last three centuries.
83 Martin Nosàl, "The Gadamerian Approach to the Relation between Experience and Language", *History and Theory* 54, 2 (2015), 195–208, esp. 196.
84 Is this the knowledge of the loss of eternity, which is associated with the loss of paradise? Not only in Christianity but in all kinds of cultures and religions, some notion of loss exists. Is time not the binary counterpart of eternity? See for the binary aspects of time: Landwehr, "Die vielen, anwesenden und abwesenden Zeiten", 238.
85 Nosàl, "The Gadamerian Approach to the Relation between Experience and Language", 205.
86 Landwehr, "Die vielen, anwesenden und abwesenden Zeiten", 235–236. Nosàl, "The Relation between Experience and Language", 205, note 24. "*Im Lernen einer Sprache, im Hineinwachsen in unsre Muttersprache artikuliert sich uns die Welt*".
87 Maurice Halbwachs, *The Collective Memory* (ed. and transl. Lewis A. Coser; Chicago: University of Chicago Press, 1992), esp. 22–87.
88 Frank Ankersmit, *Historical Representation* (Stanford: Stanford University Press, 2001), 157.
89 Frank Ankersmit confirms this: "there will be little hope for individual historical experience if we have to abandon collectivist or holistic . . . experience". Ankersmit, *Meaning Truth and Reference*, 179.
90 Allan Megill, *Prophets of Extremity: Nietzsche, Heidegger, Foucault, Derrida* (Berkeley, Los Angeles and London: University of California Press, 1987), 17–20, 33–35 and 110–116.
91 Ankersmit, *Meaning, Truth and Reference*, 4, note 9. Ankersmit in this note does not call them historicists but scholars reflecting on the nature of historical writing. His list includes also neo-Kantianists like Rickert, Windelband and Weber, whom he dismisses as historicists. He also includes Feuerbach, Marx and Lamprecht, whom he also does not consider historicists. He does not mention Heidegger, who plays an important role in Chakrabarty's book. Following the broad definition of Mandelbaum and Mannheim they all are, in my view, historicists. Ankersmit, *Meaning, Truth and Reference*, 5–7.
92 See: Koselleck, "Transformations of Experience and Methodological Change: A Historical-Anthropological Essay", in: idem, *The Practice of Conceptual History*, 45–83.
93 Terence Holden thus interprets Koselleck's temporality. See: Holden, "Hartog, Koselleck and Ricoeur", passim. See also the section "A preliminary definition of time" in the following.
94 Ankersmit, *Meaning, Truth and Reference*, 1; and idem, *Sublime Historical Experience* (Stanford: Stanford University Press, 2005), 144. However, Ankersmit delimits historicism mainly to what I will call in this book historicism with a romanticist perception of time.
95 Ankersmit, *Meaning, Truth and Reference*, 2.
96 Dipesh Chakrabarty, *Provincializing Europe: Postcolonial Thought and Historical Difference* (Princeton: Princeton University Press, 2007²), 22.
97 See Chakrabarty, *Provincializing Europe* and Chapter 10 of this book.
98 Ankersmit, *Meaning, Truth and Reference*, 3–4. Ankersmit's own perception of historicism is more limited than Mannheim's. According to Ankersmit the neo-Kantians do not belong to it, because of their search for universal values. They do not see, as Ankersmit observes, that "each epoch has its own set of such time-specific rules and is in need of them".

24 Introduction

99 Karl Mannheim, *Essays on the Sociology of Knowledge* (ed. P. Kecskemeti; London: Routledge and Kegan Paul, 1952), 83–88.
100 Ankersmit, *Meaning, Truth and Reference*, 10.
101 See Chapter 9.
102 Ankersmit, *Meaning, Truth and Reference*, 11.
103 See the definition of Collingwood, in the following.
104 See for Aristotle, W. D. Ross (ed.), *The Works of Aristotle II, Physics* (Oxford: Clarendon, 1947), 219b and 220a, for Augustine, *Confessions* (transl. E. B. Pusey; Arcadia Press, 20172), Book 11, chapters 14: 17–15: 19. Henri Bergson argues in the same way as Aristotle and Augustine. Henri Bergson, *Matter and Memory* (London: Allen and Unwin, 1911), 193.
105 Augustine, *Confessions*, Book 11, (transl. E.B. Pusey; Mount Pleasant, SC: Arcadia Press, 2017^2). chapter 14: 17.
106 Ross, *The Works of Aristotle II*, 219b and 220a.
107 Ricoeur, *Time and Narrative*, vol. II, 152.
108 Augustine, *Confessions*, Book 11, chapters 14: 17, 18: 23–24 and 20: 26.
109 Ibid., chapter 15: 20.
110 Ibid., chapter 28: 37–38.
111 Ibid., chapter 28: 38.
112 Possibly Augustine derived this idea from Plato's *Timaeus*, 37. There the Greek philosopher states that days, nights, months and years do not exist before the emergence of heaven. They are a imperfect image of eternity. See: Plato, "Timaeus", in: *Verzameld Werk* V, Dutch translation from: Xaveer de Win (Antwerpen: Baarn, 1980), 218.
113 Augustine, *Confessions*, Book 11, chapter 13: 15–16.
114 Gorman, "The Limits of Historiographical Choice in Temporal Distinctions", 155–162.
115 Ibid., 160–161.
116 See: Landwehr, "Die vielen, anwesenden und abwesenden Zeiten", 245–249.
117 See Chapter 8.
118 Landwehr, "Die vielen, anwesenden und abwesenden Zeiten", 249.
119 See: Jérôme Baschet, *Défaire la tyrannie du présent. Temporalités émergentes et futurs inédits* (Paris: La Découverte, 2018), which especially rejects Hartog's presentism.

PART 1
In search of new times

2
THE EMPTY TIME OF THE ENLIGHTENMENT

Isaac Newton

To unravel Koselleck's "time of the modern", we must pay attention to the society and culture at the beginning of the eighteenth century. It offers insights into the time regime of the Enlightenment.

Religious perceptions of time, like the one of Augustine, are preponderant until the rise of empiricism in the seventeenth century. Then those perceptions slowly disappear. The English scientist Isaac Newton more or less returns to the cosmological time concepts of Aristotle. His temporality is characterized by the idea that time is not created, as Augustine thought, but can be called absolute, with no beginning and end. This fits in with another Newtonian idea, namely the universality of physical laws. Those laws do not function only on earth but in the whole universe, with gravitation as its most remarkable example. Time and space are eternal categories, independent of the empirical world and human experiences.

However, these ideas are not completely irreligious. Newton comprehends time and space, as the German philosopher of history Lucian Hölscher states, "as divine principles of animation, as tools of God to give life to His creatures".[1] As such Newton's abstract perception of time is not completely irrelevant for history writing. Hölscher calls it "an abstract medium of history", allowing to measure the length of a period of time and to define eras like those of Christ and the Hijra.[2]

In the next century Newton becomes very popular. Voltaire writes an essay on the English physicist.[3] The French neoclassicist architect Etienne-Louis Boullée (1728–1799), being the most striking representative of Enlightenment architecture, designs a cenotaph for him. This funeral monument and his project for the National Library in Paris are important symbols not only for the architecture of the eighteenth century but also for the time views in that age.

Boullée's monuments[4]

In honour of Newton, Boullée builds in 1784 a sphere of 150 metres in heights, embedded in a circular base, topped with cypress trees. In the upper part are holes, through which the daylight can enter the dark hall, where the sarcophagus stands. By night this room is illuminated by a model of the globe, hanging in the centre, where it gives off a mysterious glow. Boullée glorifies the man who has studied the cosmos, claiming that there is universal gravity and absolute temporality, as a result of which he has designed a mechanized worldview. This memorial contains an empty sarcophagus placed in the lower part of the sphere. Newton is interred elsewhere; that's why his tomb is empty. Yet its emptiness is very symbolic, as we will see, because the time perception of the Enlightenment is absolute and almost without any content.

A year later, Boullée designs the Bibliothèque Nationale in Paris. It is megalomaniac a building, intended as an alternative to the tall medieval cathedrals. It has an open roof like the Pantheon in Rome, which allows air and daylight to dispel the dust and darkness of previous centuries, giving people a clear mind. An almost endless row of identical pillars creates an illuminated hall, with strict perspective lines focused on one point on the horizon. It creates the impression of a straight line into a bright future. By reading books about the past, people in the hall can get good and bad examples of how they can move towards a new, promising world. Both monuments represent the linear, homogeneous temporality of the Enlightenment, based on the physical and Aristotelian-Newtonian perception of time.

In a completely different way, the French painter Watteau also represents an empty time, with figures of the *Commedia dell'arte* with their everlasting Pierrots,

FIGURE 2.1 Etienne-Louis Boullée, *Newton Memorial*

The empty time of the Enlightenment 29

FIGURE 2.2 Design Etienne-Louis Boullée of the *National Library of Paris*

FIGURE 2.3 Jean-Antoine Watteau, *Love in the Italian Theatre*

Pierrettes, Columbinas, Dottores and Pulcinellas. The actors always must perform the same character and are not considered to embody an individual person. The French art philosopher and historian René Huyge comments the figures of the Commedia dell'arte on Watteau's *Love in the Italian Theatre* of 1718:

> Visible, fictional, they are there before us. In the mirror of their false presence, those symmetrical faces, of "never" and "always", recognize each and reconcile themselves to each other. Doubtless they have always been like this; doubtless they never existed.[5]

Especially "faces of 'never' and 'always'" represent a time of empty "nows", from which never a real story can be told, nor a shocking moment can be revealed.[6]

Pre-Adamite times

Time becomes an interesting subject in the eighteenth century. As a result of new discoveries, the Enlightenment creates: (1) an extension of time in periods before Adam; (2) a new chronology, periodization and thinking in terms of rationality and (moral) progress; and (3) a paradigm shift, produced by the combination of the previous two issues. The extension of time starts already in 1655. Then the Frenchman Lapeyrère publishes his *Praeadamitae*, wherein he evokes the hypothesis that people lived before Adam and that the book Genesis only concerns the origins of the Jewish people. Thus he introduces the possibility of two distinct chronologies: a biblical and a new one, the pre-Adamite. Lapeyrère also believes that the chronologies of Chaldeans and Chinese go further back than the Christian era. He claims defiantly:

> But as Geographers use to place Seas upon that place of the Globe, which they know not: so Chronologers, who are near of kin to them, use to blot out ages past, which they know not. They down those Countries which they know not: these with cruel pen kill the times they heard not of, and deny that which they know not.[7]

Not only the pre-biblical parts of the Chinese calendar but also fossils of fishes in mountains point in the direction of pre-biblical times. Around 1669 Robert Hooke argues that these fossils are "the greatest and most lasting monuments of antiquity, which in all probability, will far antedate all the most ancient monuments of the world, even the very pyramids".[8]

René Descartes designs a new history with regard to the origins of the solar system and the development of the earth. He also comes to the conclusion that our globe is much older than the 6,000 years of the biblical creation story. But he is prudent, fearing the punishment of the church. Therefore he begins the first section of part IV of his *Principles of Philosophy* with the statement that, although his hypothesis of the age of the globe is false, it must be retained, "to provide an explanation of the true natures of things".[9] The increasing knowledge of pre-biblical ages and of cultures outside Europe lead to theories of the development of the earth in the form of conjectures and hypotheses. Most philosophical historians try to make these theories compatible with their biblical beliefs, but none of them succeeds completely.[10]

The new discoveries and the resulting contradiction between a biblical-oriented and a secular-oriented history creates problems with regard to chronology. As a consequence, they lay the foundation not only for new chronologies but also – and that is even more important – for a new philosophical history. In the Scottish Enlightenment it is referred to as "conjectural history", whereby it is allowed to fill in the unavoidable gaps in historical evidence by interpretation and speculation.[11] The French call a similar approach *histoire raisonnée* or *histoire philosophique*. The Scottish conjectural and the French philosophical history have several features in common which can be summarized as anti-traditional perceptions of subjects, rationality and horizon.[12] We can be short about the subjects. Instead of the traditional political and religious subjects, new items come to the fore as customs and habits, modes of production, civil society and the position of women. Regarding rationality, the philosophical historians abjured the biblical basis of explanation and exchanged it for explications based on the human ratio. Horizon needs more explication.

An extending horizon with new periodizations

The extending horizon in space and time is the most important historical item of the New Age. Traditional history displays a European outlook, extended only by parts of the Middle East and Northern Africa. The new philosophical history expands its view to China, India and America.

The new history is universal in character, with stages of progress, ending in Europe in the eighteenth century. This becomes clear in the conjectural history of Adam Smith and John Millar, in the French philosophical history of Condorcet and in the German universal history of August Schlözer. In the fourth paragraph of his *Wealth of Nations*, Smith contrasts the living standards in "savage nations of hunters and fishers" with the standards of "civilized and thriving nations".[13] Hence Smith distinguishes four stages: (1) the age of hunters, (2) the age of shepherds, (3) the age of agriculture and (4) the age of commerce.[14] Millar also lists four stages in the history of progress: the first is one of barbarism and matriarchy, the second pertains a pastoral age, the third is the age of agriculture and of the useful arts and manufactures and finally he mentions the stage of "great opulence and the culture of the elegant arts".[15]

The most rounded illustration of the time perception of Enlightenment is Condorcet's posthumous published, *Esquisse* of 1795. Condorcet (1743–1794) distinguishes three stages in history. The first moves from primitivism to the development of language, the second runs from the use of language to the use of writing as it is done by the Greeks, the third stage starts with the classical period and exhibits the broadening of culture until Condorcet's own time. The last period again is partitioned in three stages. The first ends with the revival of science and the invention of printing, the second displays the throwing off of the yoke of authority in science and the third opens with new inventions in mathematics and physics, including Condorcet's own study in integral calculus.[16]

In Prussia August, Ludwig von Schlözer (1735–1809) writes a *Universal History* (*Weltgeschichte*), which is meant to be a guide for education. Schlözer wants to show those topics of the past that still can be perceived in the then present. Man has to keep factors like lifestyle, climate, food, sovereigns and priests in mind, because "life-style determines, climate and nutrition creates, sovereigns force, priests teach, and the examples inspire".[17] He distinguishes six eras in history: (1) a primeval world (*Urwelt*), from the creation to the Flood, lasting 1,600 years; (2) the dark world (*Dunkle Welt*) from the Flood to the first written sources, especially Moses with his Ten Commandments (400 years); (3) the preworld (*Vorwelt*) from Moses to the end of the Persian Empire (400 years); (4) the old world (*Alte Welt*) unto the fall of the Roman Empire in 476 AD (800 years); (5) the Middle Ages (*Mittelalter*) up to the discovery of America in 1492 (800 years); and (6) the new world (*Neue Welt*) up to the present.[18] Regarding the first era Schlözer indicates in a footnote, he assumes that the earth can be older than the creation date of 3987 BC. So he agrees with his French, English and Scottish forerunners. The rounded numbers of the periods represent the mathematical nature of his periodization, showing the emptiness of his chronology. And although this universal history contains some content, its periodization is based on presumed analogies between different stages of progress inside and outside Europe. There is no research in both fields, based on the presupposition of contingency. Without such a presupposition, I regard the temporalities at stake, empty (see the following).

A paradigm shift? Koselleck, Jordheim and synchronization

The worldview and historical belief system, founded on biblical knowledge, comes to an end in the last quarter of the seventeenth century. New discoveries are being made, which results in anomalies of the then worldview. The anomalies trouble men like Descartes, Lapeyrère and Schlözer, who need to search for an alternative belief system which solves the inconsistencies of the old one. It is found in a universal history of stages, by which it is possible to sort history anew, consistent with the newly acquired information. The universal history of the Enlightenment is the result of a kind of paradigm shift, of what is called above as Gorman's "rolling web of reality-sorting expressions".[19] For all historians "historical reality is, what we count it to be", but this is all the more true for the eighteenth-century philosophical historians.[20]

European historians are confronted with the non-synchronicity of the new discoveries with the biblical- and classical-oriented European history, thus synchronizing of temporalities becomes urgent. Moreover, all the distinct "conjectural" and philosophical histories, with their own stages of time, intensify the problem of the multiplicity of temporalities. Helge Jordheim, in Koselleck's footsteps, observes this problem in his "Multiple Times and the Work of Synchronization". He refers to the French *Encyclopédie* by Diderot and d'Alembert, which struggles with the continuous new information in the eighteenth century and the multiple temporalities connected to it. The *Encyclopédie*, according to Jordheim, faces the task of "synchronization to bring all temporalities into sync with one another".[21]

Jordheim also mentions the work of Johann Christoph Gatterer and his *Einleitung in die synchronische Universalgeschichte* (1771), wherein Gatterer addresses the problem of universal history. According to Jordheim, Gatterer claims that "the historian needs to take account of what occurs in different places in the world at the same time", notwithstanding the fact that he also has to "give an account of only one single diachronic narrative".[22] In another study, *Vom historischen Plan und der darauf sich gründenden Zusammenhang der Erzählungen* (1767), Gatterer designs rules of synchronicity. Despite several frantic attempts, Gatterer's endeavour to systematize universal history completely fails. His *Einleitung* remains a hodgepodge of chronologies, themes, schemes and regions.[23]

From here originates Koselleck's dichotomy between the plural development of states and nations and history as one, singular great change into progress. His solution of history as a "collective singular" has the advantage that it put into words the paradigm shift of "*Historien*" into "*Geschichte*".[24] The former consists of a loose totality of stories about happenings in the past, the latter is more or less a system of stories, mostly pointed to as "universal history". For such a singular narrative, synchronization of the multiple times of cultures is needed.[25]

The synchronization of multiple times in the Enlightenment concerns not only the historical times of stages but also what Koselleck calls, "natural time". He means the time of the clock, of the calendar, of chronology, of dynasties and of eras.[26] Jordheim does not want to make a distinction between natural and historical times: "neither in the seventeenth and eighteenth centuries, as the modern temporal regime emerged, nor at the present, at the moment of its collapse, can we find any similar, clear-cut distinction between natural and historical times".[27] I think, he is right if it regards the times of the Enlightenment; they are natural as well as historical. However, this does not mean that, inside Enlightenment's historical time, we have not to distinguish between the phasing, the natural and the chronological aspects of time. These different aspects are important because in the eighteenth century, from a philosophical point of view, they are perceived not only as distinct but also as influencing one another. We will see that with Kant.

The connection between natural and chronological time, on the one hand, and its phasing aspects, on the other, makes the historical time of the Enlightenment "empty", a term I derive from Hölscher.[28] Its emptiness first concerns its lack of contingency and secondly the fact that the phases evolve in time, not through (their own) time.[29] During the Enlightenment time is only the medium in which historical events occur. This also means that in the Enlightenment's philosophical history, the past has no organic relationship with the present. There is only a perceived, idealistic connection, in the form of a preordained path of phases, along which humankind moves into a better and more enlightened future.[30]

The historical time of progress is narrowly tied to chronology, because the historians of the Enlightenment connect the temporality of progress with universal history.[31] They want to know how far other countries and nations have progressed on their way to the stage of civilization, reached already by France, England and Prussia. As a consequence, in the Enlightenment there is much attention to the problem of chronological non-coevalness between cultures, nations and so on and the work of synchronization.[32] It stems from Koselleck's idea that history is a collective singular, forming a unitary whole, on the one hand, and consisting of states and nations in different stages of progress, on the other.

In this context Koselleck paraphrases Kant: "So far history has conformed to chronology. Now it is about making chronology conform to history".[33] I agree because it indicates that before the Enlightenment, history was an aggregate of separated histories without any relation to one another, each having only the chronology of some calendar.[34] Kant observes that universal history, understood as a unity (collective singular), requires a form in which the different histories are chronologically tuned. However, it still concerns the synchronization of an empty, progressive but mostly chronologically perceived time. When Jordheim discusses eighteenth-century synchronization, it is about this empty time.[35] Kant is all the more important here, because his historical, "empty" temporality is founded on a natural time, which underlines its "emptiness".

Kant's "empty" natural time

Eighteenth-century philosophical history is a preordained history, built mostly on judgements and hypotheses than on proofs or confirmations.[36] From Descartes to Kant history is hypothetical and therefore it is called "conjectural", "philosophical" and "empty". Kant's natural temporality is consistent with this kind of history and thus affected by the same emptiness. That is what I want to explain hereafter. However, Kant's judgement with regard to temporality has two aspects: first, a judgement concerning the conditioning function for objective appearances; and second, a judgement concerning the mediating function in order to connect phenomena in the world with the pure concepts in the mind.[37]

Time judged as **condition** has an objective and a subjective dimension. The subjective aspect of Kant's time consists in its form of intuition, in being a so-called *Anschauungsform*. As such it is a form of the mind and thus outside the human subject non-existent.[38] Moreover, as a form of intuition, time does not change, but change is something that exists in time.[39] So, time seems to be an *a priori* concept of the mind without any connection with, what Kant uses to call, the phenomenal world. Yet he also claims that time cannot exist without our (temporal) experiences. In Kant's words: "we can cognize of things *a priori* only what we ourselves have put into them".[40] About this objective aspect Kant states: "[Time is] in respect of all phenomena, and therefore of all things that can happen to us in experience, necessarily objective".[41] It is the objective time of the *nunc stans*, which I will discuss in the next section.

Time in its **mediating function** must bridge the sharp distinction between the world of appearance, the so-called phenomenal world, and the world of pure concepts, which resides in the mind. Time must be both spiritual and experiential.[42] The world of pure concepts consists of four basic divisions: quality, quantity, relationship and modality. With regard to the pure concept of *quality*, time, as a connection between the world of appearance and the world of pure concepts, consists of the filling of time. This concerns the question of time's content, which we already have answered above with the statement that the time of Kant is historically empty. However, this leads to the question whether there is no reality at all in Kant's temporality? There is, but only according to the rules of physics. He explains it with the statement that full and empty are only extremes, between which there are infinitely many degrees. Heat is the most obvious example. In the course of time, bodies can differ in intensity because water can exist in different degrees of heat: as ice, water or steam. But these qualities are phenomena which only can be present or absent; a middle way is not possible. Water cannot be at the same time ice or steam. As a consequence, change in content is not related to development of time. Change takes place in time, not through time. Therefore, Kant's time-content relates to physics, not to history. Water exists in time, but its change in ice or steam happens in another time. As for Aristotle, Newton's and Kant's time exists of now-points. So the change takes place in another now-point (see the next section). Moreover, because content-change is only related to now-points and phenomena are only present or absent, the present can only exist due to an absence of the past and the future.

Kant, mediating between the phenomenal world and the pure concept of *quantity*, perceives time as a magnitude. It is an understanding of time as "a successive addition of homogeneous units".[43] In its relationship to the pure concept of quantity, it must be divided in the categories of unity, plurality and totality. As stated before, time in its phenomenological status is nothing else than a "now". A specific time-span of successive "nows" can be (1) "momentary", (2) a series of "nows" or (3) a completion of "nows". It concerns respectively a *unity*, for instance a minute; a *plurality*, several successive minutes; or a *totality*, an hour as a completion of 60 minutes. It is obvious that this "quantity" time historically must be comprehended as empty as the time connected to the pure concept of quality. Yet, time as quantity can be *used* historically. Then it calls for a transfer into historical time in the form of the years of the calendar (unity: the year 1740; plurality: the years 1740, 1741 and 1742; and totality: 1740–1745). We already observed that historical time, being only chronological, is empty too.

Time, with regard to the pure concept of *relation*, perceives phenomena in three different ways: first, as enduring through time; second, as a state of affairs succeeding one another, and third, as coexisting of different objects. *Enduring* time is remaining permanent in substance "while all else changes".[44] Time as *succession* refers to the pure concept of relation in its aspect of causality. It is succession according to a rule. As soon as Kant considers time as a *coexisting* of different objects, there is a problem with regard to space. After all Kant distinguishes time and space as respectively non-simultaneous and simultaneous. Different objects can coexist in space, but not in time. Because time is a form of intuition, there cannot be different objects in the mind at the same time. As a consequence, his perception of time as simultaneous must have a special content. It concerns a synchronic interaction in an undivided "now". Here Kant has Newton's conception of mutual attraction of bodies in mind. Although change takes place in time, the "now" as a representation of phenomenal time itself remains unchanged. Henceforth, the relational aspect of time maintains its emptiness.

Kant's time in relation to the world of pure concepts in the form of *modality* sees phenomena in three ways: as possibility, actuality or necessity. As a *possibility*, an object can be considered as occupying time or not. As *actuality*, it exists in a specific part of time. As *necessity*, we must allocate time to each object. We cannot think of an object without time. Time "as modality" is about the way objects exist in time not about the modality of time itself. Here we have again: time does not change; change exists in time, which means an empty time.

Time as a mediator between the world of phenomena and of pure concepts remains as empty in its modality as in the other three (i.e. quantity, quality and relationship).

Nunc stans

Despite the emptiness of natural time in its conditional and in its mediating functions, there must be an experience of time, according to Kant. This can be derived from his statement that "we can cognize of things *a priori* only what we ourselves have put into them".[45] Then the question is: what experience fits in with an unmoving form of intuition in the mind? I think it is the continuing now, the *nunc stans*.[46] That experiential time is important for historical time, because it can answer the question whether Koselleck's historical time of the collective singular, called *Geschichte* instead of *Historie*, is supported by Kant. I will argue that for Kant the past as a category of time is as empty as the future. Hence Kant's perception of time is more related to *Historie* than to *Geschichte*. Only Kant's idea of progress is important for history as *Geschichte*, not his views on time.

Following Heidegger, I think we must search for such an unmoved experience in the endless repeating, and therefore continuing "now".[47] Heidegger understands Kant's experienced "now-time" as the phenomenal side of his temporality. He perceives Kant's "now" as the enduring phenomenon in which change evolves as a form of succession.[48] For Kant, the continuing "now" is "*das Unwandelbare im Dasein*", in which change becomes observable.[49] The continuing "now" is in agreement with Kant's Newtonian idea that time is absolute. It implies that past and future only have a phenomenological status, as far as they can be identified as a past and future "now".

Kant's empty natural time has consequences for his historical time. In historical time, the relationship between past and present is all important. But in Kant's natural perception of time, the past is only of interest for the present in its quality as a "past-now". Or to put it differently, the past is but relevant for the present with regard to its "now" aspects. There is no difference in identity between the present (as present-nows) and the past (as past-nows).[50] Kant thinks that people can learn from the past, because the past-nows have the same identity as the present-nows. Hence Kant's historical time is present-oriented. His perception of phenomenological time as merely a sequence of fleeting, instantaneous "nows" seems paradigmatic for the philosophical history of the Enlightenment. Philosophical history of the Enlightenment leads to a form of history writing without the intention to know what kind of influence the past may have on the present; the discipline of history only has to expose what stage of morality, of humanity (*Humanität*) and of culture humankind has reached. As a consequence, the past is not considered ontologically linked with the present, and the present is not perceived as a product of the past. Because history is most of all a learning process, historiography is pragmatic in the sense that it can teach people by example (*Historia magistra vitae*). Like Kant, the historians of the Enlightenment impute to historiography only a moral function, to demonstrate the good, and most of all the reasonable events and developments in the past and to condemn the bad ones.

This complies with Pauline Kleingeld's view on Kant's morality.[51] According to Kleingeld, Kant does not perceive that reason and morality develop, but only their corresponding predispositions do so. In the *Idea of Universal History*, Kant argues that man in his earliest stages of development only has an "uncultivated predisposition for moral discernment", not one that fundamentally *differs* from his original, universal reason and morality. Kant, in his "Conjectural Beginnings of Human History", similarly claims that at the beginning of history, "humans understand, 'although only dimly,' that they ought to regard their fellow humans as ends".[52] Thus, from the beginning of times man has a moral nature, but he does not understand completely all its implications. Kant's history of progress is a history of human's better understanding of his potentialities. Morality itself does not show historical change, only its understanding.

Thus there is a contrast between increasing moralization and a-temporality. This term means that every generation is born with the same faculties for moral agency. However, better understanding of its moral potentialities would imply that later generations enter the world with more highly developed preconditions and thus with better-developed faculties to recognize and obey moral standards. This improvement is against the a-temporal character of moral agency. Kleingeld, however, argues that, according to Kant, "every generation . . . must again move through the entire distance which generations before had already been covered".[53] The development of man's rational faculties is a learning process, which starts every time anew. According to Kleingeld, "For Kant, unlike Hegel, it is not morality, which needs to go through a historical process, but our understanding of it".[54] It underlines the idea that Kant presumes man to be a rational but not a historical being, in the sense historicism gives it.

In this context it is significant what Peter Fritzsche says with regard to the perception of ruins during the Enlightenment. According to Fritzsche, ruins are interpreted during the eighteenth century as part of nature: "a broken bridge span, a collapsed edifice or a crumbling wall could serve the same function as craggy rock formations and overgrown grottos to indicate irregularity of untamed nature". Ruins also have an educational function: it reminds people of the "impermanence of human effort and human pride, and it taught the moral lesson of humility". And Fritzsche concludes with regard to ruins during the Enlightenment: "Ruins stood in natural, not [in] historical time".[55] I consider Fritzsche's remarks about ruins as an underlining of my view that in the Enlightenment, historical time is most of all only natural and chronological and as such still empty. Because the past is a "past-now", the past can have an educational function for the present.

Koselleck's change brought into perspective

The new discoveries concerning the age of the world imply that the web of reality-sorting expressions demands several adjustments to have more consistency. However, these changes only regard the synchronization of the distinct chronologies of nations and states inside and outside Europe. Although the changes are rather drastic, creating Koselleck's collective singular in the form of a universal history, it does not mean that they overthrow the system as a whole. In its metaphysical aspects the new web shows remarkable conformities with the old one. Especially in its phasing character, the heavenly city of the eighteenth-century philosophers does not differ fundamentally from Augustine's *Civitas Dei*. From a historiographical point of view, Carl Becker, who makes this statement, is still right.[56] The Bible-founded history with its main stages of the Old and New Testaments, its sequence of world monarchies and apart from it also with the pre-Adamite time, remains paradigmatic for a new phasing of history. As a result, the new sequences of phases are as predesigned as the old ones. The only difference is that every historian and philosopher of the eighteenth century now designs his own series of stages. Both comprehend progress as their common, all-embracing aspect, without making room for deviant developments and contingency. As with the old phases, the newly designed ones are superimposed on what people knew of the history of their world. It is a preordained history with an *a priori* form of time perception. The historical time of the Enlightenment is the empty, phasing time of progress, including "natural" time and chronology. It is the empty time of eras, chronology and stages. Kant's natural perception of time underlines this.

The homogeneous and ascending time of Enlightenment in historiography

Kant's idea of time as an intuitive category of mind related to an objective series of nows is shared by most of his contemporaries. This means that for the philosophers and historians of the Enlightenment, time in history is not a substantial, continuous stream of intrinsically linked events but a discontinuous sequence of now-phases, in which events occur. These events are distinguished by their different context, not by being organic parts of a changing time. This makes time universal and the past a laboratory to study the continuities and discontinuities in human nature. Philosophers of history and historians view the past as a kind of scientists.

David Hume (1711–1776), for instance, sees "wars, intrigues, factions, and revolutions" as

> so many collections of experiments by which the politician or moral philosopher fixes the principles of his science, in the same manner as the physician or natural philosopher becomes acquainted with the nature of plants, minerals, and other external objects.[57]

Hume wrote a *History of England*, which is called a *locus classicus* for the (English) Enlightenment's sense of time. From a philosophical point of view, Hume surely is a representative of the Enlightenment and a forerunner of Kant. From a historiographical point of view, Hume's affiliation with the English Enlightenment is not so obvious. He is a Scot and as such a supporter of the Stuart cause. In the British political context of the eighteenth century, followers of the Stuarts are Tories and as such opposing the Glorious Revolution of 1688/9.[58] The ideas of this revolution are most of the time understood as examples of Enlightenment, because they further civil freedom. Hume does not see them that way. Is he therefore not a historian of the Enlightenment? To Hume the Glorious Revolution is an event and as such no more than an empty now-point with no causal connection to Enlightenment's politics. For some "1689" might be an example; for others like Hume, it is not.

As other eighteenth-century historians, Hume comprehends the present as the benchmark for the past. The Anglo-Saxon epoch is dismissed as a barbarous period, and the Normandian period "put the people in a situation of receiving slowly from abroad the rudiments of science and cultivation".[59] For a Scottish Tory, "Normandian" and "abroad" mean France, not having any problem with the teaching of British people with French examples. As for Voltaire, for Hume French culture of the eighteenth century is the top of civilization. His view on the past is present-oriented, fetching examples for improvement wherever you can get them. Those improvements do not need to be historically conditioned.

Voltaire (1694–1778) is also a typical representative of the Enlightenment's historiography. In his *Essai sur les moeurs*, he writes that the past is "a vast storehouse from which you must take whatever you can use of".[60] For Voltaire, like for Kant, history still is the teacher of life. The French philosopher writes in 1751 his *Siècle de Louis XIV*. In its first chapter, he specified "four happy ages": (1) the centuries of Pericles and Plato, (2) the period of Cicero and Caesar, (3) the Renaissance in the time of the Medicis and (4) the Age of Louis XIV. About the latter Voltaire writes:

> Lastly, the fourth age is that known by the name of the age of Louis XIV, and is perhaps that which approaches the nearest to perfection of all the four; enriched by the discoveries of the three former ones, it has done greater things in certain kinds than those three together. . . . In this age we first became acquainted with sound philosophy; . . . there has happened such a general revolution in our arts, our genius, our manners, and even in our government, as will serve as an immortal mark to the true glory of our country. This happy influence has not been confined to France; it has communicated itself to England, where it has stirred up an emulation, which that ingenious and deeply learned nation stood in need of at that time; it has introduced taste into Germany, and the sciences into Russia; it has even re-animated Italy, which was languishing; and Europe is indebted for its politeness and spirit of society to the court of Louis XIV.[61]

Voltaire's example of Enlightenment historiography evidently displays a finalistic and progressive conception of temporality. Time is classified into four periods, not connected with one another; it is a discontinuous phasing of historical time, whereof the last one is also the best. Yet there is some kind of uniformity of time between the ancient Greeks, the Romans and the Renaissance Medicis because they are the, although less perfect, predecessors of Voltaire's own age. Ages can learn from each other's discoveries, because time has some sort of homogeneous identity. It is the identity of the discontinuous now-points, epitomized in four static, causally non-connected periods, each with the same progressive outlook. Although there is some causality in Voltaire's approach, it has no organic character.[62] Christopher Clark underlines Becker's idea of "the heavenly city" by arguing that Voltaire's historiography is "a secularized version of the salvational succession of 'world monarchies' foretold in the Bible".[63]

Clark also elaborates on the historiography of **Frederick II of Prussia** (1712–1786). He signals that Frederick in his *Anti-Machiavel* strikingly misses a sense of historical development. Like Machiavelli himself, Frederick "deploy[s] exempla of Greek and Roman antiquity, using them as "timeless storehouse[s] of good examples".[64] Significant also are, according to Clark, the references to the sciences in Frederick's history writing. The latter often refers in his histories of states on self-repeating cyclical patterns of maturation and decay, seeing them as planets locked in circular orbits. Rise and decline are not movements of a time filled with events but abstract laws *a priori* given.[65]

The most rounded illustration of Enlightenment time perception is **Condorcet's** posthumously published *Esquisse* of 1795. We discussed his historical ideas above. Condorcet's perception of time is optimistic, although there are stages of setback:

> All peoples whose history is recorded fall somewhere between our present degree of civilization and that which we still see among savage tribes; if we survey in a single sweep the universal history of peoples we see them sometimes making fresh progress, sometimes plunging back into ignorance . . ., sometimes receiving knowledge from some enlightened people in order to transmit it in their turn to other nations, and so welding an uninterrupted chain between the beginning of historical time and the century in which we live.[66]

Condorcet feels his own time to be the pinnacle of civilization. His perception of time as an "uninterrupted chain" may be astonishing in the light of what is said with regard to the phasing of time during the Enlightenment. In my view, however, it is not an utterance of an organic causal continuity and development. For Condorcet, this chain means the stringing together of now-points, in which events take place that can have a meaning for the present as examples, sometimes as progress, sometimes even as plunging back in ignorance. He thus underlines the cosmopolitan view (the "survey in a single sweep of the universal history of peoples") that all peoples of the world live in the same upward proceeding time, but surely at different stages. As several identical links form a chain, time is a chain of several identical "now"-moments. The moment the chain receives its final link, the pinnacle of civilization is achieved.

The last but not the least representative of the Enlightenment historiography of the eighteenth century is **Edward Gibbon** (1737–1794). His *Decline and Fall of the Roman Empire* (1776–1788) seems to be the opposite of the eighteenth-century optimistic view on the world in general and especially of Enlightenment historiography. Decline and fall are not the items of a future-oriented present and a present-oriented past. Gibbon yet perceives the decline and fall of the Roman Empire like the rise and fall of all empires. It is a nature-inhering movement, resulting from "effeminacy by a lack of war, the unforeseen effects of economic exploitation, the weakness attending the expansion of empires etc". Behind this all is the idea that freedom is "the guarantor of civic health . . . and its denial the harbinger of social sclerosis".[67]

Gibbon's "freedom" implicitly refers to the constitutional settlement after the Glorious Revolution, the example of freedom on which the whole historiography ought to rest. He chastises the Romans for having lost a liberty, once won by Trajan and the Antonines. This liberty is similar to the English one, won by the Revolution of 1689. His book is a warning to his contemporaneous compatriots not to make the same mistake as the Romans once made (*Historia Magistra Vitae!*). Gibbon's time perception fits in very well with the linear and homogeneous temporality of the Enlightenment, in which the past is judged by the present and the present is warned by a past, which has great similarities with the present.

The book displays an explanation of contemporaneous causes which can be observed especially with regard to the role of Christianity in the downfall of the Roman Empire. As the mutual attraction in a magnetic field (see Kant's causal relation as a mediating aspect of time), the downfall of the Roman Empire is caused by the rise of Christianity. He explains the successes of early Christianity not in its descending "from Heaven arrayed in her native purity" but in terms of "exclusive zeal, the immediate expectation of another world, the claim of miracles, the practice of rigid virtue, and the constitution of the primitive church".[68] Because Christianity represents values the Roman Empire objects to, the rise of the first means the decline of the latter. It is like a physical process of communicating vessels.

This Kantian and scientific temporal explanation of the Roman downfall underlines Gibbon's perception of an empty temporality. Romans downfall does not express a pessimistic worldview. It only means a warning for the English to maintain their spirit of freedom and not to make the same mistakes the Romans made. Hence the opportunity to develop a happier future is not jeopardized.

In summary: Koselleck's modern time as the collective singular, moving from a difference between the space of experience and the horizon of expectation and creating a "systematic" universal history of progress, instead of the former loosely connected *Historie*, is not the great break in the view on history as he suggests it is. Kant's philosophical journeys into time do not produce a firm base for Koselleck's new history. Most historians during the Enlightenment and even the Whig-historians of the nineteenth century, who work in the footsteps of their Enlightenment forerunners, do not perceive the past as fundamentally different from the present. The past is connected to the present by a preordained conception of progress. The only form of historical judgement concerns the question how far a country, nation or state has progressed in civilization. Synchronization of chronologies is the main contribution to the Enlightenment's universal history. It demonstrates how empty the Enlightenment's temporality still is. Koselleck considers the idea that the past differs from the present, an idea from the Enlightenment. It would be the basis of modern thinking about time and history. In my opinion, that thinking lacks the idea of unforeseen events, which is crucial for time and history. Contingency gives embodiment to time and history. It is created by the Counter-Enlightenment, the subject of the next chapter.

Notes

1 Lucian Hölscher, "Time Gardens: Historical Concepts in Modern Historiography", *History and Theory* 53, 4 (December 2014), 577–591, esp. 583. This chapter has been the first part of Jansen "In Search of New Times".
2 Ibid., 84.
3 See: William F. Fleming, *The Works of Voltaire: A Contemporary Version* (New York: Dingwall-Rock, 1927), vol. XIX, Pt. I, 172–176.

4 Michelle Mille, "Cenotaph for Newton" (September 10, 2014). www.archdaily.com/544946/ad-classics-cenotaph-for-newton-etienne-louis-boullee
5 René Huyge, "L'Univers de Watteau", in: Hélène Adhémar (ed.), *Watteau, sa vie, son oeuvre. Catalogue des peintures et illustrations* (Paris: P. Tisné, 1950), 1–46, esp. 1.
6 See also: Clark, *Time and Power*, 103–105.
7 Quoted from: P. Rossi, *The Dark Abyss of Time: The History of the Earth and the History of Nations from Hooke to Vico* (Chicago and London: University of Chicago Press, 1987), 136. Lucian Hölscher has also observed remarkable similarities between historiography and geography in the eighteenth century. He states: "The analogies of the disciplines [historiography and geography] in the episteme of the Enlightenment are striking". Hölscher, "Time Gardens", 578.
8 An important part of this section is derived from: Siep Stuurman, "Tijd en ruimte in de verlichting. De uitvinding van de filosofische geschiedenis", in: Maria Grever and Harry Jansen (eds.), *De ongrijpbare tijd. Temporaliteit en de constructie van het verleden* (Hilversum: Verloren, 2001), 79–96, here: esp. 84.
9 René Descartes, *Principles of Philosophy* (ed. Jonathan Bennett 2010–2015; 1st ed. Latin: 1644, French: 1647), part 4: the earth. No page reference.
10 Stuurman, "Tijd en ruimte in de verlichting", 87.
11 A. Brewer, "Adam Smith's Stages of History", in: *Discussion paper* number 08/601 (March 2008), 1. www.efm.bris.ac.uk/economics/working_papers/pdffiles/dp08601.pdf (accessed March 6, 2015).
12 Stuurman, "Tijd en ruimte in de verlichting", 81–85.
13 Adam Smith, *The Wealth of Nations* (Toronto: Modern Library Paperback Edition, Random House, 2000), Introduction, 4.
14 Brewer, "Adam Smith's Stages of History", 2.
15 John Millar, *Observations Concerning the Distinction of Ranks in Society* (London: John Murray, 1773²). See the Contents of his book: xix–xxii.
16 Michael Bentley, *Modern Historiography* (London and New York: Routledge, 2005), 10–11.
17 "Die Lebensart bestimmt, Klima und Nahrungsart erschafft, der Herrscher zwingt, der Priester lehrt, und das Beispiel reisst fort". A. L. Schlözer, *Weltgeschichte nach ihren Hauptheilen im Auszug und Zusammenhänge I* (Göttingen, 1792–1801²), 66.
18 Schlözer, *Weltgeschichte*, 94–105.
19 Gorman, "The Limits of Historiographical Choice in Temporal Distinctions", 163.
20 Ibid.
21 Jordheim, "Multiple Time and the Work of Synchronization", 515.
22 Ibid. Koselleck ascribes to Gatterer a past with different truths and he adds to this saying that it "showed how the past could retrospectively be seen anew". Koselleck, *Futures Past*, 249. I do not think that Gatterer's schemes and chronologies have much to do with differences in truths of (perceived) past realities. His work was only new with regard to his attempts of synchronization.
23 Martin Gierl, *Geschichte als präzisierte Wissenschaft: Johann, Christoph Gatterer und die Historiographie des 18. Jahrhunderts im ganzen Umfang* (Stuttgart: Frohmann-Holzboog Verlag, 2012).
24 Koselleck, *Vergangene Zukunft*, 48.
25 Ibid., 131.
26 Koselleck, "Über die Geschichtsbedürftigkeit der Geschichtswissenschaft", in: idem, *Zeitschichten. Studien zur Historik* (Frankfurt a. M.: Suhrkamp, 2000, 1st ed. 1972), 303.
27 Jordheim, "Multiple Time and the Work of Synchronization", 511.
28 Hölscher, "Von leeren und gefüllten Zeiten", 36–49.
29 Koselleck also uses this distinction but associates it with progress and universal history. Kant is the example that makes clear that the philosophical histories of the Enlightenment show a development of stages in time and not through time. See below and Jansen, "In Search of New Times", 66–90, esp. 74–78.

30 My statement that "the time of the Enlightenment" is empty does not mean that the *concept* of "the time of the Enlightenment" is a concept without content. That would undermine my Brandomian perception of "inferential" concepts. (See the Introduction) It is simply a concept in which its *content* is a series of empty "nows", consisting of pre-determined phases at most.
31 Jordheim, "Multiple Time and the Work of Synchronization", 510–512.
32 Ibid., 514.
33 Koselleck, *Vergangene Zukunft*, 321–322; Jordheim, "Multiple Time and the Work of Synchronization", 510.
34 Koselleck, *Vergangene Zukunft*, 53 and 311–322, esp. 317. History mainly is contemporaneous history (*Zeitgeschichte*). Koselleck refers to a certain Campe, who distinguishes *"Jetztwelt"* from *"Vorwelt"*.
35 Jordheim, "Multiple Time and the Work of Synchronization", 514.
36 For Kant semantic explanation is not embedded in a doctrine of concepts but in one of judgements: "As all acts of the understanding can be reduced to judgements, understanding may be defined as the faculty of judging". Quoted from: Brandom, *Making It Explicit*, 79–80, esp. 79.
37 *"Daher wird eine Anwendung der Kategorie auf Erscheinungen möglich sein vermittelst der transcendentalen Zeitbestimmung, welche, als das Schema der Verstandsbegriffe, die Subsumtion der letzteren unter die erste vermittelt"*. Immanuel Kant, *Kritik der reinen Vernunft* (Neu herausgegeben von Theodoor Valentiner; 11te Auflage; Der Philosophische Bibliothek Bd. 37; Leipzig: Verlag von Felix Meier, 1917), B 178 (83). https://archive.org/details/kritikderreinenv19kant (accessed March 24, 2015). B stands for the second edition of the *Kritik* (1787), whereas A stands for the first edition (1781). See also what I have said on Kant's concepts in the Introduction.
38 *"Die Zeit ist also lediglich eine subjektive Bedingung unserer (menschlichen) Anschauung (. . .) und an sich, ausser dem Subjekte, nichts"*. Immanuel Kant, *Kritik der reinen Vernunft*, B 51 (90). See also: J. J. A. Mooij, *Tijd en geest. Een geschiedenis* (Kampen: Agora, 2001), 167. Most commentators have found Kant's claim that space and time are only in the mind and not at all in the mind-independent world, to be implausible.
39 *"Die Zeit verläuft sich nicht, sondern in ihr verläuft sich das Dasein des Wandelbaren"*. Kant, *Kritik der reinen Vernunft*, B 183 (187). See also: Mooij, *Tijd en geest*, 167.
40 *". . . was wir als die veränderte Methode der Denkungsart annehmen, dass wir nämlich von den Dingen nur das a priori erkennen, was wir selbst in sie legen"*. Kant, *Kritik der reinen Vernunft*, B xviii (29).
41 *". . . in Ansehung aller Erscheinungen, mithin auch aller Dinge, die uns in der Erfahrung vorkommen können, notwendigerweise objektiv"*. Kant, *Kritik der reinen Vernunft*, B 51 (90).
42 Immanuel Kant, *Critique of Pure Reason* (transl. Norman Kemp Smith; London: Macmillan and Co, 1929), 181.
43 Kant, *Critique of Pure Reason*, 185.
44 Kant, *Kritik der reinen Vernunft*, A 143, B 183.
45 Ibid., B xviii (29).
46 There are several interpretations of *nunc stans*. See for instance: (1) Christianity in which it means "eternal existence" as an attribute of God; (2) with Nietzsche in his *Also sprach Zarathustra*, it has the connotation of a now in which past, present and future meet one another. See Friedrich Nietzsche, "Also sprach Zarathustra, Dritter Teil. Vom Gesicht und Rätsel", *Werke* II (ed. Slechta), 682 and Chapter 8 of this book. See also: Robin Small, *Time and Becoming in Nietzsche's Thought* (London and New York: Continuum, 2010), 109, 139 and 159. In the context of Kant and the Enlightenment, it is nothing else than a continuously repeating "now".
47 Kant, *Kritik der reinen Vernunft*, B 183 (187). Martin Heidegger, *Kant und das Problem der Metaphysik* (Frankfurt a. M.: Klostermann, 1991[2]), 101; Martin Heidegger, *Sein und Zeit* (Tübingen: Max Niemeyer Verlag, 1927, 1986[16]), § 81.
48 Heidegger points at Kant, *Kritik der reinen Vernunft*, B 183 (187).

49 The "unchangeable in existence" as a qualification of time is the opposite from "endurance in change", an expression for temporality used by Herder (see the following). With Kant, time does not change, but change occurs in time; with Herder, time changes with and within each phenomenon; in each phenomenon only its identity endures.
50 See also what Morgan says about the nineteenth-century English historian Hallam. See the next chapter of this book.
51 Pauline Kleingeld, "Kant, History, and the Idea of Moral Development", *History of Philosophy Quarterly* 16, 1 (1999), 59–78.
52 Ibid., 63.
53 Ibid., 66.
54 Ibid., 69. See for Hegel, the applicable section in the following.
55 Peter Fritzsche, "The Ruins of Modernity", in: Lorenz and Bevernage, *Breaking up Time*, 57–68, esp. 58.
56 Carl Becker's *The Heavenly City of the Eighteenth-Century Philosophers* (New Haven: Yale University Press, 1932). According to Becker, the eighteenth-century philosophers wanted to make a sharp division between their present and medieval, dark, superstitious times. Becker, however, states ironically that the eighteenth-century philosophers were far more in tune with the philosophies and ideas; they so heavily attacked. Twenty-five years after Becker published his book, Peter Gay condemned Becker's "reckless wordplay" and "indefensible generalizations". Gay saw Montesquieu, Voltaire, Hume, Helvetius essentially as unbelievers. See: www.jstor.org/discover/10.2307/2145772?uid=2129&uid=2134&uid=2482187067&uid=2&uid=70&uid=3&uid=2482187057&uid=60&sid=21104211877247 and http://userpages.umbc.edu/~jamie/html/on__the_heavenly_city_of_eight.html (accessed March 14, 2015) In the light of Jonathan Israel's dichotomy between the Radical Enlightenment and the more moderate and deist Enlightenment after 1730, Becker's thesis has received more credibility. Anyway, Becker's book underlines a time regime of Enlightenment in which linear and metaphysical elements dominate.
57 Quoted from: D. Carrithers, "The Enlightenment Science of Society", in: Christopher Fox, Roy Porter and Robert Wokler (eds.), *Inventing Human Science* (Berkeley: University of California Press, 1995), 241.
58 Bentley, *Modern Historiography*, 11/12.
59 David Hume, *History of England from the Invasion of Julius Caesar to the Revolution of 1689*, 6 vols. (London, 1754–1762), I, 305–306.
60 Quoted from Clark, *Time and Power*, 95.
61 *The Works of Voltaire: A Contemporary Version*. A Critique and Biography by John Morley, notes by Tobias Smollett, trans. William F. Fleming (New York: E.R. DuMont, 1901). In 21 vols., vol. XII. http://oll.libertyfund.org/titles/2132 (accessed juni 11, 2016).
62 See the next three chapters.
63 Clark, *Time and Power*, 96.
64 Ibid., 99.
65 Clark, *Time and Power*, 102–103 and 112–117.
66 Jean-Antoine-Nicolas de Condorcet, *Esquisse d'un tableau des progrès de l'esprit humine* (Paris, 1795), 8. Quoted from Bentley, *Modern Historiography*, 9.
67 Bentley, *Modern Historiography*, 14.
68 Edward Gibbon, *The History of the Decline and Fall of the Roman Empire* (Dent and London: Everyman's Library, 1910), vol. 1, 438 and 484.

3
THE INCARNATED TIME OF THE COUNTER-ENLIGHTENMENT[1]

In the *Dictionary of the History of Ideas* the lemma of the Enlightenment is written by a rather unknown author named Helmut Pappe; however, the entry of the Counter-Enlightenment is written by the well-known historian Isaiah Berlin.[2] Berlin more or less coins the name Counter-Enlightenment, although Friedrich Nietzsche already uses the term *Gegen-Aufklärung*. Apart from the difference in relative fame of the two authors, there is another distinction between the two entries. Pappe constructs his story about the Enlightenment around *items* like "Underlying structural change", "Progress and Perfectibility", "Stages of Evolution" and "Nature", whereas Berlin explores the Counter-Enlightenment around *thinkers* like Vico, Hamann and Herder.[3] Although several of Pappe's items come close to perceptions of time and although Berlin says much about history and individuality, temporality is neither for Pappe nor for Berlin an item to highlight the difference between the Enlightenment and the Counter-Enlightenment. Yet temporality is a very strong benchmark for the distinction between the two.[4]

This is important because the Counter-Enlightenment does not follow upon the Enlightenment but develops cheek by jowl. It differs in several aspects from the Enlightenment, but surely not in all.[5] Allen Wood even claims regarding Johann-Gottfried Herder, one of the most outspoken representatives of the Counter-Enlightenment, that "while acknowledging the equally plain fact that when the chips are down, he is himself a part of it [the Enlightenment]".[6] Koselleck confirms this view by giving the following quote of Herder:

> All the questions about the progress of our generation . . . are answered . . . by one single word: humanity.[7]

Representatives of the Counter-Enlightenment are philosophical historians not very different from those of the Enlightenment. They all want a new history, most of the time even a history of progress, with a past, the present can learn from. Thus, although the Counter-Enlightenment is a criticism of the Enlightenment, it is a criticism from the inside.

The historiography of the Counter-Enlightenment is to a large extent determined by Herder's polemic against the philosophical history of the Enlightenment. Although we must not overstate the differences between Herder and the thinkers of the Enlightenment,[8] yet regarding historiography and temporality, there is a real distinction. This becomes obvious in Herder's *Eine Metakritik zur Kritik der reinen Vernunft* of 1792, in which he enters into controversy with his former teacher and tutor Immanuel Kant.[9] Against Kant's perceptions of time Herder defends a theory of multiple temporalities. Moreover, Herder's plurality of times is imbued with a plurality of time layers, which makes his temporality, what I would like to call (following Lucian Hölscher) "embodied" or "incarnated".[10] In my view the largest distinction between the philosophical history of Enlightenment and Counter-Enlightenment is the growing uneasiness in the Counter-Enlightenment with the Enlightenment's empty time. An alternative comes up only gradually.

An incarnated or embodied time means that time is filled with individual and collective experiences of events.[11] These events form the ontological layer of a development, which has its epistemological aspect in an historical account. From this the historicist idea arises that the nature of a thing lies in its history.[12] History is therefore nothing but embodied time, which is strongly reflected in Herder and Hegel, through whom the Counter-Enlightenment is connected with historicism.

As a consequence of this incarnation, "learning from the past" receives in the Counter-Enlightenment a different connotation. It does not mean that the past has the same identity as the present. The past becomes more and more seen as different from the present.[13] However, this perception of a difference between the past and present is accompanied by the idea that the present is in one way or another a result of the past. Studying the developments of the past can improve acting in the present.[14] Moreover, the idea of differences between past and present and the idea that the present is a result of the past are two sides of the same coin. It is the coin of a growing awareness of an incarnated time.[15] Events do no longer happen *in* time, but *through* time.[16] Only with Herder this time has received its almost complete form, which implies that for instance Leibniz and Vico (two representatives of the Counter-Enlightenment, which I will discuss in the following) are less complete representatives of the Counter-Enlightenment than Herder and Hegel.

The Clarke/Newton debate (1715–1716)

Newton (1643–1724), as we know, sees time as absolute and independent of real objects; it is only an instrument for measurement. Leibniz (1646–1716), in his discussion with Newton's disciple Samuel Clarke (1675–1729), calls time the order of things that follow one another and distinguishes it from space, which he perceives as the order of things existing at one and the same moment. Leibniz identifies time with change and states that time exists in things: "I have demonstrated that time, without things is nothing else but a mere ideal Possibility".[17] Leibniz gives time a first organic propensity, namely an existence in the form of a relationship. Time exists in its "following ordering", in its capacity as creating sequences. As such it gives historical objects extension and inner coherence. According to Hölscher, Leibniz assumes time to be "embodied" and "organic". By this he means that a sequence of events has something in common, a spirit, connecting events that have no direct effect on one another.[18] From this idea Leibniz's monadology is not far away. In his *Monadology* of 1714, Leibniz states: "And every momentary state of a simple substance is a natural consequence of its 'immediately' preceding one, so that its present is pregnant with the future".[19] Indeed, a state as a "natural consequence of a preceding state" and an expression such as "pregnant with its future" refers to an organic relationship. Nonetheless I wonder whether this can be seen as a definitive step in the direction of time as being embodied and organic.

I think Hölscher's conclusion has been drawn too quickly. First, Leibniz's statement that time without things is nothing can be Kantian, because Kant also reasoned that things exist in time (see Kant's time as modality). Second, "substance" in the latter quote can be a "now" in the Kantian sense, being a past "now" as an example to learn from. As such this "past-now" can be "pregnant" with future. Third, Hölscher also argues that Leibniz's relationship between past, present and future fits with his idea that these three temporalities are an order of things, not related in an empirical sense but in a spiritual sense by a *Zeitgeist*, a spirit of time.[20] With Hegel the *Zeitgeist* has an organic connotation (see further), but is that already the case with Leibniz? Fourth, Hölscher points out with regard to Leibniz's vision "that all parts of the historical universe are related to one another in perfect harmony".[21] This means a preordained connection and not a *contingent* relationship between events and entities in historical reality.[22] Fifth, it is not very difficult to undo Leibniz's "following ordering" from its possible ontological status and replace it in the human's mind. In that case we are close to Kant's causality as a category of the mind and as a consequence, not far from his empty perception of time. Moreover, and that is my sixth point, I think it takes a whole story for historical temporality to receive its real, incarnated status.[23] Maybe Leibniz's remark is a tiny beginning on a long path towards a really "embodied" time. It is the story of what Isaiah Berlin calls the Counter-Enlightenment and that story I am now going to tell. It starts with Vico.

Vico

It is not by accident that the Napolitanean Gianmbattista Vico (1668–1744) calls his study in the philosophy of history *Scienza Nuova* (1725–1744). *New Science* means better than past science, and as such it is an utterance of the ascending temporality of Enlightenment. However, it differs from it in not being a new glorification of the "natural" sciences, initiated by Newton. On the contrary, the *Scienza Nuova* contains a passage that seems to be against the spirit of the Enlightenment and its adoration of the sciences:

> a truth beyond all question: that the world of civil society has certainly been made by men, and that its principles are therefore to be found within the modifications of our own human mind. Whoever reflects on this cannot but marvel that the philosophers should have bent all their energies to the study of the world of nature, which, since God made it, He alone knows; and that they should have neglected the study of the world of nations, or civil world, which, since men had made it, men could hope to know.[24]

Truth can be acquired, according to the minds of Enlightenment, along three lines of knowledge. The first one is metaphysical or theological knowledge, obtained by rational intuition, faith or revelation; the second is deductive knowledge, as in logic, grammar or mathematics; and the third concerns perceptual knowledge based on empirical observation, as in the natural sciences. Vico, as a mind of the Enlightenment, acknowledges all three. Yet he claims the discovery of a fourth type, namely knowledge of social activities, of which we ourselves are the authors. The other three types of knowledge are based on an observer's point of view looking at the outside of things. Vico underlines with regard to the fourth one a participant's point of view, looking at the world from the inside, that is, from the motives and purposes of all those who participate in social life. Here Vico is the first to stress an *understanding* approach to reality; it seems identical with the *Verstehende* method of historicism. Thus Vico attacks with this idea the so-called new science of the Newtonians and becomes the first philosopher to create a dichotomy between the natural and the cultural sciences.

Notwithstanding novelties, Vico maintains in his thought about time and history aspects of the Enlightenment. He has an optimistic view on the possibility to know the past and he presents his "science" as new, which displays an Enlightened, future-oriented vision on the world. Moreover, man is next to God, co-creator of the world, and can in principle discover the truth about it – a statement that matches Enlightenment's optimism as well. Furthermore, the manmade world must be rediscovered according to Vico "within the modifications of our own human mind". Although this is a reflection about the social world, it seems to be more about intelligibility than about existence.[25] It does not directly point at an incarnated time.

Eelco Runia, however, just points to an "existential" aspect of Vico's *New Science*. According to Vico, as Runia sees it, people participate in social life by and in "institutions" ("cose" or "things"), which is important for his time perception. Institutions are "things" from the past in the present, giving the past "presence" in the present. Hence they are "repositories of time", or as Runia states, "places where history can get a hold on you".[26] Because they are places "anybody can visit them", and as visitors, people "may 'invent' their contents in order to experience 'presence'".[27] Here Runia rightly points to an embodied temporality at Vico.

Berlin observes something else. Humans can understand their history because of their faculty of language, which enables him to reconstruct the vocabularies of past civilizations and thus to understand their realities. Here lies a difference with Runia. Berlin underscores man's capacity to understand the past, whereas Runia underlines the transfer of the past into "presence" and hence the possibility to experience it in a rather direct way.[28] Yet, both authors presuppose in Vico's *New Science* an incarnated time, although Runia is with regard to this the most outspoken. He claims that Vico's institutions, "things" or places are "not empty but full, not shallow but deep, not dead but alive".[29] Thus with him, institutions are not only repositories of time but *are* time, incarnated time! When we take the views of Berlin and Runia together, time has an epistemological as well as an ontological aspect.

Berlin adds another historicist aspect to Vico's time perception: his view of history as a movement of rise, growth, decline and fall. "Our Science therefore comes to describe at the same time an ideal eternal history traversed in time by the history of every nation in its rise, progress, maturity, decline and fall".[30] Berlin perceives this as the *idée maîtresse*, the main theme, of Vico's view on history.[31] Indeed, it seems at first sight to be a very historicist perception of time when we look at Steven Smith's quote of Ranke's appeal for history:

> What could be more pleasant and more welcome to human understanding than to . . . observe in one nation or another how men's enterprises begin, increase in power, rise and decline.[32]

However, Berlin observes, too, that Vico adds to this "ideal eternal history" that it is "the single, universal pattern that all societies, in their rise and fall, are bound sooner or later to fulfil".[33] This is a remarkable utterance because it brings Vico back in a non-historicist way of thinking. The "ideal eternal history" seems to be a category of the mind, whereby we can know the time pattern of history. On the one hand, it differs from Kant's category of time as an "eternal Now", but on the other hand, it remains an *a priori* category. Although Berlin perceives this *storia ideale eterna* more as a Platonic than as a Kantian time pattern, he also claims that it is a principle, knowable *a priori*.[34] In sum, Vico's ideas about time are still in between the Enlightenment and the Counter-Enlightenment.

Herder

In his *Auch eine Philosophie der Geschichte zur Bildung der Menschheit* (*This Too Is a Philosophy of History*), published in 1774, Johann Gottfried von Herder (1744–1803) condemns the anti-traditionality, the rationality and the universal horizon of the Enlightenment historiography. He praises tradition in the form of the virtues of past times, whether the patriarchal religion of the Orient, the patriotism of Greece and Rome and last but not least the hegemony of Christianity over all spheres of life in the Middle Ages. He opposes the rationalistic criticism of the Enlightened thinkers regarding primitive cultures. Herder argues that ancient languages, such as that of Homer and the Bible, are more poetic than modern languages. These have become too intellectual, too controlled, too cut off from daily life. Herder's essay sketches the Enlightenment as an era of abstract intellect. He hates its superficiality, artificiality and mechanical way of thinking and considers it as an era of scepticism, religious disbelief and theoretical cosmopolitanism. According to him, the Enlightenment looks down on past times from above, considering itself as the ultimate goal of human history.

Herder perceives progress as *Bildung,* because he sees the development of all kinds of individualities going from childhood to maturity. This dovetails with Kant's view of history as a learning process. However, Kant sees this learning process as personal and recurring in every individual, whereas Herder perceives it as historical, enabling not only individual persons but also collectivities, nations, cultures, countries and other continuing entities (Mandelbaum) to search their own way to adulthood.[35] It is a phylogenesis in accordance with an ontogenesis, which leads to a completely different form of synchronization.

In the former chapter I discussed Jordheim's view on synchronization based on the temporality of the Enlightenment. Although he is right about that, he is mistaken about the problem of synchronization Herder meets in his *Auch eine Philosophie.* Jordheim's misunderstanding is important, because it originates in his failure to distinguish between the empty time of the Enlightened historians and the embodied times of Herder. As a consequence, he misrepresents the latter ones. Although Herder envisioned in *Auch eine Philosophie* a multiplicity of embodied times, Jordheim wants to maintain the universal form of history of the Enlightenment, with a "synchronized and strictly diachronic narrative of the progress of humankind".[36] This view seems to shipwreck with Herder's view on the history of the Egyptians and the Phoenicians. They do not precede or succeed one another, but live contemporaneously, thus, a linear, diachronic and homogeneous following in time becomes impossible. Herder chooses an "organic" solution by seeing both cultures as "twins of the same mother".[37] This synchronization of Herder is rather incidental and, because of its organic character, completely different from the chronological synchronization of the Enlightenment's historiography that Jordheim focuses on.

Herder's perception of *Bildung* as an individual process into maturity marks a sharper watershed between the time regime of Enlightenment and the time regime of the Counter-Enlightenment. First of all, there is a difference in the perception of culture. In the Enlightenment cultures are only seen as epistemological instruments or as concepts to reflect pragmatically on the past. Herder sees those cultures and the change from one into the other as what Bentley very aptly has been calling "a crucial feature of how the world worked".[38] It means an interrelationship between a multiplicity of ontological data and a more uniform (epistemological) view on it. It brings the problem to the fore of combining the multiple reality (an ontological aspect of history as *res gestae*) and the reduction of it in a story or representation (an epistemological aspect of history as *historia rerum gestarum*). Herder solves this problem by underlining the individuality (*in dividuum* = undivided) of each culture, identifying it with nation:

> Every nation is one people, having its own national form, as well as its own language: the climate, it is true, stamps on each its mark, or spreads over it a slight veil, but not sufficient to destroy the original national character.[39]

Here we have the first formulation of Mandelbaum's continuing entity. There seems to be some hesitation in Herder's underlining of the individuality of every nation. Language, on the one hand, stimulates an inner uninterrupted development of the nation, climate as a cause from the outside, on the other hand, can be a disturbance of its organic evolution. Nevertheless, this disturbance gives the evolution an open, contingent teleology. Is this a first sign of the dialectics that historicism inheres?[40]

Contrary to Kant, who conceives time as a form of intuition to observe the phenomenal world, Herder sees temporality as something of the observer's reality itself, or better: the observer is embedded in real time, and time is embedded in himself. Time is the living thing Collingwood speaks of in his definition.[41] Herder comes very close to the time regime of Romanticism, because its representatives surely would agree with and underline Herder's utterance:

> Everything has come to bloom upon the earth which could do so, each in its own time and in its own milieu; it has faded away, and it will bloom again, when *its* time comes.[42]

Here time is not only something in the mind but inside man and world. As a consequence, Herder does not want to measure the past to the present, as in the Enlightenment. For him there is no distinction between how things are and how they ought to be. Herder judged nothing; all genuine expressions of experience are valid.[43] Although he has his preferences – he prefers the Greeks to the Romans for instance – he is able to defend them all. His main purpose is to penetrate in people's actions, their goals and their circumstances, making no distinction between highly civilized Greeks or the native Indians of California. Here Berlin notes that Herder actually is the inventor of the historicist *Einfühlen*. Vico wants to "understand" the past, allowing him to become a predecessor of Ranke's *Verstehen*. According to Berlin, Herder goes a step further than Vico, because his "*Einfühlen*" anticipates the historicism of Dilthey, who assesses understanding (*Verstehen*) as based on personal experience (*Erlebnis*).[44]

This means a complete different view on past and present. In the Enlightenment past and present are the same in their "now-ness" and they are fixed givens, creating a sequence of stages. With Herder past and present differ from one another, but they still are part of the same continuing process. This process consists of governing agencies as climate, language, education, neighbours and so on, bearing within them the rule of their own destination and creating an inner process of concrete, unique individuals. "A nation is made what it is by 'climate,' education, relations with its neighbours, and other changeable and empirical factors, and not by an impalpable inner essence or an unalterable factor such as race or colour", says Herder.[45]

This remark is directly addressed against Kant and enhances the conflict with the philosopher of Königsberg. Herder thus perceives reason itself as changeable in time, whereas Kant sees it as remaining the same in the course of history, although people learn to use it better. It implies that Herder's teleology of reason is open, which is to say: reason can change, although it needs to be combined with individuality. He calls the combination of development and identity "*Dauer im Wechsel*" ("endurance in change").[46] He sees identity as the opposite of every classification in orders, classes or stages. "The creator of all things does not see as a man sees. He knows no classes: each thing only resembles itself. . . . I do not believe that nature erected iron walls between these terms".[47] As a consequence Herder creates a multiplicity of times:

> In reality, every mutable thing has within itself the measure of its time; this persists even in the absence of any other; . . . no two worldly things have the same measure of time. . . . There are therefore (to be precise and audacious) at any one time in the Universe infinitely many times.[48]

In this quote Herder demonstrates what Hölscher adequately calls an "embodied" time, a time embodied with reality, a time more historicist than Enlightened. Herder talks of multiple times and he is, I think, not really interested in synchronization of these incarnated times. This is what I read in the following passage:

> We humans have problems with the One in history, "in the perspective of humankind" – where does it stand, the One, big endpoint? Where is the direct way to it? What does it mean, "progress of humankind"? Is it enlightenment? Is it improvement? Is it perfectibility? More happiness? Where are the standards? Where are the facts to find a standard in such different times and among such different peoples, even if we have the best information from outside?[49]

Herder wants to underline here a multiplicity of embodied times, opposing the universal, empty time of the Enlightenment with its chronological synchronization. It will be Hegel's endeavour to synchronize these multiplicity of real, ontological and embodied times.

What temporality concerns, Herder is more ideal typical (in the Weberian sense) of the Counter-Enlightenment than Vico. His perception of time as incarnated and therefore palpable in continuing entities (nations, cultures etc.) is firmly directed against Kant's *a priori* conception of time and also against his phenomenal temporality of nows. And although Vico's "ideal eternal history" differs fundamentally from Kant's static category of time, it remains an *a priori* category of the mind. Herder's perception of time as existing inside world and man makes him, more than Vico, the forerunner of historicism.

Hegel as representative of the Counter-Enlightenment

Hegel is next to Herder a representative of the Counter-Enlightenment, because he sees history as a collective singular, equating the knowledge of history (*historia rerum gestarum*) with history as *res gestae*. How does Hegel do this? To investigate that question, we have to start with his *Phenomenology of Mind* (1807).[50] Therein he manifests himself as an adept of the Counter-Enlightenment, if we take into account that it does not exclude ideas of progress. Although the new spirit of the French Revolution is seen as an advancement, it nevertheless is a qualitative change, an organic break.

> But it is here as in the case of the birth of a child; after a long period of nutrition in silence, the continuity of the gradual growth in size, of quantitative change, is suddenly cut short by the first breath drawn – there is a break in the process, a qualitative change and the child is born.[51]

This whole quote breathes progress and the hope for a better future, a hope that the Counter-Enlightenment shares with the Enlightenment, the breeding ground from which it originates. Nevertheless, we perceive also typical elements of the Counter-Enlightenment. For instance, the comparison of phylogenesis with ontogenesis by comparing the time of the French Revolution with the development of a newborn child. Hegel distances himself from Kant and comes close to Herder when he continues:

> When we want to see an oak with all its vigour of trunk, its spreading branches, and mass of foliage, we are not satisfied to be shown an acorn instead. . . . The beginning of the new spirit is the outcome of a widespread revolution in manifold forms of spiritual culture; it is . . . a whole which, after running its course and laying bare all its content, returns again to itself; it is the resultant abstract notion of the whole. But the actual realization of this abstract whole is only found when those previous shapes and forms, which are now reduced to ideal moments of the whole, are developed again, but developed and shaped within this new medium, and with the meaning they have thereby acquired.[52]

By perceiving time as a movement and as an organic process in which the present and future are determined by all kinds of features of the past, Hegel asserts that it is not sufficient to explain the multiple totality of the present by pointing to one single origin. He thus shows himself an adept of Herder and an antagonist of Kant, who sees reason as the acorn of man's moral history (see previous discussion). According to Kant, it is sufficient to show reason as the origin of man's moral behaviour; man's history is no more than learning better what morality is. In the metaphor of the acorn and the oak, Hegel objects to Kant's perception of reason.[53] Hegel stipulates that if we want to comprehend the world and want to act according to that comprehension, we need to know its history. Then we become aware that reason alone is a poor instrument for improving morality. With only reason we cannot learn from history, an idea most explicitly expressed by Hegel in his *The Cunning of Reason*.[54] It shows that Reason as it works in history is something else than the reason in the human mind.

Hegel underscores this in *The Phenomenology* by taking a position against Kant's a-temporal character of moral improvement, whereby each person must individually learn the lessons from the past anew. He argues:

> This bygone mode of existence has already become an acquired possession of the general mind, which constitutes the substance of the individual, and, by thus appearing externally to him, furnishes his inorganic nature. In this respect culture or development of mind (*Bildung*), regarded from the side of the individual, consists in his acquiring what lies at his hand ready for him, in making its inorganic nature organic to himself, and taking possession of it for himself.[55]

Moral improvement, but also cultural improvement in general, displays a development through time. The individual as part of culture, or in Hegelian terms, as being part of the general Mind or Spirit, can make his *unorganische Natur* ("unorganic Nature") organic by participating in civilization (the Spirit) and learning from it. Thus, the Spirit is historical and develops itself through time. Man has as his duty to appropriate the experiences of this general Mind or Spirit. In terms of temporality this means that the living, historical time must become the living time of the historical individual. Moreover, by participating in the Spirit, civilization becomes the product of people's actions.[56] By acting, people create new times and these times incarnate in history.

This leads to a completely different perception of synchronization. Jordheim is almost right to consider the experience of non-simultaneity (*Ungleichzeitigkeit*) between cultures and the work of synchronization as the "most important new contribution in eighteenth-century thinking about time".[57] However, this is only true for the Enlightenment's thinking about time in the eighteenth century. Jordheim's synchronization is only possible with an empty time. As we have seen already, synchronization goes wrong with Herder. He does not only succeed in realizing synchronicity, he even abhors all kinds of unification.

Yet Hegel takes up the challenge with his unification of time and reason. He makes clear that all the individual temporalities of nations, states and so on come together in the all-embracing *Weltgeist,* the Spirit of the world. As we have seen earlier, Hegel describes the present in the Preface of his *Phenomenology* as a time of birth and as a direction sign to a completely new world in the near future. Birth means here the first embodiment of Reason, as *Weltgeist* in a real subject. This incarnation takes place in the *Welthistorische Persönlichkeit* ("World Historical Figure") of Napoleon, as the reconciliation of the actual and the rational and as the apotheosis of history. Because Napoleon reconciles reality and rationality, Hegel unveiled in this reconciliation his own so-called Absolute Knowledge.[58]

According to the French philosopher Kojève, Napoleon is the French doer, who has achieved the historical development by his bloody struggle. Hegel is, in the view of Kojève, the German thinker, who by his reason has revealed the meaning of this development. The Napoleon/Hegel duality is the new Christ, the incarnated Logos, reconciling in time reality and reason.[59] Hegel does so, by seeing the French Emperor in the *Phenomenology of Mind* as the (negative, but also positive) unifier of past developments and as the dawn of a new era.[60] As such he "synchronizes" the multiple embodied times, perceived by Herder. Hegel creates the collective singular (Koselleck) not by synchronization but by integration of the plural, real histories (*res gestae*) in the all-embracing Reason. Maybe the unification has not yet been completely accomplished by Napoleon, but the future will succeed in this endeavour. As such Hegel endorses "'progress' as the [incarnated and therefore] irresistible force carrying us toward the future utopia".[61]

Koselleck's transition of time from Enlightenment into historicism

Koselleck's sophisticated definition of historical time as the space of experience and horizon of expectation unconsciously enables a spectrum with ontological aspects on one side and epistemological on the other. In the Introduction I have argued that Koselleck with his time of the modern emphasizes the epistemological aspects of it, thus creating an empty time. In Chapter 2, I have confirmed this. Contrary to that empty time, the convergence of ontological and epistemological elements is the main feature of an embodied historical time, of which Hegel is the main representative. In my view the Counter-Enlightenment therefore forms the transition from the Enlightenment into historicism. Koselleck does not think in terms of empty and embodied times. In the Enlightenment he discovers a change from multiple histories (Historien) to history as a collective singular (Kollektivsingular = Geschichte) through synchronization. According to him, this collective singular continues to exist in the nineteenth-century romanticist form of historicism.

For me, the collective singular of Koselleck, in combination with an empty time, creates a non-existent divergence between two of the most important representatives of that form of historicism, namely Hegel and Ranke. The difference between both is incorrect and does not occur if we take into account the transition from an empty into an embodied time, in which epistemological and ontological aspects are brought together. That is what I want to explain in this section. First I will give Koselleck's interpretation of change from the Enlightenment into historicism and after that my own views on it.

For the transition of the Enlightenment into historicism Koselleck needs another route than synchronization. He connects Herder – in his perception a representative of the Enlightenment – with the historicist von Humboldt, who argues in his "Über die Aufgabe des Geschichtsschreibers" (1821):[62]

> The writer of history who is worthy of such a name, must represent each event as part of a whole, or what amounts to the same thing, within each event illuminate the form of history in general.[63]

Koselleck reads the above quote only as a phrase about historical representation.[64] He points to a statement of Droysen, which teaches him that "the representation of history [is] a dialectical self-realisation of the human mind".[65] In this way the ontological aspects in history writing are lifted to an epistemological level, omitting the aspects of *res gestae*. This is confirmed by Koselleck's reference to Goethe's statement that "one will, in the same city, hear an important event narrated differently in the morning and in the evening".[66] It expresses "perspectivism", which is for Koselleck a discovery of the Enlightenment. It is further substantiated by his reference to the philosopher and historian Johann Martin Chladenius (1710–1759):

> History is one, but representations of it are various and many.[67]

And Koselleck adds:

> A history as such is in his view, conceivable without contradiction, but any account of such a conception involves a break in perspective.[68]

Here Koselleck does not only emphasize the (empty) epistemological but also the multiple aspects of the collective singular. This interpretation anticipates Ranke's plural perception of history. Ranke argues:

> These many separate, earthly-spiritual communities called forth by moral energy, growing irresistibly, progressing amidst all the turmoil of the world towards the ideal, each in its own way![69]

Ranke's "each in his own way" refers to the historian as the writer of multiple histories, sometimes about nations, sometimes about institutions or religions. Koselleck perceives Chladenius as the forerunner of Ranke and thus as the patriarch of multiple histories, related to one collective singular.

This solution, however, seems to make Ranke the representative not only of a plurality of histories but also of a singular epistemological perception of it.

According to Koselleck the French Revolution confirms Chladenius's approach, because it uncouples "a past whose growing foreignness could be . . . recovered only by means of historical investigation". Historical investigation leads to historical knowledge; that is why it only can be seen as an epistemological activity. However, should Ranke be perceived as the representative of an epistemological view on history? If so, then there is a break between Ranke's view and Hegel's. As I explained before, Hegel's concept of history implies an epistemological as well as an ontological element. What went wrong?

Let me return to the quote in which Koselleck connects Herder with Von Humboldt. It can also be read as a statement about history in which the ontological (*res gestae*) and epistemological aspects (*historia rerum gestarum*) converge. Then Droysen's statement that action is incorporated into its knowledge must be read in the Hegelian sense that the human mind *realizes* itself, that it makes itself real.[70] As we have seen previously, Hegel realizes reason "in the body" of Napoleon. By the expression "self-realisation", Droysen transfers the epistemological, multiple histories into an objective perception of the collective singular. Historicists would regard history only to be fiction, if no correspondence is assumed between the *res gestae* and the *historia rerum gestarum*. This means a strong connection between history as knowledge and the ontological roots from which it originates. Events and their interconnections as ontological elements are inserted in an epistemologically perceived unique course of time. This interpretation creates an approach of history in which there is a balance between epistemological and ontological elements. This reading of Herder and Von Humboldt implies *an embodied historical time*.

In my view Ranke demonstrates the same balance between ontological and epistemological elements as Hegel. I think that Koselleck's view on Ranke, via Chladenius, leads to a misconception of Ranke's historical time, because it is dominated by epistemological aspects.[71] Also Ranke's adage *Jede Zeit ist unmittelbar zu Gott* is in many respects incompatible with Koselleck's time of the modern. The latter sees the future as better than the present and the past, whereas Ranke's statements consider past, present and future as equal parts of the great stream of becoming.

Hegel and Ranke both are representatives of an historical idealism in which the development of an epistemologically started idea is an ontological operation. This means nothing else than the development of an embodied time. That is the lens through which Hegel and Ranke need to be seen. Looking through that, one may observe another difference between both: Hegel underlines the singularity, whereas Ranke articulates the plural of the collective singular. Whether this is true is the subject of the next two chapters.

Retrospect and prospect

Regarding the eighteenth century we have to make several distinctions in temporality. Firstly, there is one between time in the Enlightenment and in the Counter-Enlightenment. Secondly, there are three temporalities inside the time regime of the Enlightenment: (1) natural time, put into words by Kant in his time of intuition (*Anschauungsform*); (2) chronological time and (3) historical time of stages. Natural time as *Anschauungsform* is changeless and refers to phenomena as endless repeating nows. That is why I see the time of the Enlightenment as empty. Therein the present (of the eighteenth century) is the "reasonable" benchmark for the past, and as such the past can only serve as a container of good and bad examples. Chronological time is empty, because of its purely ordering function, foremost becoming necessary by the discovery of pre-Adamite times. Historical time is empty by its preordained, staging character, in which there is no place for contingency.[72] Synchronization of historical times means in the Enlightenment predominantly coordinating the European, biblical chronologies with the "pre-Adamite" and non-European chronologies and the tuning in of the historical stages.

The times of the Counter-Enlightenment are not empty, because they are "incarnated" in reality and therefore also in history. It then becomes embodied time. Nevertheless, the tuning in of histories remains important, albeit of a completely different nature than the synchronization of empty times. "Synchronization" of incarnated times happens with Hegel in his all-embracing Reason, or *Weltgeist*, as the great unifying mover of history.

The embodied time put forward in the Counter-Enlightenment forms the basis of all the temporalities I am going to distinguish in historicism. However, this does not mean that all elements of the time of the Enlightenment are obliterated. Especially Marx, with his ambiguous time, displays reminiscences to the "time of the modern" of the Enlightenment. Hegel shows an inverse development. He abandons step-by-step the path of the Counter-Enlightenment and moves in the direction of a romanticist historicism with a plurality of times. It already starts in Tübingen (1887–1893) by his friendship with Schelling and Hölderlin. Hegel's further development in the direction of Romanticism will be the central issue of the next chapter.

Notes

1 This chapter has been the second part of Jansen, "In Search of New Times".
2 P. P. Wiener (ed. vol. II), "'IV Enlightenment' and 'Counter-Enlightenment'", in: *Dictionary of the History of Ideas: Studies of Selected Pivotal Ideas*. http://xtf.lib.virginia.edu/xtf/view?docId=DicHist/uvaGenText/tei/DicHist2.xml (accessed March 2, 2015).
3 There is a reason for this distinction in structure. The Counter-Enlightenment stems from the Enlightenment, thus several items are the same. Only in special aspects the two cultures differ. Therefore, this and the foregoing chapter have the same difference in structure as the one between the lemmas from Pappe and Berlin in the *Dictionary*.
4 Beiser also sees time as a feature of the Counter-Enlightenment's opposition to Enlightenment, but only as part of the opposition against Enlightenment's cosmopolitanism. I perceive time as being a benchmark *per se* between Enlightenment and Counter-Enlightenment. Frederick Beiser, *The German Historicist Tradition* (Oxford: Oxford University Press, 2011), 12–13.
5 Allen Wood, *The Free Development of Each: Studies on Freedom, Right and Ethics in Classical German Philosophy* (Oxford: Oxford University Press, 2014), 123.

6 Ibid.
7 *"Alle ihre Fragen über den Fortgang unseres Geschlechtes . . . beantwortet . . . ein einziges Wort: Humanität, Menschheit"*. Koselleck, *Vergangene Zukunft*, 255.
8 Allen Wood, "Herder and Kant on History: Their Enlightenment Faith", in: L. Jorgensen and S. Newlands (eds.), *Metaphysics and the Good: Themes from the Philosophy of Merrihew Adams* (Oxford: Oxford University Press, 2008), passim.
9 Johann Gottfried Herder, *Metakritik zur Kritik der reinen Vernunft* (Frankfurt und Leipzig: Hartknoch, 1799). https://archive.org/details/einemetakritikz01herdgoog. The differences between Herder and Kant come from Kant's later works. Herder was influenced by Kant's precritical works, which are more naturalistic, pragmatist, empiricist and antimetaphysical. See: Jack Zammito, *Kant, Herder and the Birth of Anthropology* (Chicago and London: University of Chicago Press, 2002).
10 Hölscher, "Time Gardens", 584–585.
11 Just like Hölscher, I do not delve deeper into Gadamer's *Leere und erfüllte Zeit*, because I do not want to start a philosophical discussion here about differences between Gadamer's substantiation of empty and full-filled times and my interpretation of empty and embodied times. However, there certainly is a relationship. Hans-Georg Gadamer, "Concerning Empty and Full-filled Time", transl. R. P. O'Hara, in: E. G. Ballard and C. E. Scott (eds.), *Martin Heidegger in Europe and America* (The Hague: Martinus Nijhoff, 1973), 71–86. See also chapter 9 of this book.
12 Ankersmit, *Meaning, Truth and Reference*, 1.
13 Collingwood in the footsteps of Hegel asserted the same: "that different periods in history are really different – not only chronologically, but different in their fundamental characteristics". See: J. van der Dussen, *History as a Science: Collingwood's Philosophy of History* (unpublished ed.: Leiden, 1980), 456.
14 There is a big difference between the pragmatism of the Enlightenment, which works by historical examples, and the "pragmatism" of historicism. Ranke for instance wants to show the present as a product of past developments, by giving the Idea of it. The Idea is a principle of life, from which politicians could learn and by learning could develop it further. As Ranke states: *"Demnach ist es der Aufgabe der Historie, das Wesen des Staates aus der Reihe der früheren Begebenheiten darzuthun und dasselbe zum Erkenntniss zu bringen, die der Politik aber nach erfolgtem Verständnis und gewonnener Erkenntniss es weiter zu entwickeln und zu vollenden"*. Leopold von Ranke, "Über die Verwandtschaft und den Unterschied der Historie und der Politik", in: idem, *Sämtliche Werke*, Bd. 24 (Leipzig, 1872), 288. The historians of the Enlightenment do not want to give an Idea or trend, only examples of more or less great statesmen, or of better or worse behaviour. I would like to thank Reinbert Krol for this reference.
15 Although Koselleck sees this problem, he does not connect it to an embodied time but to a history of progress. Koselleck, *Futures Past*, 140.
16 Koselleck, *Vergangene Zukunft*, 321. *Nicht mehr in der Zeit, sondern durch die Zeit vollzieht sich dann die Geschichte.* "Time is no longer simply the medium in which all histories take place; it gains a historical quality. Consequently, history no longer occurs in, but through, time". Koselleck, *Futures Past*, 236. Unfortunately, Koselleck does not make a distinction in the eighteenth century between the Enlightenment and the Counter-Enlightenment. As a result, he does not perceive the difference between a change *in* time and a change *through* time as the forerunner of the historicist distinction between an *empty* and an *embodied* time. See the penultimate section of this chapter.
17 Gottfried Wilhelm Leibniz, "Fifth Paper", in: *Samuel Clarke, A Collection of Papers*, which passed between the late learned Mr. Leibniz and Dr. Clarke, In the Years 1715 and 1716 (London, 1717), number 55. Published online: 2006. www.newtonproject.sussex.ac.uk/view/texts/normalized/THEM00234 (accessed April 4, 2015).
18 Hölscher, "Time Gardens", 584 and 586. See also: Hölscher, "Mysteries of Historical Order: Ruptures, Simultaneity and the Relationship of the Past, Present and Future", in: Lorenz and Bevernage, *Breaking up Time*, 134–151, esp. 141–143.

19 Gottfried Wilhelm Leibniz, *The Principles of Philosophy Known as Monadology* (ed. J. Bennet), principle 22. www.earlymoderntexts.com/assets/pdfs/leibniz1714b.pdf (accessed December 14, 2015).
20 Hölscher, "Mysteries of Historical Order", 141.
21 Hölscher, "Time Gardens", 585. See also: Hölscher, "Mysteries of Historical Order", 141. He refers here to § 61 from Leibniz's *Monadology*, in which resounds an interconnection of things in reality. Nevertheless, it is a connection of souls and moreover preordained, thus not far from a connection *a priori*.
22 See for the significance of contingency for historicism: Koselleck, *Vergangene Zukunft*, 170–175.
23 Isaiah Berlin sees Leibniz as a historian of the Enlightenment, not of the Counter-Enlightenment, because his perception of history was nothing else than "satisfying curiosity about origins, disclosing the uniformity of nature, doing justice to men of worth, offering support to Revelation, and teaching useful lessons by means of examples". Isaiah Berlin, *Two Studies in the History of Ideas* (New York: Random House, First Vintage Books Edition, 1977), 142.
24 *The New Science of Giambattista Vico* (1744) (transl. Thomas Bergin and Harold Fisch; Ithaca and London: Cornell University Press, 1948) [Section III, 331], 85.
25 Berlin's interpretation has made of Vico a direct forerunner of historicism. He saw Vico's phasing of history not only as a "pursuit of an intelligible purpose", which can still be seen as an epistemological issue, but also as an "effort to understand himself and the world, and to realize his capacities in it". Isaiah Berlin, *Vico and Herder: Two Studies in the History of Ideas* (New York: Vintage Books, 1977), 32–35.
26 Eelco Runia, "Presence", *History and Theory* 45, no. 1 (2006), 1–29, esp. 13.
27 Ibid.
28 It is remarkable that Croce and Meinecke with regard to historicism seems to display a similar difference. Croce defended, albeit in the eyes of Meinecke, an epistemological form of historicism in which logical categories regarding individuality – like for instance the individual as a man of action, led by reason – make it possible to understand historical man in the different periods of the development of humankind. Meinecke himself adheres to a historicism as a principle of life ("*eine neue Schau menschlichen Lebens überhaupt*"), wherein individual phenomena are inapprehensible and irrational. See: Reinbert A. Krol, *Het geweten van Duitsland. Friedrich Meinecke als pleitbezorger van het Duitse historisme* (Groningen, Dissertation, 2013), 140.
29 Runia, "Presence", 13.
30 *The New Science of Giambattista Vico*, 93 [Book I, 349].
31 Quoted from Berlin, *Vico and Herder*, 64.
32 Leopold von Ranke, *The Theory and Practice of History* (ed. Georg Iggers and Konrad von Moltke, transl. Wilma Iggers; London and New York: Routledge, 2011), 78; see also: S. Smith, "Historical Meaningfulness in Shared Action", *History and Theory* 48, 1 (2009), 2, note 2.
33 Berlin, *Vico and Herder*, 65.
34 Ibid., 113. Moreover, he also refers on the same page to Pythagorean, neo-Platonic and Renaissance roots.
35 See for continuing entities: Maurice Mandelbaum, *The Anatomy of Historical Knowledge* (Baltimore and London: Johns Hopkins University Press, 1979), 11.
36 Jordheim, "Multiple Times and the Work of Synchronization", 517.
37 Ibid.
38 Bentley, *Modern Historiography*, 22.
39 Johann Gottfried Herder, *Reflections on the Philosophy of the History of Humankind* [F. E. Manuel, ed. selections from T. O. Churchill's translation of J. G. Herder's *Ideen zur Philosophie der Geschichte der Menschheit*; 2 vols., 1800–1803] (Chicago: University of Chicago Press, 1968), 166.
40 Ankersmit has pointed to this dialectic in historicism by arguing that the individuality of every phase in history (see Ranke's "*Jede Epoche ist unmittelbar zu Gott*") is an element

of synchronicity in an overall diachronic organicist movement. See Ankersmit, *Historical Representation*, 132–133; idem, *Sublime Historical Experience*, 144; see also: Krol, *Het Geweten van Duitsland*, 119.
41 See Collingwood's definition at the end of Chapter 1. My impression is that Herder does not develop a participant's point of view, as Vico did.
42 Hayden White, *Metahistory: The Historical Imagination in Nineteenth-Century Europe* (Baltimore and London: Johns Hopkins University Press, 1975), 75.
43 Krol, *Het geweten van Duitsland*, 118–119.
44 Berlin, *Vico and Herder*, 163.
45 Quoted from Berlin, *Vico and Herder*, 173. See also: Krol, *Het geweten van Duitsland*, 118.
46 Berlin, *Vico and Herder*, 134.
47 Gottfried Herder Johann, *Sämtliche Werke* (ed. B. Suphan; Berlin, 1877–1913), vol. VIII, 177. English quoted from: Berlin, *Vico and Herder*, 164.
48 *"Eigentlich hat jedes veränderliches Ding das Mass seiner Zeit in sich; dies bezieht, wenn auch anderes da wäre; keine zwei Dinge der Welt haben dasselbe Mass der Zeit . . . Es gibt also im Universum zu einer Zeit unzählbar viele Zeiten"*. Quoted from: Koselleck, *Vergangene Zukunft*, 10. English transl.: Kimberley Hutchings, *Time and World Politics: Thinking the Present* (Manchester: Manchester University Press, 2008), 39.
49 Quoted from: Jordheim, "Multiple Times and the Work of Synchronization", 516. Jordheim observes here the same non-synchronicity as I do. But I don't agree with his solution of the problem. See my: "In Search of New Times", 87–88.
50 Georg W. F. Hegel, *Phenomenology of Mind* (transl. J. B. Baillie [1910]; Mineola, NY: Dover Publications Inc., 2001).
51 Ibid., 5–6.
52 Ibid., 6.
53 Collingwood states: "[t]he true nature of an institution is shown not in its beginnings but in its developments". Quoted from: van der Dussen, *History as a Science*, 339.
54 See also: Koselleck, *Vergangene Zukunft*, 58–59.
55 Hegel, *Phenomenology of Mind*, 11–12.
56 Georg Lukács, *Der junge Hegel. Über die Beziehungen von Dialektik und Ökonomie*, 2 Bände, Bd. 2 (Zürich: Suhrkamp Taschenbuch Wissenschaft, 1973), 723–725.
57 Jordheim, "Multiple Times and the Work of Synchronization", 514.
58 I do not want to discuss here the question whether, according to Hegel, Napoleon was the incarnation of the demon of power, steering the fate of himself and the state entrusted to him, or that he was only an instrument of the *Weltgeist*, ignoring his voice in the end and thus losing his power. The fact that Hegel in his *Philosophy of Right* smoothly replaced Napoleon by the Reformation does arise the surmise of the last option. See: Krol, *Het geweten van Duitsland*, 168/9.
59 Alexandre Kojève, *Hegel, Kommentar zur Phänomenologie des Geistes* (Stuttgart: Suhrkamp Taschenbuch Wissenschaft 97, 1975), 294–295.
60 Lukács, *Der junge Hegel*, 701–703. Historically seen, it is the dawn of a new era; philosophically seen, it is, according to Kojève, the end of the history of philosophy, because Hegel's philosophy has accomplished whatever can be said about the relationship between concept and time. See: *"Als adäquate Beschreibung des Wirklichen negiert sie nichts und schafft daher nichts Wirkliches: sie hat keine wirkliche oder geschichtliche Zukunft vor sich"*. Kojève, *Hegel, Kommentar zur Phänomenologie des Geistes*, 292. Kojève here agrees with Heidegger and Koyrè.
61 Quoted from: G. Blix, "Charting the 'Transitional Period': The Emergence of Modern Time in the Nineteenth Century", *History and Theory* 45, 1 (2006), 51–71, esp. 66.
62 Wilhelm Von Humboldt, "Über die Aufgabe des Geschichtsschreibers", in: idem, *Gesammelte Schriften* IV, 41.
63 *"Der Geschichtsschreiber, der dieses Namens würdig ist, muss jede Begebenheit als Teil eines Ganzen oder, was dasselbe ist, an jeder die Form die Geschichte überhaupt darstellen"*. Koselleck, *Vergangene Zukunft*, 54. See also: Koselleck, *Futures Past*, 35.

64 See also: Frank Ankersmit, "Koselleck on 'Histories' versus 'History' or: Historical Ontology versus Historical Epistemology". It is the lecture Ankersmit held at the conference of Outo Preto, August 2016. I would like to thank the author for his kindness to send it to me.
65 Koselleck, *Futures Past*, 32.
66 Koselleck, *The Practice of Conceptual History*, 114.
67 Koselleck, *Vergangene Zukunft*, 185. "*Die Geschichte ist einerlei, die Vorstelling aber davon ist verschieden und mannigfaltig*". Keith Tribe translates: History is one, but conceptions of it are various and many". I think the term "representations" is better than "conceptions". Koselleck, *Futures Past*, 135.
68 Koselleck, *Futures Past*, 135.
69 Ranke, *The Theory and Practice of History*, 74.
70 Droysen: *die Vorstellung von der Geschichte als einer dialektischen Selbtshervorbringung des menschlichen Geistes*. . . . Quoted from: Friedrich Jaeger and Jörn Rüsen, *Geschichte des Historismus: eine Einführung* (München: C.H. Beck, 1992) 34. See also: Koselleck, *Vergangene Zukunft*, 48 and note 65 above.
71 See also the Introduction.
72 For this character Jordheim gives an important quote from Schlegel against Condorcet's *Esquisse*, where we read: "The real problem of history is the inequalities between the different strands of human development". Jordheim rightly sees this quote as a proof of the eighteenth-century non-simultaneity of historical time. Jordheim, "Multiple Times and the Work of Synchronization", 514.

PART 2
The romanticist time of politics

4
HEGEL'S TIME OF THE STATE

Herder, Hegel's fellow-representative of the Counter-Enlightenment, considers rivers, trees, all kinds of objects, states and nations as embodied by time. Hegel, on the other hand, perceives the incarnated time almost exclusively in the state and its institutions. It is a flowing time of becoming that runs from the past, through the present into the future. This will be illustrated by discussing the development of Hegel's time concepts, evolving from an Aristotelian, cosmological temporality into a more musical, Augustine-oriented one. From this change results a time of becoming, which is reinforced by Hegel's reconstruction of Kant's epistemological thinking about organicism. Hegel's time thus changes into a more ontological, romanticist concept.

Let me start with the observation that an important difference exists between Hegel's *Phenomenology of Mind* of 1807 and his *Philosophy of Right*, published in 1820. It can be displayed as the watershed between the time regime of the Counter-Enlightenment and the one of Romanticism. In 1807 Hegel still believes in progress, understanding that the idea of reason is not yet completely and perfectly realized but that it will come autonomously in due time. This will change in his *Philosophy of Right*, wherein an organicist state is conceived. Such a state is needed, because there are lots of problems to be solved. They originate in Germany's disintegrating societies, in which all kinds of traditional structures disappear. As a consequence of Napoleonic domination and the bureaucratic character of the post-revolutionary new states, home towns (*Heimatstädte*) and estates (*Stände*) are in danger of disappearing.[1] Organicism and conservatism seem to be the best medicine against these social ills. They will bring coherence in society and restore the *polis*. It means tackling societal problems by political measures, which implies the restoration of a society of estates. Before I come to that, I will follow the development of Hegel from 1807 to 1820. In those years he slowly approaches the ideal type of a romanticist temporality.

Hegel's philosophical perception of time

Hegel starts his philosophical reflections with an Aristotelian, cosmological time. It displays few similarities with the temporality he ends with, namely a romanticist, homogeneous temporality, based on slowly changing entities. In his *Enzyklopedie der philosophische Wissenschaften* (1817), Hegel still considers space and time as Kantian *Anschauungsformen* and underlines the abstract, invisible character of both. Nevertheless, he admits that they can make things visible.[2] Their most important feature is being external to each other; they are "*das ganz abstrakte Aussereinander*".[3] Space represents the positive aspect of this abstract *externality*, which means that the negation of it is an abstract multitude of points. Space is "punctuality". But, in its punctuality, one point spreads itself open to all other points. Time unfolds in a continuous denial of points and so of a negation of punctuality. Hegel's rather opaque definition of time is interpreted by Heidegger:

> The point "gives itself airs" before all the other points. According to Hegel, this negation of the negation as punctuality is time.[4]

Time is the negative unity of externality: time is the being that is, when it is not, and when it is not, it is: "*sie ist das Sein, das indem es ist, nicht ist, und indem es nicht ist, ist*".[5] According to Heidegger, Hegel starts with a point, a spatial definition of time, like Aristotle's "cosmological" conception of it. Hence he sees Hegel's temporality still as "a vulgar consciousness of time".[6]

The change of Hegel's view on temporality becomes more clear in his *Vorlesungen über die Aesthetik* (1817–1829). There he explains the problem of the difference between space and time with regard to music. He observes that music instruments, as spatial objects, produce sounds. Music itself, however, is only time. Like the patriarch Augustine, he comprehends notes as points, to which we listen by combining them with preceding and subsequent notes. In Hegel's philosophical terms, time is negative externality. This means that time comes about when the externality of the points of time is annulled. In the *Vorlesungen über die Aesthetik*, he puts it like this:

> the negative externality: the transcended apartness of punctuality and as negative activity the transcending of this point of time into another, which also transcends itself into another etc.[7]

However, already in his *Phenomenology of Mind* (1807), Hegel discloses a historical time. Heidegger admits that, although he still emphasizes the Aristotelian character of Hegel's temporality. He describes Hegel's time as "contemplating becoming", in which a historical time is comprehended.[8] "Becoming" is in Hegel's philosophy the ontological result of the dialectics between being and non-being, an unreflective movement, that takes time. "Contemplating" means the reflection on this process by the Spirit or Mind that can be identified as super-personal Culture. This brings historical time into existence. Heidegger observes a very close relationship between Hegel's dialectics of the Spirit (i.e. Culture) and time.[9] He refers to a passage in Hegel's *Phenomenology of Mind* in which the Spirit shows itself as incomplete, because not everyone with self-consciousness participates in the Mind as consciousness. To say it simple: not everyone makes the fullness of Culture his own. Reason and non-reason compete for priority in everyone's personal mind as well as in the super-personal Spirit, Mind or Culture. This means a development by interaction between self-consciousness and the super-personal Spirit.

> Time therefore appears as Spirit's destiny and necessity, where Spirit is not yet complete within itself; it is the necessity compelling Spirit to enrich the share self-consciousness has in consciousness.[10]

Then *historical* time is not far away:

> The process of carrying forward this form of knowledge of itself is the task which Spirit accomplishes as actual History.[11]

As a result, we can say that there is already a historical time in the *Phenomenology of Mind* of 1807. Maybe Lessing contributes to Hegel's transformation of time. Lessing's division of arts in temporal (music, theatre and literature) and spatial (painting and sculpture) forms visualizes time and space.[12] Music, theatre and literature can give time an alignment of past, present and future after another, which is impossible in the visual arts. In fact, Hegel's perception of time changes. He increasingly leaves the cosmological time of Aristotle and opts for an embodied and organic temporality with a process-like character. By living in the present, the past is slowly left behind, expecting a better future. It is a Hegel in between modernism and historicism.[13]

Hegel's organicism compared with that of Kant and the origins of an embodied time

Long before 1817, Hegel is already engaged with organicism, although he is not completely aware of its meaning for his view on time. Beiser observes that around 1800 he has religious reasons to be interested in organicism.[14] He wonders, first, how the finite originates in the infinite and, second, how the divine trinity is possible. The first question is solved by referring to the gospel of St. John 1 1–4: "In the beginning was the word and the word was with God, and the word was God . . . What has come into being in him was life, and the life was the light of the people". Here we have incarnation, the intermingling of epistemology and ontology. For Hegel this gospel means a metaphor for organicism, showing how the spirit incarnates in matter. Thus, organicist thinking solves the problem of how the infinite results in the finite. The problem of the trinity makes clear how the One can differentiate into the many. Here we return to the collective singular with its multiplicity of times.

Although Hegel in his *The Spirit of Christianity* considers organicism as a means to understand the mysteries of Christendom, he soon exchanges mysticism for metaphysics.[15] In a discussion with Schlegel in 1801, Hegel announces his philosophical system, in which the One and Absolute is conceived as organic life. In the "Absolute One" the finitude and difference are included, because life is a process from unity to difference and from difference to unity within difference.[16] This idea will return in his constitution of the state. It also illuminates how an undulating time is already latent in this organicist thinking.

Around 1800 Hegel still belongs to the Counter-Enlightenment because of his ambiguous attitude towards Christianity and his discussion with Kant.[17] In that discussion lies another reason for Hegel's interest in organicism. In his *Critique of Judgement*, Kant anticipates on this topic. The Königsberger philosopher states that the concept of organism goes beyond that of mechanism, because an organism is self-generating and self-organizing, whereas a mechanism only explains by the working of two different things upon one another. Moreover, an organism is an indivisible unity, a *totum*, where the whole precedes its parts, whereas a mechanism is a *compositum*, where the parts precede the whole. Kant even asserts already that organicism implies that matter has an inherent purpose. He thinks that such an ideal element can bridge the Cartesian rift between mind and matter, between the intelligible and the empirical, between the world of freedom and the world of necessity and between the subjective and the objective. In his *Encyclopedia* (§ 55R), Hegel admits that Kant already embraces in his organicism all the characteristics of philosophical idealism.[18]

One fundamental distinction between Kant and Hegel remains. For Kant organicism is a regulative principle, a heuristic device for the study of nature, only existing on an epistemological level. Hegel's organicism, however, is not only a heuristic instrument but a *constitutive principle*; for him, organism is a reality, in nature as well as in culture. This distinction has consequences for his perception of time. Kant's organicism makes time only a regulative principle to explore change in nature and culture. To him organicism is not incarnated in reality and time, not embodied. Hegel's constitutive perception of organicism means that *reality is incarnated time and time is embodied with reality*. This idea is important to understand nature, but most of all to apprehend the cultural world of the state and its institutions.[19] Nature and politics are incarnated time, both showing an epistemological and an ontological component.

The difference between the phenomenology of mind and the philosophy of right

Already before 1817 Hegel's organicism is intensified by his communitarianism. This has consequences for his temporality. In his study about Hegel, Beiser sees him in his Berne and Frankfurt years (1793–1801) struggling between opposite streams: liberalism and communitarianism.[20] As we know, until approximately 1807, Hegel manifests himself a representative of the Counter-Enlightenment, in which freedom and progress are still at the forefront. Then liberalism wins from communitarianism. Hegel comes closer to romanticist conservatism after 1817. Does this imply that communitarianism gradually overrules liberalism? That question is important because communitarianism provides the entities in which time incarnates. To answer it, we have to investigate Hegel's assumptions regarding state and civil society, albeit always in their relations to time. The combination of communitarianism with the aforementioned organicism makes the embodied time a slowly, but continuously unfurling phenomenon.

In the *Philosophy of Right* (*Grundlinien der Philosophie des Rechts*, 1820), Hegel elaborates on the state as the concrete means to unite passion and liberty. Here Reason is no longer realized in a world historical figure like Napoleon but in the state of his time, the constitutional monarchy. In the *Philosophy of Right*, the history of the state embodies the entelechy of time. Thus, Hegel conceives a narrow connection between the movement of time and the organic development of the state. Time in the *Philosophy of Right* still has liberal aspects of progress, but the more-or-less conservative thinking of communitarianism prevails. As such Reason is no longer the opposite of past reality, as it still is in the *Phenomenology*, but already incarnates in reality after a long-lasting process. In that process not Napoleon but the Reformation is the apotheosis of history, reconciling religion and state in a balanced way. This cannot exist in Catholicism, because there – as in oriental despotism – the state is subservient to the church. In the Reformation the state is superior to religion, because the religious disunity of the Reformation brings about the true nature of the state as the realization of "universality of thought". This disunity makes the state self-conscious and strong and as such liberal and tolerant in matters of religion. A self-conscious state apprehends the individual as a universal person; it counts a man as a man, not because he is a Jew, Catholic, Protestant, German, Italian and so on.[21] Moreover in and through the Reformation the state is looked at with deference and thus receives *continuity*. The Catholic state is founded only on mightiness, which does not raise reverence, but rebellion and revolution.[22] Hegel here displays an interesting mix of future-oriented liberalism and past-oriented religion. In Protestantism they are mingled in an ever-changing continuity.

If Napoleon is the only incarnation of Reason yet a lot of work must be done, hence time remains future-oriented. The *Phenomenology of Mind* has the intention to know the path to the future. Since in the *Grundlinien der Philosophie des Rechts* the Reformation is a first realization of the idea of freedom, Hegel focuses on the state to know how Reason and Freedom already are – slowly but continuously – differentiating and perfecting themselves.[23] Reality has become more rational since the Reformation. Reason and freedom are not subjective anymore, because they are as ideas on their way to objectivity. They are becoming more and more realized in institutions like those of law, education and government. In this context we must see Hegel's statement: "What is rational is actual and what is actual is rational".[24]

This does not mean that everything that is existing is rational and legitimized as such. In the first paragraph of his *Philosophy of Right*, Hegel distinguishes *Wirklichkeit* and *Existenz*, actuality and existence:

> Philosophy . . . shows that only ideas and not concepts . . . have reality. All else, apart from this actuality established through the working of the idea itself, is ephemeral existence, external contingency, opinion, unsubstantiated appearance, falsity, illusion and so forth.[25]

Hegel's philosophy is an in-between; the past is not a mere past of passions but also the past of the Idea, which is to say, the reality of the already incarnated rationality. The idea of freedom has to deal with the present of passions, and in that contradiction the idea of freedom has to be further developed and perfected. The state is the instrument to realize the self-development of reason in reality.

This orientation on the future receives an antithetical part in the past. The state is not an arbitrary human artefact, created by a (mythical) contract, but a product of a long historical process. That makes time a burden, but also audacious and tenacious. The last two properties are mainly due to the state and its settings. That is why Hegel shows confidence, both in institutions in general and in the state in particular. Being a believer, Hegel formulates in his *Philosophy of Right* the state as "the march of God in the world".[26] Thus, the historical process of bringing the state into existence is for Hegel part of a divine strategy.[27] I will explain this statement in more detail in the following section. For now, it is enough to perceive how close Hegel comes to Ranke's *Jede Epoche ist unmittelbar zu Gott* and his *ahnen* (presumption) of God's hand in history. In the Introduction of his *Philosophy of Right*, Hegel abandons his more-or-less utopian political philosophy. Now he has become an almost full-fledged historian with regard to his perception of time, comprehending the present as well as the future as a product of the past:

> One word more about giving instructions as to what the world ought to be. Philosophy in any case always comes on the scene too late to give it. As the thought of the world, it appears only when actuality is already there cut and dried after its process of formation has been completed. The teaching of the concept, which is also history's inescapable lesson, is that it is only when actuality is mature that the ideal first appears over against the real and that the ideal apprehends this same real world in its substance and builds it up for itself in the shape of an intellectual realm. When philosophy paints its grey in grey, then has a shape of life grown old. By philosophy's grey in grey it cannot be rejuvenated but only understood. The owl of Minerva's spreads its wings only with the falling of dusk.[28]

In Hegel's *Phenomenology of Mind* the present is the dawn – but also the heavy birth – of a new era. In his *Philosophy of Right* the present displays evening glow instead of dayspring.[29] In 1820 the incarnated time leads to a perception of temporality as an enduring transition, in which the present is less a place of birth and more the product of the past.[30] Here Hegel leaves important elements of the time of progress and embraces a more-or-less romanticist time. Already in his *Phenomenology of Mind* Hegel succeeds in synchronizing the multiple, embodied times, so manifestly present with Herder. In Napoleon he perceives the compelling incarnation of the *Weltgeist*. In his *Philosophy of Right*, time is not only incarnated but also unified in the constitutional monarchy as the "hieroglyph of Reason".[31] This monarchy is the incarnation of God's plan with the world.[32] In 1820 he is a conservative liberal.[33] He now has got a new perception of historical time, which becomes burdensome and stubborn and almost forces to political withdrawal and waiting.[34]

The connection between Hegel's perception of time and politics

In a passage in his *Vorlesungen über die Philosophie der Geschichte* (1825), Hegel reinforces the relationship between time and state. He postulates a period in which Kronos, being the god of time and the creator of other gods and the cosmos, rules the world.[35] It is a time without a state, a time of chaos and destruction, without any structural morality (*sittliche Werke*). With Kronos as its representative, time is only devouring itself. Kronos's time is tamed when he creates Jupiter. The latter replaces the empty time of destruction with the historical time of the state, being an embodied time of wisdom (Minerva) and art (Apollo and the Muses).[36] Here we have the connection between time and politics.

The appearance of the state does not mean that chaos and irrationality disappear out of history. In the *Vorlesungen*, Hegel argues that reality is a spectacle of actions (*Schauspiel der Tätigkeit*), a confused mass of ruins (*verworrene Trümmermasse*), and history is a slaughterhouse (*Geschichte als Schlachtbank*).[37] Time remains a burden. Irrationality does not only originate in evil but also in good intentions. As a consequence corruption and "decay are not the work of mere nature, but also of the human will itself".[38] The human will is the origin of good as well as bad things. That is why the embodied time is both powerful and burdensome, being the result of the split human nature. Therefore, it is also a time of rise and fall. Here lies a big difference with Tocqueville and Marx, discussed hereafter. Hegel always believes in the mind of man, influencing reality personally or through politics, whereas Tocqueville and Marx have an eye for impersonal processes, not completely controlled by the human mind.

Let us return to Hegel's perception of history. Out of his slaughterhouse of passions, the history of the "Idea" arises. Passions and Idea are "the woof and the warp of the arras-wide-web of world history".[39] Passions can lead to misery but can also transcend into the necessary conditions of real liberty. They can be ruled by the Cunning of Reason.[40] However, it requires a mediator. Hegel finds it in the state as the union of the universal will and the subjective will. The state incorporates both, thus becoming "*Sittlichkeit*", objectified morality.[41] As *Sittlichkeit* the state can push back the chaos created by Kronos, although the passions do not disappear. With the help of God (Jupiter), the state brings time into a flow of rise and decline.[42] That is why Hegel sees the state as the march of God in the world, by which time is substantiated.

Hegel's relation to historicism and romanticist conservatism

Before we continue with the question about the relationship between Hegel's political ideas and time, another problem arises. Do Hegel's political ideas lead to a glorification of the state, or even to the defence of the conservative Prussian state? This is important, because I do not want to position Hegel as a conservative, neither as a complete, romantic conservative. I only want to present him as associated to a romanticist temporality.

For a long time Hegel has been considered the defender of the conservative Prussian regime. In his *Hegel und seine Zeit* (1857), Rudolf Haym, being a defender of German's unification, creates the myth that Hegel accommodates with Prussia, having in mind the idea that Prussia is the archenemy of German's unity and modernization. His views do not hold true, because after 1870, Prussia becomes the champion of national unification. After Haym, Hegel is reflected as the advocate of German nationalism.[43] Hegel's so-called conservatism has neither to do with a defense of the Prussian regime nor to do with the defense of whatever German government. Shlomo Avineri even remarks that the section in Hegel's *Philosophy of Right* on representation "can be viewed as an oblique critique of Prussian conditions".[44] So Hegel's past-orientation in the *Philosophy of Right* is not connected to Prussia. When he starts that study, Hegel is lecturing at the university at Heidelberg in Baden. Thus, he is not associated with the still rather conservative Prussian Regime. In the 1820s, Prussia is not as modern as Bavaria or Württemberg, and at that time, the country has no constitution and no national representative body. Nevertheless, already since the reforms of 1806 it is on its way to modernization. Prussia is not that retarded government various authors make of it.[45]

All these anachronistic approaches need to be replaced by a perception of Hegel as belonging to a romanticist time regime. The first half of the nineteenth century is fed up with the utopianism of the time culture of Enlightenment, in which the present is the starting point of a new era with a promising future. Counter-Enlightenment and most of all Romanticism perceive the present as the product of the past, and an incarnated time as an ocean, which needs a ship of state that slowly can be steered in the direction of a better future. Especially romantic conservatism, as put into words by Karl Mannheim, represents this time regime. It is the regime of traditionalism that has become reflective by the

French Revolution.[46] Romanticist historicism emerges from this conservative cocoon.[47]

Although Hegel cannot be considered entirely as a romantic conservative, he surely can be perceived as a representative of historicism in the way Beiser describes it. Beiser defines historicism as a way of thinking in which "everything in the human world has a history, that society has an organic structure and that all human beliefs and practices derive of necessity from their specific historical context".[48] Hegel completely fits in this definition. The only exception is that Hegel's reflections are metaphysical, whereas historicists reflect on history's epistemology.[49] Ranke, Humboldt, Dilthey and Weber fuss about the scientific status of history and its methodology, while Hegel and other philosophers speculate about the meaning, the ends and the laws of history itself.[50] Nevertheless, Hegel is a historicist, as a consequence of his organicism and his embodied time perception of the Counter-Enlightenment. This brings him under the spell of the romanticist time culture in which the present is a product of the past and in which the world exists of organic wholes.

Hegel's organicist state as an utterance of its vicinity to a romanticist time regime

Hegel's organicism concerns the transcendence of the dichotomy between the subjective and the objective, overcoming the dualistic legacy of Descartes.[51] This dichotomy can be found in the contradictions of the infinite and the finite, the one and the plural, the rational and the real, the state and the civil society. Their reconciliation exists in a perception of development, consisting of self-differentiation. "Life is a process, by which an inchoate unity becomes more determinate, complex and organized; it is the movement from unity to difference, and from difference to unity within difference".[52] Thus, his organicism is basic for an embodied perception of time.

Hegel's formulation of his organicist political ideas points in the direction of a romanticist time regime. In his *Philosophy of Right*, Hegel elucidates his organicist solutions of the dichotomy between state and civil society. To control the human passions of civil society, Hegel objects to every kind of atomism. People then do not belong to organic, coherent groups, but to classes, which means a return to Kronos's time.[53] Fearing these developments, Hegel seizes the past in order to cope with the possibilities of a chaotic future. Individuals must belong to an estate, which mediates between man's individual existence and those parts of society that anticipate the state. This anticipation means "prior to" as well as "aiming at". "Prior to" refers to a past in which estates still exist, and "aiming at" to a future in which they enable people to act politically. Although coming from the past, estates give political future to people. With regard to the latter, we have to look at the addition of paragraph 207 in the *Grundlinien der Philosophie des Rechts*. Hegel asserts there: "When we say that a man must be a 'somebody', we mean that he should belong to some specific social *estate*, since to be somebody means to have a substantive being". In Hegel's view a man outside an estate is a mere private person without past and future.

According to Shlomo Avineri, the German civil society at the beginning of the nineteenth century is an old, closed system of estates, dominated by inherited privilege. One can wonder if the German society in Hegel's days is as closed as Avineri assumes. Since the times of Napoleon, there already exists disintegration. Although princes, state reformers and bureaucrats, after the disappearance of the French, try to re-establish a society of estates and corporations, they do not completely succeed. Germany remains disintegrated. Hegel's solution is maintaining a society in which next to birth also merit has its influence. Hegel sees in the continuation of an old "communitarian" society, reinforced by future-oriented liberal elements, nothing else than the continuation of a process that is already underway. Therein, a "modernizing" estate is important, forming the reasonable part of reality

> to which an individual is to belong [being] one on which natural capacity, birth and other circumstances have their influence, though the essential and final determining factors are subjective opinion and the individual's arbitrary will, which win in these sphere their right, their merit, and their dignity.[54]

By such an estate a disruptive, chaotic, "chronic" time can be prevented.[55] Hegel's civil society of estates embraces the philosophical articulation of a society that modernizes in a rather conservative way.[56] It guarantees continuity in change by connecting the future through the present with the past, without major shocks or interruptions.

Hegel distinguishes three estates in society: the agricultural, the business and the bureaucratic estate. In society the unity of the state comes via the cooperation of different estates. Because of their anticipation of the state, the estates create a unity within difference. Here we have an organic process, where orientation towards the past, the present as well as the future is crucial. Being societal organizations, the estates receive a political functionality by and in the state.

The agricultural estate gets its substance from the natural products of the soil. It owns the soil privately, which poses a danger because it has to do with a whimsical nature. That makes it subservient and little inclined to reflection. Hegel's account of the agricultural estate differs in the *Philosophy of Right* from his discussion about it in an earlier publication, the *Realphilosophie*. In that study about the agricultural estate, the aristocracy has been omitted, as a result of the French Revolution. In the *Philosophy of Right* this estate returns. Avineri considers this clearly as "a bow in the direction of the Restoration".[57] Possibly Avineri is right, but it is only half an explanation. To me the reason for Hegel's bow is his inclination to the romanticist time regime of a present, created by the past.[58] Hegel incorporates the landed aristocracy in the agricultural estate on the basis of romanticist-conservative arguments, without becoming a romantic conservative. Aristocrats are relatively free from the fluctuations of the market and from the interference of the state. As "gentlemen of independent means", they are suited for public office and as such optimal political actors. These arguments are already used during the pre-revolutionary period.

Hegel's next estate practices trade. It is subdivided in (1) the class of craftsmen (*Handwerkstand*), meeting the needs of individuals; (2) the class of entrepreneurs, working for a market; and (3) the commercial class of exchange. This estate represents a higher order than the so-called "subservient" agricultural estate, in which "the individual is thrown back on himself". In Hegel's order of trade, the individual is related to others, whereby he possesses a sense of freedom that a member of the agricultural estate lacks. And he adds: "The sense of freedom and order has therefore arisen above all in towns".[59] This seems to be a reference to the medieval estates, in which the towns come above the peasantry in its hierarchy. Hegel also places the aristocracy above the trade estate, reinforcing a reference to the medieval past. It brings him close to the romanticist historians of historicism. Does not Romanticism idealize the medieval three-order society, which probably never existed in the Middle Ages?

Hegel's third estate, the one of the civil servants, surely is not medieval. This estate fits in with Hegel's philosophy of reconciliation of reality with the Idea of Reason, because it is the crucial link between the "passionate" particularism of civil society and the universality of the state.

> The universal estate, or, more precisely, the estate of the civil servants, must purely in virtue of its character as universal, have the universal as the end of its activity[60]

This is about the future-oriented element, which functions as a counterweight against the two more past-oriented, other estates, underlining Hegel's state as the (organic) representation of an incarnated time.

The reconciliation of particularism and universality of the state leads to a system of political representation in which mediation is crucial, and omitting it would mean despotism.

> The real significance of the Estates lies in the fact that it is through them that the state enters the subjective consciousness of the people and that the people begins to participate in the state.[61]

Hegel's estates can be considered as the continuing entities that become so important in Ranke's philosophy of time (see the next chapter). In the philosophies of Hegel and Ranke, the continuing entities are the carriers of time. They form the plural in history, which is itself the collective singular.

Hegel's romanticist-conservative aversion against atomism

Hegel's representative system is bi-cameral, consisting of an Upper House – composed of members of the nobility – and an elected Lower House. By making the Upper House aristocratic, Hegel bows to the past again. He does something similar with the elected Lower House. Elections are not viewed individual but based on groups: "society is not dispersed into atomic units. . . . [O]n the contrary, it is a society, articulated into associations, communities and corporations, which although already constituted for other purposes, acquire in this way a connection with politics".[62] Especially in his explanation of the way in which the House of Representatives must be elected, Hegel displays a romantic aversion to atomism. It is the terrible dystopian future of the French Revolution, from which Germany must be spared. In contrast to his forward-looking *Phenomenology*, which allows discontinuity, Hegel perceives in the *Grundlinien der Philosophie des Rechts*, the evil of a quick and abrupt break with the past. France's example deserves no imitation:

> France lacks corporations and local government, i.e. associations wherein particular and universal interests meet. It is true that these associations won too great a measure of self-subsistence in the Middle Ages, when they were states within states and obstinately persisted in behaving like independent corporate bodies. But while this should not be allowed to happen, we may none-the-less affirm that the proper strength of the state lies in these associations. In them the executive meets with legitimate interests which it must respect.[63]

Only in its corporate structure the state is a real totality, the incarnation of Reason and Freedom. This corporate structure is the product of a long process, in which the inchoate "wills" of the individual members of the civil society are transformed into a *volonté generale*, a will of the state. Then the state is no more a means to an end but a *personality*, which can decide and act. This all is made possible by the constitutional monarchy:

> The truth of subjectivity . . . is attained only in a subject, and the truth of personality only in a person; . . . [h]ence the absolutely decisive moment of the whole is not individuality in general, but a single individual, the monarch. . . . The last re-absorbs all particularity into its single self, cuts short the weighing of pros and cons between which it lets itself oscillate perpetually now this way and now that, and by saying "I will" makes its decision and so inaugurates all activity and actuality.[64]

Adam Müller is one of the protagonists of Mannheim's romantic conservatives. When we compare Hegel's organic conception of the state with the latter's, we see remarkable agreements. According to Müller:

> A people is a sublime community of past, present and future generations, which all cohere in an all embracing unity of the living and the dead . . .[,] displaying a community of customs and laws in thousands of blessed

institutes, *connecting times by long exquisite and flowering families* ending in the one immortal family, standing in the middle of the state.[65]

And further on:

> Every true, organic state of law, ought . . . to be restricted in space, in order to become a real, vivid and closed individuality.[66]

Although, there may be a difference between Hegel's metaphysical organicism and the religious organicism of the romantic conservatives, there is hardly any distinction in the resulting perception of the state. Conservatives and Hegel are both of the opinion that the state after a long period of time is realizing unity and individuality in the person of the monarch. This also makes clear that time itself is embodied in the development of the organic state. A strong organic state is the incarnation of time. Hegel's state itself displays a mix of a rather traditional communitarianism and a more modern liberalism, by which it moves slowly but steadily and continuously into the future.

Hegel's philosophical history

This brings us to Hegel's *Vorlesungen über die Philosophie der Geschichte* and more specifically to his view on historiography. In his *Philosophical History*, Hegel comes close to the time regime of romanticist historicism. He understands history as a spectacle of passions, inevitably leading into monstrous sufferings. Nevertheless, history also displays the implementation of reason and a growing recognition of freedom. This kind of optimism proceeds from Hegel's belief that every existing state actualizes a Spirit consisting of freedom and rationality. People living in the state actualize it. This process does not run into progress along a straight line. Here Hegel's view on history comes about as a move of rise and fall:

> In the course of history, the preservation of a people, a state and the preservation of the ordered spheres of its life, is one essential moment. . . . The other moment, however, is that the stable persistence of the spirit of the people, as it is, is broken because it is exhausted and overworked; that world history, the world spirit proceeds. . . . But this is tied to a demotion, demolition, destruction of the preceding mode of actuality. . . . It is precisely here that the great collisions occur between the prevalent, recognized duties, laws and rights and, on the other hand, possibilities which are opposed to this system.[67]

All these Hegelian contradictions and changes take place in an embodied time, characterized by political, cultural or philosophical ideas. This is about a homogeneous time, being the "self-development of the Idea", while maintaining its own identity.[68]

The French philosopher Louis Althusser notes that Hegel considers change as consisting of ever-altering things that still are *in* a period and remain *of* a period. This is even true for periods of transition.[69] There is constant difference, but everything changes within the self-identical consciousness. Althusser's co-author, Etienne Balibar, underlines this view by arguing that Hegel's thinking cannot outrun its period because his philosophy entirely comprehends it in its philosophical idea.[70] However, he wonders: is the Spirit thus locked in its time and thus not completely free? He admits that the freedom of the Spirit is characterized by its capacity to self-activation. As such it is in contrast with the mechanical interaction of the Enlightenment. That interaction is featured by a change, effected from the outside. Hegel's "self-development of the Idea of the Spirit" is free from such an external constraint.[71] As a result of this, we can say that Hegel's time is homogeneous.

The Spirit blows wherever it wants. It can embrace little things to exemplify something comprehensive, according to the organic rule that little things are representative parts of a greater whole. Hence it is possible to ascribe to Hegel the idea that to understand ancient Athens, one only has to read Plato. Balibar says about Hegel's approach that he does not need to examine Athens's economic basis but only has to look at the contrast between the unity of the polis and the freedom of the individual.[72] This implies a homogeneous and continuous temporality. The Frenchman Michael Gordy summarizes it as follows:

> The result is that (Hegel's) historical time is not only homogeneous; it is continuous as well: the tempo and rhythm of all the social structures display an absolute synchronization such that no structure can "out-run" or lag behind any of the others. That is why, for Hegel, thought cannot "run ahead of its time".[73]

Undulating time

There exists a distinction between the incarnated time of the Counter-Enlightenment and that of Romanticism. The first maintains the linear idea of progress, whereas the latter replaces it by the romantic wheel of fortune with its rise and fall. The abandonment of the idea of progress is completely visible with Ranke, however, not with Hegel.[74] He maintains the idea of advancement as efficacious in history. More than the historians of the Enlightenment, however, he pays attention to the unreasonable workings of it in reality. Unlike them, Hegel does not see a pure Reason as the main mover in history, but an incarnated Reason, the *Volksgeist*, which specifies itself further in the Spirit of the State. The Spirit of the People and the Spirit of the State consist of the deeds of all those who participate in the collective of nation and state. The *Volksgeist* can deteriorate but can also transcend itself into a different and often a higher form of itself.

Each civilization must therefore perish, to exist merely as an echo in what follows it, for each is a living contradiction".[75]

The Spirit of the People is like a natural person; "it flourishes, is strong, declines and dies".[76] We will see in the next chapter that this organic metaphor, and the individualistic and actionist context in which it is uttered, is fully consistent with the politics of identity, which romanticist historians pursue.[77]

Hegel's undulating conception of history can be noticed in Part 2 of his *Philosophy of History*. The histories of Greek and Rome display a pattern of birth and growth, of maturity, succeeded by decline and fall. In the history of the Greek World for instance, the idea of freedom finds its birth in festivals and the Olympic Games. The Greeks are first meant to enjoy the individual as a private person, but their individuality becomes more objective, first, as part of religion and, second, by embedding them in the state. The state itself develops from monarchy through tyranny into a democracy. As a mature democratic state, the Greek fight the Persians. The Peloponnesian War and the incorporation in the Macedonian Empire mark the decline of the Greek world. Its fall comes in the year 146 BC, when Perseus, the last Macedonian king, is defeated by the Romans.[78] We discover the same pattern in Hegel's treatment of Roman history. Only the history of the German People does not end in fall, but in the philosophy of Hegel itself.[79]

We will see that historians such as Barthold Niebuhr and Ranke make use of the same undulating pattern of time as Hegel. Still there is a difference between the latter and the romanticist historians. The first two give only imperfect and partial accounts of the past and do not pretend to contribute to an all-embracing truth. Hegel insists that Reason can claim the authority to extract such a truth from the accounts romanticist historians bring about.[80] Reason can exhibit progress, albeit slowly. Hence the undulating pattern of Hegel's perception of time takes the form of an ascending spiral. The romanticist historians do not have such high hopes of Reason. For them, not Reason but their own reasonings can extract some truth from the past. This explains why their undulating time remains horizontal.

There is another difference: the romantic historians such as Ranke do not consider Reason as a comprehensive march of God in the world. Every state, nation, church, religion or collectivity has its own individual idea and a corresponding development. Looking at history as collective singular, they emphasize the plurality of it. Hegel's development of Reason as a comprehensive process in itself maintains foremost its singularity, being the realization of freedom and reason.

> Thus progress appears in existence as proceeding from the imperfect to the more perfect, whereby the imperfect does not need to be perceived in an abstract way as only imperfect, but also as the contrary of itself, where it has the perfect in itself as a germ, as an incentive.[81]

Although imbued with universality and progress, Hegel's perception of time is not the empty one of the Enlightenment. It is an incarnated and burdensome temporality, organic as well as homogeneous. The state, organized as a hierarchical organism, is the main protector against atomism, which is constantly lurking. Hegel's perception of time is the development of that organism. It originates in the embodied time of the Counter-Enlightenment and runs into a romanticist time, characterized, firstly, by the incarnation of an Idea in reality, especially in the State. It is featured, secondly, by the wavy path it takes and, thirdly, by a past that is formative for present and future. Romanticist historicism shows almost the same features, as we will see in the next chapter. The explicit expressions of an undulating time in Hegel's philosophy of history are less the result of a conscious choice than the consequence of participation in a romanticist culture of time. This demonstrates how strong the influence of a time regime can be.

With Hegel starts historicism, and, as Ankersmit observes in the footsteps of Mannheim, this *Weltanschauung* exchanges "a static conception of society for a dynamic one".[82] For historical time it means that change and dynamics are no longer only connected to the empty time of progress but also to the embodied time of historicism. As such it can fall after a rise, it can accelerate and retard and it can get waiting people into motion. That, I will show in the next chapters.

Notes

1 Werner Conze (ed.), *Staat und Gesellschaft im deutschen Vormärz 1815–1848* (Stuttgart: Klett Verlag, 1978³); Hans-Ulrich Wehler, *Deutsche Gesellschaftsgeschichte I, Vom Feudalismus des alten Reiches bis zur defensiven Modernisierung der Reformära 1700–1815* (München: C.H. Beck, 1987); Harry Jansen, "Duitsland, een geval apart" en "Krachtig, maar ook flexibel? – Politiek-institutionele voorwaarden voor industrialisering", in: Hans Righart (ed.), *De Trage Revolutie. Over de wording van industriële samenlevingen* (Heerlen: Boom, Open Universiteit, 1991), 137–179.
2 Georg W. F. Hegel, *Enzyklopedie der philosophischen Wissenschaften im Grundrisse*, vol. II (1817 1st edition and the G. Bolland ed., Leiden, 1906), § 254–259, esp. 47–50. See also: Heidegger, *Sein und Zeit*, 428–436; Martin Heidegger, *Zijn en Tijd* (Nijmegen: SUN, 1998), 532–541.
3 Hegel, *Enzyklopedie der philosophischen Wissenschaften*, § 254.
4 Martin Heidegger, *Being and Time* (transl. John Macquarrie and Edward Robinson; Oxford and Cambridge, MA: Blackwell, 2001), 482 (430). Idem, *Zijn en Tijd*, 534–535.
5 Hegel, *Enzyklopedie der philosophischen Wissenschaften*, vol. II, 254–259 en Mooij, *Tijd en geest*, 171.
6 Heidegger, *Zijn en Tijd*, 536–537.
7 . . . *die negative Äusserlichkeit: als aufgehobenes Aussereinander das Punktuelle und als negative Tätigkeit das Aufheben dieses Zeitpunktes zu einem anderen, der sich gleichfalls aufhebt, zu einem anderen wird usf.* Hegel, "Vorlesungen über die Aesthetik III", *Werke* 15 (Frankfurt a. M.: Suhrkamp, 1970), 164. See also: Mooij, *Tijd en geest*, 171, n. 6.
8 Heidegger, *Zijn en Tijd*, 536.
9 Ibid., 540.
10 Hegel, *Phenomenology of Mind*, § 801. www.marxists.org/reference/archive/hegel/works/ph/phc4.htm.
11 Ibid., § 803.

12 Gotthold Lessing, *Laokoon oder über die Grenzen der Malerei und Poesie* (1776) quote in English by: Stephen Kern, *The Culture of Time and Space 1880–1918* (Cambridge, MA and London: Harvard University Press, 2003²), 21.
13 There is an incorrect identification of modernism and historicism. See for example: Esposito, "Transformationen Geschichtlicher Zeitlichkeit nach dem Boom", 52–57 and Chakrabarty, *Provincializing Europe*, 6–16. This may be based on Hegel's ideas between 1807 and 1820.
14 Frederick Beiser, *Hegel* (New York and London: Routledge, 2005), 80–109.
15 Ibid., 88–89.
16 Ibid., 94–95.
17 Ibid., 131. Hegel changes in his Frankfurt years his hostile view on Christianity into an unorthodox Christianity, writing his *The Spirit of Christianity*. He distances himself from Kant's view, in which the essence of religion is morality. Hegel then sees in Christianity the religion of love. In 1821 he calls himself even a Lutheran. Beiser, *Hegel*, 132–152, esp. 139.
18 Beiser, *Hegel*, 97–98.
19 Ibid., 239–258.
20 Ibid., 224–233.
21 Georg W. F. Hegel, *Grundlinien der Philosophie des Rechts* (Frankfurt a. M.: Suhrkamp Verlag, 1970), par. 209, 360.
22 Ibid., par. 270, 415–431. See also: Georg Lukács, *Der junge Hegel*, Bd. 2 (Frankfurt a. M.: Suhrkamp, 1973), 710.
23 Georg W. F. Hegel, *Vorlesungen über die Philosophie der Geschichte* (Frankfurt a. M.: Suhrkamp, 1970), 492–520.
24 Hegel, *Grundlinien der Philosophie des Rechts*, Vorrede, 24. "*Was vernünftig ist, das ist wirklich; und was wirklich ist, das ist vernünftig*".
25 Ibid., par. 1, 29. I don't follow Avineri's translation here. Shlomo Avineri, *Hegel's Theory of the Modern State* (Cambridge: Cambridge University Press, 1974²), 127. Avineri uses to translate Hegel's "Idee" with "concept"; I think that a translation with "idea" is more adequate. "Idea" is a "realized concept". Avineri in his quote does not translate Hegel's "blosse Begriffe".
26 "*Es ist der Gang Gottes in der Welt, dass der Staat ist*". Hegel, *Grundlinien der Philosophie des Rechts*, par. 257, 403.
27 See for this interpretation: Avineri, *Hegel's Theory of the Modern State*, 176–177.
28 Hegel, *Grundlinien der Philosophie des Rechts*, 28. The English text is cited from: Avineri, *Hegel's Theory of the Modern State*, 128.
29 Lukács, *Der junge Hegel*, 704.
30 "The concept of transition brings these two vectors (birth and decline) together, and ascribes progress and decadence simultaneously to the same time". Blix, "Charting the 'Transitional Period'", 63. The concept of transition can bring these two vectors together, because transition is an aspect of an incarnated and undulating time perception.
31 Hegel, *Grundlinien der Philosophie des Rechts,* § 279 *Zusatz*.
32 See: Avineri, *Hegel's Theory of the Modern State*, 177. Unlike Hegel, historicists like Ranke and Humboldt returned to a multiplicity of times, only unified by God's invisible hand in history.
33 Hegel, however, opposed a conservatism in which several romantic attempts occurred to revive old Teutonic mythology and imagery and thus to restore a pristine Germanic Ur-Volk. See: Avineri, *Hegel's Theory of the Modern State*, 22.
34 Hayden White, "The Burden of History", *History and Theory* 5 (1966), 119, and Blix, "Charting the 'Transitional Period'", 66. His translation.
35 Hegel surely makes here no distinction between Kronos and Chronos. He stands in a long Greek-Roman tradition of confusion of both gods. See: www.waggish.org/2013/father-time-chronos-and-kronos/
36 Hegel, *Vorlesungen über die Philosophie der Geschichte*, 101.

37 Ibid., 34–35.
38 Ibid., 34.
39 Ibid., 38.
40 *"Das is die List der Vernunft zu nennen, dass sie die Leidenschaften für sich wirken lässt. . ."* Hegel, *Vorlesungen über die Philosophie der Geschichte*, 49.
41 Ibid., 56.
42 Ibid., 104.
43 Avineri, *Hegel's Theory of the Modern State*, 115.
44 Ibid., 117.
45 L. Krieger, *The German Idea of Freedom: History of a Political Tradition* (Chicago and London: The University of Chicago Press, 1972²), 147–165.
46 *"Das der Traditionalismus zum Konservatismus wurde, d.h. dass er anstatt wie vorher eine in allen Individuen mehr oder minder lebendigen formale Haltung zu sein, zum Strahlungszentrum, zum treibenden Keime einer 'Bewegung' wurde, die in ihren geistigen und seelischen Gehalten einen bestimmten, wenn auch historisch sich abwandelnden Strukturzusammenhang sich aufweist, liegt daran, dass unmittelbar vorher das 'Fortschrittswollen' in einer ähnliche Weise zu einer 'Strömung' mit einem eigenen Strukturzentrum geworden war"*. Karl Mannheim, "Das Konservative Denken I", in: *Soziologische Beiträge zum Werden des politisch-historischen Denkens in Deutschland* (Tübingen: Mohr, 1927), esp. 78–79. See also: 105, 112–114 and 120.
47 See: Ankersmit, *Meaning, Truth and Reference*, 10.
48 Beiser, *Hegel*, 262, see also: 29–31. Also Beiser, *The German Historicist Tradition*, 9–18.
49 That is the reason why Beiser leaves the philosophers out of his definition of historicism. He sees the historicist tradition as essentially epistemological. Beiser, *The German Historicist Tradition*, 8.
50 Beiser, *The German Historicist Tradition*, 8–9. Weber fits completely in my broad view on historicism. See the Introduction of this book.
51 Beiser, *Hegel*, 104.
52 Ibid., 94.
53 It is rather confusing that Avineri Hegel's German term "Stand" in the *Grundlinien der Philosophie des Rechts* translates with "class". Avineri, *Hegel's Theory of the Modern State*, 156. I prefer to use therefore the English term "estate". Although he uses the term "class" in the English translation of the *Grundlinien der Philosophie des Rechts* (*The Philosophy of Right*), Avineri is fully aware of the difference between the two concepts. In *Hegel's Theory of the Modern State,* he notes that Hegel in his *Realphilosophie* uses only class to denote the workers; otherwise, he always uses the term "Stand". See: Avineri, *Hegel's Theory of the Modern State*, 149, note 49.
54 *Grundlinien der Philosophie des Rechts*, par. 206; Avineri, *Hegel's Theory of the Modern State*, 156.
55 Here we see how deeply Hegel is imbued with romantic anti-rationalistic feeling, although he maintains believing in rationalist solutions. Robert Brandom calls this Hegel's "synthesis of Enlightenment inferentialism and Romantic expressivism"? Brandom, *Making It Explicit*, 92–93, esp. 93.
56 Georg W. F. Hegel, *Political Writings* (ed. T. Knox; Oxford: Clarendon Press, 1964).
57 Avineri, *Hegel's Theory*, 156.
58 This explanation will receive substantiation, when we discuss romanticist historians like Niebuhr and Ranke.
59 Hegel, *Grundlinien der Philosophie des Rechts*, par. 204, 357.
60 Ibid., par. 303, 473.
61 Ibid., par. 301, *Zusatz*, 471.
62 Ibid., par. 308, 476.
63 Ibid., par. 290, *Zusatz*, 460.
64 Ibid., par. 279. Quoted from: Avineri, *Hegel's Theory of the Modern State*, 187.
65 *"Ein Volk ist die erhabene Gemeinschaft einer langen Reihe von vergangenen, jetzt lebenden und noch kommenden Geschlechtern, die alle in einem grossen innigen Verbande zu Leben und Tod zusammenhängen . . . welch schöne und unsterbliche Gemeinschaft sich den Augen und den*

Sinnen darstellt . . . in gemeinschaftlichen Sitten und Gesetzen, in tausend segenreichen Instituten, in viele noch besonderer Verknotung, ja Verkettung der Zeiten, besonders ausgezeichneten lange blühenden Familien endlich in der einen unsterblichen Familie, welche in der Mitte des Staates steht". Adam H. Müller, *Elemente der Staatskunst. Sechsunddreissig Vorlesungen* (Leipzig: Handel Verlag, 1808, ed. 1936), 92. My translation and emphasis in the English text.
66 Müller, *Elemente der Staatskunst*, 123.
67 Hegel, *Vorlesungen über die Philosophie der Geschichte*, 96–105, esp. 97–98. Walter Kaufmann, *Hegel, a Reinterpretation* (New York: Anchor Books, 1966), 269.
68 Jason Read, "The Althusser Effect: Philosophy, History and Temporality", *Borderlands e-Journal* 2, 4 (2005), section 5.
69 Louis Althussser and Etienne Balibar, *Reading Capital* (transl. Ben Brewster; New York: 1970), 94.
70 Althusser and Balibar, *Reading Capital*, 95.
71 Michael Gordy: "Thus the term 'spiritual' is demystified as soon as it is understood that in the tradition of Western thought the spiritual is that which is self-activating, as contrasted with the mechanical, which is other-activated. But to say that something is self-activating, that the principle governing all its changes is contained within its concept, is to say that it is free, free from external coercion and restraint." See: Gordy, "Reading Althusser: Time and the Social Whole", 1–21, esp. 2.
72 Read, "The Althusser Effect", section 6.
73 Gordy, "Reading Althusser: Time and the Social Whole", 4.
74 Von Humboldt also maintains believing in progress.
75 Gordy, "Reading Althusser: Time and the Social Whole", 3.
76 Hegel, *Vorlesungen über die Philosophie der Geschichte*, 100.
77 See for instance Hegel's statement about the deeds of the English people and its identity: "*Was ihre Taten sind, das sind die Völker. Ein jeder Engländer wird sagen: Wir sind die, welche den Ozean beschiffen und den Welthandel besitzen, denen Ostindien gehört und seine Reichtümer, welch Parlement und Geschworenengerichte haben usf*". Hegel, *Vorlesungen über die Philosophie der Geschichte*, 99.
78 Hegel, *Vorlesungen über die Philosophie der Geschichte*, 275–338.
79 See also: White, *Metahistory*, 123–131.
80 Ibid., 102.
81 Hegel, *Vorlesungen über die Philosophie der Geschichte*, 78.
82 Ankersmit, *Meaning, Truth and Reference*, 11.

5
RANKE'S UNDULATING TIME OF CONTINUING ENTITIES

The romanticist time regime

To get access to a full-fledged romanticist time regime, we must observe in the first place Hölderlin (1770–1843), and especially his poem *Half of Life* (1843), because it demonstrates the undulating time of rise and fall.

> **Half of life**
>
> Yellow with pears
> Heavy with wild roses
> The land hangs in the lake
> Magnificent swans
> Drunk with kisses
> You dip your heads
>   ---------------
> In the holy sober water.
> Where will I find flowers this winter
> And where will I find
> The sunshine and shade
> of the earth? Speechless and cold
> The walls stand, and the weathercocks rattle in the wind.

In his novel *Hyperion, oder der Eremit in Griechenland*, Hölderlin gives voice to the same waving perspective:

> Or I look out to the sea, and ponder my life, his rise and fall, his bliss and sorrow, my past often sounds to me like a psaltery where the maestro goes through all the tones and mixes conflict and unison with one another in a hidden order.[1]

FIGURE 5.1 Caspar David Friedrich, *Strandszene in Wiek*

As with Augustine, Hölderlin also uses the metaphor of music to represent his view on time. It is a time of rise and fall. Novalis (1772–1801) experiences in his *Die Christenheit oder Europa* his time as a "nadir between the unified Christianity of the Middle Ages and the dream of a future cosmopolitan state".[2] Unlike Hölderlin, with his view of rise and fall, Novalis perceives the wave as a valley between two peaks. Whatever it may be, these undulating metaphors are reminiscent of the painting *Strandszene in Wiek*, by the famous German painter Caspar David Friedrich (1774–1840). He paints himself four years before his death, overlooking the sea. His painting gets the subtitle *Lebensstufen* (Stages of Life), indicating his romanticist perception of time.

The picture exposes the painter in three different stages of life. First as a little boy with his mother and his sister, holding up a flag and sitting just before the top of the hill.[3] On the top of the hill, he displays himself in the second life stage as a mature man, looking freely into the world. The third stage shows Friedrich as an old man, leaning on his Malacca, while looking back on his life and viewing the eternal sea with several ships coming ashore or disappearing at the horizon.

Friedrich's romanticist perception of time is indicated by three different stages of life and most of all by its wavy pattern. The painter himself, standing at the beach of Wiek on Rügen, looking at the arriving and departing ships at sea, feels that his own inner time and the time of the world coincide. The curved shape of the hill, intensified by the skirt of the woman, the leaving and arriving ships and the ships disappearing at the horizon display the same undulating pattern,

88 The romanticist time of politics

FIGURE 5.2 Jean Charles Pellerin: Images d' Epinal, *Degrees of Ages*

underlining that the organic temporality does not only apply for people but also for events in the world. Or better: people are embedded in the wavy pattern of reality.

The first two stages up the hill, the last one down the hill and the movement of the ships reminds us of old, traditional pictures of stairs of life such as the one above.

In the town of Epinal in the French Vosges, father and son Pellerin publish their famous *Images d'Épinal* in 1821. *Degrees of Ages* is one of them. Men and women first walk up the stairs and then down. In this way they point to an organic and wavy pattern of time, embodied in birth, growth, rise, decline and fall. We will perceive that Ranke's historiography is cast in the same homogeneous and wavy temporality as in this *Image of Epinal*. Before I am going to deal with that, I first want to investigate Ranke's relationship with the Enlightenment, the Counter-Enlightenment and Hegel.

Ranke's roots in the Counter-Enlightenment

A discussion about Leopold von Ranke's (1795–1884) ideas about time and history writing has to start with the historicist's rejection of the historiography of the Enlightenment. Early historicists, like Ranke, argue that in the historiography of the Enlightenment only individuals are actors in the past.[4] They add to it that historians in that epoch who use non-individual factors or events in their historical explanations only label them as external causes. In that view the fall of the Roman Empire is the result of the Great Migration around 500 AD. The decline of it is not an event caused by ideas or internal non-personal forces. In short, historicism objects to the perception of the Enlightenment that historical explanations only are based on causes or on the characters and intentions of individual actors.[5] It is a rather mechanical, not an organicist, approach of history.[6]

Ranke perceives states, nations, churches or religions as the main actors in history. Some titles of his comprehensive work may illustrate this: *History of the Romanic and Germanic Peoples From 1494 to 1514* (published 1824), *The Last Roman Popes in the Last Four Centuries* (1835), *The Ottoman and Spanish Empires in the Sixteenth and Seventeenth Centuries* (1843),[7] *A History of England Principally in the Seventeenth Century* (six volumes, 1875) and *World history: The Roman Republic and Its World Rule* (2 volumes, 1886). Ranke populates his studies with, what Ricoeur calls, *entités de premier ordre*, or to say it in English with Mandelbaum: *continuing entities*.[8] Ricoeur remarks that there is an oblique reference to the individuals, where the continuing entity consists of. And he states: "This oblique reference, in turn, allows us to deal with the society itself as one great individual, analogous to the individuals who make it up".[9] He refers to Husserl in his *Cartesian Meditation*, who calls historical communities "personalities of a higher order". Here we have Ricoeur's quasi-personages of the historical narrative.[10] Ranke comprehends them governed by ideas and hence as the protagonists in history.[11] As the last title suggests, he does not fully neglect world history, but he perceives it as based on a multiplicity of continuing entities.[12] In a note of 1816/7 he claims:

> It cannot be the purpose of the historian to explain all events from the minds of the acting persons. There must be something above them and that rules them – whether we call it fate, providence or God – just as an event stands above them which they do not produce but to which they consciously or unconsciously contribute. One can call the circumstances under which people become what they are contingent; but that higher development of human life is necessary. This development[,] however, extends to the whole epoch in which people live, to the great event in which they participate, to the overview of the general fate of humanity.[13]

The "whole epoch in which people live" refers to Ranke's famous adage *Jede Epoche ist unmittelbar zu Gott*. "The great event in which they participate" points in the direction of continuing entities.

Continuing entities seem to mark the difference between Hegel and Ranke. Ranke has a lot of them, whereas Hegel has only one: the state. Indeed, Ranke observes states, nations, churches, movements and so on as continuing entities; however, Hegel also has a plural of them in corporations and estates. We find these *within* the state, but yet they have the same organic characteristics. They form the plural of Hegel's collective singular. Continuing entities are basic for an embodied time. That is why the connection between Ranke and Hegel points to their common ground in the Counter-Enlightenment. In the following, I will discuss more agreements between Ranke and Hegel.

The fragment from Ranke above is not only about super-personal actors in history but also about time. This becomes clear when Ranke refers to the "circumstances" as "the whole epoch in which people live". In another passage, written at the same time, Ranke speaks of "the spirit of time", "the power of ideas" or "the divine, idea, which governs human beings everywhere and at all times".[14] Ranke conceives history as the instrument to decipher the "divine hieroglyph", as Beiser puts it.[15] Remember that Hegel considers the development of the constitutional monarchy as the "hieroglyph of Reason".[16] The source of the hieroglyph metaphor must be sought with Herder and Hamann, thus in the Counter-Enlightenment.[17] It illustrates that the roots of romanticist historicism and philosophical idealism spring from within that culture. It points in the direction of an idealistic form of explanation, only possible on the basis of an embodied time, coming about in a term like "tendency".

Ranke puts this into words in 1847: "The succession of these ideas and their tendencies form the great structure of universal history". This seems similar to Hegel, with whom the multiplicity of ideas is unified in the all-embracing Idea of Reason and its march through history. Ranke derives the relationship between time and ideas not from Hegel but again from the Counter-Enlightenment. It is not quite clear whether Ranke takes them from Herder or from Humboldt. Both claim that the ideas originate in soil, climate and powers. This is important because it shows that they are not closed teleological instances, but agents of a time, preconditioned by the past, but open to the future. We have seen how Herder worded it:

> A nation is made what it is by "climate," education, relations with its neighbours, and other changeable and empirical factors, and not by an impalpable inner essence or an unalterable factor such as race or colour.[18]

Humboldt does it in a similar way:

> . . . vast, serried turmoil of affairs of this world, in part arising out of the nature of the soil, human nature, and the character of nations and individuals, in part springing up out of nowhere as if planted by a miracle, dependent on powers dimly perceived and visibly activated by eternal ideas rooted deeply in the soul of man – all of which composes an infinitude which the mind can never press in a single form.[19]

The idealism of Herder and Humboldt stems from the perception that reality has three qualities: (1) it is constantly changing, (2) powers and ideas are an essential working part of it and (3) the present is the result of the historically formed character of states and nations.[20] In particular this latter topic indicates how important the developments in the past are for the present. These ideas from the Counter-Enlightenment change the function and character of history.

Like Humboldt, Ranke denies that historical knowledge has only an exemplifying aim, telling "what to do and what to avoid".[21] The reader has to be immersed in the past. Although the past can be very different from the present, the past must have presence. The historian must write in such a way that the reader feels imbued in past events. Then he can identify himself with experiences which differ from his own. History requires "stirring up reader's emotions".[22] Here again we perceive the assumption of an ontological time, in which past, present and future form a real, inclusive stream. It is the embodied time of the Counter-Enlightenment.

The main task ("office") Ranke aims at is the quest for the diverse ideas that are at work in nations, states, churches and religions. This brings him close to Hegel, although Ranke objects to his reduction from a multitude of ideas to one, single comprehensive Idea, the march of Reason in world history. Still there is an equivalent with Ranke, namely God's all-embracing hand in history.

Ranke's embodied time against the time perception of the Enlightenment

That the task of history changes becomes obvious in a quote from Ranke's *Histories of the Latin and Teutonic Nations* 1494–1514, written in 1824. There we find the well-known sentence of Ranke:

> To history has been assigned the office of judging the past, of instructing the present for the benefit of future ages. To such high offices this work does not aspire: it wants only to show what actually happened ("*wie es eigentlich gewesen*").[23]

Ranke's utterance sounds modest and self-depreciating but is in fact more the self-conscious statement of a historian who wants to tell his readers about the reality of the past. Ranke's realism often has been interpreted as a belief in objectivism, in the sense of "stick to the facts". Beiser distinguishes this objectivism from an interpretation of Ranke as a naive realist. According to Beiser, Ranke is not naive, because he does not consider the past as something in itself, "apart from and prior to our attempts to know it".[24] Ranke combines ontological and epistemological elements in his perception of history. But Beiser admits that Ranke is naive in assuming that the historian can achieve objectivity by resorting to the original documents and by effacing himself.[25] On the other side, he justifies Ranke's want to separate facts from assumptions, interpretations or inventions. He brings this in connection with the first part of Ranke's statement in which he criticizes Enlightenment's history and the partisan judgements of its practitioners.[26]

The new task Ranke assigns to history originates in his philosophical idealism. Although he only in 1847 comes to a full-fledged theory of ideas (*Ideenlehre*), Ranke comprehends from the 1830s on that past, present and future are linked with one another by the development of an idea. As we have seen above, Ranke gives two meanings of it: the leading principle of an epoch or the uniting and dynamic principle of a continuing entity.[27] In both meanings the customs, morals, laws, religion, politics and culture are joint together into an indivisible whole, hence making it the *principium individuationis* of the previously mentioned institutions and movements and the source of their developments. The idea surely has the character of an incarnated time. It qualifies the spirit of an epoch and identifies the special and characteristic development of states and nations. The latter becomes obvious when Ranke writes: "The innermost urge of spiritual life is movement toward its idea, toward greater perfection".[28] Especially the dynamic character of the idea points in the direction of an embodied time.

Pragmatism, idealism and an embodied time

Ranke's statement "to history has been assigned the office of judging the past" also means that he wants to discard the pragmatism of the Enlightenment. Wilhelm von Humboldt states something similar, writing, "history does not primarily serve us by showing us through specific examples, often misleading and rarely enlightening, what to do and what to avoid".[29] And Hegel utters the same, arguing that "peoples and governments never have learned anything from history".[30] The jurist Friedrich Carl von Savigny (1779–1861) criticizes the empty law theories of the Enlightenment and defends a historical approach to law as "the only way to a true knowledge of our situation".[31] The realism of Von Savigny, Von Humboldt, Hegel and Ranke is filled with "ideas", in which the past is more than the sum of "nows", inside which only individual people can act. The past is connected to the present not as a cause but *as part of an embodied time*. Because of an incarnated temporality, idealism can create a non-causal relationship between the past and the present.

This becomes even clearer when we look at one of the functions Ranke ascribes to historiography. That function is no longer pragmatic in the sense of instructing the present with examples from the past. In his famous speech of 1836, Ranke underlines:

> It is the task of history, to display the idea of the state from previous developments and to bring it to understanding, by which politicians, after successful comprehension are capable of continuing and further developing it, and in the end to accomplish it.[32]

This is another kind of historical pragmatism. History then gives politicians knowledge of past developments of the state in the form of an idea that needs to be further developed by politicians. This means an embodied time and implies a big difference with the pragmatism of the Enlightenment, which works by historical examples. Beiser also sees that Ranke objects to the pragmatism of the Enlightenment, but his explanation differs from mine. He perceives Ranke's rejection as a consequence of his refraining from moral, religious or political partisanship, whereas I see it as a consequence of his assumption of an embodied time.[33]

Ranke does not understand the past as a box in which the historian can arbitrarily grab to find examples of how to act in the present. He aims at a form of history writing that displays the present as result of the past. The past is governed by an idea that functions as a life principle (organic thinking), from which politicians can learn. Because of this the past requires scientific study to discover a real trend from the present into the future. Showing "how the past actually was" is, for Ranke, not a simple display of the facts but the discovering of the idea in reality.[34] The idea evolves from the past into the present, to surmise what the future might be. The historian must, among other things, explore the development of a political idea to help the politician in the further development of it.

Agreements and differences between Hegel and Ranke

Michael Bentley in his *Modern Historiography* perceives remarkable agreements between Hegel and Ranke. He argues that "on several occasions Ranke sounds as though he were a pupil of Hegel more than a critic".[35] Like Hegel, Ranke has its roots in the Counter-Enlightenment. Both view history as the collective singular in which different individualities develop. Ranke:

> World history does not present such a chaotic tumult, warring, and planless succession of states and peoples as appear at first sight. Nor is the often dubious advancement of civilization its only significance. There are forces and indeed spiritual, life-giving, creative forces, nay life itself, and there are moral energies, whose development we see. They cannot be defined or put in abstract terms, but one can behold and observe them. One can develop a sympathy for their existence.[36]

Ranke places individual life in a universal-historical context that he formulates as: "Everything is universal and individual spiritual life".[37] It means that history consists of a mix of ontological and epistemological movements, with general and single, but also with multiple aspects. In a less dynamic view, the same mix can be perceived in *Jede Epoche ist unmittelbar zu Gott*. The individual reality of each era has been realized at the "universal-historical" level through their involvement with God. For Ranke, therefore, history does not dissolve into a chaotic plurality of phenomena without a context.

However, Hegel and Ranke perceive the context of that plurality as a political-cultural reality, not as an economic-social one.[38] Moreover, both see that political reality exists directly under God's custody. Hegel defines the state as "*Der Gang Gottes in der Welt*", and Ranke perceives it as positioned under God's providence.[39]

These agreements are confirmed by Beiser, who observes that Ranke and Hegel quarrel about statements on which they actually agree. Ranke firmly states that whereas the philosopher views the particular in the universal and the finite in the infinite, the historian recognizes the infinite in the finite. As a result, he makes the distinction that the philosopher works deductively and *a priori*, starting with something universal, while detracting something specific from it. The historian works inductively or *a posteriori* and deduces generalizations from specific cases.[40] Beiser does not corroborate Ranke's view. He remarks that although Ranke's ideas are very influential, they are misconceived with regard to Hegel's philosophy. In his *Philosophy of World History*, Hegel clearly claims that in history the general comes from the particular. The historian should proceed inductively by first examining the facts for their own sake and then perceive something general in the particular.[41] This underlines my thought that for both Hegel and Ranke, there must be an ontological aspect behind an idea, which means that time is embodied.

The other way around is also true. Hegel blames the historian for stacking detail upon detail without understanding the whole. But Beiser assures that Ranke "insists that understanding the unity and development of events is no less important than establishing the facts themselves".[42] The quote given earlier from Ranke in his *The Great Powers* confirms this.[43]

Here, as with Hegel, we perceive the coexistence of chaos and passions on one side and reasoning and planning on the other. Ranke also considers time as burdensome and the state as the solution to the problems enclosed in it. In Hegel as well as in Ranke, we see the same attention for inner forces and moral energies in states and peoples, the same patterns of decay and rise or the reverse: rise and fall. For both, time unfolds as an idea in the historical process. The protagonists in that process are the *Volksgeist*, a concept Hegel borrows from Herder, and Ranke from Savigny's historical school of law.[44] Hegel therefore states: "*Der konkrete Geist eines Volkes ist es den wir bestimmt zu erkennen haben*".[45] To discover the concrete Spirit of a people, one has to know how the idea works. That makes it possible to discover the general principles in the specific facts of the history of a people.[46] Hegel claims that Kepler gathers knowledge in the same way. The latter had to be familiar with ellipses and cubes, with squares and relationships before he could subsume his data under eternal covering laws.[47]

When we compare this passage from Hegel's *Philosophy of History* with a quote from Ranke's *Politische Gespräche*, we discover a striking resemblance:

> These many separate, earthly-spiritual communities called forth by moral energy, growing irresistibly, progressing amidst all the turmoil of the world towards the ideal, each in its own way! Behold them, these celestial bodies, in their cycles, their mutual gravitation, their systems![48]

The organicist development of "earthly-spiritual communities", each with its own incarnated idea, does not result in chaos of specific facts and overall turmoil, but in cycles and systems of orderly relationships. Hegel and Ranke here point to what has been called the *Real-Geistige* of German Idealism. Going from the past, through the present into the future, there is discontinuity, but the idea makes the evolving transformation homogeneous. Despite change, the continuing entity maintains its identity: *Dauer im Wechsel*. Moreover, both Ranke and Hegel refer to the world of the sciences to underline that the effects of the development of a diversity of communities are not necessary mayhem and welter. Do they want to accentuate the scientific nature of their writings in this way?

To grasp the idea, and thus the embodied time, of a state, a people, a church and so on, it is necessary that these entities have accomplished their mission. Then the ideas of states, people, churches and so on have succeeded in becoming their historical form and thus becoming cognizance. Like Hegel's, Ranke's owl of Minerva also spreads its wings at dusk.[49] Moreover, the dusk of the idea is the dawn of its comprehension.[50] For Hegel as well as for Ranke, the state is the vehicle of the idea. Both are convinced that history has the function of bringing about the essence of the idea, so that people become aware of it.[51]

Hegel's as well as Ranke's "dawn of the state" takes place in the sixteenth century. Then the march of God in the world becomes "visible". For Hegel, it happens in the Reformation, in the Protestant state. For Ranke, it occurs in the early modern state. The apogee for Ranke as well as for Hegel is the incarnation of the idea in "the reality of their own time". What Hayden White asserts for Ranke is also true for Hegel; both make "the reality of their own time, the ideal for all time".[52] Hegel and Ranke focus on political history, because the state is the bearer of the developing idea. Hence, both are moderate conservative thinkers, seeking the middle road between a policy of abstract and general principles and a policy of only sticking to tradition.[53] The same is true for their historical and temporal views. Both reject an empty time, and both do not want a history of collecting facts. Both perceive the present as the result of the past and the future as the indefinite extension of the present. Thus past, present and future are embedded in one and the same movement, and as such time is homogeneous.[54]

Hegel and Ranke have teleological presuppositions in their thinking about time, but here Hegel and Ranke differ. Hegel discusses the ultimate end, considering it in the complete incarnation of Reason and Freedom in reality. He is convinced that in his system he can conceptualize the entire history and have knowledge of its general plan. Ranke is more sceptical and modest with regard to such a comprehensive teleology. He does not want to deal with end goals but with ideas that move as trends in continuing entities such as states, nations, religions and so on. They exist in reality but also emerge in the mind of the historian after contemplating a mass of historical facts. The entire world history is unreachable, and the purpose of studying history is "to have insight into existence itself".[55]

An undulating time

Notwithstanding his scientific approach to past reality, Ranke maintains to be part of the time regime of Romanticism. As such, he perceives continuing entities as participating in the undulating time of romanticist historicism. Ranke's definition in his *Die grossen Mächte* clarifies this:

> They [states and nations as continuing entities HJ] unfold, capture the world, appear in manifold expressions, dispute with, and check and overpower one another. In their intersection and succession, in their life, in their decline and rejuvenation, which then encompasses an ever greater fullness, higher importance, and wider extent, lies the secret of world history.[56]

Elsewhere Ranke gives an even stronger quote regarding an undulating time:

> What could be more pleasant and more welcome to human understanding than to . . . observe in one nation or another how men's enterprises begin, increase in power, rise and decline.[57]

Both quotes demonstrate not only an undulating pattern of time but also a linear temporality because past, present and future are not simultaneous. They pertain to an order in which the past is situated before the present and the latter before the future.

In a warning against philosophical idealism, Ranke demonstrates a romanticist undulating temporality:

> To be sure, historians are especially interested in certain times when "the hand of God" is particularly seen shaping the course of events in "rise" and "decline"; but this shaping of human affairs should not become the theme of history in a politically or speculatively tendentious way.[58]

There can be no other conclusion: Ranke must be perceived as a representative of a romanticist time regime. He explicitly speaks of a real, experienced, homogeneous, embodied and even burdensome temporality with a wavy pattern. Thus he comes close to the *Strandszene* by Caspar David Friedrich in Wiek, in which the painter is included as a young and old man in a world of arriving and departing ships.

The last part of Ranke's quote, however, refers to his scientific approach. Rise and fall may not be demonstrated as a shorthanded paradigm *a priori*. Ranke's *wie es eigentlich gewesen* seems to me a rejection of such an Enlightenment's approach to history. Hence it is difficult to find in Ranke's studies a text in which a wavy pattern too obviously is displayed.

Conclusion

In his *Sublime Historical Experience*, Ankersmit perceives romanticist historicism as the result of a trauma, originating in the awareness of being no longer part of a traditional world in which the subject is embedded in objectivity. Henceforth the subject has been loosened of the pre-revolutionary, pre-industrial and still predominantly religious life of the so-called naturalness. Although the past remains a part of his identity, the past also has become a "paradise lost".[59] As such, time has become burdensome, which points at an embodied time. The arduous experience of a lost paradise is one of dissociation, from which the necessity arises to apply the "art of association". Historical understanding, research and narrative can help to overcome the dissociation, of which the identity suffers. The roots of it can be found in romanticist historicism, fully represented by Hölderlin and Ranke and partly by Hegel.[60] Its association rests on an Augustinian temporality of a continuous, fleeting sequence of past, present and future, which results in an embodied, homogeneous and undulating time of history.

Because of the lost paradise, representatives of romanticist historicism are convinced of the impossibility of a return to the past. But by being included in institutions such as cities, states, estates and so on, they hope to preserve something from the past and to remain part of it in an indivisible way. As individuals, they are involved in higher individuals because these institutions are in turn also indivisible (Latin: *in dividuum*). Time is incarnated in those indivisible, coherent *Personae*.

In this temporal individualism, space only plays the role of the background of an ontological experience. Koselleck is right when he defines time's past as the space of experience. This gives context to an epoch and to the development of continuing entities. The epistemological element of this embodied time is the idea. As such, it transcends space, becoming time's dominating element in the end. As a result, time maintains the aspect that it is "the being that is, while it is not, and the not-being, while it is". This demonstrates a continuous, fleeting time, indivisible and homogeneous. In Germany time has become a moving force, not an accelerating one, as Koselleck assumes, but one changing from rise to fall or the inverse. This is because it is embodied.[61] Hegel and Ranke are the participants in the heavy, embodied, romanticist time of rise and decline. Yet other historical temporalities are possible, as we will see in the next chapters.

Notes

1 Friedrich Hölderlin, "Hyperion, or the Hermit in Greece", in: idem, *Hyperion and Selected Poems* (ed. Eric L. Santner; New York: Continuum, 1990), 37. "Half of Life" is from the same edition.
2 Blix, "Charting the Transitional Period", 62.
3 The flag makes sure that Friedrich painted himself on this *Strandszene in Wiek*. Although it is not very clear with regard to the picture above, Friedrich as a boy is keeping up a Swedish flag. Friedrich was born in Greifswald, a town that was Swedish on the day of his birth in 1774.

4 This is not completely true. In France the use of the term "esprit" indicates that historians there already use super-personal instances in history. Montesquieu wrote in his *L'esprit des lois*: "When I went back to antiquity, I tried to meet its spirit". In defence of historicism must be said that this is not a spirit filled with (organic) reality but only with a certain degree of rationality.
5 See also: Beiser, *The German Historicist Tradition*, 12.
6 See in the previous chapter what is said about Kant's organicism.
7 Does Ricoeur borrow his interpretation of Braudel's *The Mediterranean and the Mediterranean World in the Age of Philip II* from this study from Ranke?
8 "A society, I (Mandelbaum) shall hold, consists of individuals living in an organized community that controls a particular territory; the organization of such a community is provided by institutions that serve to define the status occupied by different individuals and ascribe to them the roles they are expected to play perpetuating the continuing entities of the community", Mandelbaum, *The Anatomy of Historical Knowledge*, 11.
9 Ricoeur, *Time and Narrative*, vol. I, 197–198.
10 Ibid., 198.
11 "It is ideas that appear throughout the centuries, which are accepted or fought. They appear . . . in the activity of states and churches, which apply them practically". Leopold von Ranke, *Aus Werk und Nachlass*, vol. IV (ed. W. P. Fuchs; München: Oldenburg, 1965; 4 Bände), 191, note q. English: Beiser, *The German Historicist Tradition*, 282.
12 The quote of note 11 is followed by: "The succession of those ideas and their tendencies form the great structure of universal history".
13 Ranke, *Aus Werk und Nachlass*, vol. I, 234. English from: Beiser, *The German Historicist Tradition*, 280.
14 Ranke, *Aus Werk und Nachlass*, vol. I, 235–236.
15 Beiser, *The German Historicist Tradition*, 281.
16 Hegel, *Philosophy of Right*, addition to § 279. See the previous chapter.
17 Beiser, *The German Historicist Tradition*, 281, note 94.
18 Qouted from: I. Berlin, *Vico and Herder*, 163.
19 Wilhelm von Humboldt, "On the Historian's Task", *History and Theory* 6 (1967), 57–71, esp. 60.
20 Ankersmit, *Meaning, Truth and Reference*, 11–14.
21 White, *Metahistory*, 180.
22 See also the end of the chapter about the Counter-Enlightenment. Therein the pragmatic, educational aspect of history is foregrounded.
23 Ranke, *Geschichten der romanischen und germanischen Völker von 1494 bis 1535*, v–vi. Transl.: Himmelfarb, *The New History and the Old: Critical Essays and Reappraisals*, 17.
24 Beiser, *The German Historicist Tradition*, 275.
25 Ranke: "I wanted, as it were, to extinguish myself, and to let the facts speak for themselves". Leopold von Ranke, "Englische Geschichte, vornehmlich im 16. Und 17. Jahrhundert", in: idem, *Sämtliche Werke*, vol. 15, 103. ("*Ich möchte mein Selbst gleichsam auslöschen und nur die Dinge reden, die mächtigen Kräfte erscheinen lassen*".)
26 Beiser, *The German Historicist Tradition*, 275–277, esp. 277. See for Ranke's criticism of pragmatic history also: Allen Megill, "Historical Representation, Identity, Allegiance", in: S. Berger, L. Riksonas and A. Mycock (eds.), *Narrating the Nation: Representations in History, the Media and the Arts* (New York: Berghahn Books, 2013), 19–34, esp. 21.
27 Beiser, *The German Historicist Tradition*, 282.
28 Leopold von Ranke, *Sämtliche Werke* (herausgeb. Alfred Dove; Leipzig: Duncker und Humblot, 1867–1890, 54 Bände), XLIX/L, 337. English from: Beiser, *The German Historicist Tradition*, 282.
29 Arthur Alfaix Assis, *What Is History For? Johann Gustav Droysen and the Functions of Historiography* (New York: Berghahn Books, 2016[2]), 41 and 98.
30 "*Was die Erfahrung aber und die Geschichte lehren, ist dieses, dass Völker und Regierungen niemals etwas aus der Geschichte gelernt und nach Lehren, die aus derselben zu ziehen gewesen wären, gehandelt haben*". Hegel, *Vorlesungen über die Philosophie der Geschichte*, 17.

31 *"Die Geschichte ist dann nichts mehr bloss Beispielsammlung, sondern der einzige Weg zur wahren Erkenntnis unseres Zustands"*. Friedrich Carl von Savigny, *Vermischte Schriften* 1 (Berlin: Veit, 1850), 109–111.
32 See: *"Demnach ist es der Aufgabe der Historie, das Wesen des Staates aus der Reihe der früheren Begebenheiten darzuthun und dasselbe zum Verständniss zu bringen, der Politik aber, nach erfolgtem Verständniss und gewonner Erkenntniss es weiter zu entwickeln und zu vollenden"*. See: Leopold von Ranke, "Über die Verwandschaft und den Unterscheid der Historie und der Politik", in: idem, *Sämtliche Werke*, Bd. 24, 288–289. My translation. See also: Koselleck, *Vergangene Zukunft*, 58–59.
33 The rest of the quote supports my assumption. This does not affect the possibility that both explanations can be true.
34 See also: Ankersmit, *Meaning, Truth and Reference*, 12.
35 Michael Bentley, *Modern Historiography: An Introduction* (London and New York: Routledge, 2004), 40.
36 Leopold von Ranke, *Die Grossen Mächte* (ed. Friedrich Meinecke; Leipzig: Insel-Verlag, 1916, Erst Ausgabe 1833), Kap. 7. Wiederherstellung. http://gutenberg.spiegel.de/buch/die-grossen-machte-3017/7. Schlußworte nach dem Texte der Historisch-politischen Zeitschrift 2. Band, 1833.
37 Ranke, *Samtliche Werke*, Bd. 14/15, IX.
38 Helmut Berding, "Leopold von Ranke", in: Peter Koslowski (ed.), *The Discovery of Historicity in German Idealism and Historism* (Berlin, Heidelberg and New York: Springer, 2005), chapter III, 41–58, esp. 43.
39 Berding, "Leopold von Ranke", 45.
40 Beiser, *The German Historicist Tradition*, 260.
41 Hegel, *Vorlesungen über die Philosophie der Geschichte*, 87. See also: Beiser, *The German Historicist Tradition*, 262.
42 Beiser, *The German Historicist Tradition*, 264. I don't completely agree with Beiser. Reading Ranke, you surely get the impression that he is piling up detail upon detail.
43 See Ranke, *Die Grossen Mächte*.
44 Beiser, *The German Historicist Tradition*, 248.
45 Hegel, *Vorlesungen über die Philosophie der Geschichte*, 96. "We have decisively to learn and acknowledge the Spirit of a people". My translation.
46 *"Wir gingen von den Behauptung aus, dass in der Weltgeschichte die Idee des Geistes in der Wirklichkeit als eine Reihe äusserlicher Gestalten erscheint, deren jede sich als wirklich existierendes Volk kundgibt"*. Hegel, *Vorlesungen über die Philosophie der Geschichte*, 105.
47 Hegel, *Vorlesungen über die Philosophie der Geschichte*, 87.
48 Ranke, *The Theory and Practice of History*, 74. See also: White, *Metahistory*, 168.
49 Beiser, *The German Historicist Tradition*, 283. Beiser about Ranke's *Ideenlehre*: "Since the idea is the whole structure and generating force behind a culture, it should be the result rather than [the] starting point of explanation. We only know the idea after examining and explaining its many parts".
50 *"Ferner ist zu bemerken, wie die Erkenntnis, die denkende Auffassung des Seins, die Quelle und Geburtsstätte einer neuen Gestalt ist, und zwar einer höheren Gestalt in einem teils erhaltenden, teils verklärende Prinzip"*. Hegel, *Vorlesungen über die Philosophie der Geschichte*, 103.
51 *"[Es ist] die Aufgabe der Historie das Wesen des Staates aus der Reihe der früheren Begebenheiten darzuthun un dasselbe zum Verständnis zu bringen"*. Leopold von Ranke, "Abhandlungen und Versuche", in: *Sämtliche Werke*, Bd. 24 (Leipzig, 1867–1890), 288–289. See for Hegel: Hegel, *Vorlesungen über die Philosophie der Geschichte*, 96, 105.
52 For Ranke see: White, *Metahistory*, 173; for Hegel see: *Philosophie der Geschichte*, 104.
53 See for Ranke: Beiser, *The German Historicist Tradition*, 278–279 and for Hegel: Beiser, *Hegel*, 220–221.
54 Although Hegel sometimes uses the term "phases" ("Stufen") to define the course of world history, time also for him moves in an organicist way, uninterruptedly and continuously.
55 Beiser, *The German Historicist Tradition*, 264–266, esp. 266.

56 "*Sie blühen auf, nehmen die Welt ein, treten heraus in dem mannigfaltigsten Ausdruck, bestreiten, beschränken, überwältigen einander; in ihrer Wechselwirkung und Aufeinanderfolge, in ihrem Leben, ihrem Vergehen oder ihrer Wiederbelebung, die dann immer größere Fülle, höhere Bedeutung, weiteren Umfang in sich schließt, liegt das Geheimnis der Weltgeschichte*". Ranke, *Die grossen Mächte*, Kap. 7. *Wiederherstellung*.
57 Ranke, *The Theory and Practice of History*, 78; see also: Smith, "Historical Meaningfulness in Shared Action", 2, note 2.
58 Quote from: Fritz Stern (ed.), *The Varieties of History: From Voltaire to the Present* (New York: Meridian Books, 1972), 54–62, esp. 60.
59 Ankersmit, *Sublime Historical Experience*, 333.
60 Ibid., 343–344.
61 Hartog, "The Modern Régime of Historicity in the Face of Two World Wars", 126.

PART 3
The ambiguous time of societies

6
TOCQUEVILLE'S TIME OF AN ARISTOCRATIC AND DEMOCRATIC SOCIETY

A time of transition in Germany and France

In Germany as well as in France the period between 1815 and 1850 is considered an age of transition. In France, François-René de Chateaubriand (1768–1848) experiences the French Revolution as a defeat. He feels "condemned to live amidst the ruins of what once had been a noble existence".[1] Literally, before the French Revolution, a ruin is comprehended as part of nature, after it is an unprecedented loss. This shows that natural time has become historical time and also how its burden is experienced.[2] So Chateaubriand knows what he is talking about. Although he is aware of living in historical times, he feels not at ease in this age of alteration. In his despair he states: "it is not clear whether one is present at the creation or at the end of the world".[3] Here we presumably have a first utterance of an experience of synchronicity of the non-synchronous.

Alfred de Musset (1810–1857) in his *La Confession d'un enfant de siècle* (1836) expresses something else: "everything that was, is no more; and everything that will be is not yet", assessing the time he lives in as transitional.[4] Musset's statement reminds of the definition of time in general (see Augustine), and he thus underlines its character of elusiveness. The perception of time in France could have taken the same route as in Germany, but it does not. De Musset formulates the intangibility of the period of his lifetime as an "ambiguous angel of twilight . . . half mummy, half fetus". He juxtaposes past and future and observes great uncertainties in the direction history moves. On the other side of the Rhine, there are similar moods. Schlegel wonders "whether the period really is an individual" (and as such being coherent) or that it might be only "the point of collision of other periods".[5] Thus, synchronicity of the non-synchronous is not only a French invention. Perhaps Hegel and Ranke's historical idealism, consisting of supra-personal individualism and constant volatility of time, is an attempt to combat the uncertainty of a collision of different periods.

German conceptions of time lead to feelings of romantic *Weltschmerz* and waiting, but not to complete political quietism. The organic perception of reality makes traditionalism reflective, put into words by Karl Mannheim as Romantic Conservatism. Because in Germany the French are defeated and no repetitive revolutions occur (in the nineteenth century), the passage of time gives a less bad feeling than in France. Although the German romantic conservatives think time to be burdensome, they want to deal with it. Their guideline becomes *ein sich mitbewegen mit der Wirklichkeit*. In Germany time is not understood as a foe but as a fellow traveller that you need to come along with.

Quietism in France

On both sides of the Rhine, the first half of the nineteenth century is experienced as a juxtaposition of loss and progress. But in France, the feeling of loss is stronger. It is deeply felt by people like Chateaubriand, De Maistre (1753–1821) and Bonald (1754–1840). Contrary to the German conservatives, who accept their lost world, the French conservatives are called reactionaries. Against all knowledge they maintain believing in the possibility of a return to the Ancient Regime. This results in a difference between the French and the Germans with regard to their perceptions of time.

In France the Revolution and the Restoration, with their turmoil and death, lead to quietism and powerlessness. As shown by the utterances from Chateaubriand and De Musset at the beginning of this chapter, the French conservatives become politically more passive and waiting than in Germany. It is caused by the fact that eighteenth-century France does not have the experience of a Counter-Enlightenment, which means that time maintains its empty nature and change is felt separately from time. This creates the illusion that time is not an obstacle to realize change. However, the French Revolution has taught them differently and thus also France learns that time is embodied. In post-revolutionary France, more than in the German Counter-Enlightenment, time is felt as a burden. It becomes an obstacle to change. The transition of time is apprehended as crossing a desert or an ocean.[6] Here lies the origin of the almost uncontrollability of an embodied time.

Opposite to the conservatives are the French progressives, who, in the footsteps of the great revolution, want to proceed in modernizing the world. The failure of the revolution is their experience of a burdensome time. They consider the reactionaries and conservatives as representatives of decadence, dragging on a useless, vanishing old world.[7] Nevertheless, even the former revolutionaries cannot break the spell of a rigid and surly temporality. Progress, even in the more neutral form of modernization, loses its real influence and does not encourage people to take action.

The Dane Göran Blix asserts that the Restoration of Louis XVIII in France means a disappointment for the revolutionaries as well as for the reactionaries. He observes that "depictions of *le mal du siècle* are a dime a dozen".[8] "Transition" in

France means discontinuity, which becomes manifest in metaphors like "death throes" or "birth pangs". The reactionaries opt for a complete withdrawal, because modernization should mean only distress and misery. The modernists, disappointed by the failure of the revolution, are still giving lip services to progress, albeit without any political action. One of them, Michelet, reformulates progress as "becoming" and as "civilization on the march".[9] He suggests that a better future is on its way and will come without doubt, but he still does not discover its path.

Writers like Musset, Chateaubriand, Michelet (1798–1874), Flaubert (1821–1880) and Renan (1823–1892) experience transition as a passage, as an interstitial state devoid of a proper identity, "as a passing evil to be *endured* [my italics] until a stable state is reestablished".[10] This results in quietism with reactionaries and modernists. The young nobleman Alexis de Tocqueville (1805–1859) moves to action. He takes the middle road between a reactionary and a modernist attitude and lectures both for their lethargy.

Tocqueville's perception of transition and his journey into the future

Tocqueville's middle road is, firstly, characterized by a certain perception of modernization; secondly, by a burdensome time, because of the lethargy of his countrymen, thirdly, by the dualistic and static analysis of society in an *état aristocratique* and an *état démocratique*; and fourthly, by a temporality of a synchronicity of the non-synchronous. In 1840 Tocqueville publishes the second volume of his great study *The Democracy in America*. In its last part (chapter VIII. "General Survey of the Subject") he makes clear that he wants to redeem his contemporaries of their slackness.

> I am aware that many of my contemporaries maintain that nations are never their own masters here below, and that they necessarily obey some insurmountable and unintelligent power, arising from anterior events, from their race, or from the soil and climate of their country. Such principles are false and cowardly; such principles can never produce aught but feeble men and pusillanimous nations.[11]

This sounds as a statement about a burdensome time, but opposite to what we have learned from Herder, Hegel and Ranke. Tocqueville opposes (German) conservatives as well as (French) reactionaries. This suggests that we are here on a different ground than in the foregoing chapters, which makes the search for a distinct temporality all the more interesting.

In 1831 Tocqueville makes a journey to America with his friend Gustave de Beaumont (1802–1866). This results in the first volume of his *Democracy in America*, published in 1835. In its Introduction Tocqueville explains what is going on in his life time: "It is evident to all alike that a great democratic revolution is going on amongst us".[12] In a letter to his friend Eugene Stoffels dated February 21, 1835, he states the same, accompanied by a clear warning for the idealist but lethargic progressives as well as for the timorous reactionaries.

> To those who have fancied an ideal democracy, a brilliant and easily realized dream, I endeavoured to show that they had clothed the picture in false colours; that the republican government which they extol, even though it may bestow substantial benefits on a people that can bear it, has none of the elevated features with which their imagination would endow it. . . . To those for whom the word democracy is synonymous with destruction, anarchy, spoliation, and murder, I have tried to show that under a democratic government the fortunes and the rights of society may be respected, liberty preserved, and religion honoured; . . . I attempted to prove to them that whatever their opinions might be, deliberation was no longer in their power; that society was tending every day more and more towards equality, and dragging them and every one else along with it.[13]

Although Tocqueville calls for equality and democracy, his reason is not their goodness but their inevitability. A democratic future surely will not be rosy, but fear for it is senseless, because equality is an irresistible movement.[14] Here we see how Tocqueville's philosophy of history is based on a temporal assumption that is characterized by a long-term trend of egalitarianism and democratization, developing between two opposite poles: "stubbornness" and "malleability".

The main reason for his journey across the ocean is not in the first place an interest in America or its democratic constitution, but an interest in a democratic society as such. So his curiosity is selective and specialized. He wants to experience America's problems personally, checking his idea that the French and English monarchies represent the past and the American democracy the future.[15] He distances himself from Guizot, who sees the monarchy as the best *political* solution for the future.[16] Tocqueville makes a distinction between a political and a societal system. He comprehends Restoration France in its social system as democratic and in its political system as aristocratic. In America he observes that all the systems are democratic, *"sans partage"*.[17]

That is the reason why Tocqueville's thinking can be called rather sociological than political.[18] Is he therefore a sociologist and not a historian? The Dutch sociologist Peter Buiks answers this question in the affirmative. He perceives Tocqueville as one of the founding fathers of sociology. The French historian Furet juxtaposes Guizot and Tocqueville, considering the first a historian and the latter a sociologist. Tocqueville is more often denied the title of historian. Hayden White ascribes this idea to the fact that Tocqueville "seemed more interested in structure and continuity than in process or diachronic variation".[19] Nevertheless this does not mean that Tocqueville cannot be both: a historian as well as a sociologist. White thinks a separation anachronistic, "since *in his own time* there is nothing inconsistent in a historian's attempt to rise above a mere interest in the past to a theoretical analysis of forces that makes of individual events elements of general processes".[20] I think Tocqueville is one of the most outstanding representatives of a form of history that wants to explore society. His historical assumptions are equipped with the ambiguous time of synchronicity of the non-synchronous. To show that is the main aim of this chapter.

Modernization

In the nineteenth century, modernism and historicism develop side by side. Tocqueville and Marx let them interfere without mixing them.[21] Tocqueville regards modernization as irresistible, irreversible and partly uncontrollable. He observes how about 700 years ago all of the French land is owned by a few families. Land is the sole source of power, and land and power are conveyed from generation to generation. This changes when the power of the clergy soars, because their ranks are in principle open to everyone, to the rich and the poor, to nobility as well as to "common people". Gradually feudalism is losing ground and society becomes more complicated. Social relationships and agreements have to be arranged by contract, improving the power of lawyers. With some venom, Tocqueville adds to this:

> Thence the want of civil laws was felt; and the order of legal functionaries soon rose from the obscurity of the tribunals and their dusty chambers, to appear at the court of the monarch in their ermine and their mail.[22]

It is not the sudden change of the French Revolution that causes the nobility and the aristocratic institutions to lose their power but an age-old gradual development that brings democracy and equality to the forefront of the social scene:

> In perusing the pages of our history, we shall scarcely meet with a single great event, in the lapse of seven hundred years, which has not turned to the advantage of equality. . . . If we examine what has happened in France at intervals of fifty years, beginning with the eleventh century, we shall invariably perceive that a twofold revolution has taken place in the state of society. The noble has gone down on the social ladder, and the roturier has gone up; the one descends as the other rises. Every half century brings them nearer to each other, and they will very shortly meet.[23]

Sure, there is some romanticist time of fall and rise in this passage, but also some linearity of the Enlightenment, especially with regard to growing equality and modernization. Yet, Tocqueville does not base his ideas on secularization as Comte does, who wants to replace theological or metaphysical postulations by social science. Tocqueville also stays away of a modernization founded on

Marxist economic development. His ideas are based on a change in the societal field of social events, institutions, religion and psychology.

> The gradual development of the equality of conditions is therefore a providential fact, and it possesses all the characteristics of a divine decree: it is universal, it is durable, it constantly eludes all human interference, and all events as well as all men contribute to its progress.[24]

Tocqueville paints this development as a waterflow from aristocracy into democracy. It is a "stream descending to us from afar, swollen and accompanied by flashes of lightning".[25] Does this come from the idea that God has created a desire for equality in the human soul? Remarkable in the quoted text are the expressions "providential" and "divine decree", because Tocqueville does not appear to be religious. Several explanations occur. Most likely is the idea that for Tocqueville religion belongs to human nature and can therefore help to keep democracy on the right track.[26] Maybe he thinks it a succinct way either, to convince his contemporaries of the need to abandon their impotence and to participate in the "democratic revolution". It also may be a manner to take the wind out of the sails of the ultra-conservatives, who consider each derivation of the old order as a violation of "the will of God". Tocqueville wants to walk in the shoes from the "*hommes de nos jours*", to convince all of them, progressives and conservatives, to cooperate in the process of democratization.[27] Again it is a sign how old and new, tradition and modernism are juxtaposed in Tocqueville's France.

Nonetheless modernization and egalitarianism are not tendencies he only applauds: "Is it credible that the democracy which has annihilated the feudal system and vanquished kings, will respect the citizen and the capitalist?"[28] Tocqueville is convinced it does not. We will see that for him one of the most fearful features of democracy is "the tyranny of the mob". His study is not only a clean analysis of his view on modernization, it also is a warning against the dreadful aspects of it. Tocqueville insists that there are great dangers in the process of equality, with anarchy on one side and servitude on the other. But man can overcome these: "I firmly believe that these dangers are the most formidable, as well as the least foreseen, of all those which futurity holds in store: but I do not think that they are insurmountable".[29] Although irresistible and irreversible, modernization does not mean that man has no chance whatsoever to influence the process.

Two models of society

In his study of modernization, Tocqueville uses two models of society: an aristocratic and a democratic one. These are not only political or constitutional orders but complete societal systems. Instead of aristocracy and democracy, he speaks about *un état sociale aristocratique* and *un état sociale démocratique*, where the aristocratic system represents the past and the democratic one the future. Thus, both systems have temporal connotations and can be compared with Tönnies's analysis of *Gemeinschaft* and

Gesellschaft. This underlines the socio-historical approach that Tocqueville practices in his studies. He confronts a model of society that will belong more and more to the past with a model that – in his view – surely will be real in the future. As an aristocrat, his love, but also his criticism, surely is on the side of the *état aristocratique*, but he tries to depict the *état démocratique* as objective as possible. He regards the democratic society of America as being Europe's future and thinks that the aristocratic society of the Ancient Régime belongs more and more to the European past, which will not return. Like Tönnies, he is less interested in the development from the aristocratic system into the democratic one. His description is synchronic, only analysing the coherence of each of the two systems.[30]

In a provisional version of his manuscript about *The Democracy in America*, Tocqueville conceives the aristocratic and democratic society as follows:

- In an aristocratic society there is a hierarchy of rather isolated social groups, whereof the status is determined by birth and almost unchangeable. Social relations are more or less particularistic, aimed at oblique advantages of the group, with an "ascription" of social roles. Thinking and acting are guided by the values and norms of the ruling classes. In politics the aristocratic society displays love for the monarch, dedication to authority and to virtues and obligations.
- In a democratic society there is more equality in material and cultural conditions, more social mobility, social relations are less particularistic and more universal, based on concrete social-economic aims, determined by individual interests. Social roles are more "acquired" and information and education are far more important in a democracy than in an aristocracy.[31]

Tocqueville wants to analyse two opposite *settings*. Buiks compares them with Weber's ideal types. However, Weber does not only want to analyse settings or models but also to comprehend patterns of actions.[32] Tocqueville does not aspire to observe patterns of actions but gives a concrete picture of both aristocratic and democratic *situations*.[33] He is convinced that America is the most egalitarian society of his time. The United States can realize that egalitarianism "in tranquil growth of society". Hence Tocqueville can perceive it as a laboratory for analysing Europe's future. "Providence has given us a torch which our forefathers did not possess, and has allowed us to discern fundamental causes in the history of the world which the obscurity of the past concealed from them".[34] Hayden White observes that for Tocqueville "America offers a kind of hothouse environment for the full development of a social system that was only beginning to take shape in . . . Europe".[35] By analysing American society, Tocqueville "embodies" Europe's future.

Tocqueville's analytical system

Tocqueville develops a more-or-less sociological apparatus to give structure to his analysis of past and future, albeit less explicit than in Marx's economic-based systems theory. Tocqueville's socio-historical device does not only illustrate his synchronic approach but also his assumptions about the almost uncontrollable, "ontological" modernization beneath it. He distinguishes four subsystems in both *états*: (1) a subsystem of material conditions, (2) a political, (3) a civil and (4) a religious and ethical subsystem. The (sub)system of the material *conditions* entails commerce and industry. The political system concerns on one side the relationships between the government and the citizens (*lois*) and on the other the interactions between the nation as a whole and the distinct parts of it. The civil system consists of the contacts between the citizens (*moeurs* and *opinions communes*). The religious and ethical system embraces the relations between the members of the different religious organizations and the bond between God and man (*opinions* and *croyances dogmatiques*).

On October 29, 1831, Tocqueville observes in the note "On the superiority of the *moeurs* above the laws" that "the laws cooperate with the *moeurs* to produce the character of a people".[36] He points towards the interaction between material conditions, habits, laws and common opinions to research the type of *état* of a people. The reverse is true for him either: "we need the knowledge of the whole system of a people to understand its *conditions*, *moeurs*, *lois* and *opinions*". Tocqueville sees a mutual determination of the whole and its parts.

Interdetermination of subsystems. The examples of America and 1848

Tocqueville's analysis of the beginnings of the *état démocratique* in America is an example of this interdetermination. It concerns the interacting of material conditions, *moeurs*, institutions and common opinions, playing an important role in every specific historical situation. Applied to the beginnings of American history, he sees that the country steeped in equality based solely on material conditions. It stems from the fact that America has never had feudal relationships.[37] It implies a weak coherence in the political (sub)system and hence also in society as a whole (*état*). Being an aristocrat, Tocqueville considers this regrettable, because feudal society once has shown how hierarchy strengthens political bonds.

However, American society creates an alternative for it in the Puritan religion. It is not without reason that the Dutch historian Jacques Presser calls this first period of American history "Americanaan", recalling that for the Puritans influenced by the Old Testament, America is the Promised Land. For Tocqueville, the Puritan churches form a substantial part of the American *croyance dogmatique* and the Protestant churches the core of its institutions. In want of political institutions, the American society in its early years is dominated by material conditions, puritan opinions and religious institutions. They determine American habits and its later constitution. Tocqueville does not perceive this interrelation merely as a fact but also as a must. In a letter to his friend Gustave Beaumont, he writes: "What a weakness is shown, when opinions and habits (*moeurs*) do not feed the institutions".[38] Nevertheless, the "must" of the interdetermination is not ethical but functional; it refers to the want to be successful. This becomes obvious when Tocqueville talks about France and its revolutions in the nineteenth century, which are ineffective because "with us [France] the democratic revolution is achieved in the material conditions of society, without change in the laws, the opinions, and the habits, which was needed to make the revolution effective".[39] Here we have synchronicity of the non-synchronous, because the material conditions already are in the future, whereas the laws, opinions and habits still remain in the past. This form of time here even has the function of explaining the poor results of the consecutive revolutions in France.

It is of special interest to see how Tocqueville's scheme of interdetermination works for the revolution of 1848. Hereafter, in the chapter about Marx, I will compare his insights with Marx's *Eighteenth Brumaire*, dealing with the same part of French history. In his *Souvenirs*, Tocqueville distinguishes general and secondary forces, causing in his view, the February-revolution in 1848. The general forces firstly must be sought for in the subsystems of the material conditions and in the system of politics. The initial causes of the revolution are formed by industrialization, with its changes in working conditions and the centralization of power in state and bureaucracy. Secondly, there are changes in the common opinion about the causes of social distress. According to this, the misery of the people no longer has its origin in a divine order, whether it is a personal Christian God or a Hegelian *Geist*. The causes must be found in economic and political factors, brought forward by economic and sociopolitical theories. Another aspect of the change in general opinion is, according to Tocqueville, the contempt of the people towards the ruling classes. Here the complexity of society confirms the idea how difficult it is to control an embodied time.

In addition to these general forces are accidental ones, such as the clumsy way the monarch comes to reforms in the administration and the excessive way he suppresses the people's revolt. Other accidental forces are the sudden retreat of several ministers and the incompetence of the military leaders, by which the stability of government is corroded.[40] Tocqueville is convinced that the accidental forces can do nothing without the preparations of previous facts of working conditions, the change in the nature of the institutions and the change of opinions and habits; these facts form the general forces which make the unexpected possible.[41]

> But I am firmly convinced that chance can do nothing unless the ground has been prepared in advance. Antecedent facts, the nature of institutions, turns of mind and the state of mores are the materials from which chance composes those unexpected events that surprise and terrify us.[42]

Long-term trends in material circumstances, institutions, habits and opinions are the more general and fundamental forces of the past, which make possible the accompanying chance events in the present and the future.

Tocqueville's static analysis of the two *états* and their meaning for temporality

The distinction between Tocqueville's general and accidental forces exhibits some similarity with Marx's distinction between basis and superstructure. As I will argue hereafter, they bring Tocqueville close to Marx, being his fellow-thinker in the synchronicity of the non-synchronous. As Marx's basis provides the dominant causes of changes in society, Tocqueville's general forces are featured by the same dominance. They create the trends into the future, which can be interrupted by accidental events.

Yet there are also big differences between Tocqueville and Marx. Marx's theory of modernization is mainly economic and dialectic, as we will perceive in the following, whereas that of Tocqueville is, besides socio-economic, mainly cultural and political in nature and more dualistic than dialectic.[43] Marx's view on history cannot be loosened of his dialectic development of production forces and production relations. Tocqueville's analysis cannot be qualified as a development of contradictory forces. He analyses the *état aristocratique* and the *état democratique* in a rather static way as respectively the past and possible future of Europe. Hayden White observes that for Tocqueville the central question in the history of Western civilization from the Middle Ages to his own time is: "What is the nature of the *process* [italics H.W.] within which *these two essentially changeless types* (the *état aristocratique* and *démocratique*) arise, interact, and conflict with each other?"[44] White's interpretation of Tocqueville's process of modernization purports the interaction of two static models of society by which the decline of the aristocratic model implies the rise of the democratic one. They are functionally related as in a closed system, "containing", as White claims, "a finite amount of energy, in which whatever is gained in any process of growth must be paid by some loss in another part of the system".[45] It reminds us to Gibbon's communicating vessels, showing how modernism has penetrated Tocqueville's historicism. Here the synchronicity of the non-synchronous comes into play.

The two systems and its parts are conceived in mechanical terms.[46] Tocqueville comprehends the present of his days not as a process from the aristocratic past into a democratic future, but as a mix of aristocratic and democratic forces, thus as a synchronicity of the non-synchronous. To put it in judoka terms: they keep each other "in a headlock". That is the reason why Hayden White does not want to speak of a dialectic process with Tocqueville, but only of dualistic systems.[47]

In the nineteenth century, politics and culture are viewed much more malleable than nature and economics. Hence Tocqueville can fiercely oppose deterministic theories which reduce the role of people in history into a "passive acceptance of the course of things":

> For my part, I hate all those absolute systems that make the events of history depend on great first causes linked together by the chain of fate and

thus succeed, so to speak, in banishing men from the history of the human race. Their boasted breath seems to me narrow, and their mathematical exactness false.[48]

Tocqueville's view on historiography

The distinction between the aristocratic and democratic system has consequences for Tocqueville's view on history. Historians who write in aristocratic ages "are wont to refer all occurrences to the particular will or temper of certain individuals", whereas in the democratic system, historians "assign great general causes to all petty incidents". In the aristocratic system the historian focuses on a small number of prominent actors. In the democratic system, in which "all the citizens are independent of one another, and each of them is individually weak", historians are "not only prone to assign a great cause to every incident, but they are also given to connect incidents together, so as to deduce a system from them".[49] Because in aristocratic ages the attention of historians is constantly drawn to individuals, "the connection of events escapes them; or rather, they do not believe in any such connection. To them the clew of history seems every instant crossed and broken by the step of man".[50] In democratic ages, on the contrary, the historian "may easily establish some kind of sequence and methodical order" amongst individuals and events.[51] The historian of an *état aristocratique* tries to teach that man must be master of himself to become master of his fate, whereas the "democratic" historian holds that "man is utterly powerless over himself and all around him".[52]

By analysing history from the dichotomy of an aristocratic and a democratic society, Tocqueville tries to come up with a new kind of historiography. In this way he makes a distinction between general, democratic forces and "aristocratic" more-or-less accidental problems in history. According to him the general forces are irresistible, but the accidental forces deliver the possibilities to steer them in the right direction. This would produce a history not "busied for tomorrow only, but for the whole future". It means that he does not only want to research the past but also the future. White even adds, that Tocqueville "attempted to treat the *future as history*" (italics H.W.).[53] The *future as history* means that not only the past and the present are embodied, as they are with Hegel and Ranke, but the future as well. This is the reason why he goes to America. According to Tocqueville, history has a forecasting function, a view he shares with Marx.

The ancient regime and the revolution in France

The forecasting function of history is also clear in a letter that Tocqueville writes to his friend Count Kergorlay on December 15, 1850. He wants to start a new book, but not in the form of an ordinary history. He identifies such a history with "historical curiosities that suffice idle and erudite societies". Although he sees difficulties, he still prefers to analyse the (then) present to find something about its probable future.[54] Although Hegel and Tocqueville both assume an embodied time, their temporalities differ. Hegel studies a political and institutional incarnated past, to comprehend which idea of freedom rules his own time and its future; Tocqueville explores a societal and institutional incarnated past (the Old Regime) and an incarnated future (the American Democracy) to analyse the divided structure of his own time. Although Tocqueville uses the metaphor of time as birth, development, decline and fall, a metaphor so popular with Hegel and Ranke, he does not refer to it as a drama but as a painting. The aforementioned events are not described one after another but juxtaposed in "painted" time-space before and after the French Revolution.

This becomes all the more obvious in a letter of a few weeks later on January the tenth of 1851 to De Beaumont, the friend with whom he has been making his great and fruitful journey into America.

> But now the subject has presented itself in a form which has seemed to me more approachable; I have been thinking that, instead of undertaking to write the history of the empire, I must try to exhibit and to explain the cause, the character, and the import of the great occurrences which form the chief links in the chain of events of that time; the facts to be no more than a sort of solid unbroken foundation . . . *not only concerning the empire, but on the period by which it was preceded and succeeded.*[55]

Here Tocqueville opts for a structural, not for a linear, approach. He intends to write a comparative study of the Old Regime before and the New Regime after the French Revolution.

Tocqueville tells these observations not chronologically but analytically. He does not want to write a historical narrative, but a so-called "philosophical history". Here we see the influence of Enlightenment in his work again. In the Introduction of the *Ancient Regime*, he proclaims that he desires "to make clear in what respects [the present social system] resembles and in what it differs from the social system that preceded it; and to determine what was lost and what was gained by that vast upheaval".[56] Here we clearly have the announcement of a comparative and thus a more-or-less sociological approach to the history of France. Although he sees continuity between the Old and the New Regime with regard to the centralization of power, Tocqueville still understands the French Revolution as "that vast upheaval" in the history of France. As Hayden White states: "Tocqueville sought to show how the transition from the old regime to the new had taken place, not dialectically, but rather cataclysmically, in a process by which human consciousness becomes reconciled with the conditions in its social existence".[57] The latter section of this sentence refers to the fact that the social conditions, the institutions and the *croyance dogmatique* have already been altered before the revolution (by the Enlightenment). According to Tocqueville during that revolution the names of the institutions and its conditions and moeurs also change, thus reconciling the economic and institutional foundations with the cultural upper structure.

Synchronicity of the non-synchronous in the aristocratic society before the French Revolution

Before the French Revolution, France can be called an aristocratic society. Yet there are trends into a new, more democratic one. In 1851 Tocqueville becomes aware that the striving for egalitarianism in France does not come from Napoleon (Consulate and Empire), however important the man may have been. It even does not stem from the French Revolution of 1789.[58] Egalitarianism is, according to Tocqueville, the result of a process of ages. It begins during the Ancient Regime with the gradual disappearing of the society of estates and the improving conditions of the common people.[59] Although the French Revolution creates a new type of society that is fundamentally different from the society of the Old Regime, the foundations of the latter regime disintegrate long before 1789. Before the French Revolution the habits and common opinions of the people already have been changing, the revolution needed only to overthrow the remnants of the feudal-aristocratic institutions.

Tocqueville first observes that during the Old Regime in the whole of Europe, it is common that the chief-landholders govern and administer the country, even in the tiniest affairs. Especially since the eighteenth century, this is no longer the case in France. There, the landowner – the *seignor*, as Tocqueville calls him – has lost the relationship with the national government. He does not "figure any longer as the king's deputy in the parish".[60] Officials of the state, such as the intendants, are appointed to govern the provinces, and in turn these intendants appoint local officials, who manage the parishes. The *seignor* is in fact no more than a simple individual. Equality has entrenched itself in a feudal society, because clergy and nobility no longer have any governmental power. More forward-looking democratic forms settle in the old aristocratic society. This synchronicity of the non-synchronous will repeat itself continuously. Even the old monarchy supports this process by making Versailles the centre of power, by creating new bureaucratic functions and selling them to non-noble people. The powers of the *noblesse d'épée* are weakening and those of the *noblesse the robe* become stronger. Local authorities see their powers flooding away to Paris and Versailles. Paris turns out to be France, as Tocqueville notes at the end of his book.[61] He concludes that long before the French Revolution, a "revolution in administration" has taken place, with features like rationalization and bureaucratization.

Moreover, centralization and bureaucratization undergo a process of self-sustaining growth, because the more functionaries, the more money is needed to pay them. The soaring wages create the necessity for more taxes, which raise the demand for more functionaries and so on. It surely is a modern process, in 1958 put into words by Parkinson, in the law with his name on it.[62] Although the old feudal society maintains, modern society irresistibly sneaks beneath it and undermines it. Not only the increase in power of the central government but also the subdivision of property among the peasantry is the reason for the decline of the feudal society. Both developments make the nobleman no more "than the first peasant in the parish".[63]

There is another ambiguity to be observed. Although the old feudal civil society has been undermined by the political system of the central government, the cultural system of *moeurs* and institutions of that society mainly remains (not completely as we will see). This means a discrepancy between the modern political subsystem and the more traditional social and religious subsystems.[64] Depriving members of the noble classes of their feudal powers and functions implies an atomization of the social structure. According to Tocqueville, this phenomenon fits in a democratic society. Hence, inside the aristocratic society with its *moeurs* and institutions of tradition, new egalitarian potentialities gain more and more actuality: synchronicity of the non-synchronous.

There is an exception with regard to the loss of power of the nobility: they still have a hand in the administration of justice. This gives them the opportunity to compensate their political losses by improving their financial situation.[65] Although the feudal ranking is undermined, a fierce social ranking maintains. This development is reinforced by the central government on one side, robbing provincial and local organs of their political power, whereas on the other side, the members of these organs are pacified by granting them financial privileges. This means a social ranking based on money, which also points towards modernity: synchronicity of the non-synchronous again.

According to Tocqueville, centralization is meant to be favourable for the aristocratic society, because it can realize a balance of power between outworn feudal institutions and a reinforced royal power. However, it has a levelling effect on the conditions of its existence, thus yet undermining the *état aristocratique*. As an unintended consequence of the measures of the central government, a social and cultural climate arises, in which the aristocracy becomes involved in ideas of independence, individuality, equality and human rights. These ideas strengthen the craving for a more egalitarian and democratic society. Thus the aristocratic society becomes the delver of its own grave.

Before the French Revolution, the society in France turns out to be a mix of old, aristocratic and new, democratic aspects. It is reinforced by the political philosophers of the eighteenth century. The essence of their message is "that it was necessary to substitute simple and elementary rules, based on reason and natural law, for the complicated and traditional customs which regulated society in their time".[66] They forecast a bright future which finds a willing ear amongst the masses![67] In former times the aristocracy is the leader of opinion, but it loses a big part of its social and cultural power and prestige to the eighteenth-century philosophers. Thinkers about the future are changing places with the powers of the past, albeit in a still existing aristocratic society.

There is an interesting picture of Dali showing exactly what Tocqueville apprehends by the synchronicity of the non-synchronous as it is reinforced by those philosophers.

Tocqueville's time 117

FIGURE 6.1 Salvador Dali, *Slave Market with the "Invisible" Bust of Voltaire* © Fundacion Gala – Salvador Dali, c/o Pictoright Amsterdam 2019

Dali's painting *Marché d'esclaves avec l'apparition du buste invisible de Voltaire* displays a landscape with women in eighteenth-century garb, seemingly merchant-women buying slaves at a slave market. Looking to these women according to Jastrow's rules of Gestalt-change, the head of Voltaire appears. The meaning of it is that Voltaire in his *Essais sur les Moeurs et l'Esprit des Nations*, especially in the section "Esclavage", advocates the abolition of slavery.[68] Thus Dali demonstrates synchronicity of the non-synchronous by painting a slave market that shows at the same time the head of the man who looks in a future without slavery.

A spatial form of the synchronicity of the non-synchronous

Tocqueville's analyses very clearly substantiate the synchronicity of the non-synchronous. There even are passages in which this temporality takes a spatial form. Around Paris he observes the most modern part of France. "The extant archives of the old district of Ile de France prove that the old regime was soonest and most thoroughly reformed in the neighborhood of Paris".[69] On the other side, the liberty and property of the peasant are nowhere more secure as around the Loire and in the Vendée. There the Old Regime most obviously persists. For Tocqueville:

> On the other hand, the old regime was nowhere in so high a state of preservation as on the borders of the Loire, especially near its mouth, in the swamps of Poitou and the moors of Brittany. That is the very place where

the civil war broke out, and the Revolution was resisted with most obstinacy and violence.[70]

Distributing past, present and future in space underlines the synchronicity of the non-synchronous. As we have seen with Hegel, time can only be defined as one after the other; thus, spatial synchronicity of past and future does not belong to Hegel's perceptions of time. Tocqueville's juxtaposing spatially past and future also makes the inverse true: the synchronicity of the non-synchronous underlines the connection between time and space. This is important for the history of former Western colonies. For a long time they are saddled with Western times and now have to look for their own time.[71]

Buiks also perceives differences between Tocqueville and Kant with regard to spatiality of time. With Kant, time and space are different forms of intuition. Tocqueville, as Buiks states, brings them together: "time and space . . . are empirical coordinates behind which a concrete historical period and a concrete societal type are hidden".[72] In my view precisely this is the case: time is embodied and can be partitioned in past, present and future and these three aspects can coexist in an ambiguous, society-exploring form of history writing.

Synchronicity of the non-synchronous in the democratic society after the French Revolution

In French society after the revolution, the *état démocratique* is becoming increasingly visible, especially with regard to the material and social circumstances of the civil subsystem. The associated institutions, laws, ideas and *moeurs* on the other hand lag behind. Here we see the reverse of aristocratic society before the French Revolution. Still, the synchronicity of the non-synchronous remains. In the society after the French Revolution, the monarchy and aristocracy continue to dominate the political subsystem through the Bourbon restoration. In contrast, the democratic society is increasing because the revolution has abolished many feudal rights that existed before the revolution.[73]

Maybe even more important is the rise of commercialization and industrialization in France. These make the country even more modern than what the French Revolution has done. As we have seen before, Tocqueville makes a distinction with regard to France between its political subsystem on one side and its material and civil subsystems on the other. Because of the latter, industry and most of all commerce still can develop, despite its aristocratic political subsystem from the past. As a result, French society after the revolution is split between a past- and a future-oriented subsystem.

In France the synchronicity of the non-synchronous is far more obvious than for instance in England. This seems rather odd, because in the eyes of Tocqueville, England is a more complete aristocratic society than France, whereas industry there has been further developed. In a footnote Tocqueville solves this problem. He points to the fact that the English aristocracy "hurry into trade and manufactures".[74]

In England the social and political system remains a unity because the aristocracy embraces industry and commerce.[75] Past, present and future maintain in the same flow without great discontinuities. In France the aristocratic society is preserved until the French Revolution, although modernity is obviously on its way. The revolution brings discontinuity in time perception, especially in the material and civil subsystems. In the political subsystem, Tocqueville underlines continuity, because of the Bourbon restoration, but most of all in the long-term trend of centralization and bureaucratization. Before the revolution, the administrative revolution is "a future-oriented past", but after the revolution, it is creating "a past-oriented future".

What does Tocqueville consider a "past-oriented future" and how does the political system support it? To understand the term "past-oriented future", we must bear in mind that Tocqueville's vision of modernization is founded on his belief that equality is the future. During the Old Regime the administrative revolution reinforces egalitarianism by setting aside all kinds of feudal rights. After the French Revolution industrialization seems – together with democracy – to reinforce equality. In America Tocqueville has perceived how much that democratic society is tuned on commerce and industry.[76] Thus he links an industrializing society with democracy and hence with equality. Nevertheless, his journeys into England and America show him otherwise, namely how industry creates new social inequality between rich capitalists and poor proletarians. Important in this trend is the way Tocqueville puts the new inequalities into words. He takes a term from the past to outline a modern future:

> Thus, in proportion as the mass of the nation turns to democracy, that particular class which is engaged in manufactures *becomes more aristocratic*. Men grow more alike in the one, more different in the other; and inequality increases in the less numerous class in the same ratio in which it decreases in the community. Hence it would appear, on searching to the bottom, that aristocracy should naturally spring out of the bosom of democracy. . . . The *small aristocratic societies* that are formed by some manufacturers in the midst of the immense democracy of our age contain, like *the great aristocratic societies of former ages*, some men who are very opulent and a multitude who are wretchedly poor.[77]

This new aristocracy is worse than the older one:

> The territorial aristocracy of former ages was either bound by law, or thought itself bound by usage, to come to the relief of its serving-men and to relieve their distress. But the manufacturing aristocracy of our age first impoverishes and debases the men who serve it and then abandons them to be supported by the charity of the public.[78]

Two things are important here. First, the observation of a growing disparity between the rich and the poor brings Tocqueville close to ideas of Karl Marx, ideas I will discuss in the next chapter. Second, in America the state is very supporting with regard to industry and its new aristocracy, but it does not relieve the misery of the impoverished proletarians:

> As a nation becomes more engaged in manufactures, the lack of roads, canals, harbors, and other works of a semi-public nature, which facilitate the acquisition of wealth, is more strongly felt; and as a nation becomes more democratic, private individuals are less able, and the state more able, to execute works of such magnitude.[79]

The latter two quotes display a mirrored view of society before and after the French Revolution. Before it, egalitarianism – with the help of the centralizing state – makes the aristocratic society fit for democracy. After it, industrialization creates in modern, more egalitarian and democratic societies, new "aristocratic" systems with the help of the same centralizing state. This does not only mean that Tocqueville's time can be considered a synchronicity of the non-synchronous but also as burdensome.

De Tocqueville and Hegel

There are some similarities between Tocqueville and Hegel. Both authors focus on political and cultural freedom, albeit that Hegel, unlike Tocqueville, does not accept democracy. Hegel thinks the constitutional monarchy of his time the safe haven for freedom, whereas Tocqueville accepts democracy as the only possible constitution that can be realized in the future. The reason for this difference is the distinction between their perceptions of equality. Hegel speaks of "equality" in legal and institutional terms, Tocqueville in societal terms. The latter wants *égalité des conditions* and detests the inequality he has seen in the United States. In America he "collected a hatred against all those, who, after more than thousand years of equality have introduced slavery in the world again".[80]

Because of the differences in perceptions of equality and especially because of Tocqueville's perception of time as a synchronicity of the non-synchronous, which differs fundamentally from Hegel's view on temporality, it is important to observe whether he has uttered himself about the German philosopher. On a journey in Germany in 1854, Tocqueville objects to Hegel. In a letter written that year, he argues that according to Hegel "all established facts ought to be submitted to as legitimate; and that the very circumstance of their existence was sufficient to make obedience to them a duty".[81]

Tocqueville has two reasons to oppose Hegel, which both are related to his perception of time. First, contrary to Hegel he encloses the future in his time perception. Hegel's embodied time perception ends in a fully incarnated present, because freedom, the great mover in his philosophy of history, is in principle realized in it. The future of freedom can be one of rise and fall, but in the end there will be a new rise, because Hegel considers freedom as developing in an ascending spiral. Despite that new rise, Hegel's future remains the same; the freedom in it differs in principle not from the freedom in his own present. It is not an empirical future but one based on a reflection of present and past. Tocqueville's view on the future is different. He investigates the American democracy because he thinks it to be the laboratory where he can perceive Europe's future. As we have seen, Hegel becomes more and more a conservative historian, and from the start, Tocqueville intends to be a forecasting one.[82] Hegel, though conservative, remains an optimist with regard to the future. Tocqueville, on the contrary, is not very pleased with what he perceives in America, and he hopes that Europe will realize democracy in a distinct way.

Tocqueville's second reason for rejecting Hegel is closely related to the first one. His research is based on his view on modernization, wherein the focus is on the drive to equality.[83] Egalitarianism is the assumed ontological stream beneath his time perception. As we will see, Marx and Nietzsche also believe in the existence of such an ontological stream. Hegel and Ranke do not believe in it. They look at historical reality from an idealistic point of view and identify history and politics. Hegel and Ranke's embodied pasts are political, constitutional and religious, and so are their presents. Their "body politic" forms their incarnated and thus substantial past and present; their futures form an extrapolation of it.

In contrast to Hegel and Ranke, Tocqueville and Marx embark on a societal approach to reality. Their temporality embodies the future, not only by extrapolation but also by some sort of empirical research. Tocqueville is doing it by investigating America, Marx by studying the laws of capitalism. With his study of the democracy in America, Tocqueville, more than Marx, has been giving Europe an incarnated future, with all the flaws that inhere egalitarianism and democracy.

A summary

Tocqueville gives a new face to the great historicist stream of becoming. This is a complete deviation of the perceptions of time during the Enlightenment and Romanticism in Germany. As we remember, Kant understands time as a form of intuition by which we take up impressions only "in so far as the mind distinguishes the time in the sequence of one impression upon another". The same is true for Hegel. He perceives past, present and future always as a "one after the other", a *nacheinander*, with the consequence that there can be no past, present and future at the same moment. Thus in Germany historical thinking is embedded in a homogeneous time regime, in which past, present and future are ontologically seen as a fleeting stream from past, into present and future. Epistemologically perceived, this means that in retrospection, the complete realization of the idea is projected in the future or in a mitigated form in the present. The past is considered as giving a development of the idea from almost non-existence into its full evolution.

Tocqueville's alignment of modernization and egalitarianism is embedded in a heterogeneous time regime in which past, present and future are juxtaposed. The pre-revolutionary past of Tocqueville has already elements of the present and the future in its craving for an egalitarian and a democratic society by the de-feudalization, bureaucratization and centralization of the aristocratic system. The post-revolutionary present with its continuing egalitarianism and democratization is still hooked to the past by its aristocratic political system and by the fact that industrialization creates a new "aristocracy". As a consequence, the "narrative" structures of Tocqueville's *The Democracy in America* and *The Old Regime and the Revolution in France* are dominated by a time construction of the synchronicity of the non-synchronous. Tocqueville does not seem to be very aware of the novelty of his temporality. Although it is very explicit in his text, he does not explicitly speak about it. He is the counterpart of Ranke, who is very conscious of his new temporality in relation to the one of the Enlightenment. His use of the new romanticist temporality in his texts, however, is hidden behind stories full of facts.

Next to Tocqueville, Karl Marx is an explorer of the synchronicity of the non-synchronous. He does not only transform Hegel's historical idealism into a historical materialism but also changes his homogeneous and continuous time in a heterogeneous and discontinuous one. More than Tocqueville, he is aware of what he is doing.

Notes

1 Fritzsche, "The Ruins of Modernity", 60. Also see: Hartog, *Regimes of Historicity*, 89–95, esp. 92.
2 Fritzsche, "The Ruins of Modernity", 60.
3 Both quotations come from Blix, "Charting 'the Transitional Period'", 63.
4 Ibid., 58–59.
5 Ibid., 62.
6 Ibid., 64.
7 Ibid., 54.
8 Ibid., 58.
9 Ibid., 67.
10 Ibid., 68–69.
11 Alexis de Tocqueville, *Democracy in America*, vol. II, Book Four, chapter VIII (transl. Henry Reeve; London, 1840). www.marxists.org/reference/archive/de-tocqueville/democracy-america/ch44.htm (written: 1840; Source: Project Gutenberg, www.gutenberg.org; E-text: by David Reed, haradda@aol.com, February 1997;HTML Mark-up: by Andy Blunden), fourth section.
12 Alexis de Tocqueville, *Democracy in America*, vol. I (transl. Henry Reeve; New York: Allard and Saunders, 1862), Introductory chapter, third section.
13 Letter to Eugène Stoffels, February 21, 1835, Paris, in: Alexis de Tocqueville, *Memoir, Letters and Remains of Alexis de Tocqueville*, transl. from the French by the translator of Napoleon's Correspondence with King Joseph. With large Additions. In Two Volumes (London: Macmillan, 1861), vol. 1. http://oll.libertyfund.org/titles/2435 (accessed

augustus 18, 2015), 397–398. See also: J. P. Mayer, *Alexis de Tocqueville, Analytiker des Massenzeitalters* (München: Beksche Verlagsbuchhandlung 19723), 36.
14 François Furet, "Naissance d'un paradigme: Tocqueville et le voyage en Amérique (1825–1831)" *Annales, Économie, Civilisations* 39, 2 (1984), 225–239, esp. 234.
15 Furet, "Naissance d'un paradigme", 228 and 236.
16 Guizot's remark strongly resembles Hegel's view on the constitutional monarchy.
17 Furet, "Naissance d'un paradigme", 234.
18 Ibid.
19 White, *Metahistory*, 226.
20 Ibid.
21 These moments of interference do not justify to identify modernism and historicism by hindsight. See Chapter 12.
22 Alexis de Tocqueville, *Democracy in America*, vol. I, Introductory chapter, 2. See also: idem, *La Démocratie en Amerique* (Paris: Institut Coppet, 2012), 13.
23 Tocqueville, *Democracy in America*, vol. I, section 8.
24 Ibid., section 10.
25 *Drafts*, Yale, CVb, paquet 13, 27.
26 Carson Holloway, "Tocqueville on Christianity and American Democracy", *The Heritage Foundation. Report the Constitution* (March 7, 2016). www.heritage.org/civil-society/report/tocqueville-christianity-and-american-democracy. Horst Mewes, "The Function of Religion in Tocqueville's Theory of Democracy". https://sites01.lsu.edu/faculty/voegelin/wp-content/uploads/sites/80/2015/09/Horst-Mewes1.pdf (both accessed December 2019).
27 Tocqueville, *La Démocratie en Amerique*, 5.
28 Alexis de Tocqueville, *Democracy in America*, vol. I, Introduction, 4.
29 Ibid., vol. I, Book IV, chapter VII, 329 and: White, *Metahistory*, 211.
30 This is not an ideal-typical approach, thus different from the one Max Weber has developed. The latter sees ideal types as being dynamic and diachronic. See note 32.
31 *Drafts*, Yale, CVh, paquet 3, cahier 3 (probably 1835), 110–111.
32 Peter Buiks, *Alexis de Tocqueville en de democratische revolutie* (Assen: Van Gorcum, 1979), 205. In my view settings or models have a function in observation, ideal types in comprehension. I elaborated on the differences between the two in my *The Construction of an Urban Past*, where they appear in the guise of closed and half-open systems. See with regard to the Weberian ideal types, pages 121–134 and with regard to models 203–213. See Harry Jansen, *The Construction of an Urban Past: Narrative and System in Urban History* (Oxford and New York: Berg Publishers, 2001).
33 Buiks, *Alexis de Tocqueville*, 147. In my view: Models create pictures; ideal types create stories most of the time.
34 See also: Tocqueville, *Democracy in America*, vol. I, chapter 2, Part I, no page indication.
35 White, *Metahistory*, 209.
36 Alexis de Tocqueville, *Mélanges, Fragments Historiques et Notes sur l'Ancien Régime, la Révolution et l'Empire, Voyages, Pensées Entièrements Inédits par Alexis de Tocqueville* (1865, 2010), 286–287.
37 Tocqueville, *La Démocratie en Amerique*, 13.
38 *Correspondance d'Alexis de Tocqueville et de Gustave Beaumont, texte établi, annoté et préfacé par André Jardin* (Paris: Gallimard, 1967), 543.
39 Tocqueville, *La Démocratie en Amerique*, 16.
40 Buiks, *Alexis de Tocqueville*, 80–81.
41 ". . . mais je crois fermement que le hasard n'y fait rien, qui ne soit préparé à l'avance. Les faits antérieurs, la nature des institutions, le tour des esprits, l'état des mœurs, sont les matériaux avec lesquels il compose ces impromptus qui nous étonnent et nous effraient". Alexis de Tocqueville, *Souvenirs* (ed. Calman Lévy; Ancien Maison Michel Lévy Frères, 1893), 89. See also: John Lukacs, *Alexis the Tocqueville: A Bibliographical Essay*. http://oll.libertyfund.org/pages/alexis-de-tocqueville-a-bibliographical-essay-by-john-lukacs#tocquevilleIIIv. Without reference to pages. See also: Buiks, *Alexis de Tocqueville*, 81.

42 Tocqueville, *Souvenirs*, 89.
43 Hayden White speaks of an antidialectic dualism in Tocqueville's thinking, which he ascribes to Tocqueville's conception of human nature. He refers to a letter of Tocqueville to a friend: "Whatever we do, we cannot prevent men from having a body and a soul . . . You know that the animal is not more subdued in me than in most people, [but] I adore the angel and would give anything to make it predominate". White, *Metahistory*, 197. The editor of Tocqueville's *Ouevres Complètes* (Paris: Gallimard, 1964), J. P. Mayer, perceives Tocqueville's view on history indeed as dialectic. The examples that Mayer gives are more accidental forms of dialectic reasoning than structural for whole Tocqueville's thinking. See: Mayer, *Alexis de Tocqueville*, 42–43. I prefer White's view.
44 White, *Metahistory*, 195. My italics.
45 Ibid.
46 Ibid.
47 Ibid., 206.
48 Lukacs, *Alexis the Tocqueville: A Bibliographical Essay*, III. Last section: Tocqueville's Historical Genius in the "Souvenirs". Without reference to pages. See also: Buiks, *Alexis de Tocqueville*, 86. In the last sentence of his *Democracy in America*, Tocqueville makes the same reproach to social determinism: "Providence has not created mankind entirely independent or entirely free. It is true that around every man a fatal circle is traced beyond which he cannot pass; but within the wide verge of that circle he is powerful and free; as it is with man, so with communities. The nations of our time cannot prevent the conditions of men from becoming equal, but it depends upon themselves whether the principle of equality is to lead them to servitude or freedom, to knowledge or barbarism, to prosperity or wretchedness". Alexis de Tocqueville, *Democracy in America*, vol. II. Fourth Book; chapter VII (transl. Henry Reeve; London: Saunders and Otley, 1840), 353.
49 Alexis de Tocqueville, *On Democracy, Revolution and Society: Selected Writings* (eds. J. Stone and St. Mennell; Chicago and London: Chicago University Press, 1980), 160.
50 Tocqueville, *Democracy in America*, vol. II. First Book; chapter XX, 92.
51 Tocqueville, *Democracy in America*, vol. II. Third Book; chapter II, 178. and White, *Metahistory*, 201.
52 White, *Metahistory*, 204. Compare this with Nietzsche's herd people and supermen.
53 Ibid., 205.
54 "But which contemporary subject to choose? One that would . . . be an ensemble of reflections and insights on *the current time*, a free judgement on *our modern societies* and *a forecast of their probable future*. . . . I see parts of such a work, I do not receive the whole; I have the threads well in hand, but lack the woof to make the cloth" (my italics). Alexis de Tocqueville, *Selected Letters on Politics and Society* (ed. Roger Boesche, transl. James Toupin and Roger Boesche; Berkeley, Los Angeles and London: University of California Press, 1985), 254–255. See also: https://books.google.nl/books?id=QNcUXU wtQeMC&pg=PA252&lpg=PA252&dq=Letter+from+De+Tocqueville+to+Kergorla y+15+December+1850&source=bl&ots=co89ks6aPv&sig=OGzFuF_22W1caNlaKPB 15xtqY4Y&hl=nl&sa=X&ved=0CCAQ6AEwBGoVChMIpNTfi-i5xwIVizkaCh0__ wPy#v=onepage&q=Letter%20from%20De%20Tocqueville%20to%20Kergorlay%20 15%20December%201850&f=false
55 Tocqueville, *Memoir, Letters and Remains of Alexis de Tocqueville*, 68–69. My italics.
56 White, *Metahistory*, 213.
57 Ibid.
58 The ideas about the new book he intended to write were not completely new. On instigation of John Stuart Mill, Tocqueville already in 1836 wrote an article in the *London and Westminster Review* about centralization in France.
59 Contrary to the ideas of his time, Tocqueville was convinced that not impoverishment but the increasing prosperity of the people was the main cause of the French Revolution.
60 "The execution of the laws, the assembling of the militia, the levying of the taxes, the promulgation of the king's commands, the distribution of his alms, were no longer intrusted to the seignior". Alexis de Tocqueville, *The Old Regime and the Revolution in*

France (transl. John Bonner; Online Library of Liberty), 43. See: http://oll.libertyfund.org/titles/2419.
61 Buiks, *Alexis de Tocqueville*, 48.
62 Parkinson's law can be conceived as "the self-satisfying uncontrolled growth of the bureaucratic apparatus in an organization". C. N. Parkinson, *Parkinson's Law: The Pursuit of Progress* (London: John Murray, 1958).
63 Tocqueville, *The Old Regime and the Revolution in France*, 44.
64 "In the old feudal times people looked upon the nobility as they now look on government: they bore its impositions for the sake of the protection it afforded. If the nobility possessed inconvenient privileges and exacted onerous duties, it secured public order, administered justice, executed the laws, succored the weak, managed public affairs. It was when it ceased to do these things that *the burden of its privileges began to be felt*, and its very existence became inexplicable". Tocqueville, *The Old Regime and the Revolution in France*, 47–48. My italics.
65 Ibid., 45.
66 Ibid., 171.
67 In the form of a rhetoric question Tocqueville wondered: "How did it happen that, instead of lying buried in the brain of philosophers, as it had done so often, it became so absorbing a passion among the masses, that idlers were daily heard discussing abstract theories on the nature of human society, and the imaginations of women and peasants were fired by notions of new systems?" Tocqueville, *The Old Regime and the Revolution in France*, 171.
68 F. M. Arouet, *Oeuvres complètes de Voltaire*, tome XXXI "Commentaire sur l'Esprit des Lois. Section Esclavage" (1756).
69 Tocqueville, *The Old Regime and the Revolution in France*, 213. See also: H. White, *Metahistory*, 217.
70 Tocqueville, *The Old Regime and the Revolution in France*, 214.
71 See Chakrabarty, *Provincializing Europe*. Charles Mayer has earmarked the concept of "Territorial Regimes" as a pendant to Hartogs, *Regimes of Historicity*. See: Charles S. Mayer, "Transformations of Territoriality 1600–2000", in: Gunilla Budde, Sebastian Conrad and Oliver Jansz (eds.), *Transnationale Geschichte. Themen, Tendenzen und Theorien* (Göttingen: Vandenhoeck & Ruprecht, 2006), 32–56, esp. 39. See also: Ogle, *The Global Transformation of Time*, 99–119.
72 Buiks, *Alexis de Tocqueville*, 159. My translation.
73 Tocqueville gives a long list of it. See: Tocqueville, *The Old Regime and the Revolution in France*, 335–340.
74 "Some aristocracies, however, have devoted themselves eagerly to commerce, and have cultivated manufactures with success. . . . This is the case in England, where men seek to get rich in order to arrive at distinction, and seek distinctions as a manifestation of their wealth". Tocqueville, *Democracy in America*, vol. II. 2; chapter XIX. Electronic edition deposited and marked up by *ASGRP*, the *American Studies Programs* at the University of Virginia, June 1, 1997. From the Henry Reeve Translation, revised and corrected, 1899, 399–400.
75 Is this the cause of the long tradition of the Whig-interpretation of history in Great-Britain? See Chapter 10.
76 Buiks, *Alexis de Tocqueville*, 102.
77 Tocqueville, *Democracy in America*, vol. II, Section 2, chapter XX. (From the Henry Reeve Translation, revised and corrected, 1899). 100. My italics.
78 Ibid.
79 Ibid., vol. II, Section 4, chapter V.
80 Buiks, *Alexis de Tocqueville*, 59.
81 A. de Tocqueville, *Memoir, Letters and Remains of Alexis de Tocqueville* II (1861), 270. See also White, *Metahistory*, 220.
82 Buiks, *Alexis de Tocqueville*, 121–122. Forecasting does not mean prediction by means of a law or prophesying by (religious) inspiration but looking to the future based on a thorough studying of the past and the present, taking contingency into account. (Like weather forecasting.)
83 I derive the concept of "modernization" from Buiks, *Alexis de Tocqueville*, 73.

7
MARX'S SYNCHRONICITY OF THE NON-SYNCHRONOUS

Time, space and the synchronicity of the non-synchronous

Lucian Hölscher understands the First World War as the great rupture between a linear and homogeneous perception of time and a more heterogeneous relationship of past, present and future. He argues:

> For most of us history no longer moves in a coherent way, as it did in the eighteenth and nineteenth centuries, from some very distant past to some remote future. . . . [W]e can no longer view history as unfolding in one coherent, evolutionary stream. . . . Historical times have multiplied, each establishing a present in a historical cosmos of its own.[1]

Stephen Kern, in his *The Culture of Time and Space*, sees the systematically questioning of a homogeneous time a bit earlier, namely in the late nineteenth century, but none perceives it already around the 1830s.[2] Nevertheless, that is the moment I think the first rupture between a homogeneous and a heterogeneous temporality must be situated. It is the thesis I have shown in the previous chapter about Tocqueville, and the one, I defend in this chapter about Karl Marx.

Let me start with some examples that are part of the time regime that surround both thinkers. They show how synchronicity of the non-synchronous becomes manifest since 1830.

In his *Introduction à l'histoire universelle* (1830), Jules Michelet (1798–1874) introduces a three-scaled theory of world history. The first and largest scale is the world, containing Europe as a smaller, but still comprehensive scale. Therein is situated the scale of France, with Paris at its centre. Going out from Paris, you walk through the three scales, and reaching the borders of the largest one, you come closer to the vicissitudes of nature. India, in the largest scale, is almost completely subjected to the environmental effects of climate and race. It is a place where time almost has come to a standstill, whereas Paris and France know the fast beat of modern society. In the middle of Michelet's multi-scale temporality, time goes faster and faster, in the periphery slower and slower. The English mathematician and philosopher Charles Babbage (1791–1871) attunes with Michelet's Europe-centred view on space and time by saying that "ten years in modern England is worth a thousand in Old Cathay".[3]

The two examples by Michelet and Babbage expose a remarkable compatibility with the world expositions that come into fashion after the London Crystal Palace Exhibition of 1851. Especially the one held in Paris in 1867 shows the same synchronicity of the non-synchronous as Michelet's three-scaled theory of world history, albeit in an inverse form. A bird's eye view can confirm this. The exhibition space consists of seven concentric oval galleries. The centre is occupied by exotic buildings, surrounded by a palm garden, thus representing the non-Western countries, completely fulfilling the requirements of Orientalism. Walking from the centre to the outside, you come closer to the industrialized countries, exhibiting steam looms, tractors, locomotives and setting machines. This temporality differs from the romanticist one by spatiality, and as a consequence, by heterogeneity. The present does not follow the past and is not followed by the future, but past and present are situated side by side in different spaces but in the same time. Even the future exists in the present, because the so-called "underdeveloped" countries can see "their" future in the galleries at the outside of the space of the exhibition.

These spatial forms of the juxtaposition of past, present and future still are compatible with the views on development in the eighteenth century. Countries outside Europe do not have a relationship with progress, except that they lag behind. As we have seen, Tocqueville is already creating a relationship between progress and backwardness, by distinguishing places and institutions in Europe,

FIGURE 7.1 Paris Universal Exposition, 1867

and in particular in France, that impede a more egalitarian society or even create new forms of inequality.

Marx goes still a step further. In his view, regions outside Europe have a relationship with more progressive countries, because first forms of globalization (colonialism) make them technically lagging behind and thus vulnerable. This becomes obvious when we, for instance, read his article in the *New York Tribune* of August 8, 1853, titled, "The future Results of British Rule in India".[4] The relationship between the Indian past and the British capitalist future has fatal consequences for the Indian society.[5] Here, progress destroys the past with its traditions. However, Marx often also analyses situations in which the past hinders progress. All in all, he creates a relationship between tradition and modernization, which points at an embodied time that differs fundamentally from the eighteenth-century empty time of progress.

The paradigmatic rupture brought about by Marx

To get a correct view on Marx's temporality, one needs to look at the following four elements. First, Marx begins by applying the antique theory of atomism to people and divides them into submissive, Democritian atoms and self-aware, Epicurean ones. Second, he says goodbye to an incarnated time, based on an organically and harmoniously conceived society, solving problems of integration (Hegel). Therefore, he creates an embodied temporality, consisting of a base and a superstructure, wherein the two sorts of atoms are working differently. In the base they are almost completely subjected to economic laws; in the superstructure they can choose between change and tradition. After all, in the present there are emancipatory, future-oriented atoms and non-emancipating (Democritian) particles that are stuck in the past. Third, it means the coexistence of present, past and future. Fourth, he explores as a result of this, a new onto-epistemological continent, in which the "collective singular" (Koselleck) consists of a phased economic "singular" with a dialectical development of established relations of production and innovative forces of production and a "collective" superstructure with very diverse actions to maintain the past or to anticipate the future (the so-called "practice").

Tocqueville realizes a fundamental break in the thinking about time by comprehending the past in the present and searching the reality of the future in the structural democratic aspects of French society and most of all in the United States of America. He does so in a rather practical way, by travelling and writing. Marx adds to this a theoretical rupture, searching for a new ontological foundation of society and a new onto-epistemological time. Instead of continuing entities like states, churches or other institutions, his objects of investigation are economically "determined" formations of society.[6] Although Marx perceives these formations developing in time, they are not characterized by a homogeneous temporality. From a spatial point of view, national borders disappear, internationalism comes into focus and ideas about identity become irrelevant.

Due to their lack of identity, the formations of Marx also lack homogeneity, and this also applies to the development over time. Just like Ranke, he wants a scientific approach to present and past, not in an idealistic way but in a structural way, whereby he removes his social formations from any teleology. This does not mean that teleology has completely disappeared from its approach. With Marx, we must distinguish between a philosophical and a structural perception of time. His philosophical perception has a *telos*, namely an egalitarian communist society; his structural approach is non-teleological. Both temporalities remain coexistent, framed in a socio-economic view on reality. It creates a tension between multiple temporalities and a progressive time of the modes of production.

Marx's views on a burdensome time and a socio-economic reality

In *The Eighteenth Brumaire*, Marx makes a remark by which he distances himself from the optimism of the thinkers of the Enlightenment and also of those of the Counter-Enlightenment as Vico and Hegel. They all are optimistic about the role of reason in the understanding of nature, man and history.[7] Even in the Counter-Enlightenment, people think that by knowing the past, man can design his own future. Here is the remark of Marx I would like to point to:

> Man makes his own history, but he does not make it out of whole cloth: he does not make it out of conditions chosen by himself, but out of such as he finds close at hand. The tradition of all past generations weighs like an alp upon the brain of the living.[8]

Especially the remark of a tradition weighing "like an alp upon the brain of the living" makes clear how much Marx stands in the tradition of a burdensome time.[9] Friedrich Engels, the lifelong friend of Marx, also considers him the discoverer of a new historicist continent, because not identities and actions with a purpose rule history, but irrational conditions and unforeseen consequences of actions:

> we have seen that the many individual wills active in history for the most part produce results quite other than those intended – often quite the opposite; that their motives therefore, in relation to the total result are likewise of only secondary importance. [Then] the further question arises: What driving forces in turn stand behind these motives.[10]

Marx and Hegel have a comparable start in philosophy. Like Hegel and the romantic conservatives, Marx also objects to the empty perception of society by the Enlightenment and hence of its time.[11] They all feel their own time (their present) as burdensome. However, in Hegel's idealism, the state is in the end the incarnation of reason and time is the process of the embodiment of reason in the state. It means that in the first half of the nineteenth century, the state is the solution of the temporal problems.[12]

Marx and Engels, on the contrary, perceive the state not as a solution but as part of the burden itself. The state is a problem because it originates in the past, that is in the feudal landed property, taken by force. Remnants of feudalism still exist in the new state of the first half of the nineteenth century, especially in Germany, in which the landowners are still in power. Thus feudalism and the belonging state continue to exist in an economically modernizing society. As a consequence, state and time are burdensome, because they are determined by powers and politics which have their bases in an outdated feudalistic form.

The West-European industrialization brings Marx and Engels to the insight that there are economic drives behind political motives. Their arguments are simple and fit with the society they are living in. They perceive two classes – bourgeoisie and proletariat – which *both* have no power whatsoever and yet they do emerge (next to the landed aristocracy). Hence Marx and Engels wonder how the bourgeoisie and the proletariat can come up without any power or political opportunities. Their answer is that the ascent of these new classes is the result of the transformation of economic conditions. The rise of a new mode of production, namely industrial capitalism, is the cause of a new societal phenomenon, the contradiction of two new classes: a class of entrepreneurs, the industrial capitalists; and a class of labourers, the industrial proletariat.[13] Not power and politics are the most important determining factors in society, but economics and material needs. Here the embodied time takes the form of a self-sustaining process, in which good and bad developments coexist.

This again confirms Engels's statement of the discovery of a new historicist continent. It differs in specific ways from the former, mainly politically predicated historical landscape of the Enlightenment, of Hegel and romantic conservatism. Historical materialism differs by its anti-political and societal foundations, although it shares with them a burdensome, incarnated time.

Atomism and the origins of a materialist synchronicity of the non-synchronous

In one aspect the young Marx and Hegel agree. They both want to get rid of the Platonic split in reality between a world of appearances and a real world of ideas. Hegel chooses for an Aristotelian solution to comprehend ideas embodied with reality; Marx wants to disclose a world in which matter provokes ideas. He inverses Hegel's idealism and enters the new continent of historical materialism.[14] It is founded on atomism, which, as we have discussed earlier, is fiercely rejected by Hegel (but also by Tocqueville). For Marx it is important, because it forms the base of his perception of time.

To get a clear view on Marx's atomism, we have to go back to November 1837. After studying Hegel, Marx starts his dissertation on the Greek philosophers Democritus and Epicurus.[15] Abandoning idealism, he wants to study realism *ab ovo* again. Atomism is therefore important because it is a farewell to an organic structure of reality. The differences between Democritus and Epicurus give Marx the possibility to create a materialism, split between a base and a superstructure. In Marx's view, Democritus reflects on human beings as atoms, completely subjected to nature and social conditions. Epicurus also perceives human beings as atoms, but they can evade their natural as well as their social conditions of oppression, associating themselves with networks of people with self-awareness. For Marx, such a network is the realization of the Free Spirit, having the possibility and energy to act.

> It is a psychological law that the self-liberated, theoretical spirit becomes practical energy and as *will*, stepping out from Amenthes' shadow-realm, opposes the secular reality.[16]

Here we spot Marx in between idealism and materialism. He presumes a spirit – an idea so to speak – that works against reality. He adds to it a positive attitude towards atomism. In the next chapter, we will see that there are similarities between Marx's views and Nietzsche's.

Atomism means that some people remain completely determined (Democritus) whereas others can free themselves of oppressive conditions (Epicurus). It implies that at least two societies coexist (remember Tocqueville): a traditional one with oppressed people and a more modern, utopian one with free, forward-looking persons. This double-sided society evolves into an embodied, but ambiguous perception of time: a society in which a modern part is juxtaposed to a traditional one. This is the atomistic foundation of a composite concept of time. Past, present and future are no longer perceived as a sequence in which the past is gone and the future is not yet there. Marx, together with Tocqueville, makes past, present and future coeval or synchronous. His perception of time has got several names: the synchronicity of the non-synchronous, the simultaneity of the non-simultaneous or the coevalness of the non-coeval.[17] I will use the first expression for Marx's new historicist temporality.

Essential sections, *coupes d'essence*

The French philosopher Louis Althusser supports Marx's idea of time as a synchronicity of the non-synchronous. He stipulates the distinction between Hegel and Marx as a difference between a homogeneous and a heterogeneous temporality. Althusser's first instrument to make this clear is his concept of "the homogeneous continuity of time" and its application on Hegel's diachronic perception of historical time. He asserts that Hegel refers to the development of history as a process, in which the idea remains the same over time.[18] In the dialectical process the idea arises as a phoenix out of its ashes of negation. Although for instance the form of freedom may differ in Hegel's distinct periods in history, because of its different ontological context, its *idea* remains the same. Marx's time is heterogeneous because of its ambiguous atomistic origins.

Althusser regards "simultaneity of time" another aspect of Hegel's homogeneous temporality. This becomes clear when we exert Althusser's second instrument, his so-called *coupe d'essence* on Hegel's philosophy. By cutting a section in the stream of history, we can observe a contemporaneity, of which we can investigate the relationship between the parts and the whole. Such an "essential section", applied on Hegel's "present", would show that his state, civil society and the associated consciousness are related to each other in a harmonious way. All parts and structures directly agree with the essence, the idea of freedom.[19] The civil society as built along the lines of estates and representative bodies is functional for the freedom of his constitutional monarchy. And the freedom of this monarchy is identical with the freedom Hegel advocates in his philosophy. Althusser argues further that if we should apply a *coupe d'essence* on Marx's philosophy of history, the result would be completely different. This becomes clear when we look at the scheme of Marx's perception of society.

Superstructures	1. Culture and Ideology (Philosophy, religion etc.) 2. The legal system 3. Political superstructures and the state	
Base or infrastructure	4. The economic, or Mode of production	Relations of production (classes) Forces of production (technology, ecology, population)[20]

About these four levels and practices Althusser writes:

> the relations between ideology and the other practices, between the different practices in general, between the elements in each practice, and between ideology and science, are, in principle, relations of *dislocations*, staggered with respect to one another: each has its own time and rhythm of development.[21]

This *coupe d'essence* cannot be a real "essential section" because it does not display an essence.[22] Every mode of production has its own time and its own history, moulded in a special way by the development of the forces of production. In the same way, the relations of production have their own time and history, and the same is true for the superstructural elements of politics, philosophy, art and science. Every part has its own rhythm of time and its own history.[23] The following passage makes clear that it is impossible for Marx to perceive in a process of development a continuous and homogenous time. Michael Gordy says it pithily:

> Abandon the possibility of an "essential section" and you abandon the homogeneity and continuity of historical time.[24]

Heterogeneity does not mean a complete independency of the parts; only a relative independency is at stake. There must be some coherence, although not visible at the surface of the phenomena. Therefore we have to uncover behind the superficial clock time or the time of life, the existence of invisible times and its rhythms and moulds.[25] This can only be done by conceptual *construction*. Such a construction leads to a perception of history, consisting of distinct times at different levels of society (modes of production, political practices and philosophical systems). It is an encounter of correspondence and non-correspondence, of relationship and separation, of hierarchization and levelling, all together functioning in the structure of a whole. It is not possible to speak of a history in general, but only of specific structures of historicity, founded in last instance on the specific structures of different modes of production.[26]

In Althusser's approach to Marx's worldview, historical materialism loses its teleological drive, because a mode of production has no purpose or *telos*. It is a condition for the different planes of society, not an aim, although there is a moving forward by the discovery of new forces and modes of production. Moreover, it is related to economics in which identities play a subordinated role and actions are far less important than in politics and culture. Still the thinking in terms of a totality remains. This raises the question of how the whole of Marx differs from the previous romantic-organic one, which also implies the question of how he sees the transition from one totality to another. These questions are hidden behind an Althusserian sentence like this: "The totality is the theory of their articulation together, so it cannot be discovered by making an 'essential section' through the current of historical movement at any time one (as with Hegel). This dislocation plays an important part in the theory of transition".[27]

Marx's temporality is incarnated in formations of society, which encompass regions with different rhythms and speeds of time. It shows how his temporal constructions come close to those of Michelet, Babbage, Tocqueville and the Paris's exposition of 1867. This implies concepts like "uneven development", "backwardness" and "residual elements". In Hegel's totality no aspect of society can "run ahead of its time". Marx's whole can only be approached by the concept of unevenness. It is the concept through which we can know the history of social formations, although we cannot take it as a characteristic of the historical process itself.[28] In the base as well as in the superstructure, we discover through the idea of unevenness various practices, each with its own history, tempo and rhythm.[29]

A plurality of times and histories?

Marx distinguishes several levels of society, maintaining their independent existences, with their own laws of development, resulting in a plurality of times. This might give the impression that Marx creates an ordinary form of pluralism.

Althusser strengthens this by considering each superstructural plane as relatively autonomous. The consequences for historical time are obvious. Althusser states:

> it is no longer possible to think the process of the development of the different "levels" of the whole in the same historical time. Each of these different "levels" does not have the same historical existence. On the contrary we have to assign to each level a peculiar time, relatively autonomous and hence relatively independent, even in its independence, of the times of other levels . . . for each mode of production there is a peculiar time and history . . . philosophy has its own time and history . . .; aesthetic productions have their own time and history . . .; scientific formations have their own time and history, etc.[30]

It is obvious that Althusser argues against a Hegelian conception of time, especially against its homogeneous character.[31]

Does Althusser's heterogeneous temporality rule out the possibility for Marx of a singular historical time? This question has triggered different approaches. Sean Homer concludes from Althusser's statement that there are not only "different temporalities, but also that there are different histories corresponding to the different levels of the social totality".[32] It appears to lead to an ordinary form of pluralism, with a multitude of time speeds and rhythms. It looks as if we thus regain a Herderian world with millions of temporalities. Or, to mention another possibility: history becomes a discipline of a multitude of specialized histories. This raises questions as: should not a relationship be maintained between superstructure and the economic base? And if so, how must that relation be perceived? Frederic Jameson, an American literary critic and Marxist political theorist, solves these problem as follows: in Marx's philosophy of history (as perceived by Althusser) exists an *experience of necessity* through which we "envisage" reality. It is not a single cause and not narrowly economic, specified in for instance the forces of production, but it is the whole base, consisting of different layers. It is the experience of "an absent, nonrepresentational cause".[33] From that point of departure, he rewrites Marx's original scheme of the relationship between basis and superstructure as follows:

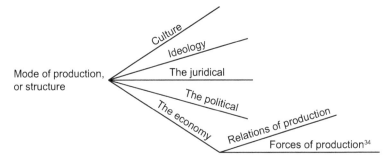

In this scheme the mode of production is an all-embracing system. Culture, ideology, the juridical, the political and the economic are all subsystems of it.

As a consequence, they are no longer independent of the mode of production. The relations of production and the forces of production are subsystems of the economic and sub-subsystems of the mode of production.[35] Subsystems and sub-subsystems have a certain autonomy with regard to each other, but they all are still dependent on the mode of production. In the transition from one mode of production to another, one singular history can be traced.

In Jameson's scheme it becomes quite clear that the relative autonomy of the subsystems "is based on a certain type of articulation in the whole, and therefore on a certain type of dependence with respect to the whole".[36] This has consequences for Jameson's view on temporality. He follows Etienne Balibar, who states that

> in the history of different social formations there is a multiplicity of "times," each contemporary with one another, some of which present themselves as a continuous progression, whereas others effect a "short circuit" between the most ancient and the most recent. This "overdetermination" . . . is the very form assumed by the singularity of history.[37]

"Overdetermination" is realized by Jameson's mode of production. It means an assignment to the base of a primordial temporality, distinguished and relatively independent from the temporalities in the subsystems.[38] In Jameson's view history seems to be a development of modes of production, in which the subsystems and sub-subsystems change with them. This development implies what Althusser calls the "hierarchization of effects" (*Hierarchie der Wirkung*).[39] He perceives a dominant structure of production powers, creating new modes of production, breaking up existing formations of society and creating new ones. This process makes history discontinuous. Althusser ascribes this dominant base to Marx himself, referring to his statement:

> In each formation of society there is a special production that dominates all others, whereof the [social] relations determine as a consequence the rank and order of all others.[40]

The modes of production, with all its belongings, have a dominant function. Each of them has its own time and its own history, which is embedded in the development of production forces.[41]

Summarizing, Althusser's followers sometimes ascribe to Marx a plurality of historical times in base and superstructure, without any hierarchization. Jason Read, like Sean Homer, attributes to Althusser the intention to get rid of any standard timeline whatsoever. Maybe he is right in refusing the possibility of a simple standard timeline. However, although Marx's historical materialism acknowledges no continuous and homogeneous time, it surely observes a certain sequence of society formations with the associated modes of production. This concerns a development from primeval communism, from ancient slave and feudal societies to modern capitalist societal formations. This is Marx's theory of modernization. After reading Jameson's explanation, Homer retraces his steps. He agrees that, despite different temporalities in different levels, there still remains one History with a capital *H*.[42]

Kant, social practice and determination in last instance

Jameson's reduction, bringing all subsystems and sub-subsystems under the umbrella of the modes of production, leaves unanswered how the system of the mode of production is dependent on its subsystems. There must be some mutual dependency; otherwise, we would return to a vulgar economist form of Marxism. Therein all that happens in the spheres of culture, ideology, politics and so on is dependent on the economic interpreted mode of production. Conversely, by disposing the mode of production of an economic interpretation, Hegelianism returns. If we strictly follow Jameson's theory, it could result in the idea that there is no separation of the knowledge of an object (belonging to the subsystem of culture) from the real object (belonging to the material world of economics), because all fits in the same mode of production, albeit within different subsystems. This would be a resurrection of Hegel's incarnated Reason in the guise of an all-embracing mode of production! That is why Althusser defends a totality, with subsystems that are *relatively* independent. Each has an existence ruled by laws, governing its own specific development.[43] To evade the idea that knowledge is only a reflection of a historically perceived mode of production, we must consider knowledge as a product of intellectual activity, situated elsewhere than in the Jameson's mode of production. Marx places it in the head:

> The concrete totality is a totality of thoughts, concrete in thought, in fact a product of thinking and comprehending, but not in any way a product of the concept which thinks and generates itself outside or above observation and conception; a product, rather, of the working-up of observation and perception into concepts . . .
>
> The totality as it appears in the head, as a totality of thoughts, is the product of a thinking head, which appropriates the world in the only way it can, a way different from the artistic, religious, practical and mental appropriation of this world. There the real subject (i.e., the real object) retains its autonomous existence outside the head.[44]

Marx makes here a certain return to Kant. The latter distinguishes between a phenomenal world and a *noumenal* world. Kant considers the *noumenal* world of the *Ding an sich* as unknowable. Marx's distinction between *practice* (practical and mental appropriation of the world) and theory comes close to Kant's distinction between respectively a *noumenal* and a phenomenal world. The return of Marx to Kant becomes corroborated by Jameson's experience of necessity as "an absent, nonrepresentational, cause" (see earlier discussion). Jameson points here to a *noumenal* world. However, by an epistemological move, he immediately elevates it into the phenomenal world of the all-embracing mode of production. Hence, he makes the Kantian split undone.

Marx (and after him Nietzsche, as we will see in the next chapter) retains the Kantian split, but with one enormous difference. Kant's *noumenal* world can, according to Nietzsche and Marx, be experienced and explored not on an epistemological plane, but on the level of the mode of production (as the absent, nonrepresentational, cause) *in relation to social practice*.[45] It means that Marx establishes a scientific discourse about the phenomenal world, through categories like base-superstructure, relations of production and modes of production. The *noumenal* world is approached causally and *practically*. This is the way philosophy and epistemology have arrived a new historicist continent. It is the way of "the science of history", which studies society in its transformation.[46] So Marx tries to comprehend society theoretically and practically.

Theoretical comprehension pertains to an understanding of every societal formation as in last instance dominated by an economically perceived mode of production. Changes in it come from the introduction of new production forces, that is, technological innovation. In terms of social practice, there is a tendency to support or reinforce the existing relations of production or to undermine or destroy them.[47] The practical handling of things contains the viewpoint that there is no such thing as class struggle in general, but as Gordy states:

> only various antagonistic engagements between the classes within the different practices that comprise a social formation. There are a variety of class struggles taking place simultaneously within a society, each with its own rhythm and tempo, its own specific set of contradictions, its own history. From this point of view, the various social practices can be regarded as sites of contention between antagonistic social classes. The class struggles conducted on these sites relate to one another according to their respective positions in a hierarchy of effectivity. As we have just seen, this hierarchy is formed into a whole, a social formation, through the determination in the last instance by the economy of that society.[48]

In his *Capital*, Marx calls this development the "*Entwicklung der Formen*".[49] This "development of forms" is constructed along the lines of a dominant basic time of economic development (of production forces, modes of production and production relations) interdetermined by the divergent times of the superstructure.[50] Thus there is a coexisting plurality of times with a "relative autonomy", but this coexistence is in "last instance" determined by the "level" of the economy.[51] In the first chapter of the first volume of *Capital*, Marx formulates these manifestations as follows:

> Bourgeois society is the most developed and the most complex historic organization of production. The categories which express its relations, the comprehension of its structure, thereby also allow insights into the

structure and the relations of production of all the vanished social formations out of whose ruins and elements it built itself up, whose partly still unconquered remnants are carried along with it, whose mere nuances have developed explicit significance within it. . . . The intimations of higher development among the subordinate animal species . . . can be understood only after the higher development already known. The bourgeois economy thus supplies the key to the ancient.[52]

Here we meet Marx's approach to modernization, which implies two issues. First, a synchronicity of the non-synchronous ("whose partly unconquered remnants are carried along with it"), which I will discuss in the next section. Second, a global, irreversible and real development of a phenomenally represented but noumenally experienced time. According to Althusser:

> This concept [the concept of historical time] can only be founded on the composite structure of the societal totality – a structure with a dominant and with differential levels – forming a formation of society assigned to a determined mode of production.[53]

Althusser here clearly refers to a composite society, which implies a hierarchized temporality, in which the base plays a dominant role. Nevertheless, it includes also the times of politics, law, religion, philosophy and so on. These superstructural times play their roles in the structuring of the composite temporality of the whole formation of society.

An example may illuminate this. C. R. Friedrichs, in his *Urban Society in an Age of War. Nördlingen 1580–1720* and in his article "Capitalism, Mobility and Class Formation in the Early Modern German City", shows how the development in the direction of early capitalism is retarded by Nördlingen's citizenry.[54] Early capitalism exists in the introduction of the putting-out-system (*Verlagssystem*) around Nördlingen and the selling of its products in the city itself. It leads to the rise of a non-artisan production, which forms a threat for the artisans inside Nördlingen in the first part of the seventeenth century. After all they are bound to various guild regulations, which the merchant-entrepreneurs easily can avoid.

The artisans, however, do not lose completely their economic position because the town council of Nördlingen in 1667 forbids its citizens to buy stuff outside the city. The argument given is that citizens

> should stand by one another through thick and thin and must partake of each other's joys and sorrows [and should not] cause any further diminution of each other's livelyhoods (sic), which are already far too difficult to obtain by granting a foreigner their money.[55]

This means that the citizens of Nördlingen are obliged to buy their products from artisans in the town itself. By this order of the town council, the system of the *bürgerliche Nahrung* is introduced in Nördlingen. As long as the *bürgerliche Nahrung* exists, the guilds and the artisans maintain their late-medieval mode of production. A class struggle in the field of politics therefore interferes in the development of capitalism. In the following we will see that this synchronicity of the non-synchronous can take on a completely different form in Chakrabarty's *Provincializing Europe*.

The synchronicity of the non-synchronous

Marx deletes a time of ascent and descent of his historical menu, (re)constructing it as the synchronicity of the non-synchronous. In contrast with Hegel's concept of social totality (a totality of interconnected rationalizing and therefore identical spheres), Marx's totality can be spatially expressed as a "'topography' of base and superstructure", which implies a synchronicity of the non-synchronous.[56] Already in his *Zur Kritik der Hegelschen Rechtsphilosophie*, we can find this synchronicity of the non-synchronous. He pinpoints there that the German situation of 1843 has reached merely the French situation of 1789.[57] In his *German Ideology*, Marx gives a still clearer statement:

> It goes further, but slowly: the different [losing] levels and interests are never completely overcome, they drag on continuously next to the winning ones, even for centuries.[58]

Marx's utterance can be considered an assertion about historical materialism, in which the development of the production forces is understood as the real force in history. New production forces create new modes of production. In Marx's perception, a specific sequence can be discovered in it, which affects the corresponding formations of society. But this does not mean that old and traditional modes of production immediately disappear when new ones arise. Marx's historical materialism is not only the reversal of Hegel's historical idealism; he (Marx) accentuates that past modes of production can remain in the present, whilst new production forces have already arisen, thus making past and present coeval.

This becomes still more clear since Ernst Bloch, in Marx's footsteps, in his *Philosophische Aufsätze zur objektiven Phantasie*, says about a heterogeneous concept of time:

> In a single sentence of Marx almost the entire theory of nonsynchronism is included: however, this sentence is far away from a unilinear succession (and nothing but succession) of an idealistic dialectic. In the Introduction to his "German Ideology" Marx noted the development of productive forces: "It goes further, but slowly: the different [losing] levels and interests are never completely overcome, they drag on continuously next to the winning ones, even for centuries".[59]

What does non-synchronism signify? It means synchronicity of the non-synchronous. According to Ernst Bloch, synchronicity means existing in the same present. Non-synchronicity is more difficult, because it appears to have an objective and a subjective side in Bloch's perception. Objective *Ungleichzeitigkeit* means that vestiges of the past remain to exist in the present. According to Bloch, subjective *Ungleichzeitigkeit* exists in a certain repugnance of the present, often turning into rage. Bloch's interpretation is supported by Frederic Jameson's observation that there never have existed pure modes of production with pure formations of society. Jameson argues that

> every concrete historical society or social moment is in fact a coexistence of a number of distinct modes of production, the dominant one, but also those which . . . conveniently [have been] termed "residual" and "emergent": the mode of production in the process of eclipse and dissolution, and that which is already in Utopian emergence within the interstices of the new dominant.[60]

This is, in my view, the synchronicity of the non-synchronous, as Marx wants to have it, consisting of an objective, but also of a subjective, experiential side.

A rhetoric synchronicity of the non-synchronous

The structural analysis of the synchronicity of the non-synchronous does not mean an obliteration of a perspective on the future. It also implies an experiential side. The perspective consists of the intentionality of proletarian actors – who give history a *telos* – and of the development of new production forces and new means of production. By this change the existing bourgeois society will be undermined.

Modern industry, therefore, cuts from under its feet the very foundation on which the bourgeoisie produces and appropriates products. What the bourgeoisie, therefore, produces above all is its own grave-diggers. Its fall and the victory of the proletariat are equally inevitable.[61]

Apart from his belief that economic forces will create a new society, Marx also wants to create a fear for the communist proletariat by exclaiming at the start of his Communist Manifesto:

> A spectre is haunting Europe – the spectre of communism. All the powers of old Europe have entered into a holy alliance to exorcise this spectre: Pope and Tsar, Metternich and Guizot, French Radicals and German police-spies.[62]

Marx's spectre is real in its future-directed belief that once there will be a communist society. In his perception utopia already has a certain ontic existence in the present by the economic movement of society. But this also is rhetoric, because Marx knows that the coming existence of a communist society only lives in the now as a fear of the bourgeois society for its enemies.

The experiential side results in a rhetoric, which implies also less optimistic spectres in Marx's thinking. They refer to a burdensome past, weighing "like an alp upon the brain of the living", where he continues:

> At the very time when men appear engaged in revolutionizing things and themselves, in bringing about what never was before, at such epochs of revolutionary crisis do they anxiously conjure up into their service the spirit of the past, assume their names, their battle cries, their costumes to enact a new historic scene in such time-honoured disguise and with such borrowed language.[63]

In the *Eighteenth Brumaire*, Marx corroborates this:

> A whole people, that imagines it has imparted to itself accelerated powers of motion through revolution, suddenly finds itself transferred back to a dead epoch, and, lest there be any mistake possible on his head, the old dates turn up again; the old calendars; the old names; the old edicts, which long since had sunk to the level of antiquarian's learning; even the old bailiffs, who had long seemed mouldering with decay.[64]

Here we have the disappointed rhetoric of an unsuccessful revolution, overstating the return of its ontic past in the present. Thus Marx's synchronicity of the non-synchronous also happens to be a combination of rhetoric and ontology, merging in the trope of the spectre. Here we have the spectral time Derrida talks about in his *Spectres of Marx*.[65]

Tocqueville and Marx

Tocqueville appears to be a fierce opponent of socialism, albeit of the utopian blend of Fourier and Louis Blanc. He reads their books after 1847. It is unknown whether he is familiar with the works of Marx at that moment, but I think he also would detest them. He condemns socialism because of its aiming at materialism and its attack on private property, which Tocqueville considers the foundation of man's independency from the state. Despite this all, Albert Salomon views Tocqueville as a "conservative Marxist".[66] Considering what is said above with regard to Tocqueville's "industrial aristocrats", I think Salomon's qualification is adequate. But there is more. In the second volume of his *Democracy in America*, Tocqueville perceives a development in social conditions to equality and a softening of *moeurs* (customs). For him the question arises: "Are these two things merely contemporaneous or does any secret link exist between them so that the one is unable to advance without the other?" He answers his own question:

> Several causes may concur to render the customs of a people less rude but of all these causes the most powerful appears to me to be the equality of

> conditions. Equality of conditions and greater mildness in customs are, then, in my eyes, not only contemporaneous occurrences, but correlative facts.[67]

In my view this may not be a Marxist, but surely a "Marxian" perception of the relationship between basis and superstructure. It also means a synchronicity of the non-synchronous because the mildness of the customs can accelerate the realization of equality of conditions. It thus brings the future in the present. In the field of politics and society, for instance, mildness can break down hierarchical dividing lines. In chapter XIV of the same volume he gives an example of this relationship:

> Among aristocratic nations, all who live within reach of the first class in society commonly strain to be like it, which gives rise to ridiculous and insipid imitations. . . . In democracies manners are never so refined as among aristocratic nations, but on the other hand they are never so coarse. Neither the coarse oaths of the populace nor the elegant and choice expressions of the nobility are to be heard there; the manners of such a people are often vulgar, but they are neither brutal nor mean.[68]

Yet we must keep in mind that Tocqueville and Marx differ greatly. For Marx basis and superstructure are separated, often displaying distinct times, albeit still connected. Moreover, the economic base remains dominating. Tocqueville does not make such a sharp distinction. Material conditions correlate with ideological phenomena, and sometimes he considers institutions or *moeurs* as determining factors. Buiks states: Tocqueville "tried to withstand the 'seductions' of materialism as well as those of spiritualism".[69]

Notwithstanding that Marx and Tocqueville reason from different ontologies (respectively materialist and "institutionalist"), they have corresponding epistemologies. Marx practices a split in base and superstructure, and Tocqueville in general and accidental forces. This comparable split leads to agreements with regard to temporality. Synchronicity of the non-synchronous is constituted by Marx in a chronological sequence of modes of production and by Tocqueville in the succession of *états* before and after the French Revolution. Marx's non-synchronicity exists in the lagging behind of old modes of production, whereas a new mode already has become dominant. Tocqueville discovers non-synchronicity before the French Revolution in the modernizing government, whereas the classes are still semi-feudal. After the revolution the inverse is the case: the aristocratic-monarchical government lags behind a modernizing society.

Nevertheless, there are differences in the explicitation and implicitation of it. We discern that Tocqueville's synchronicity of the non-synchronous remains hidden in his historical texts. He does not make a theory out of it. Marx does the opposite. His synchronicity of the non-synchronous is a consequence of his new epistemology. In several quotes he demonstrates that he is fully aware of the temporal consequences of his new historicism. His *Eighteenth Brumaire* makes explicit use of it.

Ambiguous and romanticist time. A conclusion

This part of the book ends with the similarities and differences between Tocqueville and Marx. Both authors agree with their predecessors Hegel and Ranke that time is embodied and burdensome and that there is some teleology in history. Hegel perceives it in a dialectical growing of rationality and freedom, realized in and by the state, Ranke in the development of states with an uncertain future, but always guided by divine providence. Tocqueville's idea of the future contains the idea that social equality will grow, whether for better or for worse, while Marx projects the future in a communist society.

However, important differences occur. Hegel and Ranke perceive time as continuous and homogeneous, founded as it is on an organicist, holistic, political and institutional view of past, present and future. They consider the organic state as a solution for a disintegrating society. Tocqueville and Marx do not focus on disintegration, but on social revolutions and industrialization. Both analyse neither states nor institutions, but *états* or formations of society, perceiving them as intermittent and abrupt changing. In the sequence of society formations, each of them differs fundamentally from its predecessor. Their view on society can be called discontinuous, structural and analytical. Hegel and the romantic conservatives have an assumption of time as a continuous flux; Marx's and Tocqueville's historical temporality focuses on its synchronicity. They believe that past, present and future can coexist, although in different spaces, layers of society or institutions.

Hegel and Marx differ on specific points. Hegel's historical philosophy remains purely reflective, Marx wants to make his historical philosophy practical in a way, whereof Hayden White states "that men should not [only] try to understand the world, but that the sole test of their understanding of it was their capacity to change it".[70] Hegel's time, incarnated in political and cultural entities, constituting organic wholes, becomes visible when we make an "essential section". A similar *coupe d'essence* in Marx's embodied time is impossible. Base and superstructure exhibit different layers with different temporalities. Marx seems to return to Kant with a superstructure of phenomena and a *noumenal* base. The basis of Marx only differs from Kant's *Ding an sich*, by being able to be experienced, to be explored in concepts and to be transformed by collective action of the proletariat. Friedrich Nietzsche makes a similar movement into Kant's direction, seeing his *noumenal* world as one of wills and drives. He propagates a heterogeneous temporality as well, although its features differ fundamentally from those of Marx's and Tocqueville's synchronicity of the non-synchronous.

Notes

1 Hölscher, "Mysteries of Historical Order", 134.
2 Kern, *The Culture of Time and Space 1880–1918*, 60–108, esp. 61–64.
3 I derive this quote and incidentally this whole passage from: G. C. Bowker, "Altogether Now: Synchronization, Speed and the Failure of Narrativity", *History and Theory* 53, 4 (December 2014), 563–576, esp. 573.

4. Karl Marx, "The Future Results of the British Rule in India", *The New-York Daily Tribune* (August 8, 1853). Quoted from: Karl Marx and Friedrich Engels, *On Colonialism* (Moscow: Foreign Languages Publishing House, without year), 83–90.
5. In Chapter 10, we will see how Dipesh Chakrabarty thinks to solve the problems of this synchronicity of the non-synchronous, which lasts until the twenty-first century.
6. "Determined" and "determines" are between quotation marks because to determine is a discussed issue in the Marxist debate. I will return to this in the following.
7. J. Balmuth, "Marx and the Philosophers", in: R. Freedman (ed.), *Marxist Social Thought* (New York: Harcourt, Brace & World Inc., 1967), xxv–xxxiv, esp. xxviii.
8. Karl Marx, "The Eighteenth Brumaire of Louis Bonaparte", in: Freedman, *Marxist Social Thought*, 188–211, esp. 188.
9. Marx begins here with an idea that twentieth-century philosophers as Hermann Lübbe and Aleida Assmann have referred to as "Kompensationstheorie" (compensation theory). That theory is characterized by the idea that time is no longer considered linear as an arrow, but in the form of contradictions, in which the disadvantages of progress must be compensated by human measures. See: Assmann, *Ist die Zeit aus den Fugen?*, 209–228, esp. 226–227.
10. Friedrich Engels, "Ludwig Feuerbach and the End of Classical German Philosophy", in: Freedman, *Marxist Social Thought*, 110–114, esp. 110. See also: idem, "Engels to J. Bloch" (September 21–22, 1890), in: Freedman, *Marxist Social Thought*, 130; and idem, "Engels to H. Starkenburg" (January 25, 1894), in: Freedman, *Marxist Social Thought*, 133.
11. "In this society of free competition, the individual appears detached from his natural bonds etc., which in earlier historical periods make him the accessory of a definite and limited human conglomerate. Smith and Ricardo still stand with both feet on the shoulders of the eighteenth-century prophets, in whose imaginations this eighteenth-century individual – the product on one side of the dissolution of the feudal forms of society, on the other side of the new forces of production developed since the sixteenth century – appears as an ideal, whose existence they project into the past. Not as a historic result but as history's point of departure. As the Natural Individual appropriate to their notion of human nature, not arising historically, but posited by nature. This illusion has been common to each new epoch to this day". Karl Marx, *Grundrisse, Foundations of the Political Economy* (1857–1861; transl. Martin Nicolaus; London: Penguin Books and New Left Review, 1973) https://www.marxists.org/archive/marx/works/1857/grundrisse/
12. See Chapter 4.
13. Freedman, *Marxist Social Thought*, 111–112.
14. The term "historical materialism" is under discussion. See: Allan Megill and Jaeyoon Park, "Misrepresenting Marx: A Lesson in Historical Method", *History and Theory* 56, 2 (June 2017), 288–306. According to the authors Marx was not a materialist. I think Marx can be considered a materialist in respect to his atomism. Moreover, historical materialism is used here as opposite to Hegel's historical idealism. It refers to the economic base of Marx's philosophy. I maintain the term because it is commonly used and my book is about time, not about materialism.
15. Karl Marx, "Doktorsdissertation: Differenz der demokritischen und epikurischen Naturphilosphie nebst einem Anhänge", in: *Marx, Engels, Werke. Ergänzungsband I* (Berlin: Dietz Verlag, 1968), 257–373.
16. Ibid., 327. Italics from Marx. Amenthes's shadow-realm stands for the Egyptian realm of the dead. See for the "spirit of the will" the next chapter about Nietzsche.
17. In English there are several translations of the German "Ungleichzeitigkeit". See Ernst Bloch, "Nonsynchronism and the Obligation to Its Dialectics", *New German Critique* 11 (Spring 1977), 22–38; and idem, "Non-contemporaneity and Obligation to Its Dialectic", in: idem, *Heritage of Our Times* (Cambridge: Polity Press, 1991), 97–148.
18. Louis Althusser and Etienne Balibar, *Das Kapital lesen* I (Reinbeck bei Hamburg: Rowohlt, 1972), 122–124.

19 Ibid., 123.
20 See also: Frederick Jameson, *The Political Unconsciousness: Narrative as a Socially Symbolic Act* (Ithaca, NY: Cornell University Press, 20023), 32.
21 Althusser, *Glossary*, "Dislocation" (transl. Ben Brewster, 1969). www.marxists.org/reference/archive/althusser/glossary.htm (accessed September 2017).
22 Gordy, "Reading Althusser: Time and the Social Whole", 7.
23 Althusser and Balibar, *Das Kapital lesen* I, 130–131.
24 Michael Gordy, "Reading Althusser: Time and the Social Whole", 7.
25 Althusser and Balibar, *Das Kapital lesen* I, 132.
26 Ibid., 143.
27 Althusser, *Glossary*, "Dislocation".
28 Gordy, "Reading Althusser: Time and the Social Whole", 13.
29 Ibid.
30 Louis Althusser and Etienne Balibar, *Reading Capital* (London: Verso, 1979), 99–101, esp. 101. See also: Althusser and Balibar, *Das Kapital lesen* I, 143.
31 Althusser and Balibar, *Das Kapital lesen* I, 138 and 162. See also: Jameson, *The Political Unconsciousness*, 17, where Jameson writes "that the so-called Hegelian idealism . . . emerge[s] from interpretations that assimilate levels to one another and affirm their ultimate identity".
32 Sean Homer, "Narratives of History, Narratives of Time", in: Caren Irr and Ian Buchanan (eds.), *On Jameson: From Postmodernism to Globalization* (New York: State University New York, 2006), 71–94, esp. 85.
33 Jameson, *The Political Unconsciousness: Narrative as a Socially Symbolic Act* (Ithaca, NY: Cornell University Press, 2002³), 20. Jameson formulates it as: "history is not a text, not a narrative, master or otherwise, but that, as an absent cause, it is inaccessible to us except in textual form, and that our approach to it and to the Real itself necessarily passes through its prior textualization, its narrativation in the political unconscious."
34 Jameson, *The Political Unconsciousness*, 21.
35 Jameson, *The Political Unconsciousness*, 36.
36 Homer, "Narratives of History, Narratives of Time", 86.
37 Etienne Balibar, *The Philosophy of Marx* (London: Verso, 1995), 108. See also: Homer, "Narratives of History, Narratives of Time", 86.
38 The traditional list can be rapidly enumerated: first, primitive communism, or tribal society, generally subdivided into the two distinct moments of the paleolithic *horde* of nomadic hunters and gatherers and the neolithic *gens* of an already more hierarchical and sedentary village society; second (but the order is not a chronological one), the asiatic mode of production or the so-called oriental despotism, the great hydraulic empires of the Near and Far East and of pre-Columbian Mexico and Peru, tributary societies that organize a network of villages around the centred power of the sacred god-king with his clerical bureaucracy; third, the ancient mode of production, or the slave-holding oligarchic republic or polis or city-state; fourth, feudalism; fifth, capitalism; and sixth, socialism or communism. Even on the traditional conception, these various modes of production are all conceived as each having a cultural dominant specific to it: myth and the ideology of kinship for primitive communism, the sacred for the asiatic mode, "politics" in the classical sense for the ancient polis, relations of personal domination for feudalism, commodity fetishism for capital itself and community and self-management for communism. Frederic Jameson, "The Ideological Analysis of Space", *Critical Exchange* 14 (Fall 1983), 1–15, esp. 3. See also: Ira Chernus, "Frederic Jameson's Interpretation of Postmodernism" (without page reference). http://spot.colorado.edu/~chernus/NewspaperColumns/LongerEssays/JamesonPostmodernism.htm, where she states: "A Marxist analysis (in a sentence before this quote, Chernus observes that Jameson is a Marxist) of the totality of our world starts with a basic premise: our lives are shaped, above all, by the mode of production that exists in our society. The mode of production means the various tools available to produce goods and services (human labor, natural resources, technologies, investment capital, etc.) and the way we organize those tools.

This includes the way we organize ourselves when we use the tools; i.e., the way we relate to each other as producers and consumers of goods and services. We only have real power when we can control our own mode of production. We must be able to produce things we really want in the ways we really want. Therefore, we must study various modes of production, freely decide which one we want, and be able to implement our decision. 'We' here means all the people of the society, working together. The only way to really improve the world is to give everyone a share of real power. Otherwise inequality, injustice, and oppression are bound to continue".

39 Althusser and Balibar, *Das Kapital lesen* I, 129–130.
40 Ibid., 129. See also: Althusser, "Schets van het begrip historiese tijd", in: *Ter elfder ure* 31 (Geschiedenistheorie 1, Nijmegen: SUN, without year of ref.), 380–415, esp. 390. My translation.
41 Althusser and Balibar, *Das Kapital lesen* I, 130. My translation. With Nietzsche, we will find a similar reasoning. He sees a comparable relationship between the genealogical time of becoming as the basic structure and the historicist time of the phenomena as a kind of superstructure. Nietzsche also holds the existence of a certain interdetermination between the two levels. See the next chapter.
42 Homer, "Narratives of History, Narratives of Time", 86.
43 Althusser and Balibar, *Reading Capital*, 97.
44 Karl Marx, *Grundrisse*, "Introduction" (Late August – Mid-September 1857; transl. Martin Nicolaus), 101.
45 Karl Marx and Friedrich Engels, *The German Ideology* (New York: International Publishers, 1970), 48. "when reality is depicted, philosophy as an independent branch of knowledge loses its medium of existence".
46 Louis Althusser, *Politics and History* (transl. Ben Brewster; NLB, 1972), 167.
47 Gordy, "Reading Althusser: Time and the Social Whole", 11.
48 Ibid., 12. See also: Althusser and Balibar, *Reading Capital*, 101.
49 Karl Marx, *Das Kapital* I (Ungekürzte Ausgabe nach der zweiten Auflage von 1872. Mit einem Geleitwort von Karl Korsch aus dem Jahre, 1932), § 13. See also: Althusser, *Das Kapital lesen* I, 142. With "Formen", Marx adresses something in, what Kant would call the "noumenal" reality, although Kant himself uses the term "Formen" in *Anschauungsformen* for the construction of the phenomenal world.
50 Althusser, *Das Kapital lesen* I, 127–143.
51 Althusser and Balibar, *Reading Capital*, 105.
52 Karl Marx, *Capital*, vol. I (Moscou: Foreign Languages Publishing House, n.d.), 60.
53 Althusser, "Schets van het begrip historiese tijd", 402.
54 C. R. Friedrichs, *Urban Society in an Age of War: Nördlingen 1580–1720* (Princeton: Princeton University Press, 1979); idem, "Capitalism, mobility, and Class Formation in the Early Modern German City: A Cross Cultural Analysis", in: P. H. Abrams and E. A. Wrigley (eds.), *Towns in Societies, Essays in Economic History and Historical Sociology* (Cambridge: CUP, 1978).
55 Friedrichs, "Capitalism, Mobility, and Class Formation", 199.
56 "Topography" is a term used by Read, "The Althusser Effect", section 7; According to the Dutch philosopher Martin Terpstra, Althusser uses consciously spatial terms to indicate a shift in the perception of time. Martin Terpstra, "Het geschiedenisbegrip bij Althusser", in: *Te elfder ure* 31, 420–450, esp. 445. See also: https://larvalsubjects.wordpress.com/2010/07/04/the-bp-oil-disaster/, where an anonymous states: "Marxism attempts to formulate a four-dimensional topography of the present that maps attractors, bifurcation points, or tendencies within the social field through which change might be produced. By 'four-dimensional' I am referring to the unfolding of time in the present. Through such a topography of tendencies it hopes to strategically intensify these tendencies through political practice".
57 Koselleck, *Vergangene Zukunft*, 325.
58 Karl Marx, "Deutsche Ideologie I. Feuerbach", *Marx Engels Werke* 3 (Berlin: Dietz Verlag, 1969), 72.

59 Ernst Bloch, "Ungleichzeitigkeit, nicht nur Rückständigkeit", 41–49, esp. 44–45. "*Obgleich in einem einzigen Satz von Marx fast die ganze Theorie der Ungleichzeitigkeit enthalten ist: dieser Satz is von einlinigen Nacheinander (und nichts als Nacheiander) idealistischer Dialektik freilich weit entfernt. In der Einleitung zur Deutschen Ideologie notiert Marx zur Entwicklung der Produktivkräfte: Sie geht ferner nur sehr langsam for sich: die verschiedenen Stufen und Interessen werden nie vollständig überwunden, sondern nur dem siegenden Interessen untergeordnet und schleppen sich, noch Jahrhunderte lang, neben diesen fort*".
60 Jameson, "The Ideological Analysis of Space", 3.
61 Freedman, *Marxist Social Thought*, 188.
62 Karl Marx and Frederick Engels, "Manifesto of the Communist Party", in: *Marx/Engels Selected Works*, vol. I (Moscow: Progress Publishers, 1969, first ed.: February 1848, ed. Andy Blunden, 2004), 14.
63 Freedman, *Marxist Social Thought*, 188–189.
64 Karl Marx, *The Eighteenth Brumaire of Louis Bonaparte* (New York: Cosimo Classics, 2008 [1852]), 2.
65 See: Nchamah Miller, "Hauntology and History", Jacques Derrida's *Spectres of Marx*. www.nodo50.org/cubasigloXXI/taller/miller_100304.pdf.
66 Albert Salomon, "Tocqueville 1959", *Social Research* 26, 4 (Winter 1959), 449–470, esp. 458.
67 Tocqueville, *Democracy in America*, vol. II, section 3, chapter I.
68 Ibid., chapter XIV.
69 Buiks, *Alexis de Tocqueville*, 157.
70 White, *Metahistory*, 284.

PART 4
The kairotic time of cultures

8

NIETZSCHE'S *AUGENBLICK*

Nietzsche makes his ideas about a passing time and forgetfulness crystal clear in the preface of his "On the Use and Abuse of History for Life":

> Observe the herd which is grazing beside you. It does not know what yesterday or today is. It springs around, eats, rests, digests, jumps up again, and so from morning to night and from day to day, with its likes and dislikes closely tied to the peg of the moment, and thus neither melancholy nor weary. To witness this is hard for man, because he boasts to himself that his human race is better than the beast and yet looks with jealousy at its happiness. For he wishes only to live like the beast, neither weary nor amid pains, and he wants it in vain, because he does not will it as the animal does. One day the man demands of the beast: "Why do you not talk to me about your happiness and only gaze at me?" The beast wants to answer, too, and say: "That comes about because I always immediately forget what I wanted to say." But by then the beast has already forgotten this reply and remains silent, so that the man wonders on once more.[1]

This quote not only illustrates how Nietzsche thinks about forgetfulness and time but also demonstrates – albeit in translation – Nietzsche's beautiful, almost poetic rhetoric. A summary of it can be: the past is a burden and man must do his best to forget it.

Nietzsche's burdensome time concerns a continuous fleeting perception of reality, as the Greek philosopher Heraclitus put it in the statement *pantha rhei* ("everything flows"). Hence man can never step into the same stream. To get a grip on this fleeting reality, Nietzsche makes time discontinuous. He comprehends the flow of time staccato, consisting of a continuous movement interspersed with striking moments. Moreover, Nietzsche resists romanticist philosophy of continuing entities; he prefers a philosophy of personal emancipation. Implicitly he also objects to Marx's collective proletarian emancipation. Nietzsche just wants to free humanity from economic forces.

According to Mannheim's definition, Hegel and Marx are historicists. Does this also apply to Nietzsche? Given his plea for personal emancipation and forgetfulness, Nietzsche's philosophy seems a-historical. Although there is a strong tendency to forgetfulness and to an affirmation of life in Nietzsche's work, it does not mean that his philosophy is a-historical. Even his stance towards an antiquarian form of history is nuanced, as we will see. In his *Untimely Meditations*, especially in the second one, Nietzsche appears to be a historicist. By reading his *Thus Spoke Zarathustra*, it becomes clear that Nietzsche wishes to create a new historicism with a new perception of time, based on an ontology that is distinct from that of Hegel as well as of Marx.

An overview of this chapter can show how Nietzsche achieves this new form of historicism. He starts the fight against the cultural crisis of his time by a new, anti-staticist ontology of becoming, which he connects to a time theory of will points. At first glance, this gives the impression of an empty time, but at second glance, it is a burdensome time that must be overcome by tenacity and will power. Nietzsche illustrates this in particular by the Spirit of Gravity in *Thus Spoke Zarathustra*. The burden consists of conflicts between past and future and can be relieved by "genealogy". It is a new vision on the past that creates a new view on the future, featured by "eternal recurrence", in which choices have to be made. This dual view of genealogy gives time a twofold form: an unconscious background and a conscious, intentional foreground time. Herd people only perceive the background time and keep waiting, whereas supermen take both times into account and by acting realize a kairotic time. This double-sided, kairotic time must be applied in the practice of history writing. Nietzsche rejects a historicist historiography that is only based on a romanticist conception of time. His own historicism is a combination of ordinary historiography and genealogy. It even makes antiquarian historiography acceptable.

Difference between Darwin's and Nietzsche's naturalism. A cultural crisis

According to Allan Megill in his *Prophets of Extremity*, the cultural crisis Nietzsche responds to is nihilism. Megill perceives how Nietzsche distinguishes two types of it: one of supermen and one of herd people. The nihilism of herd people, which Megill regards as passive, originates in secularization and the shock of Darwinist evolutionism.[2] It results in a nihilism that suffers from the devaluation of religion, morality and theory ("the will to truth"). In contrast to this, the nihilism of the "*Übermensch*" wants to "return to myth". The crisis of devaluation of traditional values then becomes a challenge to invent new ones. "Instead of drawing back from the void, we dance upon it", as Megill expresses it.[3] By believing in Nietzsche's own nihilistic myths it is possible to throw off the burden of age-old times and to fly into the future.

Marx's reacts on the societal crisis of his time with temporal perceptions, embedded in the atomism of his historical materialism. Nietzsche responds to the cultural crisis of his generation with a conception of time, inserted in naturalism. Naturalism has two aspects: first, it understands man as a part of nature, which implies a form of evolution, similar to that of Darwin and secondly, it regards the origins of our ideas about social behaviour as non-metaphysical. Religion and morality are perceived without reference to supernatural entities, like God or gods. For Nietzsche as for Darwin, man is not created but is a product of a naturalist selection, which is a selection for continuous success, giving "functions to organs and goals to organic processes".[4]

Nonetheless at least there are two important differences between Nietzsche's naturalism and Darwin's. (1) The natural selection of the latter produces instincts for survival, Nietzsche's natural selection creates, what he calls a Dionysian world of drives and instincts for power.

(2) Darwin's natural selection results in "reproductive fitness" that of Nietzsche often changes into its counterpart: "social selection". Unlike natural selection, social selection favours people's propensities of cohesiveness, by which society receives homogeneity. By selecting "herd habits, it gives us the drive to be similar to one another". This forms a successful behaviour for society as a whole but not for me as a person. It makes us "herd animals". According to Nietzsche, social selection is a kind of virus with purposes of its own, unaware of our real will and desires. In his view Christianity is one of the most terrible viruses. "It appeals to certain weaknesses and sicknesses for entry into persons, but then aggravates that weakness for purposes of its own".[5] It is the virus "do as others do", developed during primeval times, long before the 4,000 years, with which we are more or less known. Although inaccessible for ordinary history, those years are approachable to genealogy, a new form of history, which will be discussed in the following. Social selection belongs for Nietzsche to the real burden of his time.

Past, becoming, evolution and time. Nietzsche's ontology

The base of Nietzsche's thinking about time can be revealed by pointing to his creation of a new ontological field, which he gives the name "becoming". Its novelty seems odd, because Hegel already has characterized the term "becoming" by perceiving it as the synthesis of being (thesis) and non-being (anti-thesis). However, Nietzsche's "becoming" takes on a completely different outlook. At first glance it has nothing to do with being. Manuel Dries, an expert in Nietzschean thought, labels Nietzsche's view on the world as "anti-staticism". According to Nietzsche, being is not only the opposite of becoming, but it is most of all fake. It belongs to a world of permanence, achieving in the end truth and happiness, by which every form of movement stops. Hegel, in Nietzsche's perception, "aims at a becoming [that is] one with being". Hegel's existing world is "the world, as it ought to be".

To Nietzsche, Hegel's real world is "only error, – this world ought not to exist".[6] Nietzsche's becoming must be considered without being, because being is fiction.[7] Becoming is the substratum of a new Dionysian world, in which Hegelian Reason does not rule, but man's wills and drives. In that world there is no real past, present and future, in the Hegelian sense, but only a world of origins and evolution. Origins, however, point towards being; hence Nietzsche has a problem here. His solution is rather simple: we cannot study the world of becoming without the fiction of staticism. Although being is fake, it still is a necessary concept and as such a condition of life.[8] Nietzsche utters this dual view on reality in a twofold form of aestheticism. Next to the disharmonious, Dionysian world of becoming, he perceives a harmonious world, which he calls Apollonian.

There is still another difference between Nietzsche and Hegel. The latter investigates becoming from a historical point of view, which is to say in hindsight (the owl of Minerva), displaying how the rational present has its precedents in the past. His future is the end of a way, paved by freedom and reasonableness. In short: his becoming has a *telos*. Nietzsche's becoming is "a continually pattern of conflict and concord", having three properties.[9] First, becoming is the opposite of "being", and as such it has neither a purpose nor a final state. Second, being is an illusion, so becoming "must be the sole reality".[10] Third, becoming has the same value in every moment, or better: it has no value at all, because the total value of the world cannot be evaluated. Thus, ideas about progress or pessimism about the world's future are nonsense.[11]

Nietzsche's becoming cannot be grasped directly. It can only be comprehended by time. Becoming as a conflict between forces displays differences in intensities, and the greater the difference, the more the sensation of becoming. But this sensation is not yet time: "Intensity is a becoming without time".[12] Differences in intensity are accompanied by variation in tempo, because they follow each other faster or slower. But these differences also cannot be understood in terms of time. The rotation of a wheel shows it. Points on the inner and the outer periphery of a wheel move with different speeds, but they complete their revolution in the same time.[13] The most essential phenomenon that entails the possibility to let time appear out of becoming is rhythm. Rhythm is a dynamic process, "an interaction of forces giving rise to a patterning of time".[14] To Robin Small, Nietzsche's perception of rhythm is the alternation of Dionysian disharmony and Apollonian harmony. It can be observed in music. Through Apollonic forms of harmony, the unfathomable Dionysian process of becoming takes the form of time. Because of Nietzsche's time-atom theory, this is not evident at first sight.

Nietzsche's time theory of will points

Nietzsche starts his ideas about time with the present, which is the only genuine form of time for him.[15] But the present is continuously fleeting away.

> Imagine the extremest possible example of a man who did not possess the power of forgetting at all and who was thus condemned to see everywhere a state of becoming: such a man would no longer believe in his own being, would no longer believe in himself, would see everything going asunder in moving points and would lose himself in this stream of becoming: like a true pupil of Heraclitus, he would in the end hardly dare to raise his finger.[16]

Although continuous fleeting is a clear metaphor for becoming, it is not for time. Time, in Nietzsche's early years, is not a continuum but consists of separate instants.[17] This seems in complete contradiction with becoming. However, it must be viewed from Nietzsche's endeavour to create an alternative for the ruling materialist and positivist epistemology of his days. His "new" epistemology consists of replacing the Humean causality with an "acting upon" (*Wirken*). This comes close to the way romanticist ideas work, although Nietzsche's "acting" does not take place with ideas or a spirit (*Geist*), but with wills and drives. The romanticist ideas of Hegel and Ranke only act in historical times, while those of Nietzsche originate in pre-historic times.

Nietzsche perceives the ontology of becoming as an antagonism of wills, resulting in the distinction between supermen and herd people.[18] This sounds to me in accordance with Marx's antagonism between Epicurean and Democritean atoms. Democritean atoms are driven by circumstances, being as lethargic as Nietzsche's "herd animals". The latter maintains a traditional (religious and moral) past.[19] Epicurean atoms are self-conscious and forward-willing instances.[20] They can be seen, as some do, like those early capitalists Marx describes in his *Communist Manifesto*. Nietzsche's supermen and Marx's early capitalists have the same secularizing, demystifying and active willing nature.[21]

We have observed how Marx's atom theory forms the base of his materialism. It probably intends to explore Kant's noumenal world of the *Ding an sich*. Nietzsche wants to do the same, not in a Marxian way, but in the footsteps of Schopenhauer.[22] To Marx, differences in atomistic matter are part of his perception of time, enabling a more-or-less spatial synchronicity of the non-synchronous. Nietzsche perceives that matter and space are ruled out in time, and hence there also is no material or spatial synchronicity of the non-synchronous. According to his time-atom theory, action (*Wirkung*) at distance is a force, but not in Newton's gravitational perception. It is the rhythm of actions at distance which produces changes in time.

Nietzsche's time-atom theory is rather vague, and in the end, it changes in a theory of "will points". It is a will-based theory of time, based on an ontology of *Willens-Punktationen*, culminating in a process of power activities and power-relations, endlessly recurring and never ending.[23] Nietzsche identifies action at distance not only with the inner Dionysian life of drives and wills but also with sensations coming from the outside. He assumes that we, as human beings, construct our world via a vocabulary of visual appearances, which is a world of stable, identical objects, moving and interacting in space.[24] Our interpretive constructions of time, as well as those of space and force, are representations. Kant would call it "the world of phenomena". According to Nietzsche, the will with its fluctuations is the most important thing behind this world.

Here Nietzsche makes his Schopenhauerian move. Schopenhauer considers the world of the will and its drives as the *noumenal* world of Kant, which the latter assumes to be not investigable. In this world without time and space, Nietzsche finds the basis for intensity, speed and rhythm, giving it a sequential pattern so that becoming turns into time. Yet successive sensational impressions cannot be perceived without some "spatiality". Nietzsche reintroduces space, but he does so in a metaphorical way (see the following). He argues that we need metaphorical language to indicate things like time and space. They form the conditions of perceiving things. Just like Kant, Nietzsche makes time and space separate categories. That is why his atomic time theory and theory of will points consist of non-spatial time nodes. Inner experiences and encounters from the outside touch our wills and drives, through which we feel a new time-knot.[25] Although later on, Nietzsche abandons his theory of will points, he maintains the idea of decisive time nodes. At first glance this appears to be an empty time, but at second sight, it is embodied.

A burdensome time with conflicting aspects

Nietzsche's theory of will points is blown away by a huge time node. At the Surlej-rock in Silvaplana (1881, Switzerland), Nietzsche enjoyed an ecstatic moment of indescribable completeness. Nietzsche describes this moment of revelation in *Ecce Homo* (1888).

> The concept of revelation, in the sense that suddenly, with unspeakable certainty and subtlety, something becomes visible, audible. . . . One hears, one does not seek, one takes, one does not ask who gives, like a lightning bolt a thought flashes up, with necessity, in form without hesitation. – I have never had a choice. A rapture (*Entzückung*) whose tremendous tension occasionally discharges itself in a storm of tears . . . a complete being-outside-of-oneself (*Aussersichsein*). . . . Everything happens involuntarily to the highest degree, but as in a storm of a feeling of freedom, of being unconditioned, of power, of divinity – The involuntariness of image, of metaphor, is the most curious of all; one has no more concept, what is an image, what is a metaphor, everything offers itself as the nearest, most correct, simplest expression.[26]

In my view this is Nietzsche's kairotic moment, in which he discovers "eternal recurrence". In the next chapter I will discuss who Kairos is and what a kairotic moment involves. For now, it is enough to know that Kairos is the god of the right moment, in which past experiences and expectations of the future tell us that it is now the time to act. For Nietzsche the experience of Silvaplana leads to the kairotic moment of creating his greatest work: *Thus Spoke Zarathustra* (1883–1885).

"Eternal recurrence" needs an explanation via a detour. I will discuss it in the context of Nietzsche's thinking about genealogy. For now, I want to deal with a question that is related to eternal recurrence, namely the burdensome and conflicting aspects of Nietzsche's time. He elaborates on it in *Thus Spoke Zarathustra*, especially in the paragraph "On the Vision and the Riddle". There he introduces, next to Zarathustra, a blind dwarf-like creature called "the Spirit of Gravity". I think that the dwarf represents the same embodied and burdensome time, felt by Hegel, Marx and other German and French thinkers in the first half of the nineteenth century. The dwarf is lame and sits on Zarathustra's shoulders, pouring "leaden drips of thoughts" (*Bleitropfen-Gedanken*) in his ears, thus burdening him physically and mentally.[27]

Next to time, the conflict of forces is the main issue of *Thus Spoke Zarathustra*. Time and the conflicting forces even are related. This becomes obvious in the beginning of Zarathustra's story, where he is climbing a mountain path. It contains a contradiction between the climber's first and second step and between the second and the third step and so forth. Each step means a conflict within Zarathustra between his ambition to climb the ever-higher mountain and his fear for the ever-deeper abyss. Nietzsche compares this conflict with the times of yesterday and today, referring to them as parts of time. "You contradict today what you taught yesterday – But that is why yesterday is not today, said Zarathustra".[28] The contradiction between yesterday and today and between today and tomorrow is simultaneously a succession in time, as Kant already knew.[29] But Nietzsche does not want to perceive it that way. Contradictions ought not to be solved. Conflict is a polarity of force, with an experience of disagreement between eye and feet and an inner conflict of striving to the top and fearing the depth. Striving to the top is the way to the future, burdened by what we have experienced in the past. The change of days with their contradictions represents not only the rhythm but also the burden of time. As we shall see hereafter, when I discuss for instance Chakrabarty's "Indian time", an important element of kairotic time is its contradictory aspect.

The gateway and the *Augenblick* as aspects of an embodied but also conflicting time

Climbing up the mountain, Zarathustra makes a stop at a gateway, and there he speaks to the dwarf:

> "Behold this gateway, dwarf!" . . . It has two faces. Two ways come together here: no one has yet followed either to its end. This long way stretches back for an eternity. And that long lane out there, that is another eternity. They contradict each other, these ways; they offend each other face to face; and

it is here at this gateway that they come together. The name of the gateway is inscribed above: "Moment".[30]

With this statement, Zarathustra adds to the succession of the *parts* of time (before the moment, the moment itself and after the moment, as in yesterday, today and tomorrow) a construction of *forms* of time (past, present and future). The gateway does not stand only for the "Moment" (*Augenblick*) but also for the "present". The eternal way backward represents past time, and the eternal way forward stands for the future. This transition from a formal succession of *parts* into a construction in *forms* of time gives time an aspect of perspective, of vision. It undergoes a transition of a logical proposition of succession into a dialogical relation between interlocutors. It is a conflicting encounter between the past and the future. Conflict does not only mean a difference between today and yesterday but a distinction between "It was" and "It will be".

Referring to the logical time of parts and succession, Nietzsche refers to an empty time: "All is empty, all is the same, all has been".[31] He refers to an embodied time of forms when he speaks of the past as "It was" and about the future as "It will be".[32] Small gives the following clarifications for this view. First is a remark in Nietzsche's notebook where he says: *die Vergangenheit ist nicht vergangen*; that is, the past has not passed away. As a consequence, the past is incarnated in the present. The second elucidation is from Zarathustra:

> Willing liberates; but what is it that puts even the liberator himself in fetters? "It was" – that is the name of the will's gnashing of teeth and most secret melancholy. Powerless against what has been done, he is an angry spectator of all that is past. The will cannot will backwards; and that he cannot break time and time's consciousness, that is the will's loneliest melancholy.[33]

At first sight this statement gives the impression to be contradictory, because the past seems over and out. However, at second sight, it is a new argument with regard to an embodied, burdensome time. The past has such a strong impact on the present that it is impossible to change it by the will in the present. This inability of the will expresses itself in frustration about time's burden: "That time does not run backward, that is its wrath".[34] In this view the past is the dominating aspect of time as a whole. Heidegger articulates Nietzsche's temporality in that way.[35] According to Heidegger, Nietzsche observes the past as time's overall character.[36] Heidegger resents Nietzsche's backward-looking temporality. He presents time as *Sorge* (care), which means a future-oriented temporality.

But, another interpretation is possible. Hannah Arendt, in *The Life of the Mind*, refers to a short parable of Franz Kafka in which two counteracting forces are at stake:

> He has two antagonists: the first presses him from behind, from his origin. The second blocks the road in front of him. He gives battle to both.

> Actually the first supports him in his fight with the second, for he wants to push him forward, and in the same way the second supports him in his fight with the first, since he drives him back.[37]

The gateway is the Now in which past, present and future are interacting forces. It is not a halt between the backward lane of the past and the forward lane of the future. It also is not a given, but the product of a conflict of forces: the product of a collision between a drive forward into the future (hope?) and a power that wants to remain (fear?). Thus, Nietzsche here is more Heideggerian than Heidegger likes to understand him. Nietzsche, the thinker of hope and fear, is aware of the necessity to make choices.

The conversation between Zarathustra and the Spirit of Gravity is illuminating for the ambiguity in Nietzsche's spatial aspect of time. Zarathustra asks whether the two ways contradict each other eternally. The dwarf answers: "All that is straight lies. All truth is crooked, time itself is a circle".[38] Although he reintroduces space immediately by the metaphor of the circle, the dwarf dismisses the spatial aspect of time (as a straight line). By the words of the dwarf, Nietzsche wants to dismiss space as an element of time. However, as a form of appearance, he cannot speak about time without spatial terms, and therefore he uses the metaphors of the gateway, the circle and the paths.

With the circle, he also dismisses the time of progress and the romanticist temporality of rise and fall. Both are linear, homogeneous times, whereas Nietzsche wants a time of shocks and heterogeneity. More than with space, Nietzsche identifies time with motion and force as in Kafka's parable.[39] Motion and force, experienced in the gateway of the "Moment", make the moment in general not a Now with a before and an after, as with Aristotle, but a tipping point in which experiences are lost and new will come. Moreover, motion and force also connect time with becoming. We have already noticed that, according to Nietzsche, becoming is expressed by intensity, speed and rhythm. These experiences do not form directly an utterance of time. They become so by the relationship between motion and force on one side and rhythm on the other. It contains Nietzsche's difference between genealogy and history, but also their interrelation.

The past as a burden and genealogy as the panacea against herd principles

According to Nietzsche, the past leaves the present with heavy burdens. It does so with retrospection, history, memory and punishment. They are the instruments of social selection through which we acquire habits that separate us from our innate drives. These tools are designed to remember the rules, in order that we are *in thrall to our past*.[40] According to Nietzsche, ordinary history does not expose that "the meaning of what we do logically is formed by selection from the past". Romanticist history shows only the way we are controlled by herd viruses, such as Christianity. Even more than religion, ethics cultivates piety for the founders of our customs and laws, which we have made into gods, to whom we owe gratitude. In this way we turn our drives against ourselves and reinforce the habit of tormenting ourselves.

In addition to the role of religion and morality, there is another stance with regard to reality that Nietzsche views with suspicion. That is the "will to truth", manifesting itself in reason and cognition, and moreover in a theoretical attitude. Nietzsche wonders whether the will to truth, with the associate asceticism, does not bring about a separation between our false intentions and our real "Dionysian" drives.[41] In the third essay of the *Genealogy of Morals*, Nietzsche identifies this attitude with the ascetic ideal. He asks: "Do we really become acquainted with the Dionysian world of drives and wills?" No, is his answer, because of the ascetic stance, which inheres retrospective theory and cognition. In religion and morality, people constitute conscious, but "false" intentions and drives; in the will to truth, they mostly turn their retrospective eye to the Apollonian world, exploring values which also kill our real wills and drives. As a consequence we do not really direct ourselves, as we naively suppose, but we have been directed.[42] The will to truth strengthens our (scientist but also romanticist) retrospective powers and also our slave instincts.

All these forms of retrospection do not kill our false intentions; they kill our genuine, Dionysian strives and wills.[43] Studying the past even makes it worse. It diverts us, as John Richardson interprets Nietzsche, "into a stance that undermines our natural drive-effort, co-opting it for social ends".[44] The so-called civilizations make us herd people.

Therefore the past is harmful and disturbs us, because "there is a degree of sleeplessness, of rumination of the historical sense" in it.[45] Still it cannot be ignored, because it has a kind of "presence" in our personal lives.[46] In *Human, All Too Human*, Nietzsche states:

> Direct self-observation is not nearly sufficient for us to know ourselves: we require history, for the past continues to flow within us in a hundred waves; we ourselves are, indeed, nothing but that which at every moment we experience of this continued flowing [*Fortströmen*].[47]

The significance of this passage is that Nietzsche acknowledges the importance of history. He explains how a continued flowing is moving within us, as the result of a long cultural history of creating supermen or herd people. Thus he considers time as embodied with history; as a consequence, he can be perceived as a post-Enlightenment philosopher.

Nietzsche even accuses contemporary philosophers of thinking about humanity from a very limited time frame. "A lack of historical sensibility is the original failing of all philosophers".[48] Hence, he wants to imbue history with a new perspective on the past: genealogy. Genealogy is Nietzsche's new vision on history as the world of becoming. It creates a new perception of past, present and future by displaying the past as the world of origins. Nietzsche's genealogy is "the highest achievement of the will to truth, inasmuch as it penetrates to the most hidden, most difficult, and most important truths – the facts of what and why we are (as we are)".[49]

Genealogy, the gateway and eternal recurrence

Does not genealogy work in the same way as the will to truth? In his *Genealogy of Morals*, Nietzsche reveals the negative way we deal with our memory and retrospection.[50] Moreover, in its retrospective character, genealogy can be viewed as a burden to our "forward-pushing" will. Nevertheless, despite its retrospective view, or just because of it, genealogy can further the prospective drive of becoming.[51] Richardson underlines the relevance of genealogy for Nietzsche's thinking. For him, as for Small, the passage of "On the Vision and the Riddle" in *Thus Spoke Zarathustra* is important. Richardson also discusses the "Gateway of the Moment" and the two lanes departing from it.[52] He perceives the lane ahead not only (and even not mainly) as referring to the future but to the projective thrust of the will to a personal end. He considers the lane backwards as referring to the retrospection of the genealogical approach. "The moment then becomes the 'retrospective' pause in this willing, which distinguishes humans from animals and reaches its fullest form in our knowing".[53]

In genealogy Nietzsche denies what romanticist historicism propagates: intentionalism.[54] We do not determine what we want and think by our acts of intending. "A thought comes when 'it' wants, not when 'I' want".[55] Nietzsche does not only struggle with the past but also with the future. He attacks Hegel's teleology, which has as *telos* (aim) the freedom for the world. In Nietzsche's "teleology", hundreds of waves of wills and drives are moving forward, without a clear aim. His view at the world of becoming would lead to a future in which there is only a "free individual, liberated from any spiritual-transcendental impulse".[56] Nietzsche's personal freedom is anti-metaphysical and autonomous. It differs completely from Hegel's metaphysical idea that freedom is embedded in Absolute Reason, regarding the individual and the world as one.

The moment of the gateway illuminates the possibility of reconciling the retrospective and prospective views of time. Retrospection can lay bare how the willing is suppressed in the past, creating the possibility to choose. Nietzsche's "eternal recurrence" is a recurrence of choice. Hence the self can make choices with regard to rules and virtues we commit ourselves to and thus realize our identity and self-awareness in the future. Richardson thinks Nietzsche's genealogy is of great help in this endeavour: "By genealogy, we can judge those designed-in purposes of our ways of thinking and acting – and decide whether we favour those purposes. And if we don't favour them, we can try, at least, to redesign those thoughts and acts for different ends".[57] We even can decide to honour commitments pertaining to traditional rules. Then we still display power over our drives "and pride [ourselves] in being able to override those drives to follow those rules".[58] Thus genealogy confers a self-understanding that opens a way to freedom. Small joins Richardson by not identifying the retrospective "moment" (*Augenblick*) with a short lapse of time but with a timeless "hour" (*Stunde*), in which past and future, prospect and retrospect are incorporated, constituting a kairotic time, which no clock can tell us.[59] It is untimely and opens a way of greatness.[60]

Genealogical retrospection "visualizes" our human circumstances, making it possible to revise habits. Richardson states: "The upshot indeed is that Nietzsche uses his 'conditions' [mental categories] for an opposite purpose than Kant: Kant identifies conditions to validate them for science, but Nietzsche identifies them in the hope of freeing himself from them".[61] Nietzsche's attention shifts from a historical past into a personal past. The "way of greatness" is the personal path we have chosen. By that way we shake off the burden of ages of religion, morality and conceptualization and also of (romanticist) historicism.[62] By flying or dancing, we can abandon it, because the burdensome time has been overcome.[63]

Eternal recurrence does not refer to a circular time but to experiences that have occurred in the past and must occur in the future. It points to a life embedded in becoming, which can give us the lowest but also the highest feeling:

> How, if some day or night, a demon were to sneak after you into your loneliness and say to you: "this life, as you now live it and have lived it, you will have to live once more and innumerable times more: and there will be nothing new in it, but every pain and every joy . . . must return to you – all in the same succession and sequence – even this spider and this moonlight between the trees, even this moment and I myself". . . . Would you not throw yourself down and gnash your teeth and curse the demon who spoke thus? Or have you once experienced a tremendous moment when you would have answered him: "you are a god and never did I hear anything more godlike!" . . . The question in each and everything, "do you want this once more and innumerable times more?" would weigh upon your actions as the greatest stress. Or how well disposed you would have to become to yourself and to life to *crave nothing more fervently* than this ultimate eternal confirmation . . .?[64]

The highest feeling does not subject us to religion, to fate, to socialism, even not to secularism, because they all narrow our perspective to what is "at hand both in space and time".[65] A life embedded in becoming is a life of changing into "what you are".[66] This is the way of greatness, being like "the course of a ship through the sea or a bird through the air".[67] This way has no destination; its only sense is overcoming a burdensome past and constituting a future by the will to power. This is the way Nietzsche wants to lose a burdensome time, making it into a kairotic one.

Time thus becomes a series of nodes in which genealogical retrospection in the present creates the opportunity to make the right choices for the future. This is what the "Behold this gateway, dwarf" implies. However, as we will see hereafter, not everyone makes these choices. A lot of people wait, making themselves into herd people. Those who choose to live in a kairotic time have to take into account two different temporalities: the time closely connected to becoming and an intentional temporality to make choices.

Genealogical background time and conscious, intentional time

Kevin Hill, a specialist in the philosophies of Kant and Nietzsche, argues that Kant perceives time mostly as a form of intuition (inside the mind), whereas Nietzsche defends a real time. The latter's eternal recurrence is an affirmation of an embodied time, because repetition of kairotic moments means a time full of experiences.[68] Hill attributes to Nietzsche a vision of Kant, in which the latter makes the world of appearances unreal, and the *noumenal* world of the unknowable, *Ding an sich*, real. Nietzsche claims, according to Hill, that Kant, by making time transcendentally ideal [i.e. a form of intuition and thus empty of most of reality], distinguishes "between an apparent world, in which there is destruction, and a real world, in which there is no destruction".[69] Hill asserts that Nietzsche considers Kant's empty time as lacking historical sense, thus displaying a hatred for life and the very idea of becoming.[70] Nietzsche corroborates *avant la lettre*, what we have discussed in Chapters 2 and 3.

As a consequence, Nietzsche commits himself to two appearances of time. First, a time beyond human control, in which the human intellect is produced and embedded in the "natural" world of becoming.[71] Second, a time produced by the human intellect and connected with the world of appearances, coming close to Kant's form of intuition.[72] However, Nietzsche's time "of appearances" has only a superficial resemblance with Kant's *Anschauungsform*, because Nietzsche's second temporality differs from it by its possibility to change. The present changes continuously and therefore also its past and future. The time belonging to becoming manifests itself in genealogy, whereas the time of appearances (*res gestae*) is an object of study in history as *historia rerum gestarum*.

Dries, in his "Towards Adualism", also discovers two notions of time with Nietzsche: a pre-conscious temporality of becoming, which he calls a "background time", and a conscious temporality existing in the world of appearances.[73] The conscious time concerns a "sum of selves", that is, a group of subjects with intentions.[74] Having an aim, worth pursuing, they create "directional" time.[75] The pre-conscious time of becoming is "the multi-directional temporality of the physical-spiritual whole, in which even inorganic matter participates".[76] This leads to the idea that history can be studied in an intentionalist and a genealogical way. In "*Vom Nutzen und Nachteil der Historie für das Leben*", the second essay of his *Untimely Meditations*, Nietzsche elaborates on this distinction (see the following).

Dries goes one step further. He proposes an "adualistic interdetermination" of the background and conscious time. This comes to the fore when we, being engaged in a targeted action, discover at a certain moment that we are involved in something completely different. It can reveal itself also in an inverse way, as

Dries states: "you find yourself engaged in an action, you had not been consciously aware of, and from that 'moment' on you are 'interrupting' and 'determining' this action, thereby taking it in a different direction".[77] This interrelation between the background time of becoming and the conscious, intentional one is a heterogeneous time. It is a time of tipping points in which essential moments of the stream of becoming penetrate into the phenomenal time of being. These tipping points are featured by a coexistence of past and present. Pasts, belonging to the world of becoming, penetrate into the phenomenal present. We can perceive this in the involuntary memories of Marcel in Proust's *In Search of Lost Time*, which are popping up out of background time to become conscious in the phenomenal time. On the other side of the time spectrum, becoming is imbued with a drive to acting. Thus, in the present the future manifests itself. Nietzsche's heterogeneous time consists of tipping points in which past, present and future coincide.

Genealogical time, romanticist-historicist time and historiography

Dries does not notice how his interdetermination between the genealogical background time and the "phenomenological", conscious time of intentions determines Nietzsche's historiographical views. Therefore, I want to propose the following question: can we find the interdeterminated perception of times, as proposed by Hill, Richardson and Dries, in Nietzsche's historiographical attitudes?

Already in the *Birth of Tragedy*, Nietzsche conciliates by interdetermination the Dionysian, fleeting world of becoming and the Apollonian world of appearances. The Dionysian world of wills and drives calls for the Apollonian one of substances (beings) and forms to control reality, not in a theoretical and technical way but in an aesthetic way. Nietzsche, standing in a long German, Graecophilic tradition, wants a return to the myth of ancient Greece: seeing life as a classical tragedy. In the tragedies of Sophocles and Aeschylos, the optimistic Apollonian forms make the dramatic world of Dionysos, with its struggles and cruelties, visible and bearable. Nietzsche wants, that

> from the foundations of existence, from the Dionysian substrates of the world only so much become into human individual awareness, that they can be overcome by Apollonian power of explanation; thus in such a way that these two artistic drives are compelled to unfold their powers *in mutual proportion* [my italics] and according to the law of everlasting righteousness.[78]

Already in his first big essay, *The Birth of Tragedy*, Nietzsche seems not to prefer the Dionysian world to the Apollonian one; he only wants their interdetermination. At the end of the essay he makes Aeschylos say:

Tell also this, you wondrous stranger: how much had this people to suffer to become so nice! However, come and follow me now into tragedy to bring a sacrifice with me in the temples of both deities [Dionysos and Apollo]![79]

Genealogy is not a sufficient alternative to romanticist history. It has too far a distance to ordinary history, and therefore Nietzsche designs a combination of both in his genealogical history. It is a temple of history, in which Clio brings a sacrifice to history as well as to genealogy.

In Nietzsche's view, traditional history concentrates on the micro-consciousnesses of micro-subjects looking ahead to micro-goals.[80] This history studies the past of appearances in a romanticist-historicist way. We cannot ignore that past, although it ought not to be studied in that romanticist-historicist manner, which Nietzsche calls in *Untimely Meditations* the way of the "polemic micrologists".[81] Those historicists want to stick to the facts, and thus they reinforce the burden of memory by assuming that we cannot afford to forget parts of the past. Nietzsche as a philologist knows it all too well, and he even practices it, albeit from the perspective that some great men are capable of reconciling their micro-goals with their natural drives and wills to power. These men appear in ancient Greece and in the Renaissance. Beneath superficial stability, these stories display the internal power conflicts, characterizing the changes in historical phenomena.[82] In rejecting a romanticist philology and history, Nietzsche advocates in his *Use and Disadvantages of History*, a genuine history which combines traditional, romanticist history from the world of appearances with the genealogical history of the world of becoming.

In the second essay of his *Untimely Meditations*, Nietzsche reveals the differences between romanticist history and genealogical history. He analyses three forms of historical practice in his time: monumental, antiquarian and critical history. His analysis has nothing to do with methodology but with the psychological-cultural aspects of these three forms.[83]

1. Monumental history is romanticist-historicist and false when it tends to romanticize the past and perceives common greatness in every individual.[84] It is genealogically right when it "provides exemplars of human nobility and teaches that, since a great thing once existed, it was therefore possible, and so *might be* possible again".[85] This remark is meant to be optimistic opposite to Schopenhauer's pessimistic view.[86] Its "genealogical truth" lies in the fact that this form of monumental history furthers the drives and wills to power. The true monumentalist historian acknowledges something great and can describe it as worthy of imitation.[87]

2. Antiquarian history in its false romanticist-historicist form leads to *indiscriminant appreciation* of everything in the past. It values anything old, *just because* it is old.[88] In its creative, genealogical form (a comprehensive structuring of the past cannot do without the "artistic impulse" of the inquiring

historian),[89] it promotes the "feeling of the tree that clings to its roots, the happiness of knowing one's growth to be not merely arbitrary and fortuitous but the inheritance, the fruit and the blossom of a past that does not merely justify but crowns the present".[90] Thus it "engenders a respect for origins".[91] Antiquarian history in its genealogical form "serves life by adding value to what is inherently valueless".[92]

3   Critical history in its romanticist-historicist figure implies a "deification of triviality, by having shown that nothing is noble".[93] In its Schopenhauerian form, critical history may lead to the terrible idea that "everything that is born is worth of being destroyed" and hence to the conclusion "better were it that nothing should be born". In general, critical history and philology in the romanticist sense has an analytic drive, which can be destructive, especially with regard to the Greek culture of antiquity.[94] In its genuine, genealogical historicist shape, critical history can teach that it requires great strength to be able to live and forget how far life and injustice are one. It also can bring the past (of appearances; *res gestae*, H.J.) "to the bar of judgement, interrogate it remorselessly, and finally condemn it".[95] This is especially true for a past, inhabited by Christian and moral-ideological pieties and their claims on the present. "[H]e who constructs the future has a right to judge the past".[96]

Nietzsche displays an overall heterogeneous temporality in his work, consisting of the interdetermination of the time of appearances with the time connected with becoming. This heterogeneity comes to the fore and is intensified by the three approaches of his "Second Untimely Meditations". There he combines ordinary history with genealogical history and thus objects to its romanticist form, such as that of Ranke. The latter is lifeless and boring, and the genealogical history accentuates special people, events and moments which have created tipping points in history. These points embrace past, present and future. They can turn history (*res gestae*) in a different direction, indefinite and unforeseeable. Its study requires a cultural anthropological approach. Then history writing is not about the past but from within the past, enabled by its presence.

Retrospect and prospect

Nietzsche's temporality is rooted in becoming, in an ontological stream; therein he perceives it as opposite to being. The stream has no *telos* or value, existing of alternations of Dionysian disharmony and Apollonian harmony, displaying patterns of conflict and concord. This stream of becoming is not time. To say it in Kantian terms, becoming is the *noumenal* plane of reality and time is its phenomenal face. Although Nietzsche comprehends reality as continuous becoming, he is aware that only in the form of being can it be spoken about. It implies a metaphorical approach to reality, which is mainly expressed in time and genealogical history. Nietzsche is a preacher of forgetfulness, but also a historicist.

The phenomenal face of becoming is uttered in metaphorical terms of being. Hence it becomes understandable how Nietzsche's Heraclitean ontology ends in a rather staccato perception of time. He first makes time visible in his theory of time atoms and willing points. He perceives it as a sequence of separate instants, contradicting today what has been taught yesterday. In *Thus Spoke Zarathustra*, Nietzsche chooses definitely for a complete metaphorical approach to time. He illustrates it by the image of climbing a mountain, whereby striving to the top is combined with fearing the abyss. It is a spatial image for time, because fearing the abyss stands for a past that is not yet over, and striving for the height stands for a future that is already there. Thus, past and future are incarnated in the moment of the present. Nietzsche also clarifies it in the riddle of the gateway. It is the "place-time" where past and future meet and interact.

Past and future are not empty concepts but embodied with will and striving. As such, they are opposing forces: the future drives man forward and the past holds him in the present, making the present a "presence" of past, present and future. This struggle between a projective thrust (future) and the necessity of retrospection (past) makes the gate a reflective break in the forward craving. The past as a burden for the striving, changes time into a Manichean struggle. It means a choice between an ordinary life without questioning the illusion of being and a life of *amor fati*, which demands the ultimate recognition of pain and joy to attain the status of superman. These are the moments that Nietzsche refers to in his *Beyond Good and Evil*. Those who choose the eternal repetition of a life without fundamental choices are called the *Wartenden*, those who wait. They are the herd people, who endure to live in the time of Kronos. Those who choose to become superman behave like Kairos, the god of the right moment. Kairos creates a turning point, leading to a "jump up" and a change of life. We can observe that Nietzsche's philosophy of becoming is permeated with a new temporality. It makes Nietzsche the prophet of a new kairotic time regime that he almost creates from scratch. In the next chapter I will analyse Kairos and try to display how Nietzsche and the Dutch historian Johan Huizinga are thinkers of the "right moment".

Notes

1 Friedrich Nietzsche, "Unzeitgemässe Betrachtungen. Zweites Stück: Vom Nutzen und Nachteil der Historie furs Leben", Abt. 1, *Werke* I (K. Schlechta ed.; Franfurt a. M., Berlin and Wien: Ullstein Buch, 1976⁶), 211. Friedrich Nietzsche, "On the Use and Abuse of History for Life" (Rev. ed. 2010, transl. Ian Johnstone; Nanaimo, BC, Canada: Vancouver Island University), 1. https://records.viu.ca/~johnstoi/nietzsche/history.htm
2 Megill, *Prophets of Extremity*, 33.
3 Ibid., 34.
4 John Richardson, "Nietzsche's Problem of the Past", in: Manuel Dries (ed.), *Nietzsche on Time and History* (Berlin and New York: Walter de Gruyter, 2008), 93.
5 Richardson, "Nietzsche's Problem of the Past", 94. See also: Nietzsche, "Der Antichrist", Abt. 7, *Werke* III (Schlechta ed.), 614. English: *The Antichrist* (1895, transl. H. L. Mencken, 1920), esp. section 7 and Nietzsche, "Zur Genealogie der Moral", *Werke* III

(Schlechta ed.), Abt.: 17, 243–244. English: idem, *On the Genealogy of Morals*, section 17. www.inp.uw.edu.pl/mdsie/Political
6 Manuel Dries, "Nietzsche's Critique of Staticism. Introduction to *Nietzsche on Time and History*", in: idem, *Nietzsche on Time and History*, 1–19, esp. 5. See also: Small, *Time and Becoming in Nietzsche's Thought*, 25–33.
7 Although we cannot deny that we need fiction. See the following.
8 Dries, "Nietzsche's Critique of Staticism", 8. In his "Towards Adualism", Dries elaborates on the contradiction between being and becoming. Dries argues that the contradiction Nietzsche so heavily articulates must be seen in the context of his fight against passive nihilism. In the end, the contradiction between the two is not so fierce as it seems. Nietzsche even abhors the either-or dilemma, as Dries sees it. See: Manuel Dries, "Towards Adualism: Becoming and Nihilism in Nietzsche's Philosophy", in: idem, *Nietzsche on Time and History*, 113–145, esp. 135–141.
9 Small, *Time and Becoming in Nietzsche's Thought*, 11.
10 Ibid., 25.
11 Ibid., 24–25.
12 Ibid., 46.
13 Ibid., 45–49.
14 Ibid., 52.
15 Ibid., 55.
16 Friedrich Nietzsche, *Untimely Meditations*. Section 2. "On the Uses and disadvantages of History for Life; Texts in the Philosophy of History" (ed. Daniel Breazeale, transl. J. Hollingdale; Cambridge: Cambridge University Press, 1997), 62.
17 Small, *Time and Becoming in Nietzsche's Thought*, 56. Later on (after 1875) Nietzsche will return to continuity as a corollary to his doctrine of becoming. See: Small, *Time and Becoming in Nietzsche's Thought*, 74–75.
18 Dries, "Towards Adualism", 132.
19 Andrea Orsucci, "Nietzsche's Cultural Criticism and His Historical Methodology", in: Dries, *Nietzsche on Time and History*, 23–34, esp. 29.
20 See Marx, *Marx Engels Werke. Ergänzungsband*, 327. See also the previous chapter of this book.
21 Martin A. Ruehl, "'An Uncanny Re-Awakening' Nietzsche's Renascence of the Renaissance Out of the Spirit of Jacob Burckhardt", in: Dries, *Nietzsche on Time and History*, 231–272, esp. 235–236.
22 See: Small, *Time and Becoming in Nietzsche's Thought*, 58–60.
23 Dries, "Towards Adualism", 127–129. Dries text implies two remarks: first, his eternal return differs from Richardson's, because the latter sees it as a reconciliation of the prospective view of becoming and the retrospective view of genealogy, whereas Dries perceives eternal return as an endless struggle between will points; second: language does not admit a complete explanation of the world of becoming with its struggle of will points, because "language's semantic units and grammar always confirm that [interrupted] structure [of isolated substantive subjects and objects] and with it the paradigm of being itself". Dries, "Towards Adualism", 129.
24 Small, *Time and Becoming in Nietzsche's Thought*, 76.
25 See for a more sophisticated explanation of Nietzsche's atom theory of time: Small, *Time and Becoming in Nietzsche's Thought*, 55–77.
26 Nietzsche, "Ecce Homo. Wie man wird, was man ist" (Abt. 3: "Also sprach Zarathustra"), *Werke* III (Schlechta ed.), 577. English from: Will Dudley, *Hegel, Nietzsche and Philosophy: Thinking Freedom* (Cambridge: Cambridge University Press, 2002), 224.
27 Small, *Time and Becoming in Nietzsche's Thought*, 80.
28 Ibid., 92.
29 Ibid., 92–93.
30 Nietzsche, "Also sprach Zarathustra, Dritter Teil. Vom Gesicht und Rätsel", 682. English from: Small, *Time and Becoming in Nietzsche's Thought*, 95.

31 Small, *Time and Becoming in Nietzsche's Thought*, 100.
32 Ibid., 98–100.
33 Nietzsche, "Also sprach Zarathustra. Zweiter Teil: Von der Erlösung", 668. English from: Small, *Time and Becoming in Nietzsche's Thought*, 99.
34 Nietzsche, "Also sprach Zarathustra. Zweiter Teil: "Von der Erlösung", 668. English from: Small, *Time and Becoming in Nietzsche's Thought*, 106.
35 See for the relation between Nietzsche, Heidegger and kairotic time: Felix O. Murchadha, *The Time of Revolution: Kairos and Chronos in Heidegger* (London: Bloomsbury Press, 2013). Murchadha speaks of kairological time, instead of kairotic time.
36 Small, *Time and Becoming in Nietzsche's Thought*, 100–101.
37 Ibid., 112.
38 Nietzsche, "Also sprach Zarathustra. Dritter Teil. Vom Gesicht und Rätsel", Abt.: 2, 682.
39 Small, *Time and Becoming in Nietzsche's Thought*, 114–126.
40 Richardson, "Nietzsche's Problem of the Past", 95–97.
41 Friedrich Nietzsche, "Zur Genealogie der Moral, Dritte Abhandlung: Was bedeuten Asketische Ideale?", Abt.: 27 and 28 *Werke* III (Schlechta ed.), 343–346.
42 John Richardson, "Nietzsche's Problem of the Past", 101.
43 Ibid., 102–103.
44 Ibid., 104.
45 Friedrich Nietzsche, "Unzeitgemässe Betractungen, Zweites Stück. Vom Nutzen und Nachteil der Historie für das Leben", *Werke* I (Schlechta ed.), 209–285, esp. 213. English from Richardson, "Nietzsche's Problem of the Past", 87.
46 Richardson, "Nietzsche's Problem of the Past", 91.
47 Nietzsche, "Menschliches, Allzumenschliches. Ein Buch für freie Geister", in: idem, *Werke* I (Schlechta ed.), Zweiter Band, I. "Vermischte Meinungen und Sprüche", Abt.: 223, 823. English from: Richardson, "Nietzsche's Problem of the Past", 91.
48 "*Alles, was der Philosoph über den Menschen aussagt, ist aber im Grunde nicht mehr als ein Zeugnis über den Menschen einer sehr beschränkten Zeitraumes. Mangel an historischen Sinn ist der Erbfehler aller Philosophen* ". Nietzsche, "Menschliches, Alzumenschliches", *Werke* I, Erster Band 2, 448. Emphasis Nietzsche.
49 Richardson, "Nietzsche's Problem of the Past", 107.
50 Allan Megill sees genealogy as an approach to past, present and future that is illuminating and frightening at the same time. He argues that it would force man "to think out from its beginnings every act that he wished to perform". And he continues: "to act without continually trying to make explicit the grounds and assumptions of one's actions . . . is an absolute necessity in both social and individual life". Megill, *Prophets of Extremity*, 83.
51 Richardson, "Nietzsche's Problem of the Past", 105.
52 Ibid. See note 30 of this chapter.
53 Richardson, "Nietzsche's Problem of the Past", 105. Richardson leaves out the last sentence of this quote from Zarathustra – The name of the gateway is written above: "Moment" – but this sentence is in my view not unimportant. It shows that the retrospection is conscious for us at a due moment, becoming then a tipping point for acting. In every life of every man in all times these moments will occur and that is what is meant by eternal return.
54 Intentionalism means the inclusion of unintended consequences. Nietzsche abolishes unintended consequences, because intentions do not exist in the world of becoming.
55 Nietzsche, "Jenseits von Gut und Böse. Vorspiel einer Philosophie der Zukunft", Abt.: 16 and 17, *Werke* III (Schlechta ed.), 26; English in: *Beyond Good and Evil*, Part I, Aphorism 17.
56 White, *Metahistory*, 345.
57 Richardson, "Nietzsche's Problem of the Past", 108.
58 Ibid., 109.
59 Small, *Time and Becoming in Nietzsche's Thought*, 151–169, esp. 157–158.

60 Ibid., 156–157.
61 Richardson, "Nietzsche's Problem of the Past", 110.
62 Kern, *The Culture of Time and Space 1880–1918*, 63.
63 Small, *Time and Becoming in Nietzsche's Thought*, 156–161.
64 Nietzsche, "Die fröhliche Wissenschaft", in: Schlechta, *Werke* II, Aphorism 341 (Das grösste Schwergewicht), page 202. Translation from Kern, *The Culture of Time and Space*, 86–87.
65 Small, *Time and Becoming in Nietzsche's Thought*, 145.
66 Ibid., 146.
67 Ibid., 152.
68 Ibid., 140.
69 R. Kevin Hill, "From Kantian Temporality to Nietzsche's Naturalism", in: Dries, *Nietzsche on Time and History*, 75–85, esp. 85.
70 Hill, "From Kantian Temporality to Nietzsche's Naturalism", 85.
71 This "time" is between quotation marks, because it belongs to becoming in the form of rhythm, tempo and intensity. It is not yet the completely realized time of appearances. See also the section "Past, becoming, evolution and time" of this chapter.
72 Hill, "From Kantian Temporality to Nietzsche's Naturalism", 78.
73 Dries, "Towards Adualism", 130–132.
74 Selves are also called by Dries: "will points" with the following structure: subject → affect → intentional object. Dries, "Towards Adualism", 129.
75 Ibid., 132.
76 Ibid.
77 Ibid., 132–133.
78 "*Dabei darf von jenem Fundamente aller Existenz, von dem dionysischen Untergründe der Welt, genau nur soviel dem menschlichen Individuum ins Bewusstsein treten, als von jener apollinischen Verklärungskraft wieder überwunden werden kann, so dass diese beiden Kunsttriebe ihre Kräfte in strenger wechselseitiger Proportion, nach dem Gesetze ewiger Gerechtigkeit, zu entfalten genötigt sind*". See Nietzsche, "Die Geburt der Tragödie oder Griechentum und Pessimismus", *Werke* I (Schlechta ed.), 21–134, esp. 133. My translation.
79 "*Sage aber auch dies, du wunderlicher Fremdling: wieviel musste dieses Volk leiden, um so schön werden zu können! Jetzt aber folge mir zur Tragödie und opfere mit mir im Tempel beider Gottheiten!*" Nietzsche, "Die Geburt der Tragödie", 134. My translation.
80 Richardson, "Nietzsche's Problem of the Past", in: Dries, *Nietzsche on Time and History*, 87–111, esp. 93.
81 Anthony K. Jensen, "Geschichte or History? Nietzsche's Untimely Meditation in the context of Nineteenth-Century Philological Studies", in: Dries, *Nietzsche on Time and History*, 213–230, esp. 222.
82 Orsucci, "Nietzsche's Cultural Criticism and His Historical Methodology", 28–29.
83 Jensen, "Geschichte or History?", 213–230, esp. 221. Here, I ignore the idea of Jensen that Nietzsche responded to the philological discussions about his time. See also: Ernst Schulin, "Zeitgemässe Historie um 1870. Zu Nietzsche, Burckhardt und zum 'Historismus'", *Historische Zeitschrift* 281 (2005), 33–58.
84 Nietzsche, "Unzeitgemässe Betractungen, Zweites Stück. Vom Nutzen und Nachteil der Historie für das Leben", in: *Werke* I (Schlechta ed.), 209–285, esp. 222–225. See also: White, *Metahistory*, 349.
85 Nietzsche, "Vom Nutzen und Nachteil der Historie für das Leben", 221. White, *Metahistory*, 349.
86 Jensen, "Geschichte or History?", 225.
87 Ibid., 226.
88 Nietzsche, "Vom Nutzen und Nachteil der Historie für das Leben", 225–229, esp. 228. White, *Metahistory*, 350.
89 Jensen, "Geschichte or History?", 223.
90 Nietzsche, "Vom Nutzen und Nachteil der Historie für das Leben", 227. White, *Metahistory*, 350.

91 White, *Metahistory*, 350.
92 Jensen, "Geschichte or History?", 223.
93 White, *Metahistory*, 350.
94 Jensen, "Geschichte or History?", 222–223.
95 White, *Metahistory*, 350.
96 Nietzsche, "Vom Nutzen und Nachteil der Historie für das Leben", 229. Jensen, "Geschichte or History?" 225 .

9
HUIZINGA AND THE HISTORICAL SENSATION

FIGURE 9.1   Kairos, Fresco, in the Palazzo Sacchetti in Rome (1552–1554)

Kairos

This picture shows a detail of a fresco in the Palazzo Sacchetti in Rome, made by Francesco de' Rossi of Salviati (1510–1563) between 1552 and 1554. It represents Zeus's youngest son, Kairos, the god of chance. Not completely visible is the balance Kairos holds in his right hand to weigh the precise moment for action. Kairos is the god of due time, but more than by the balance, it is symbolized by his forelock. This must be grasped to use the appropriate instant for change.

Kairos is the opposite of his grandfather, Kronos.[1] The latter is the god of eternal repetition, of continuity, of chronology, of the countable time of the clock. In my view, he also represents the empty, horizontal time of continuous advancing. Kairos, on the contrary, stands for an embodied time of change, for discontinuity, for the vertical time of rupture. This concerns the present as an interval between the past and the future in which, according to Heidegger, the "full moment" is revealed. Then Kronos is erased and a consciousness of a till-then-unconscious past arises, which has nevertheless shaped our existence. The Dutch philosopher Veronica Vasterling observes that in Heidegger's full moment the straight line of temporality changes into a loop.[2] The past meets us from the future, which occurs in its most extreme form in a post-traumatic stress disorder. Traumatic experiences in the past can then lead to deviant behaviour in the future. In my view, she speaks here of a kairotic time. In a more moderate form, this time contains moments of *Entschlossenheit*, which literally in English means "unlocking". Hidden aspects of our past are opened through *Entschlossenheit*. In a more figurative sense it means determination, which refers to the future as an *anfängliche Zeit*, an initial time, in which new insights and opportunities emerge.[3] These are the moments in life which the Heidegger expert Jonathan Rée calls "countless pathways of memory and anticipation".[4] Gadamer's *erfüllte Zeit* has the same connotation. His empty time is seen as continuity (*Dauer*), as a time that is available and measurable. *Erfüllte Zeit* is the time of an experience of farewell and beginning, which comes close to the moment between the past and the future as the borderline between two eras.[5] We experience this temporality in its most optimal form in the face of death. In the confrontation with the end, our life seems to pass in a flash.[6]

Heidegger's full moment comes close to Nietzsche's *Augenblick*. Remember how Zarathustra at the gate interrupts his quest to the future and takes a "moment" of genealogical reflection. Reflection means here *reculer pour mieux sauter*, laying bare the way wherein the will is suppressed but also opening the "way of greatness", in which we can change our life in the man or woman we "are". Nietzsche does not use the term "kairotic moment" in relation to the gateway. Yet Nietzsche knows about Kairos, as we will see in this chapter. He interprets him as the god of the "right moment", which fits in with the moment of the gateway.

Kairos is not only an initial moment of acting, it can also be the start of a new way of thinking, of looking to ordinary things in a completely new manner. This does not mean that it is always a conscious moment of choice. Sometimes it is a moment that takes us by surprise, giving the opportunity to make a choice. It creates an opening to an unpredictable and unimaginable future. This brings us close to the awe-inspiring sensation, Ankersmit elaborates on in his *Sublime Historical Experience*. Ankersmit's study observes how we lose the experience of reality in language. In that loss he detects a moment of "sublime indeterminacy in the relationship between language and reality", and he adds to it: "at that very moment the past makes its entrance in our minds".[7] That moment of historical experience "transcends . . . time as the Kantian *Anschauungsform*, defining [in a new way] our relationship to the past".[8] This becomes obvious in Proust's novel *In Search of Lost Time*, in which involuntary memories emerge. They show how Kairos lets the past to unexpectedly enter in our mind. But then something new is not far away. In this case it results in an uncommon and unusual "intrigue".[9]

The kairotic moment brings the historian another experience of the past than the one he gets when reading and interpreting historical documents. It moves him into the past, thus bringing the past and the present together. This "presence of the past" can be found in the studies of the Dutch historian Johan Huizinga. His "historical sensation" is the kairotic time that philosophers as Nietzsche and Heidegger think about. Historians like Burckhardt and Huizinga experience it and try to express it in their writings. As a result, they do not tell historical narratives but give representations of the past. Kairotic time brings Huizinga and Nietzsche together, although Huizinga is often critical of Nietzsche.

Differences between Huizinga and Nietzsche

Huizinga has several objections against Nietzsche.[10] The first concerns antiquarian history. Nietzsche grasps (genealogical) antiquarian history as "serving life by adding value to what is inherently valueless".[11] This comes close to a statement from the philosopher Theodor Lessing (1872–1933), to whom history is the *Sinngebung des Sinnlosen*. This is to say "meaning is given to the meaningless". Huizinga refers to Lessing's utterance and retorts that the historical discipline is *Sinndeutung des Sinvollen*, that is, "interpreting the meaning of the meaningful".[12] Although Huizinga does not mention Nietzsche anywhere in this context, he may be the real opponent here.

Huizinga's second objection concerns Nietzsche's evolutionary ideas, which start in mythical times and continue until his own days. Their main issue is the fission of humankind in a few empowered heroes and a majority of herd people. Huizinga, however, dismisses such an evolutionary and mythical thinking. He finds it contradictory to critical scholarship.[13]

As a consequence, a third difference emerges. Nietzsche explains his philosophy in *Thus Spoke Zarathustra* in literary images. Although Huizinga does not deny a metaphorical aspect to the writing of history – "scholarship cannot do without it"[14] – he criticizes historical explanation in literary forms. He argues against mythical and literary history in the third section of his essay "The Task of Cultural History":[15]

> The utterly sincere need to understand the past as well as possible without any admixture of one's own is the only thing that can make a work history. Judgment has to rest on an absolute conviction that what is described must have been that way.[16]

The fourth distinction concerns the fundamental rift between Nietzsche's and Huizinga's ideas about history and historical thinking. Nietzsche, dividing humankind in "supermen" and "herd people", gives history a philosophical substratum, based on a collective psychology. Huizinga's history is not based on an *a priori* philosophy or psychology. For him it is a discipline occupying itself with individuals without psychological patterns. According to Huizinga, the relationships between people are not ruled by "what man holds together inwardly, the 'psychosomatic principle of his actions', but by 'events' they share".[17]

The last difference between Nietzsche and Huizinga concerns an attack of the latter on the former. Living between the two World Wars, Huizinga refers to the dangers of the one-sided use of the Nietzschean concepts of the superman and the will to power.[18] They easily can be misused by the spirit of anti-intellectualism, which rules those days. He even wonders whether Nietzsche himself is not imbued with anti-intellectualism, referring to his statement that "abstaining from wrong judgments would make life impossible".[19] Huizinga, explaining the behaviour of medieval persons like several dukes of Burgundy, comes to the same judgement. Ironically he adds to it: "In our own day, in times which require the utmost exertion of national force, the nerves need the help of false judgment".[20] This addition is ironic and not meant to be positive. It also shows how Huizinga experiences his own time as burdensome.[21] His historical practice can surely be seen as a nostalgic flight into the past.

Misunderstanding and confirmation

At some points Huizinga has completely misunderstood Nietzsche, especially with regard to the antiquarian interest of historians. Huizinga argues at several places that Nietzsche disdainfully deals with that interest as "an inferior form of history".[22] Huizinga does not grasp Nietzsche's whole reasoning. Antiquarian history is part of a triptych of philosophical forms of history writing. If he had taken notice of Nietzsche's monumental and his critical history, he would have appreciated them. Nietzsche's monumental history, with its underlining of human nobility, would have found a connection with Huizinga's statement that "professional scholarship can never be for more than a few: it is aristocratic".[23] Huizinga perceives false sentimentalism and passion as belonging to the plebeian intellectual attitude. He argues:

> An aristocratic culture does not advertise its emotions. In its forms of expression, it is sober and reserved. . . . In order to be strong it wants to be

and needs to be hard and unemotional, or at any rate to allow the expression of feelings and inclinations only in elegant forms.[24]

This does not only adhere to Nietzsche's monumental history but also to his critical one, which wants to interrogate the past remorselessly.[25]

At some other points, Huizinga confirms a statement of Nietzsche. In "Een kleine samenspraak over de thema's der Romantiek" ("A small dialogue about the issues of Romanticism"), he ascribes to Nietzsche with regard to historical realism "an awakening from sleeplessness". The Romanticists – and Huizinga encloses Nietzsche in that category – manage "in seeing things historically" ("*in het historisch zien der dingen*"), which he indeed meant positively.[26] But there are more conformities between Nietzsche and Huizinga.[27]

Conformities between Nietzsche and Huizinga with regard to time

The most important agreement between Nietzsche and Huizinga is to be found in the field of temporality. Both have an almost common perception of time, consisting of eight aspects: first, a rejection of teleology; second, a wavy pattern, without being a romanticist one; third, a dualistic view at the past, being partly objective and partly personal; fourth, the recognition of the past as an experience, albeit an unaesthetic one; fifth, the view that the past is an ecstatic part of the present, thus bringing it close to the world of becoming; sixth, the use of metaphors to demonstrate the otherness of time-periods; seventh, the combination of the past and the present in "kairotic" time; and eighth, a cultural-anthropological approach, researching the past as being present.

Rejection of teleology

Huizinga is very critical with regard to Darwin's evolutionary theory.[28] He studies the concept of evolution in the second section of his essay "The Task of Cultural History". It gets the extensive title: "The concept of evolution is of little utility in the study of history, and frequently has a disturbing, obstructive influence." This title already demonstrates how he disapproves evolution and evolutionary theories.[29]

Huizinga explains that the origins of evolutionary thinking must be sought in the philosophical history of the eighteenth century. Its path is prepared by Voltaire, Turgot and Condorcet, with their views on the historical process in the form of transition and progress of stages.[30] In the first half of the nineteenth century, the concept is combined with that of organicism. It is then linked with the age-old, primitive, mythological-biological metaphor of endogenous evolution. "It is implicit in the ('organic') metaphor that the inherent tendencies are the ones that determine a process".[31] This is already unacceptable for Huizinga, but it becomes still worse in the second half of the nineteenth century. Then the concept of evolution is usurped by the natural sciences, thus "[t]he earlier vague, idealistic concept of evolution is now filled out by the biological aspect". And he adds: "Every situation, every relationship – in society and in nature alike – introduces itself *a priori* as a product of evolution".[32]

Ernst Bernheim's *Lehrbuch der historischen Methode und der Geschichtsphilosophie* displays for Huizinga how the biological "superficial concept of evolution" has been spread "among the rank and file in the historical discipline".[33] The main mistake of Bernheim, according to Huizinga, is to identify history with *genetische Geschichtsbetrachtung*.

> By making this concept "genetic" interchangeable with "evolutionary," Bernheim, it seems to me [Huizinga], makes a double mistake. He misjudges the full cognitive value of the older phases of historical study and overestimates that of modern historical thought, as if the latter were constantly maintained by a higher principle unknown in earlier times.[34]

The reproach Huizinga makes to Bernheim could also have been made by Nietzsche. The latter designs a naturalism that is fundamentally distinct from Darwin's. He thinks modern times are not of a higher order than earlier ones. All times are characterized by the same contradiction between supermen and herd people.

Huizinga's main demur against Bernheim is that

> the biological science . . . prescribes that the organism must be thought of as set off from its environment, that the constant interdependence of the object and its environment is only of token importance and the object's evolution be considered as a closed causal process.[35]

Nietzsche's *Genealogy* means the study of "becoming" as a process of continuous conflicts and concords, allowing influences from the outside.[36] Closed causal processes are not in Nietzsche's dictionary. For Huizinga, "There are no closed historical organisms. . . . Viewed historically, in every contact between man and man and between man and nature *everything* is an influence from the outside".[37] According to Huizinga, there is no inherent teleology in history, which is in agreement with Nietzsche's rejection of all teleology, especially the Hegelian one.[38]

A wavy pattern

Nietzsche's as well as Huizinga's undulating patterning of time is remarkable, because both do not want a return to a romanticist temporality. Nietzsche objects to it in his demurs against romanticist historicism, Huizinga in his objections against evolutionism. The undulation they aim at has nothing to do with a long-term wave of rise and fall. We know that Nietzsche's thinking about time consists of "hundreds of waves of wills and drives, moving forward, but without a clear aim".[39] It is an undulating pattern of contradictory powers, figuring in Kafka's parable of the two men opposing each other. It is a struggle to reach for the heights of the future, while at the same time fearing the increasing abyss of the past. It is the wave of a desire to become the superman or superwoman you want to be, while leaving your past of the safe herd behind. It is a process of two steps forward, one step back and the reverse.

The wavy time of Huizinga appears to be comparable to that of Nietzsche. His view on transition from the Middle Ages to the Renaissance is not one of rise and fall, symbolized by the rotation of a great wheel, but by "a long succession of waves rolling onto a beach, each of them breaking at a different point and a different moment".[40] Huizinga explains this image:

> Everywhere the lines between the old and the news are different; each cultural form, each thought turns at its own time, and the transformation is never that of the whole complex of civilization.[41]

The transition from the Middle Ages to the Renaissance is a period in which old and new coexist. Huizinga understands it as a struggle between the preceding old Middle Ages and the future-oriented Renaissance. Sometimes the more modern dominates but usually the Renaissance seems to be no more than a Sunday suit.[42]

The dualistic perception of the past

This coming together of the past and the more modern time is the result of Huizinga's third characteristic of temporality, namely the dualistic perception of the past, which is at the same time objective and personal. In a long text, Huizinga demonstrates how an objective and a subjective form of time come together. The passage runs as follows:

> This brings us to the essence of the issue. There is in all historical awareness a most momentous component, that is most suitably characterized by the term historical sensation. One could also speak of historical contact. . . . This contact with the past, that is accompanied by the absolute conviction of complete authenticity and truth, can be provoked by a line from a chronicle, by an engraving, a few sounds of an old song. It is not an element that the author writing in the past deliberately put down in his work. It is beyond and not in the book the past has left us. . . . Indeed this sensation, vision, contact, *Ahnung*, is limited to *moments* of special intellectual clarity, *moments* of a sudden penetration of the spirit. This historical sensation is apparently so essential that it is felt again and again as the true *moment* [my italics] of historical cognition.[43]

Remarkable of this quote is the fact that Huizinga speaks of the historical sensation as a moment in which the past penetrates the present. Past and present coexist. That is the same with the short waves between the Middle Ages and the Renaissance. Both temporal moments coincide. Another remarkable element in the text is that the historical sensation lies outside the history book. It belongs to the sphere of the *res gestae*, not to that of the *historia rerum gestarum*. The past is no longer only the result of historical insight. It can be experienced and as such it has an objective existence. However, the past as an experience is also subjective and personal. Nietzsche's genealogical encounter with the past has the same personal aspects.

The past as a personal, but non-aesthetic experience

The past as a personal experience is not a psychological process of re-experiencing; it is an authentic moment (*Augenblick*) of penetration from the past into the present, which gives a feeling of truth. Here we have Huizinga's fourth aspect of time. Gadamer would say of this personal encounter of the past and present: "it is the lifting of reality into truth" ("*Aufhebung der Wirklichkeit in die Wahrheit*").[44] It is truth by seizing the past for a moment, at which Gadamer would exclaim: "so it is".[45] Huizinga underlines that it is not a process or a part of it but the experience of a moment, which comes as a flash of lightning. In the following passage, Huizinga describes this experience:

> During long years I had a weakness for the print work by Jan van de Velde. Not a master of the very first rank. Certainly, it is costly to connect in the rigid copper with needle and burin so strong and great effects to so many tenderness and sensitivity, but . . . he's also still awkward, parochial, primitive in the decreasing sense, furthermore he repeats himself excessive. . . . There is a very important element in historical understanding, which might best be indicated by the term "historical sensation". . . . It may be that such a historical detail, in an engraving, but it could just as well be in a notary deed . . . suddenly gives you a feeling of an immediate contact with the past, a sensation as profound as the pure enjoyment of art, a (do not laugh) almost ecstatic sensation of not being myself, of a flowing over into the world outside me, of getting contact with the essence of things, the experience of Truth through history. . . . You walk in the street, and there plays a barrel organ. . . . You would be ashamed to call it musical enjoyment . . . but it is a pathos, an intoxication of a moment.[46]

Huizinga, understanding the historical sensation as a brief, sudden experience, also considers it non-aesthetic. This produces a remarkable agreement with Nietzsche, who writes:

> Perhaps our great virtue of historical sense is necessarily opposed to good taste, at least to the very best taste, and it is only poorly and haltingly,

only with effort, that we are able to reproduce in ourselves the brief and lesser as well as greatest serendipities (Glücksfälle) and transfigurations of human life as they light up every now and then: these moments and marvels (*Augenblicke und Wunder*) when a great force stands necessarily still in front of the boundless and limitless-, the enjoyment of an abundance of subtle pleasure (*Überfluss von feiner Lust*) in suddenly mastering and inscribing in stone (*Bändigung und Versteinerung*), in settling down and establishing yourself on ground that is still shaking.[47]

Nietzsche describes here the kairotic moment as grasped by an "abundance of subtle pleasure", which ought not to be comprehended as aesthetic. Nietzsche objects to an aesthetic pleasure in a more-or-less cognitive sense. The same goes for Huizinga's historical sensation. Both, however, do not reject it in the ontological sense. Nietzsche expresses it in the Dionysian aesthetics of a "ground that is still shaking", whereas Huizinga uses a phrase like an "almost ecstatic sensation of not being myself, of a flowing over into the world outside me, of getting contact with the essence of things".

The past as an ecstatic part of the present

In this context we come to the fifth aspect of the agreement between the concept of temporality of Nietzsche and Huizinga. Frank Ankersmit points out that Huizinga's historical sensation comes close to Nietzsche's *Rausch*, a description I approve, because Ankersmit refers to it as a "moment of enrapture and of being carried away by the intensity of experience".[48] *Rausch* has the effect that "[t]he determinations of space and time have changed; immense distances are grasped within one single overview and become only now perceivable, it offers an expansion of view comprising many things both close and remote".[49] Significant here is the change of the determination of time. The *Rausch* of Huizinga's historical sensation lifts him out of the ordinary trajectory of practicing history – romanticist history, I would say – and seems to pull him in the world of becoming, in which disappears the seriality of the past and present. Or, to put it in Ankersmit's words: "Historical experience pulls the faces of past and present together in a short but ecstatic kiss".[50] Nietzsche does not understand it in that romantic way but as a clash between "it was" and "it will be".[51]

In romanticist-historicism, past and present follow each other continuously. Ankersmit explains it as a constructivist form of history writing. "Constructivist" means here the want to contextualize historical events by telling what happened before and after them. He calls this the dimension of "horizontality", which he describes as "connecting through time the different phases of a historiographical tradition".[52] "Through time" refers to a diachronic approach which is, as I have explained, a romanticist form of temporality. To explain the opposite, Ankersmit refers to a "paradigmatic rupture". Huizinga's historical sensation is justified by the fact that Ankersmit perceives it as the Kuhnian "anomaly", which terminates a "period of normal science" and creates a "scientific revolution".[53] I can approve Ankersmit's need to underline the discontinuity in history writing, which is brought about by Huizinga's historical sensation. Nonetheless, Huizinga's "verticality" is not only a breach with the traditional, constructivist approach to the past but most of all the introduction of a new temporality. The "paradigmatic" rupture Ankersmit observes in Huizinga's historical experience (Ankersmit replaces Huizinga's "sensation" by "experience") consists in the elimination of the "horizontal" dimension and the bringing about of a "vertical" relationship between the historian and the past.[54]

Although Huizinga makes no difference between a *noumenal* world of becoming and a phenomenal world of *res gestae*, he yet approaches the past with great responsibility, wanting to reach objective truth. He argues:

> And as soon as the past is converted into the language of the novel, into the form of an imaginative literary work, the *sacred essence of history has been adulterated*, although the author may still believe that he is writing history.[55]

He feels something of the past inside him, although he is aware that the result of his approach can only be subjective. Thus Huizinga displays a certain piety with regard to the past, because it transcends his ordinary experiences. His piety is underscored by his historical sensation in which the past displays an impact on the present. Ankersmit is right in perceiving a difference between historical insight and historical experience.[56] Does Huizinga's historical sensation come out of something *noumenal*, breaking into the phenomenal world of the *res gestae*? Does Huizinga assume a world beyond the ordinary history of the *res gestae*? Ankersmit's *Rausch* with regard to Huizinga's historical sensation, points in the direction of something like Nietzsche's becoming.

Metaphoric language

We have seen how Nietzsche, since his *Thus Spoke Zarathustra*, wants to perceive the world metaphorically. Although he has an aversion of a romanticist historicism with a diachronic approach to time, he cannot completely comprehend the world without staticism. Therefore, he speaks metaphorically in spatial objects and actions. He climbs mountains and waits at gates. Huizinga's historical sensation also wants to make a rupture in the succession of events. He distances himself from the historicist *Nacheinander*, in which an organic view is substantiated. Nonetheless, and here I come to my sixth conformity between Nietzsche and Huizinga, metaphorically they cannot completely do without. This becomes obvious in the Dutch title of the *Waning of the Middle Ages – Herfsttij der Middeleeuwen –* in which an organic metaphor is enclosed. As we remember from Hegel and Ranke, we know that organicism regards subjects, actions and their rise and fall, but it does not mean that Huizinga and

Nietzsche have an organic view of reality or temporality. Huizinga uses his organic metaphor not to point at a fall of a civilization but to reveal the splendour of contrasting colours as an autumn shows. Both Nietzsche and Huizinga need metaphorical language to reveal a completely different temporality than the romanticist one.[57]

Kairotic time with Nietzsche and Huizinga

How can we connect Huizinga's historical sensation with the time of Kairos and especially with Nietzsche's perception of it? It makes sense to look first at a passage of Nietzsche in which he unfurls his perception of kairotic time:

> *The problem of those who wait.* Strokes of luck (*Glücksfälle*) and many incalculable factors are needed for a higher human, in whom the solution to a problem sleeps, to go into action at the right time – "into explosion" you might say. This does not usually happen, and in every corner of the earth people sit waiting, hardly knowing how much they are waiting, much less that they are waiting in vain. And every once in a while, the alarm call will come too late, the chance the event that gives them "permission" to act – just when the prime of youth and strength for action has been depleting by sitting still. And how many people have realized in horror, just as they "jump up," that their limbs have gone to sleep and their spirit is already too heavy! "It's too late" – they say, having lost faith in themselves and being useless from that point on. What if in the realm of the genius, the "Raphael without hands" (taking that phrase in the broadest sense) is not the exception but, perhaps, the rule? Perhaps genius is not rare at all: what is rare is the five hundred hands that it needs to tyrannize the kairos, "the right time," in order to seize hold of chance by grasping the forelock![58]

The "Raphael without hands" refers to a passage in Gotthold Lessing's *Emilia Gaiotti* (1772), where the painter Conti reflects on the importance of form above matter. He says:

> What a pity that we do not paint directly with our eyes. How much is lost on the long path from the eye, through the arm, into the brush, . . .Or do you think, . . . that Raphael would not have been the greatest artistic genius had he unfortunately been born without hands?[59]

"Raphael without hands" embodies the ideal of the Neoplatonic artist, who creates purely through his spiritual design, without the influence of the material or biological world. It is what the painter has in his brain, without the poor hands that imperfectly hold the brush. Nietzsche states that an artist or a scientist needs both the design and the matter. But most of all, he needs the kairotic moment to connect matter and design in an authentic way. Then he grasps Kairos by his forelock. Transferred to the historian, we can say that he may have a thesis and a score of books at his disposal, but without a moment in which he feels the truth of it, he remains belonging to the *Wartenden*. His study does not differ from all those other historians, who investigate the past. Huizinga grasps Kairos by his forelock by seeking his confidence not only in a thesis and hard work but also in what he feels inside himself from objective truth.

> From time to time one must rise above the limiting constraints of hard work, to feel again in the light of the theory that our powers are limited, but the history universal; to feel again the profound responsibility of the historian, who, the clearer he is aware that him is given merely a subjective understanding, the more firmly he will keep the eye focused on the ideal of objective truth, which rests in him.[60]

I think Huizinga's moment of historical sensation is similar to Nietzsche's kairotic *Augenblick*. Both see that moment as a specific experience, relating something noumenal with something that has a certain objectivity. For Nietzsche it means the link between design and material, for Huizinga it is the connection between sensation and knowledge. The latter sees the kairotic moment as the "right time" for a very special study of the past. Here the historian discovers that he has been immersed in the past, although he at the same time remains in the present. Historical insight and historical experience form together for Huizinga the 500 hands that give the historian "the chance to tyrannize Kairos".

Without using the name of the god with the forelock, Huizinga points in his *The Waning of the Middle Ages* to the kairotic moment, on which his study of the late Middle Ages is based. One day in 1902 he visits an exhibition of the so-called Flemish primitives in Bruges, with his friend André Jolles. In a quote from Huizinga's "*Het historisch Museum*" ("The Historical Museum"), we can find out what Huizinga must have experienced by observing the Van Eycks, Van der Weijden, Campin, Van der Goes and others:

> What am I enjoying here. Art? – Yes, but something else as well.[61]

That "something else" is the historical sensation of the late Middle Ages, which, combined with vision, leads to Huizinga's kairotic moment of truth, whereof we find the insights in his *The Waning of the Middle Ages*.

Kairos and Huizinga's *The Waning of the Middle Ages*

The opening phrase of *The Waning of the Middle Ages* indicates that we are entering a world completely different from ours:

> To the world when it was half a thousand years younger, the outlines of all things seemed more clearly marked than to us. The contrast between

> suffering and joy, between adversity and happiness, appeared more striking. All experience had yet to the minds of men the directness and absoluteness of the pleasure and pain of child-life. . . . Then, again, all things of life were of a proud or cruel publicity. Lepers sounded their rattles and went about in processions, beggars exhibited their deformity and their misery in churches.[62]

This passage shows how profound Huizinga's submersion must have been in the world of the late Middle Ages. In some quotes the presence of his sensation becomes even more visible. The first chapter, entitled "The Violent Tenor of Life", tells the story of the citizens of Mons, "who bought a brigand, at far too high a prize, for the pleasure of seeing him quartered". He adds a quote from a contemporaneous source, saying, "at which the people rejoiced more than a new holy body had risen from the dead".[63] Is this not the Dionysian world so dear to Nietzsche? It brings Huizinga to the kairotic moment of understanding the differences between the fifteenth century and his own time. Especially the fierce contradictions of the Middle Ages remind him of the intense colour contrasts of the autumn.

> Those Ages . . . knew nothing of all those ideas which have rendered our sentiment of justice timid and hesitating: doubts as to the criminal's responsibility; the conviction that society is, to a certain extent, the accomplice of the individual; the desire to reform instead of inflicting pain; and, we may even add, the fear of judicial errors. . . . [T]he Middle Ages knew but two extremes: the fullness of cruel punishment and mercy. When the condemned criminal is pardoned, the question whether he deserves it for special reasons is hardly asked; for mercy has to be gratuitous, like the mercy of God.[64]

Here lies the origin of the Dutch title of his book. Although *Herfsttij* has the organicist connotation of a fall, here it means the colour splendour of the autumn.

The comparison between medieval and modern justice signifies a close relationship between the historical experience and the kairotic moment of historical insight. The kairotic moment consists in the awakening from the ecstatic moment of submersion in the past, by which the historian gets insight in the otherness of it. Sometimes this otherness is fuelled by nostalgia and then it can take the form of a paradise lost. Ankersmit notices this nostalgia with the conservatives of the first half of the nineteenth century, for whom the Ancient Regime is definitively gone. According to him, they get a new identity, which exists in the loss of their traditionalist identity. They transform their loss and thus their nostalgia into historical knowledge, recreating it as a scientific discipline (Ranke) or as a historicist philosophy (Hegel). The conservative nostalgia leads to a romanticist historicism and a narrative way of history writing. Therein a move of rise and fall emerges, to bridge the distance between the past and the present in the form of an intrigue.

This is not the history writing Nietzsche and Huizinga aim at. The latter two want a discontinuous perception of history, wherein not evolution *through* time but a period *of* time is the main object of research. Ankersmit observes the same difference between romanticist historicism and Huizinga's discontinuous conception of it. He states:

> Even more so, the fact that Huizinga does not tell us a *story* in *The Waning of the Middle Ages* with a beginning and an end, but presents us instead, with a synchronic section perpendicular on the movement of time, shows that the decontextualization manifests itself no less in the form than in the content of the book.[65]

Decontextualization and historical sensation bring the past into the present. It makes a cultural anthropological approach possible, which is practised indeed by Huizinga in his *The Waning of the Middle Ages*.

The cultural anthropological approach

The Middle Ages, the seventeenth century, and his own age, the first part of the twentieth century, are the synchronic sections Huizinga is interested in. For Nietzsche the main periods are Antiquity and the Renaissance. They thus follow in the footsteps of Mink, who observes "to comprehend temporal succession means to think of it in both directions at once and then time is no longer the river which bears us along, but the river in aerial view, upstream and downstream in a single survey".[66] This deviation of romanticist historicism comes from the vertical approach of Kairos's time and of the historical sensation.

Verticalism means the articulation of the trace; the past has left behind in the present. It foregrounds the source and the event in what is called microhistory, and it considers some traces as discontinuous moments, as tipping points, leading to new periodizations.

See for instance the following passage of Jonathan Israel's *Radical Enlightenment*. It is illustrative for Israel's historical experience, which comes from it, as well as for the historical rupture Israel discovers in the seventeenth century:

> Spinoza then, emerged as the supreme philosophical bogeyman of Early Enlightenment. Admittedly, historians have rarely emphasized this. It has been much more common, and still is, to claim that Spinoza was rarely understood and had very little influence, a typical example of an abiding historiographical refrain which appears to be totally untrue, but nevertheless, since the nineteenth century has exerted an enduring appeal for all manner of scholars. In fact, no one else during the century 1650–1750 remotely rivaled Spinoza's notoriety as the chief challenger of the fundamentals of revealed religion, received ideas, tradition, morality, and what was everywhere regarded, in absolutist and non-absolutist states alike, as divinely constituted political authority.[67]

Israel states that usually Spinoza plays an unimportant role in the history of the Enlightenment. Does he attack here romanticist history with its articulation of continuity? Israel's confrontation with Spinoza, the man, his work and his followers, gives him a historical sensation by which he ascribes to him the start of a new period in history, the one of Radical Enlightenment.[68]

The time regime of romanticist historicism gives historiography the form of rise and fall. The kairotic time presents history in a discontinuous, metaphorical way as it can be perceived in microhistory and in "narrative substances", as Ankersmit conceives Renaissance, the Enlightenment and the French Revolution. Burckhardt, with his *The Civilization of the Renaissance in Italy* (*Die Kultur der Renaissance in Italien*), and Huizinga, with his *The Waning of the Middle Ages*, belong to this category of discontinuous, metaphorical historians.

The microhistorical and the metaphorical approach both result in thick descriptions of thousands of topics. Huizinga's work contains 22 chapters, while Burckhardt's has 6. However, in Burckhardt's study, the chapters are sub-divided into more than a hundred items.[69] In both works it is an avalanche of topics, and each is like a sparkling drop of water, clinging to Indra's web. They are, to put it in Leibnizian words, *monads* forming together the colligatory concept of Huizinga's autumn of the Middle Ages or Burckhardt's Renaissance. This is what is called "thick description". It refers to the work of the American cultural anthropologist Clifford Geertz (1926–2006), who describes cock fights at Bali without contextualizing them by explicit theories. He aims at a close network of relationships creating an image. Huizinga and Burckhardt work in the same way.[70]

Burckhardt and Huizinga[71]

Jacob Burckhardt, the Swiss preceptor of Nietzsche, opposes like Huizinga to the scientific objectivity of romanticist history writing. Although he was in the beginning a Rankean historian, in the end he detests Ranke's objectivist approach.[72] He also disgusts "world-historical ideas", as he states in his *Weltgeschichtliche Betrachtungen*. It is most likely he has Hegel in mind. Huizinga joins Burckhardt in his dislike of romanticist-historicist ideas. According to Ankersmit, both want "to offer cross-sections of the past, in as many directions as possible".[73] Peter Burke summarizes Burckhardt's anti-romanticist-historicist approach to history by the assertion: "Where others want to tell a story, Burckhardt's aim was to paint the portrait of an age".[74]

Both for Huizinga and for Burckhardt, this means an opposition to a diachronic history, shaped in terms of evolution and development. Burckhardt prefers a history of *Querschnitte*, of synchronic times. Maybe his disgust of romanticist history is even fiercer than Huizinga's. Ankersmit brings Burckhardt's dislike in connection with his profoundly felt link between life and history, which he transfers to Nietzsche.[75] Ankersmit observes that the Swiss has a great admiration for Eichendorff's novelle *Das Marmorbild*, which he regards "as the most subtle expression of experience of the Italian past". Burckhardt himself describes a fortuitous visit to the Santa Croce of Florence as a real historical experience.[76] He had liked to be born in Italy, the country and the culture he describes in his *The Civilization of the Renaissance in Italy*.

Both Huizinga and Burckhardt demonstrate a craving for the past they study. Huizinga acknowledges this by stating that it is most important for the historical researcher to achieve "the living contact of the mind with the old that was genuine and full of significance".[77] Burckhardt displays his affection with the past by requiring that a great historical subject "must [needs] cohere sympathetically and mysteriously to the author's inmost being".[78] Peter Burke explains Burckhardt's affinity with the urban culture of the Renaissance by his descent of a patrician family in Basel, which continues to rule that city until the 1830s. For that reason, the city-states of Renaissance Italy would appeal to him greatly. There is "an elective affinity between Burckhardt and his subject . . . stained by nostalgia for the world of his childhood."[79]

By stipulating the modernity of the Renaissance, Burckhardt articulates discontinuity between this period and the Middle Ages, underlining its continuity with Modern Times. According to the Swiss historian, the Renaissance is the beginning of new perceptions of the world, of the individual and of the state. Huizinga's perception of the fourteenth and fifteenth centuries in Burgundy, France and the Netherlands is in stark contrast with Burckhardt's view. Huizinga stresses the strong medieval character of those ages. They are even more chivalric and scholastic than the ages before. The Dutch historian searches for discontinuity between the Middle Ages and Modern Times and underscores continuity between the fourteenth century and previous centuries.

In his "The problem of the Renaissance", Huizinga confirms this thesis. There is no gap between the Middle Ages and the Renaissance. He asserts "on closer inspection, the great dividing lines might . . . prove to lie at least as clearly between Renaissance and modern culture"[80] In the eyes of Huizinga the Renaissance is a "Sunday suit" and as such a rather superficial phenomenon. "The [medieval] cultural development flows on underneath the Renaissance".[81] Huizinga ponders that Burckhardt overstates individualism and paganism and underestimates binding authority.[82] For Huizinga, "The spirit of the Renaissance is indeed much less modern than one is constantly inclined to believe".[83]

Burckhardt grasps the late Middle Ages in the metaphor of the Renaissance and considers them as a starting point for modernity. Huizinga uses the metaphor of the autumn to paint the same ages as still medieval. He brings the past into the present, loving the past more than his own present (the *Interbellum*). Burckhardt brings the past into the present because "Our topic is a past which is clearly connected with the present and with the future. . . . Actually, one ought to stress especially those historical realities from which threads run to our own period and culture".[84] While Burckhardt transfers the past into the present because of its resemblance, Huizinga does so because of its otherness. For both, it leads to a division of the past into continuities and discontinuities. The past is separate from the present, but it is precisely because of that separation that it is longed for out of nostalgia. Moreover, both adhere to the triptych: (1) historical experience, (2) a monadic, microcosmic approach to the past and (3) metaphorical comprehensibility.

Burckhardt, Nietzsche and Huizinga, as representatives of a kairotic time, differ in their application of it. Burckhardt unconsciously applies this in his writings, Nietzsche makes it explicit in his philosophy, whilst Huizinga does both. He reflects about kairotic time in the very original way of the historical sensation and also practises it in his studies. With Nietzsche, he is the co-creator, and with Burckhardt, he is the practitioner of a kairotic time regime.

Resume of parts III, IV and V

The parts concerning the three time regimes of the nineteenth century now have come to an end. Before we start with the final three chapters, I will give an overview of the time regimes so far. The culture of romanticist historicism is the heir of the Counter-Enlightenment, perceiving time as embodied. Because of this incarnation, the past is experienced as a burden for the present, which makes people hesitating to take responsibility for their future. Hence they put their fate in the hands of super-individual entities like states and estates, churches and religions. By participating in the state through estates and corporations, however, they consider it possible to steer the state cautiously in the right direction. By its organicist, political and institutionalist form, romanticist historicism develops a curvy perception of time, wherein each fall is followed by a rise and each rise by a fall. Thus, the rising time of the Enlightenment and of progress, disappears almost completely.[85] Hegel's time follows the same curve as the one of the romantic conservatives, albeit that reason and freedom still play a role in reality. As a consequence, his undulating time takes the form of a rising spiral. The undulating, embodied time of romanticist historicism remains homogeneous, linear and continuous, developing from the past via the present into the future, without a clear separation between them. However, the development of the idea is viewed from the present to the past (Minerva's owl), so the future remains without new content.

Tocqueville and Marx, like Hegel and the romantic conservatives, also feel time as burdensome. But the way they want to make it bearable differs fundamentally. Tocqueville wants to study the ever-growing egalitarianism in society, perceiving it as having an inevitable *telos*. His analysis is not framed in an organic but in a structural approach to reality and history. His *état aristocratique* and *état démocratique* are rather static models of society, designed to research the past and the present of France in his *The Old Regime and the Revolution in France*. He demonstrates the coevalness of past and future during the Ancient Regime by observing an anticipation of the future in the modernization of state and bureaucracy and by perceiving society as lagging behind. After the French Revolution the society progresses in modernization, whilst the political regimes of the Restoration and of the July monarchy are hanging back. In his *Democracy in America*, Tocqueville investigates democracy to explore Europe's future. Thus, his synchronicity of the non-synchronous dismisses romanticist historicism with its continuous flowing time. He constitutes a heterogeneous and discontinuous temporality. Its discontinuity comes to the fore in the role he ascribes to the French Revolution and to the distinction he makes between Europe and America.

Although Marx wants a society in which equality rules, he does not assume a growing egalitarianism, like Tocqueville. Equality can only be established in a communist society. Marx goes further than Tocqueville in resisting the idealist realism of romanticist historicism. He opens a new atomistic and economic field of realism whereof the state is only a part. His historicism is no longer holistic political, but reductionist, international and socio-economical, consisting of production forces, modes of production and production relations, ruling worldwide. Marx's perception of time is not linear and homogeneous, but analytical and heterogeneous, dissolving it in a coexisting of past, present and future. Like Tocqueville, he thinks about time as a societal synchronicity of the non-synchronous.

Nietzsche puts aside the continuous flowing time of the romantic historicists as he does with the discontinuous, heterogeneous temporality of Tocqueville and Marx. He designs a moving, cultural time of becoming, with heterogeneous moments. This so-called kairotic time has no *telos*, but time-knots, making the course of history contingent and the event a precious part of it. Thus, it results in a kairotic temporal approach, which opens the gate to a cultural-anthropological form of history writing. Even historiography itself is made dependent of a deeply felt experience of event(s), inviting the historian to grasp Kairos by the forelock, in giving a representation of (a part of) the world. Huizinga deepens kairotic time by his underlining of the historical sensation. Just like Burckhardt, he becomes the protagonist of a historicism of cross-sectional *Querschnitte*. Because Nietzsche as well as Huizinga have a strong contingent view on reality, seeing persons and events in their autonomy, their temporalities are tipping points in a stream of becoming. Links between them are construed through metaphors.

Now it is time to return to the Brandomian point of view, where concepts are identical with the inferences they stem from and where form and matter are one. Applied to the time of the modern that originates in the Enlightenment, it shows a temporality that is empty, homogeneous, diachronic, future-oriented and accelerating. *Historicist* times are embodied and burdensome by the revolutions from which they arise. These times are often more delaying or nostalgic than accelerating. Within historicist temporalities, the *romanticist time* is homogeneous and undulating, connected to continuing entities such as states, nations, institutions or civilizations. The time of the *synchronicity of the non-synchronous* is heterogeneous, discontinuous and connected to split and dichotomous formations of society. *Kairotic time* is also discontinuous and heterogeneous, linked to split and dichotomous cultures and mentalities, creating turning points in which horizontal developments interfere with vertical moments, giving developments a new direction or a new periodization.

190 The kairotic time of cultures

These three different temporalities, resulting from the nineteenth-century regimes of time, are so impressive that they proceed their (inferential) existence in the twentieth and twenty-first centuries. This means a revival of historicism next to modernism. Its practical consequences will be dealt with in the three final chapters of this book.

Notes

1 Also pointed to as Chronos. See Chapter 4, note 35. See also: www.waggish.org/2013/father-time-chronos-and-kronos/
2 The character of "'having been' arises, in a certain way, from the future . . . and in such a way that the future which 'has been' (or better, which is 'in the process of having been') releases itself from the present. This phenomenon has the unity of a future which makes the present in the process of having been; we designate it as *temporality*." Heidegger, *Sein und Zeit*, section 65. See also: Veronica Vasterling, "De rechte lijn en de lus", in: Grever and Jansen, *De ongrijpbare tijd*, 185.
3 See for this: Eelco Runia, *Moved by the Past: Discontinuity and Historical Mutation* (New York: Columbia University Press, 2014).
4 Jonathan Rée, *Heidegger* (London: Phoenix, 1998), 43.
5 Gadamer, *Über Leere und erfüllte Zeit*, 221–236. See also Chapter 3, note 11.
6 Heidegger, *Sein und Zeit*, section 65 and 68.
7 Ankersmit, *Sublime Historical Experience*, 177.
8 Ibid.
9 See Jansen, "Time, Narrative and Fiction", 23.
10 Johan Huizinga, *Men and Ideas: History, the Middle Ages, the Renaissance* (New York: Meridian Books Inc., 1959), 23 and 55 among others.
11 See the previous chapter.
12 Huizinga, *Men and Ideas*, 46.
13 Ibid., 41.
14 Ibid., 36.
15 Ibid., 39–51.
16 Ibid., 49.
17 Ibid., 57.
18 Johan Huizinga, "Het probleem der Renaissance", in: idem, *Verzamelde Werken*, vol. 4, (Haarlem: Tjeenk Willink, 1947), 231–275, 247 and idem, "Erasmus", in: idem, *Verzamelde Werken*, vol. 6, 3–194, 233.
19 Huizinga, "Herfsttij der Middeleeuwen", in: idem, *Verzamelde Werken*, vol. 3, 3–435, 293–294 or idem, *The Waning of the Middle Ages* (Mineola, NY: Dover Publications Inc., 1999), 215.
20 Huizinga, *The Waning of the Middle Ages*, 215.
21 See also: Huizinga, "In de schaduwen van morgen. Een diagnose van het geestelijk lijden van onzen tijd (In the Shadows of Tomorrow. A Diagnosis of the Spiritual Suffering of Our Time)", in: idem, *Verzamelde Werken*, vol. 7, 313–428.
22 Huizinga, *Men and Ideas*, 23 and 55.
23 See the previous chapter and Huizinga, *Men and Ideas*, 50.
24 Ibid., 47.
25 See the previous chapter.
26 Huizinga, "Een kleine samenspraak over de thema's der Romantiek", in: idem, *Verzamelde Werken*, vol. 4, 381–390, esp. 385.
27 Huizinga, "Twee worstelaars met den Engel", in: idem, *Verzamelde Werken*, vol. 4, 441–496, 457–458.
28 Huizinga, *Men and Ideas*, 32.
29 Ibid., 29–39.

30 Ibid., 31.
31 Ibid., 32. See also, 62.
32 Ibid., 32.
33 Ibid., 33.
34 Ibid., 34.
35 Ibid., 35.
36 See the previous chapter.
37 Huizinga, *Men and Ideas*, 36–37.
38 See the previous chapter.
39 Huizinga, *Men and Ideas*, 36–37.
40 Ibid., 282.
41 Ibid., 282.
42 Ibid., 270.
43 Huizinga, "De Taak der Cultuurgeschiedenis", in: idem, *Verzamelde Werken*, vol. 7, 35–94, esp. 71–72. Translation is partly by Ankersmit, *Sublime Historical Experience*, 120–121 and partly by me.
44 Gadamer, *Gesammelte Werke* I, 118. See also: John Sallis, "The Hermeneutics of the Art-Work", in: G. Figal, *Hans-Georg Gadamer* (Berlin: Akademie Verlag, 2007), 45–58, esp. 52.
45 It is in conformity with Merleau-Ponty's idea of chiasm. See Elm, "Schenkung, Entzug, schöpferisches Fragen", in: Figal, *Hans-Georg Gadamer*, 151–176, esp. 153–154.
46 Huizinga, "Het historisch museum", in: idem, *Verzamelde Werken*, vol. 2, 559–568, esp. 565–566. English from: Ankersmit, *Sublime Historical Experience*, 128.
47 Nietzsche, "Jenseits von Gut und Böse", Abt. 224, *Werke* III (Schlechta ed.), 134. English from: Gary Shapiro, "Kairos and Chronos: Nietzsche and the time of the Multitude", in: Keith Ansell Pearson (ed.), *Nietzsche and Political Thought* (London, New Delhi, New York and Sydney: Bloomsbury, 2013), 123–139, esp 135–136.
48 Ankersmit, *Sublime Historical Experience*, 121.
49 "*Die Raum- und Zeit-Empfindungen sind verändert: ungeheure Fernen werden überschaut und gleichsam erst wahrnehmbar; die Ausdehnung des Blicks über grössere Mengen und Weiten* ". Nietzsche, "Aus dem Nachlass der achtziger Jahre", *Werke* IV (Schlechta ed.), 347 Vert. Ankersmit, *Sublime Historical Experience*, 121.
50 Ankersmit, *Sublime Historical Experience*, 121.
51 See the previous chapter.
52 Ankersmit, *Sublime Historical Experience*, 125.
53 Ibid., 127.
54 Ibid., 125.
55 Huizinga, *Men and Ideas*, 49. My italics.
56 "Put differently, whereas in the case of the historical experience the historian's mind is formed by the past, historical insight is, on the contrary, a giving form to the past by the historian". Ankersmit, *Sublime Historical Experience*, 128.
57 Which is different from a fictional form of history writing.
58 Guy Shapiro, "Kairos and Chronos: Nietzsche and the time of the Multitude", 123. In German: Nietzsche, *Jenseits von Gut und Böse*, 192.
59 Gotthold Ephraim Lessing, *Samtliche Werke* (ed. Karl Lachmann and Franz Muncker; Stuttgart, 1886–1924, Reprint: Berlin, 1979), vol. 2, 381–384. English from Tanehesa Otabe, "'Raphael Without Hands'. The Idea of the Inner Form and Its Transformations", *Journal of the Faculty of Letters. Aesthetics* 34 (University of Tokyo, 2009), 55–63, esp. 58.
60 In Huizinga, "Het aesthetische bestanddeel van geschiedkundige voorstellingen", in: idem, *Verzamelde Werken*, vol. 7 (Haarlem, 1950), 3–28, esp. 26–27. My translation.
61 Quotation from Ankersmit, *Sublime Historical Experience*, 126.
62 Huizinga, *The Waning of the Middle Ages*, 1.
63 Ibid., 15.
64 Ibid., 16.

65 Ankersmit, *Sublime Historical Experience*, 134–135.
66 Mink, *Historical Understanding*, 56–57.
67 Jonathan Israel, *Radical Enlightenment, Philosophy and the Making of Modernity* (Oxford: Oxford University Press, 2001), 157.
68 See for a more extensive explanation of this passage: Jansen, "Research, Narrative and Representation", 85–87.
69 Harry Jansen, "Rethinking Burckhardt and Huizinga. On a Transformation of Temporal Images", *Storia della Storiografia* 70, 2 (2016), 95–112, esp. 98. In the English edition of Burckhardt's Renaissance study, the chapters are called parts.
70 See also: Harry Jansen, *Triptiek van de tijd, Geschiedenis in Drievoud* (Nijmegen: Vantilt, 2010), 69–70.
71 This section is a part of Jansen, "Rethinking Burckhardt and Huizinga".
72 Ranke, "Englische Geschichte, vornehmlich im 16. Und 17. Jh.", 103. English from Ankersmit, *Sublime Historical Experience*, 165.
73 Ibid., 165.
74 Burke, "Introduction", in: Burckhardt, *The Civilization of the Renaissance in Italy*, 5.
75 Ankersmit, *Sublime Historical Experience*, 171.
76 Ibid., 161–162.
77 Huizinga, *Men and Ideas*, 24.
78 Burke, "Introduction", 6.
79 Ibid., 9.
80 Huizinga, *Men and Ideas*, 268.
81 Ibid., 270.
82 Ibid., 271–273.
83 Ibid., 271.
84 Quoted from Ankersmit, *Sublime Historical Experience*, 165.
85 It subsisted only for some time (until 1931) in the Whig-interpretation of history.

PART 5
The time out of joint

10
HISTORICIST TIMES IN THE TWENTIETH AND TWENTY-FIRST CENTURIES 1

France and the Anglo-Saxon world

Historicism regained

In the second part of his *Time and Narrative*, Ricoeur discusses three time novels: Marcel Proust's *À la recherche du temps perdu*, translated in English as *In Search of Lost Time*; Virginia Woolf's *Mrs. Dalloway*; and Thomas Mann's *Der Zauberberg*, in English, *The Magic Mountain*.[1] Ricoeur brings all three under the same header of "discordant concordance".[2] He embraces in all three novels a single temporality, coherent and homogeneous, with an intrigue of rise and fall. Here we have the historicist time of Romanticism.

Unlike Ricoeur, I see a different time in every novel. Proust's *In Search of Lost Time* exemplifies a kairotic time, *Mrs. Dalloway* typifies synchronicity of the non-synchronous and *The Magic Mountain* epitomizes, but also ironizes, the romanticist time of rise and decline. I have elaborated on this in my "Time, Narrative and Fiction".[3] There are three reasons to mention it here. First, to show that historicism has created three different temporalities and not one, as Ricoeur assumes.[4] Second, to illustrate that time is already "out of joint" at the beginning of the twentieth century (and even earlier) and not at its end, as Aleida Assmann and François Hartog argue. Third, the three time regimes are important for bringing to light a continuation or revival of historicism in the twentieth century. Historicism is therefore not an outdated nineteenth-century philosophy of history but a way of thinking that is very suitable for the twenty-first century. Although the three times of the nineteenth century take different forms in the twenty-first century, as will be shown for example in Chakrabarty's *Provincializing Europe*, their foundations are laid in the three historicist time regimes of the nineteenth century.

The reception of historicism differs from country to country. In France, most historians, such as Langlois and Seignobos, are of a Rankean style. Tocqueville, as a non-academic exception, senses better the time regime of the society he lives in than his academic colleagues. Sometimes, however, that regime penetrates the university. Although he is a Rankean historian too, Michelet displays an interest in the synchronicity of the non-synchronous in his *Introduction à l'histoire universelle*.[5] Rankean historicism does not alter fundamentally in France's academic life until the beginning of the twentieth century. Then, change occurs under inspiration of Henri Bergson, Marcel Proust and Emile Durkheim.[6]

Only in the twentieth century, historicism wins in Britain the battle against the Enlightenment interpretation of history and its time of the modern. The miseries of the First World War give rise to the insight that time is embodied and a burden for progress. As a result, the Whig-interpretation of history is abolished and the ambiguous time of the synchronicity of the non-synchronous becomes dominant. It arises in Britain in the 1930s of the twentieth century and continues in India, England's most important former colony.

In Germany, discussed in the next chapter, the situation is more complicated. There, in the early nineteenth century, Enlightenment's approach to historiography has already been overcome by romanticist historicism. However, after the First World War various authors regard that form of historicism the great culprit of the German catastrophe. Especially Ranke is the scapegoat. After the Second World War, Koselleck completely leaves historicism to restore the Enlightenment's approach. His progressive form of history is coming to an end now. Aleida Assmann discusses its decline in her *Ist die Zeit aus den Fugen?*

I want to show that the three historicist time regimes of the nineteenth century are also visible in the twentieth and twenty-first centuries. So, when I discuss the introduction of those three temporalities in France, the United Kingdom and Germany in the last two centuries, I only do so with a few remarkable examples. Of course it is impossible and also unnecessary to fully work out the entire historiography of the three countries in one or two chapters.

Historicist temporality in France

As we noticed earlier, around the 1980s Ricoeur presses Braudel in the paradigm of a romanticist time of rise and fall. It illustrates how dominant Rankean historicism is in French historiography. Only at the beginning of the twentieth century, this is changing very slowly and not definitively, given the work of Ricoeur. The alteration at the start of the twentieth century appears to be due to the influence of the philosopher Henri Bergson, the novelist Marcel Proust and the sociologist Emile Durkheim.[7] The inspiration of the latter leads to the founding of the famous French *Annales* school in 1929. Two of its representatives, Braudel and Le Roy Ladurie, are creating alternatives for the romanticist temporalities, defended by Ricoeur. Braudel has become a clear representative of the synchronicity of the non-synchronous, and Le Roy Ladurie's work is related to kairotic perceptions of time.

In nineteenth-century France the Rankean dictum *Wie es eigentlich gewesen* is very strong. Its most remarkable representative, Seignobos (1854–1942), assures:

"As a historian one can ask questions, but it is dangerous to answer them". He comprehends questions as coming from the historian and not from the past itself. Thus, it is hardly justified for a professional historian to ask them. This means adherence to Ranke's "effacing himself".[8] Marc Bloch (1886–1944), belonging to the founders of the *Annales* school, gives Seignobos an "annalist" reaction: "A document is a witness, and like most witnesses, it seldom talks before it begins to ask questions".[9] Although Bloch's reflections on historical time remain fragmentary, he regards historical temporality as "a concrete and living reality". This is a description of an embodied time.[10] Seignobos's pupil Lucien Fèbvre (1878–1956) also attacks his former tutor by arguing that the latter blows "the cold wind of abstractions like those of . . . 'European politics' over the living history of states 'of flesh and blood'".[11] Both reactions anticipate the temporal changes, which Braudel and Le Roy Ladurie bring about after the Second World War. Braudel does so with a composite time, replacing the homogeneous time of the romanticist historicists. Ladurie does something similar, substituting the so-called dry, lifeless and political time of the Rankean historians by a "Dionysian" kairotic time. Despite these changes, a romanticist course maintains in French historiography, as Ricoeur shows. Even Braudel and Le Roy Ladurie remain historicists, although they are of a different kind than the more conventional historians.[12]

Fernand Braudel (1902–1985)

Fernand Braudel, in his *La Méditerranée et le Monde méditerranéen à l'époque de Philippe II*, analyses the Mediterranean world in the fifteenth and sixteenth centuries.[13] In the Introduction I pointed out that Ricoeur wants to read Braudel in the time mode of Romanticism, articulating the rise and fall of the Mediterranean in the fifteenth and sixteenth centuries. Although there are clues for Ricoeur's reading, I think it more adequate to look at his work through a time of synchronicity of the non-synchronous. The overall drama of the decline of an age-old Mediterranean economic, political and cultural system remains, but to Braudel, it is more a drama of structures and processes than of human intentions and actions.[14] Three mutual, related layers with different speeds of time play a role in his work: the immobile first layer comprehends the subsystems of the faster moving times of the conjuncture and the vibrating time of politics. (See also Tocqueville's systems approach.) Braudel himself underlines the importance of the first layer with a time, he calls *presque immobile*.

Braudel's layers of time are related to spaces. He connects the almost immovable time to landscapes, seas, climates or other spaces, which are characterized by difficult accessibility for human action. This is different in the layer of cyclical times, because time moves faster here, due to the change of seasons and the ups and downs of good and bad harvests. The spaces of these times are the cities with its markets and commerce and the associated human activities. The almost immobile time of the first layer changes in the second layer in a more human time of rise and fall. The cities are the spaces wherein Braudel situates an undulating time. The vibrating time of the third layer is ascribed to important governing centres, like Madrid and Istanbul. The connection Braudel makes between different times and special spaces is another way of underlining the synchronicity of the non-synchronous. This staging of time in space is intended to show the possibilities and impossibilities for human action. The impossibilities concern actions that are hardly effective, because of inaccessible spaces. The possibilities show spaces that enable rapid and successful actions. As a result, the romanticist temporal *mise and intrigue* is replaced by a spatial *mise en scene* (see the following).

The relationship between time and space is still more obvious in Braudel's *Civilisation matérielle, économie et capitalisme*.[15] Following the American economist and historian Immanuel Wallerstein, Braudel perceives a sequence of several world economies with different time-spaces, consisting of a centre, a semi-periphery and a periphery. The first world economy is Venice, with as semi-periphery the Dalmatian coast, the Greek islands and even Byzantium and as periphery the countries outside the Mediterranean coastline. The second, third and fourth world economy are respectively concentrated in Bruges and the Hanze, Antwerp and Genova. The fourth and fifth world economies of Amsterdam and London form the definitive shift from the Mediterranean to the Atlantic.

The periphery is featured by subsistence economies, with its very slow changes in material opportunities and conservative attitudes regarding the hardships of life. Braudel observes how in several regions around the globe peasants are cultivating their plots with the hoe.[16] It is a fairly fertile zone, so that people are not challenged to modernize, which is inherent in a survival economy. Time almost comes to a standstill. The world even has parts that are completely outside every temporality. The interior of India, for example, is such a quiet region.[17] Here we have the same perspective as used by Michelet and Babbage around 1830. They also consider India as the most remote country of civilization.[18]

Braudel's semi-periphery is marked by a *vie économique* with local markets, combined with yearly fairs. Life occurs in cities, subject to a faster time than in the periphery, but still a time of rise and fall. It resembles the conjunctural time of civilizations in his Mediterranean study. Life in the semi-periphery is not about survival but about earning money. Here, besides use value, goods and services also have exchange value.

The centres of Braudel's system consist of world economies possessing large banks, merchant firms and stock exchanges, all institutions of a calculating capitalism. In addition to use and exchange value, surplus value is created here by profit maximization and manipulation of underlying economies. In world centres reigns a world conjuncture with the fastest and most modern time, a *temps du monde*, which is the title of the third volume of his *Civilisation matérielle, économie et capitalisme*.

The slow time in the periphery, the faster time in the semi-periphery and the fastest world time in the centre exemplify a synchronicity of the non-synchronous in Braudel's second magnum opus. He explains this heterogeneous time by pointing to the Marxist term of the mode of production. As Marx himself, Braudel brings this concept in perspective by stating that world history is a sequence not only of modes of production but also of formations of society. Several modes of productions can coexist in such a societal formation, although one mode of production predominates the whole. Braudel then comes to his formulation of world history:

> the history of the world is an undivided procession, a cortege of coexisting modes of production which we are too inclined to think of following one another in successive historical periods. In fact the different modes of production are all attached to each other.[19]

To underline his perception of time, Braudel observes stepping stones of capitalism in the periphery and semi-periphery. Batavia in the Dutch East Indies, with its factories and colonies of merchants, forms an example of capitalism in the periphery.[20] It should be clear that Braudel here attaches the periphery with the centre of capitalism. His studies yield a form of temporality that is connected to conditions and spaces. They hardly concern continuing entities, figuring as quasi-personages.

In the Introduction I have made a distinction between the non-simultaneity of the simultaneous and the synchronicity of the non-synchronous. The former originates in the Enlightenment and belongs to an empty time; the latter fits in with the embodied time of Tocqueville and Marx. Some elements of the non-simultaneity of the simultaneous can be observed in Braudel's studies. However, the last sentence from the quote given previously is important here: "In fact the different modes of production are all attached to each other". This is of interest because in the Enlightenment's view, less and more progressive countries and regions are not linked to each other. It is Braudel's intention to follow Marx and his synchronicity of the non-synchronous. Past, present and future belong to each other, not in a homogeneous, sequential way, but in a heterogeneous and composed way. This creates new problems, especially with regard to colonialism and post-colonialism, because it creates for colonialism the problem of the "not yet". This will be discussed in the section about Chakrabarty's *Provincializing Europe*.

Ricoeur and Braudel

To understand Ricoeur's approach to Braudel's studies, we first have to explain his relationship to a homogenous temporality and then observe how it undulates. Ricoeur explains his homogeneous temporality in the two first volumes of his *Time and Narrative*, underlining it in the third part by an affirmation of Koselleck's space of experience and horizon of expectation. He agrees with Koselleck that the intrigue makes *Geschichte* a single course of events, whereby "histories" become "history" or better: "world history" (*Weltgeschichte*). Ricoeur remarks that already Droysen elaborates on this concept, connecting it with the idea of a history knowing itself.[21] It makes history a collective singular, a subject with force (*Macht*) "that propelled history according to a more or less secret plan".[22]

Ricoeur's interpretation of Koselleck's space of experience and horizon of expectation also reveals differences between the German and himself. Koselleck's "now" is a growing hiatus between an ever-faster disappearing space of experience and an ever-faster changing future. His future-oriented perception of history makes it something that must be controlled by human activity. Ricoeur does no longer believe in an accelerating march of progress.[23] Koselleck's hiatus becomes a crisis for Ricoeur: "torn between two fleeting horizons, that of the surpassed past and that of an ultimate end."[24] The mastering of history is for Ricoeur a utopian illusion.[25] Time remains a burden, which does not match with Koselleck's accelerating, progressive, modernizing time. In Koselleck's view, time is a straight line, Ricoeur makes it undulating. Ricoeur's waving temporality comes to the fore in his analysis of Braudel's *Mediterranean and Mediterranean World in the Era of Philip II*. It entails a special reading of Braudel's three layers of time. Ricoeur wants to read them in a way that highlights the second layer.

> The second part [= layer] is devoted to the long time-span . . . and serves to hold the two poles together: the Mediterranean, the referent of the first part, and Philip II, the referent of the third. In this sense it constitutes both a distinct object and a transitional structure. It is this last function that makes it interdependent with the two parts that frame it. . . . Thus, the second level is not only implied but actually anticipated in the first: geohistory is rapidly transformed into geopolitics. . . . Geography has so little autonomy that the boundaries of the space considered are continually redrawn by history.[26]

Braudel perceives the second layer as mainly dominated by economic conjunctures; Ricoeur underlines the political and cultural aspects of it.[27] The combination of economic conjuncture with political institutions and civilizations occupies for him the complete second layer of Braudel's study.[28] It makes time endless undulating.

An endless undulating time is, however, not an intrigue, as Ricoeur wants to have it. An intrigue has a beginning, a middle and an end, and therefore Ricoeur connects conjuncture to the two Mediterranean empires: Turkey and Spain. According to him, these two world powers are the main first-order entities and at the same time the super-personal actors that make the Mediterranean the stage as well as the super-personage of the fifteenth and sixteenth centuries.[29] They flourish in the fifteenth century, reach their apogee in the sixteenth century and undergo a decline in the seventeenth century.[30] After the battle of Lepanto (1571) – won neither by the Turks nor really by the Spaniards – they increasingly ignore each other out of impotence. This heralds the beginning of the decline of the Mediterranean system as a whole, being the centre of the world for more than 20 centuries.

Thus, the demise of the Mediterranean means more than the departure of two empires from the stage of the world. In Ricoeur's view, the main plot in Braudel's book is the undulating drama of the loss of a Mediterranean culture and the coming up of a new Northern culture of the Atlantic Ocean. That is how Ricoeur tries to make an undulating time of Braudel's synchronicity of the non-synchronous. Despite the *Annales* school, which is the big twentieth-century eye-catcher, Ricoeur illustrates with his interpretation of Braudel, the still strong attraction of romanticist historicism to the French historical discipline.

Le Roy Ladurie's Carnival in Romans

Carnival in Romans is about a kairotic time. It concerns two carnivals in the French city of Romans in the sixteenth century. Ladurie's book shows how a long, continuing stream of suppression of the lower layers of society is interrupted by rebellion. His vision seems to me similar to Nietzsche's *Wartenden* and its breakthrough by a kairotic time.

> In 1579, rebellious Dauphiné peasants attacked and destroyed country manors; the same thing happened during the Jacqueries of 1358 and again during the terrifying spring of 1789.[31]

What follows is also Nietzschean. Le Roy Ladurie analyses the carnivals of 1579 and 1580, in which two parties stand against each other: the commoners and the gentlefolk. He underlines its Dionysian aspects by stating the fact that between St. Blaise's Day (3 February) and Mardi Gras (16 February) in 1579, the commoners "held several great feasts, street dances, and masquerades and during the whole week in their street dances proclaimed that the rich of their town had grown rich at the expense of the poor people."

Guérin, the cunning leader of the gentlefolk, proclaims Romans *a pays de Cocagne*, the imaginary land of wine, flowing like water. In a decree he turns the entire world of food and drink upside down. This reversal implies that scarce foodstuffs can be bought for next to nothing, whereas the highest prices have to be paid for hay, wormy wine and rotten herring.[32] Guérin's main purpose is to illustrate "an order in which nature and society are soundly unchangeable or untouchable as to facts as opposed to myths".[33] When the doors of the Cockaigne castle are opened, only gentlefolk and those loyal to them are admitted. The commoners react with a parade in which funeral rites and the cry "Flesh of Christians, four *deniers* the pound" stand out.[34] The gentlefolk are named "Christians". Does this point to the given that the commoners, *avant la lettre*, have a more Dionysian view on reality?

The handling of time seems to confirm that. The term "Mardi Gras" refers to a change from a solar calendar into a lunar one. Monday February 15 becomes

Lundi Gras and February 16, the day before the beginning of Lent, Mardi Gras.[35] Regarding these things Ladurie remarks:

> Time flowed normally during the year, then ran briefly in reverse during the festive period, returning to its normal flow during the course of the following year or season. This paradigm of alternation harmonizes with the immediate experience of time flow (night and day, life and death, and so forth). The festival supposes a first "preliminary" ... phase (A), setting it off from time as experienced in normal life, or during the past year. A second or "liminary"(B) phase, is the transitional period which the threshold into festive or sacred time is crossed, a quick swing of the pendulum, into time running backwards or *role reversal* properly speaking. Finally a third phase (C) is one of *reintegration* or aggregation into profane or ordinary time, which will prevail until the next alternation and so on.[36]

Here Ladurie refers to a festive – and even ecstatic – moment in the Nietzschean sense of a kairotic time. The carnivals do not belong to a homogeneous line of events, in which there is a certain continuity with what happens before and after them. They are not to be considered as a rise or decline of a modernizing or traditionalizing trend during the Ancient Regime. The carnivals in Ladurie's Romans are discontinuous events, where the well-to-do maintain the past and ordinary people look ahead, searching for a better world to live in. The carnival's reversal of time symbolizes this in two ways. The commoners want to overturn the existing world, whereas the gentlefolk want to demonstrate the impossibility of such a change.

Le Roy Ladurie does not place the two carnivals neither in the frame of an undulating line, like Ranke, nor as a synchronicity of the non-synchronous, like Tocqueville. Ladurie does not contextualize the carnivals either, by placing them in a long evolutionary and undulating story from the Middle Ages into modernity. The carnivals are moments in time, in which something special happens, comparable to Nietzsche's experience at Silvaplana. It is a transcendence from the time of the clock and of the historicist diachronic and synchronic times of the first half of the nineteenth century.

Most historians comprehend the popular revolts as reactionary, "opposed to the growth of centralized government and the modernizing force, the progress it represented for society as a whole".[37] Ladurie rejects that time of advancement; he chooses to see the carnivals in the light of an embodied, kairotic time, taking sides with the losers, perceiving them as his contemporaries. As a former Marxist, he sympathizes with the lawyers of the South of France in the sixteenth and early seventeenth centuries, who fought with the commoners against the tax exemptions of the nobility.[38] He considers them as forerunners of his own time.[39]

This brings Huizinga's historical sensation in memory, being involved in the past he describes. Just like Huizinga, Ladurie tells the carnival stories from an almost participatory research approach, as a cultural anthropologist would do.

This is far removed from Ranke's "effacing myself". He achieves it in particular by highlighting the Dionysian aspects of the carnivals, which makes them a general human experience. His history writing implies an identification of past and present as expressed in a kairotic time. This historicist temporality, however, differs from both Ricoeur's romanticist undulating time and Braudel's synchronicity of the non-synchronous.

With Braudel's and Le Roy Ladurie's studies, Ricoeur's endeavour to press all historiography in the romanticist time of rise and fall can be rejected. Ricoeur's perception of time is ruled by the idea of discordant concordance, resulting in a homogeneous temporality. Neither Braudel's nor Le Roy Ladurie's works fit in that temporal straitjacket.[40] All this illustrates that already in nineteenth-century France, a romanticist historicism (Seignobos) can be observed, and that in the twentieth century, all three historicist times are represented.

The Anglo-Saxon way to historicism

The Whig-interpretation of history

At the start of Chapter 7, I have been denouncing Hölscher's idea that the First World War is the great rupture in the thinking about time. To me this already happens around 1830. However, Hölscher's view is true for Great Britain. On the continent the time regime of the Enlightenment disappears at the beginning of the nineteenth century, but the Enlightenment's time regime survives in nineteenth-century Great Britain.

Henry Hallam (1777–1859) writes a *Constitutional History of England from the Ascension of Henry VII to the Death of George II* (1827). In his introduction to Hallam's extensive study in three volumes, J. Morgan states:

> For him [Hallam] the thoroughly upright and enlightened man of the seventeenth century was not intrinsically different from the thoroughly upright and enlightened man of the nineteenth; the one concession he makes to time is that the historian is probably in a better, not in a worse, position to judge than the men of whom he writes – if only because he is more detached.[41]

Morgan feels that Hallam is one of the most explicit users of a homogeneous, empty temporality, which we discussed before in the chapter about the Enlightenment. According to Morgan the only difference between the past and the present is the improved consciousness of people in later days. Past-nows and present-nows are almost identical; they only differ by some form of progress. Hallam puts this into words as follows:

> England, more fortunate than the rest, had acquired in the fifteenth century a just reputation for the goodness of her laws and the security of her

> citizens from oppression. This liberty had been the slow fruit of ages, still waiting a happier season for its perfect ripeness, but already giving proof of the vigour and industry, which had been employed in its culture. I have endeavoured, in a work of which this may in a certain degree be reckoned a continuation, to trace the leading events and causes of its progress.[42]

The roots of England's liberty are constantly pushed to a further afield past. Hallam sees the Tudors as its founding fathers. Edward Freeman (1823–1892) marks its origin with William the Conqueror. He perceives similarities between William the Conqueror and William of Orange, calling the latter "the Deliverer". According to Freeman both are "the fellow-workers in the same cause". Their "revolutions" work for the same end: "the continuous being of English law and of English national life".[43] Before Freeman, John Mitchell Kemble (1807–1857) already suggests that there is continuity between the political institutions of the Anglo-Saxons and the Norman kingdom.[44]

In his *Short History of the English People* (1874), John Richard Green (1837–1883) refers to the Teutonic migrants from northern Germany as the direct "democratic" forebears of the Victorians. It illustrates how the past "now" does not essentially differ from the present "now", which is one of the main features of the Enlightenment's temporality. Michael Bentley in *Modern Historiography* points to the fact that most of the so-called Whig-historians are Christian, approaching their stories "from the standpoint of having Good News to relate". Bentley argues that their thinking in terms of progress is not yet harmed by "the barbarisms of the Somme and Paschendaele", the great slaughters of the First World War.[45]

Throughout the nineteenth century, English historiography is characterized by the so-called Whig-interpretation. Its definite end is highlighted by Herbert Butterfield's *The Whig Interpretation of History* in 1931.[46] To him the First World War is the decisive event to stop the optimism of the nineteenth century. Historians no longer perceive their own time as the best of all times, let alone as a yardstick for assessing past performances. The battles at the Somme and in the Flander Fields make Butterfield feel that it is no longer allowed to observe past centuries from the present:

> Real historical understanding is not achieved by the subordination of the past to the present, but rather by our making the past our present and attempting to see life with the eyes of another century than our own.[47]

This is Ranke *redivivus* with his *Jede Epoche ist unmittelbar zu Gott*.[48] Each era has to be understood by the norms of its own time and not by the values of a later stage. As Ranke, Butterfield is against the idea of progress in history. The reason Butterfield writes his essay is inconvenience with regard to historians who use their work to judge the past for its benefactors and malefactors. Another reason is the abridgement functioning of "progressive" history.

> The theory that is behind the Whig-interpretation – the theory that we study the past for the sake of the present – is one that is really introduced for the purpose of facilitating the abridgement of history; and its effect is to provide us with a handy rule of thumb by which we can easily discover what was important in the past. . . . [I]t serves to simplify the study of history by providing an excuse for leaving things out.[49]

Butterfield points here to the simplified, empty nature of time in the Whig-interpretation of history. The Whig-historians write inside an English time regime, in which a homogeneous, continuous progressing temporality is still not contested and thus feels as normal.[50]

Virginia Woolf's Big Ben and the non-synchronicity of Mrs Dalloway's protagonists[51]

Before Butterfield, the time novel *Mrs Dalloway* (1925) of Virginia Woolf already refers to a historicist temporality, albeit to another type of it than the Rankean, romanticist one. Here it is worthwhile to dive a bit deeper in her story and analyse its temporal aspects.[52] Ricoeur does so in the second volume of his *Time and Narrative* by posing the crucial question: "Overall, may we speak of a single experience of time in *Mrs. Dalloway*?"[53] His answer is affirmative. Above, I refer to Ricoeur's reading of Braudel, pressing the latter in the first volume of his *Time and Narrative* in a homogenous time of rise and fall. In the second volume, he does the same. There he interprets *The Magic Mountain, Mrs Dalloway* and *Remembrance of Things Past* as *Bildungsromane*, as novels about someone's formative years. He depicts Clarissa Dalloway as learning about herself and the world she lives in. According to Ricoeur, there is only one homogeneous and continuous temporality in all three novels:

> It is clear that a discontinuous structure suits a time of dangers and adventures, that a more continuous, linear structure suits a *Bildungsroman* where the themes of growth and metamorphosis predominate.[54]

Maybe Virginia Woolf's *Mrs. Dalloway* is a *Bildungsroman*, but it does not expose the continuous time of rise and decline, as Ricoeur likes to have it. It displays much more the ambiguous time, put into words by Tocqueville and Marx in the nineteenth century. This is Woolf's way to get rid of the time of the modern, so dear to the Whig-interpretation of history.

Woolf tells the story of one day in the life of Clarissa Dalloway, a woman in her 50s. That evening she is hosting a party. Her husband is an honourable Member of Parliament and her guests are therefore among London's upper class. London in 1923 still is the centre of an empire, stretching from Western Europe to India. Westminster's Big Ben plays a crucial role in *Mrs. Dalloway*. It makes the non-synchronous time of the inner stream of consciousness of the protagonists of Woolf's novel synchronous with the time of the clock and the chronological world time of monumental history. Here we have Koselleck's "time of the modern", epitomized by London as "the admirable marble decor of the capital" of a great Empire.[55]

In the morning, walking through the streets of London, Clarissa meets Dr. Bradshaw, whom she explicitly asks not to forget to come to her party. Mr. Bradshaw will spoil that party by telling all the guests about Septimus Warren Smith's suicide. Clarissa sees that same person through the window of the flower shop, though she is completely unaware of his existence, because he does not belong to her circle. Nevertheless, she is connected to him via Dr. Bradshaw, who is among Clarissa's acquaintances and also involved in Septimus Smith's treatment. In Woolf's novel, the rich and the poor depend on one another, despite being unaware of one another's existence. It looks to me a Marxian view of the world.[56]

Peter Walsh is another link. He is Clarissa's former sweetheart and will visit her that afternoon. Then Clarissa makes clear that there is no future for both of them. In a rather emotional state, Peter meets in a park Septimus Smith, who was a soldier in the First World War. His life is ruled and ruined by shell shock. For Peter, without Clarissa, there is no happy future; for Septimus, there is no future at all. They both lead an existence as Marx describes in his dissertation as the atomism of Democritus.

Like Clarissa, Peter does not know Smith. Their encounter in the park is one of the many moments of synchronicity of the non-synchronous in *Mrs. Dalloway*. Clarissa and Septimus, noticing an airplane advertising "Kreme Toffee" at the same time, experience another moment of synchronicity. The same events, simultaneously perceived by different characters and accompanied by Big Ben, sonorously striking the half and full hours, indicate synchronicity. But if we look at the inner experience of the two main protagonists, Clarissa and Septimus, it is a non-synchronous time. Clarissa's stream of consciousness is the expectation of her party that evening, an orientation towards the near future. This is in stark contrast to the spectral remembrance which haunts Septimus's mind. His fate is determined by his traumatizing wartime experiences, which force him to remain in the past. He commits suicide, for death is the only escape from that unbearable, monumental time. To a lesser degree, Peter Walsh has to stay in the past because Clarissa remains unattainable. Maybe that is why he cannot come loose from her; he is trapped in the "ecstasy of her presence".[57]

Clarissa's joyful expectation of her party has its counterpoint in Septimus's horrible past. However, Clarissa is also an atom in the Marxian sense of the word. "The same horror dwells in her, but unlike Septimus, she will confront it, sustained by an indestructible love for life".[58] Septimus is, as it were, a Democritian atom, whereas Clarissa's atomism is Epicurean, because she becomes self-assured. Notwithstanding the burden of "lost events" in the past, Clarissa's lust for life wins, whereas Septimus's lust for life is defeated. All protagonists experience, however, not a "Whig" time of progress but the burdensome time of historicism.

Ricoeur explains that there is only one time in Woolf's novel, but his assertion remains a bit vague:

> The experience of time is neither that of Clarissa nor that of Septimus; it is neither that of Peter nor that of any other character. Instead, it is suggested to the reader by the reverberation . . . of one solitary experience in another solitary experience.

According to Ricoeur the reverberation makes the experience of time in *Mrs. Dalloway* holistic.[59] He thus overlooks the different forms of atomism in which Clarissa, Septimus and Peter are caught. His inclination to interpret the experience of time without a "search for sources" results in missing Marx's synchronicity of the non-synchronous in *Mrs. Dalloway* and therefore the heterogeneity of the novel's temporality.[60]

Mrs Dalloway can still be read in another way, as a thought-experiment, making Woolf's personal and internal "soul-view" an external worldview. It consists of projecting on the novel the global problem of development and underdevelopment. My approach contains no judgement with regard to the tenure of Woolf's novel. It only functions as a clarification concerning the problems I want to discuss hereafter. By doing so, the question arises whether the synchronicity of the non-synchronous must be considered as a simultaneity in which every protagonist may have his or her own development into maturity or that Clarissa's zest for life becomes a kind of standard that other protagonists have to meet. By making Clarissa the main protagonist of her novel, Woolf suggests the latter view. This suggestion involves that the temporality of synchronicity of the non-synchronous, applied to societies, has as its main function to lift backward societies up to the most modern ones. It raises the problem of how the transition takes place from traditional societies, "trapped in the past", to modern societies that "look ahead". This view is attacked by the Indian historian Dipesh Chakrabarty in his *Provincializing Europe*.[61]

Provincializing Europe

In my opinion, Chakrabarty is one of the heroes of historicism. That seems strange, because he starts his *Provincializing Europe* with a very critical approach of it.[62] He rejects historicism firstly because it denies synchronicity. He draws this idea from Johannes Fabian, who opposes the idea that countries outside of Europe are not synchronic with the West, because they lag behind in modernity. Secondly, it results in a "not yet", because the European powers continue to rule the non-Western world in colonial times, assuming that they are not modern enough to have self-rule. With regard to colonial societies, Chakrabarty observes that even Marx is embedded in the language of "remnants" and "survivals" too. That is why Chakrabarty is sceptical about European historicism. He states that even European Marxism is a form of historicism that places colonies in "the waiting room of history".[63] Important is his conclusion that the theory of uneven development goes hand in hand with the "dated grid of an homogenous empty time".[64] Here we see what Chakrabarty understands by historicism. It is a Western philosophy in which the time of the modern dominates. In my redefinition of historicism, I reject identification historicism with a single homogeneous, and above all with an empty, temporality. My historicism comes close to what Chakrabarty calls the Heidegger's hermeneutic tradition.[65] He combines it with a form of Indian Marxism that is critical of capitalist modernization.

This double-sided historicism is applied and epitomized in his so-called subaltern, Bengal studies. On the one hand Bengal is embedded in the global, future-oriented history of capitalism and on the other in a history of its own. Thus he creates a synchronicity of the non-synchronous, whereby global history is referred to as History$_1$ or H_1 and the traditional Bengali stories are denoted as H_{2s}. H_1 is characterized by abstract labour, expressed in money, machines and commodity, but also in emancipatory aspects like opposition to labour conditions, citizenship and equality before the law. As such it leaves much room for non-capitalist elements: the H_{2s}. And Chakrabarty summarizes:

> Globalization does not mean that History$_1$, the universal and necessary logic of capital, so essential to Marx's critique, has been realized. What interrupts and defers capital's self-realization are various History$_{2s}$ that always modify History$_1$ and thus act as our grounds for claiming historical difference.[66]

Here we see the same synchronicity of the non-synchronous and their interaction as we have observed in the chapter about Marx.

Chakrabarty exemplifies the interaction between H_1 and H_{2s} in things like *adda*. It concerns a small history of "careless talk with boon companions". He underlines that when H_1 has room for sub-alternative histories, H_{2s} have it for modernity. Already in the definition of *adda*, traditional and modern elements come together: it is a "dwelling-place" and a "club" at the same time. "Dwelling-place" refers to something very old as "a settlement suggesting perhaps a dialectic of settlement and nomadology", and "club" refers to something modern, an English club.[67] The talks inside *adda* are also about nostalgic subjects and about capitalist and feminist modernity.[68] Pasts and futures coexist in the present and constitute the present: "whatever the nature of these pasts that already 'are,' they are always oriented to futures that also already 'are'".[69] Here we have the synchronicity of the non-synchronous together with a kairotic time, in which the past and the future coexist in the present.

People "living in" H_{2s} have to deal with "the metanarrative of progress" (H_1).[70] The "belief" in it is wanted to satisfy modern bureaucracies and to participate in the universal language of sociology.[71] But that belief, how indispensable it may be, remains inadequate. In the disenchanted, secular, modernizing history that "Europe" introduces in India, stories about humans' actions have to be intertwined with agency of gods and spirits. The main problem is to translate the diverse, enchanted world of the Indian and its so-called pre-capitalist time in the disenchanted language of sociology and economy.

Chakrabarty's heterogeneous temporality of synchronicity of the non-synchronous shows two important differences with the heterogeneous time I explained in the reading of Tocqueville, Marx and Braudel. First, he abandons the idea of transition from a less modern world into a more modern one. The past has no need to disappear, because it is a brake on progress. Chakrabarty even abhors the idea of a past that must be overcome. Colonizing countries use it as a "not-yet" to postpone decolonization. He accepts completely a traditional past, concomitant with the modern world of capitalism. There is no necessity to deny the existence of superhuman actors, because it is incompatible with modern science. Chakrabarty wants the so-called past to be a non-assimilable part of the present, so that there happens to be a temporality in which nonhumans and humans coexist.[72]

The second difference with the former heterogeneous time is how synchronicity of the non-synchronous is concentrated in a now that is embodied with the past and the present, which is not an empty point of time as with Aristotle or Kant. Even the future is embodied in the present, because it aligns itself with History$_1$, with its future-oriented logic and its Enlightenment universals.[73] Chakrabarty refers to Heidegger when he states that we "have a fore-conception of the fact that we live amid 'futures' that already are and which cut across the future, which is cast in the mold of a "will be".[74] Nietzsche also comes into view here.

In Chakrabarty's *Provincializing Europe*, Heidegger functions as a kind of kairotic justification for his subaltern histories. They voice the past (*adda* and the belief in gods as actors in history) to inspire present historians to resoluteness for the future in conserving valuable traditions inside a modernizing and globalizing world. Resoluteness (*Entschlossenheit*) however also implies criticism of the so-called "dead wood of the past", like the caste-system, girl-marriage or widow-burning. But Chakrabarty does not want H$_1$ to be the only form of history writing, because it has an objectifying relationship to a past, that "retains a power to haunt and deliver the shock of the uncanny".[75] In the subaltern histories still exist another past "encountered by capital as antecedents but not as belonging to its own life-process".[76]

Chakrabarty's Heideggerian approach is important, because it illuminates the essential features of a historiography, written in the kairotic mode of time, besides the synchronicity of the non-synchronous. These histories are micro-historical, because they are embodiments of a kairotic temporality of time nodes. Chakrabarty gives some examples of the manifestation of such a Heideggerian "now". He refers to the Indian Nobel Laureate physicist C. V. Raman, who embodies a "double temporality" of past and future by rushing home from his laboratory in the 1930s to "take a ritual bath ahead of a solar eclipse". When questioned about this, the physicist is reported to have simply stated: "'the Nobel Prize'? That was science, a solar eclipse is personal".[77] Chakrabarty affirms that Raman and others are serious scientists. "Yet they did not need to totalize through the outlook of science all the different life-practices within which they found themselves and to which they felt called".[78]

For history writing, this means that the past is not over and that the present is non-contemporaneous with itself.

> Thus what allows historians to historicize the medieval or the ancient is the very fact these worlds are never completely lost. We inhabit their fragments even when we classify ourselves as modern and secular. It is because we live in time-knots that we can undertake the exercise of straightening out, as it were, some part of the knot. . . . [H]ence the Bengali word shomoy-granthi, shomoy meaning time and granthi referring to joints of various kinds, from the complex formation of knuckles on our fingers to the joints on a bamboostick.[79]

Here Nietzsche's kairotic time-knots are displayed in an Indian setting. We will see something similar in the *Jetztzeit* of Walter Benjamin, a remark that completes the British historicist temporality and introduces the German one.

Notes

1 There exists a translation entitled: *Remembrance of Things Past* (transl. C. K. Scott Moncrieff, Terence Kilmartin and Andreas Mayor; New York: Random House, 1981). This one is used by Ricoeur in his *Time and Narrative*, vol. II, 100–152. I have used: M. Proust, *In Search of Lost Time* (transl. Andreas Mayor, Terence Kilmartin and D. J. Enright; New York: Modern Library, 1999), esp. vol. IV. Time Regained. Thomas Mann, *Der Zauberberg* (Michael Neumann ed., Band 5 / 1–2. Teil; Frankfurt a. M.: S. Fischer, 2002). Virginia Woolf, *Mrs Dalloway* (Adelaide: University of Adelaide, 2015). See also: https://ebooks.adelaide.edu.au/w/woolf/virginia/w91md/
2 Ricoeur, *Time and Narrative*, vol. II, 101.
3 Jansen, "Time, Narrative and Fiction", 1–24.
4 I analyse two of the three time models in relation to urban history in my *The Construction of an Urban Past*. It relates to the romantic time of rise and fall and the ambiguous time of synchronicity of the non-synchronous. Jansen, *The Construction of an Urban Past*, 237–310.
5 Michelet, *Introduction à l'histoire universelle* (Paris: Librairie Classique de L. Hachette, 1834). See Chapter 7.
6 See for this also my "Time, Narrative and Fiction".
7 See for the temporalities of Bergson and Proust: Jansen, "Time, Narrative and Fiction", 16–24.
8 See Chapter 5.
9 Marc Bloch, *Mélanges historiques* I (Paris: S.E.V.P.E.N., 1963), 20.
10 Marc Bloch, *The Historian's craft* (Manchester: Manchester University Press, 2004), 24–25.
11 Lucien Fèbvre, *Combats pour l'histoire* (Paris: Colin, 1953), 64.
12 It is even possible to put the question whether there is overall a paradigm change between Seignobos and the so-called "Annalistes". See: D. Damamme, "Un Cas d'Expertise. L'Etrange Defaite de Marc Bloch", in: *Sociétés Contemporaines* 39, 3 (2000), 95–116, esp. 107, note 17.

13 I've used, amongst others, the English translation: Braudel, *The Mediterranean and the Mediterranean World in the Age of Philip II*.
14 "For the historian everything begins and ends with time, a mathematical, godlike time, a notion easily mocked, time external to men, '*exogeneous*' [my italics], as economists would say, pushing men, forcing them, and painting their own individual times the same color: it is indeed the imperious time of the world". Fernand Braudel, *On History* (transl. Sarah Matthews; Chicago: University of Chicago Press), 48.
15 Fernand Braudel, *Civilization and Capitalism: 15th–18th Century*, Book I, II, III (transl. Siân Reynolds; Berkeley and Los Angeles: University of California Press, 1992).
16 Fernand Braudel, *Beschaving, Economie en Kapitalisme (15e–18e eeuw). De structuur van het dagelijks leven* 1 (Amsterdam: uitgeverij Contact, 1988), 48–49 and 167–169.
17 Fernand Braudel, *Civilization and Capitalism III, The Perspective of the World* (London: Harper and Row, 1984), 18, Fernand Braudel, *Temps du Monde. Civilisation Matérielle, Économie et Capitalisme. XVe-XVIIIe Siècle*, tome 3 (Paris: Armand Collin, 1979), 8.
18 See Chapters 6 and 7, about the ambiguous time.
19 Braudel, *Civilization and Capitalism III, The Perspective of the World*, 70.
20 Braudel, *Temps du Monde*, 224.
21 As we have seen above, Droysen borrows this idea from Hegel.
22 Ricoeur, *Time and Narrative*, vol. III, 209.
23 Ibid., 212.
24 Ibid., 213.
25 Ibid., 215.
26 Ricoeur, *Time and Narrative*, vol. I, 209–210. Ricoeur can find support for Braudel's underlining of the importance of the conjuncture in Fernand Braudel, *L'Écriture sur l'histoire* (Paris: Gallimard, 1969), 48. There the latter writes: "*Un mode nouveau de récit historique apparait, disons le 'récitatif' de la conjoncture, du cycle, voire l'intercycle qui propose à notre choix une dizaine d'années, un quart de siècle et, à l'extrême limite, le demi-siècle de Kondratieff*".
27 From the perspective of an undulating time, it becomes completely comprehensible that Ricoeur stresses the meaning of this second layer. Braudel gives himself here the argument in the English translation of his *La Méditerranée et le Monde Méditerranéen*: "Towns rise, thrive and decline according to the pulses of economic life". See: Braudel, *The Mediterranean and the Mediterranean World in the Age of Philip II*, vol. I (Glasgow: Collins Sons and Harper and Row, 1972), 322.
28 Ricoeur, *Time and Narrative*, vol. I, 211.
29 Ricoeur clearly has a reason to do so, because Braudel writes regarding the Mediterranean region as a whole: "*Nous saurons donc pas sans peine quel personage historique exact peut-être la Méditerranée* " and further "*son personage est complex, encombrant, hors série*"; Braudel, *La Méditerranée*, 13. In English: "We know without difficulty which exact historical personage could be the Mediterranean" and "its personage is complex, encompassing and extraordinary".
30 Ricoeur, *Time and Narrative*, vol. I, 211–217.
31 Le Roy Ladurie, *Carnival in Romans* (New York: George Braziller, Inc., 1979), xv.
32 Ladurie, *Carnival in Romans*, 190.
33 Ibid., 192.
34 Ibid., 207–208.
35 Ibid., 189.
36 Ibid., 306.
37 Ibid., 340.
38 Ibid., 346.
39 Ibid., xiv (see his comparing of the French situation of 1579 with the one in Iran in 1979) and see the pages 339–370, in which he uses many quotes from the sources, to revive the sixteenth-century past.
40 See also the way Ricoeur deals with Proust's *À la recherche du temps perdu*: Jansen, "Time, Narrative and Fiction", 16–24.

212 The time out of joint

41 H. Hallam, *Constitutional History of England From the Ascension of Henry VII to the Death of George II*. www.gutenberg.org/files/39711/39711-h/39711-h.htm. E. Rhys (ed. Everyman's Library), Hallam's *Constitutional History*, vol. 1 (With an introduction of J.H. Morgan).
42 Hallam's *Constitutional History*, 8–9.
43 Quoted in Bentley, *Modern Historiography*, 63.
44 J. M. Kemble, *The Saxons in England* (London, 1849).
45 Bentley, *Modern Historiography*, 65–66.
46 The title of William Cronon's "Two Cheers for the Whig Interpretation of History" seems to indicate the opposite, but he acknowledges Butterfields's criticisms. The only issue he approves with regard to the Whig-historians is their teleological approach. A substantial part of historiography is teleological. So, you don't need to be a Whig-historian to take a teleological stance in history writing. Therefore, I maintain the idea that the Whig-interpretation of history ends with Butterfields's attack on it. A main aspect of Butterfields's criticism concerns the "abridgements" the "Whigs" apply, which make their narratives oversimplified. In this respect Cronon agrees with Butterfield. See: William Cronon, "Two Cheers for the Whig Interpretation of History", *Perspectives on History: The Newsmagazine of the American Historical Association* 50, 6 (September 2012).
47 Herbert Butterfield, *The Whig Interpretation of History* (Harmondsworth: Penguin, 1973, 1st ed. 1931), 20–21.
48 See for Ranke, Chapter 5.
49 Butterfield, *The Whig Interpretation of History*, 25/6.
50 There are exceptions: Frederic Maitland, Charles McIlwain and especially Lewis Namier have already given a counter-sound.
51 This partly is section IV in Jansen, "Time, Narrative and Fiction", 13–16.
52 Virginia Woolf has written more time novels than *Mrs Dalloway*. In her *Orlando: A Biography* (London: Hogarth Press, 1928) we also see clock time associated with different times of consciousness. In *The Waves* (London: Hogarth Press, 1931) and *Between the Acts* (London: Hogarth Press, 1941), she combines a time of rise and fall with kairotic times. See also: Landwehr, "Die vielen, die anwesenden und abwesenden Zeiten", passim, esp. 228, 232, 239, 244 and 248–249.
53 Ricoeur, *Time and Narrative*, vol. II, 112.
54 Ibid., 81.
55 Ibid., 106.
56 See Brigitte Bechtold, "*More Than a Room* and *Three Guineas*: Understanding Virginia Woolf's Social Thought", *Journal of International Women's Studies* 1, 2 (2000). http://vc.bridgew.edu/jiws/vol1/iss2/1/ (accessed November 17, 2014). Bechtold underlines that Woolf deplores the lack of choice which women as well as soldiers have.
57 Ricoeur, *Time and Narrative*, vol. II, 112.
58 Ibid., 110.
59 Ibid.
60 In Septimus Warren Smith also a kairotic time is enclosed, because in his soul the past encroaches the present by the burdensome experiences of the First World War.
61 Chakrabarty, *Provincializing Europe*.
62 Ibid., 6–11. See also Chapter 4, about Hegel.
63 Ibid., 8–12. See also: Lorenz, "Der letzte Fetisch des Stamms der Historiker", 84.
64 Chakrabarty, *Provincializing Europe*, 12.
65 Ibid., 18.
66 Ibid., 71.
67 Ibid., 180 and 187. This looks like what Walter Benjamin said about the arcades in nineteenth-century Paris. They are modern constructions of iron, steel and glass but also resembled Christian churches and their immense glass roofs "seemed to be modelled after Oriental bazaars".
68 Chakrabarty, *Provincializing Europe*, 180–213.

69 Ibid., 251.
70 Ibid., 88.
71 Ibid., 89.
72 Ibid., 94.
73 Ibid., 250.
74 Ibid., 252.
75 Ibid., 252. In a note Chakrabarty refers to Jacques Derrida, *Specters of Marx: The State of the Debt, the Work of Mourning and the New International* (transl. Peggy Kamuf; New York and London: Routledge, 1994).
76 Chakrabarty, *Provincializing Europe*, 250.
77 Ibid., 254.
78 Ibid.
79 Ibid., 112.

11
HISTORICIST TIMES IN THE TWENTIETH AND TWENTY-FIRST CENTURIES 2

The German way

Mann, Meinecke and the end of romanticist historicism

In Germany the historiographical developments differ from those in France and Great Britain. Long before Butterfield makes an end to the English tradition of Enlightenment's historiography, the Counter-Enlightenment and historicism have finished that culture in Germany. However, there the time of rise and fall is not undisputed either. The debate about it starts especially after the First World War. Thomas Mann's *The Magic Mountain*, published in 1924, ironizes historicism in its romanticist temporality. The protagonists in Mann's time novel, Hans Castorp, his nephew Joachim Ziemssen, madam Clavdia Chauchat and her lover, the Dutch planter Mynheer Peeperkorn, go up the magic mountain to the Berghof sanatorium. Most of the time the up is followed by a down, whether in the form of descending the mountain or in the form of death. The sanatorium itself functions in Mann's novel as the continuing entity that "outlives the cadavers", to use Ricoeur's words. The ups and downs, the protagonists' dreams, which never become real and the sick, who are hardly curable, represent the romanticist intrigues of rise and fall, but at the same time ironize them.[1]

Somewhat later, during and after the Second World War, the German historian Friedrich Meinecke (1862–1954) also abandons romanticist historicism. In the beginning this is not that clear.[2] He spends a large part of his life by elaborating on German history in the Rankean way of ascent and decline. In his first great study *Weltbürgertum und Nationalstaat,* Meinecke displays it with regard to Germany in the nineteenth century, ending with Bismarck's unification in 1871. He considered *Weltbürgertum* or cosmopolitism an ambiguous concept. In its empty, eighteenth-century generality, it needs to be overcome by the national state, but incarnated in it, cosmopolitism ought to be preserved. Meinecke regrets, however, that the reason of state is more focused on power

(*Kratos*) and less on culture and morality (*Ethos*). The Wilhelminian empire does not seem the great synthesis of *Ethos* and *Kratos*, as Meinecke would like it to be.

Although this is a first disappointment in Germany's development, there is still hope to reconcile *Ethos* and *Kratos* in the form of Culture and Mass in the Naumann project. This project aims at a reconciliation between liberals and socialists, between *Bildungsbürger* and the rest of the nation. The First World War and its aftermath destroys that reconciliation and creates the complete demise of the German Empire. In *Die geschichtlichen Ursachen der Deutschen Revolution* (1919), Meinecke perceives the putting on the back burner of the *Wahlrechtreform* (electoral reform) as one of the great culprits of the defeat of the German army and the revolution of 1918.[3] For Meinecke these are aspects of a second decline in Germany's history.

In *Die Idee der Staatsräson* (1924), Meinecke comprehends the state as a personage with a vital impulse of its own, embodying instinct and reason, power and culture, *Kratos* and *Ethos*, selfishness and morality. Meinecke's recognition of the Weimar Republic brings a more harmonious perception of the reason of state. He transforms the brutal impulse of life (*Lebenstrieb*), residing in the *raison d'état*, into a softer impulse of play (*Spieltrieb*), in which *Kratos* and *Ethos* are interrelated.[4] Here is a third "up" in Germany's history, viewed from a Meineckean perspective. However, Meinecke changes his time perception before he can observe its fall.

In his *Geschichte und Gegenwart* (1933), *discontinuity* becomes prominent, instead of the undulating continuity. The full moment comes to the fore, in which time and space contract and expand.[5] By this view, Meinecke appears to break away from the horizontal stream of past, present and future and becomes absorbed in an enduring, vertical moment of time.[6] The grasping of Kairos's forelock we find in Meinecke's *Entstehung des Historismus* (1936).[7] He elaborates there on the origins of historicism during the Counter-Enlightenment and does so in the kairotic spirit of affirmation. The book is written, as he himself states, in a *bejahender Gesinnung*, which comes close to Huizinga's historical sensation and surely demonstrates a personal involvement.

Die Deutsche Katastrophe realizes a complete break with Ranke. It shows German's history before and during the Second World War, representing its definitive shift from a continuing entity and a quasi-personality with a horizontal undulating time into the Germany of National Socialism, epitomized in an enormous discontinuity, created by a vertical temporality. Meinecke does not see National Socialism as the result of an organic development in German history but as a huge incidental deviation. This is a complete break with Rankean organic thinking, and Meinecke seems aware of it. *Die Deutsche Katastrophe* is a contemporary history of Germany and an autobiography as well. His life and the history of his fatherland echo one another. The eclipse of democratic Germany reflects in Meinecke's life by the overshadowing of Ranke by Burckhardt. This comes together in a metaphor Meinecke uses about himself and his time: the creating mirror.[8]

In the 1930s of the twentieth century, Meinecke takes a first run-up to that, probably not fully aware of the implications for his conception of time. He may think he is abandoning historicism, but he is only opting for a different temporality within historicism. During the Second World War, Meinecke makes the ultimate shift. Instead of a (Rankean) time of rise and fall, he (consciously?) prefers a (Burckhardtian), personally felt, kairotic time of sudden moments, which also implies major transformations in history. Changes are no longer continuous but disruptive metamorphoses (*Verpuppungen*), resulting in completely new periods.[9]

Nietzsche, Benjamin and Heidegger

Walter Benjamin also distances himself of romanticist historicism. In thesis VI of his *Über die Begriff der Geschichte*, he explicitly objects to a Rankean form of it. "To articulate the past historically does not mean to recognize it 'the way it really was' (Ranke). It means to seize hold of a memory as it flashes up at a moment of danger".[10] For Benjamin, history is built on a discontinuous series of moments with no causal or other connections.[11] They are ambiguous in character because past, present and future are intertwined. This comes to the fore in Benjamin's concept of the Now-Time (*Jetztzeit*). The pre-figurations in the Old Testament of happenings in the New Testament form a known example of it. The exodus of the Jewish people out of Egypt and their crossing the Red Sea prefigure Jesus's baptism in the river Jordan. Being a secularized and Left-oriented Jew, Benjamin gives another example:

> Thus for Robespierre ancient Rome was a present time [a Now-Time], loaded with a past, that flashed up from continuous history.[12]

Both examples are "expressions of the wish that the present moment be redeemed and granted a dignity that survives its passage".[13] Thus Benjamin attacks romanticist historicism with its continuous fleeting time. *Jetztzeit* implies a certain suddenness in the coming together of the past and the present, articulating the contingency of time. Benjamin follows Nietzsche, which becomes clear when we take Benjamin's political messianism into account. The Italian Giacomo Marramao observes this, speaking about Benjamin's *Jetztzeit*:

> [It] is placed at the intersection between the moment (*Augenblick*) and the past (*Vergangenheit*), outside of the "future-oriented" symbolism of waiting. Every instant carries within it the energeia, the power (*potenza*) or virtuality of the messianic: on the condition that it be conceptualized – *begriffen*, literally: caught, ensnared – in its singular, unrepeatable specifity. It is only when political action can be recognized as messianic action that *Jetztzeit* is converted into *Augenblick*.[14]

In the last sentence is displayed what James McFarland and Benjamin Aldes Wurgaft perceive as a common denominator in Nietzsche's "eternal return" and Benjamin's *Jetztzeit*. Benjamin calls it "the small gate" (Nietzsche's gateway) through which pass at the same moment being and nothing, past and present, hope and despair. Through hope and despair, there is not only a past in the present of *Jetztzeit* but also a future. In the past of the present, the latter becomes a "now of recognisability" that is "a moment of awakening".[15] It is the same awakening Nietzsche underlines in his eternal return as a reflective "reculer pour mieux sauter". Like Vanessa Schwarz, McFarland and Wurgaft, I also see in Benjamin "an important way station in the journey towards a 'postmodern' historiography [whatever that may be, but surely what Hartog has been calling a time of the present], that begins with Nietzsche".[16]

Heidegger is the last representative of an anti-romanticist form of historicism during the first part of the twentieth century. He agrees with Count Yorck's opinion in his letters to Dilthey, in which the count writes about Ranke:

> Ranke is a great ocularist, for whom things that have vanished can never become actualities. Ranke's whole tribe also provides the explanation for the way the material of history has been restricted to the political. Only the political is dramatic.[17]

Here we have in a few sentences the differences between the nineteenth-century romanticist approach to history and the twentieth-century Heideggerian, kairotic approach. According to Heidegger, Ranke considers the past as being over. The only way to bring it to life is through a lively, pictorial text. Heidegger sees the past as still being there, as still existing (*gewesenes Dasein*). It only has to be faced to find the right words for it in a text. "Be faced" means that *Dasein*, in its full ecstatic presence of *Gewesenheit*, determination and openness to the future, understands history as the "recurrence" of the possible. It "knows that a possibility will recur only if existence is open for it fatefully, in a moment of vision, in resolute repetition".[18] Here we clearly have Nietzsche's "eternal recurrence" but now in the form of a still more future-oriented point of view.

Heidegger also confirms Nietzsche's genealogical perception of monumental history, formulated by the latter as providing examples of human nobility, which teaches us that "since a great thing once existed, it was therefore possible, and so *might be* possible again".[19] In Heideggerian words this sounds: "*Dasein* exists authentically as future in resolutely disclosing a possibility which it has chosen".[20] It creates a form of historiography that is contrary to the Rankean tradition. Nietzsche calls the latter apollonic-scientific, whereas Heidegger calls it aesthetic, ocular and ontic (= only in fact). Both use these terms pejoratively. Nietzsche as well as Heidegger want a history that serves life.[21] It results in a kairotic temporality, connected to a historiography that does not only aim at a contemplation of the past but wants to project our inheritance on the future, thus making it our own. This happens in a moment, which is experienced as lasting. It is the experience of being thrown in the past, directed to a future that teaches us how we can have resoluteness in the present.

Like Benjamin, Heidegger follows Nietzsche in his demurs against romanticist historicism. My explicit reference to Romanticism implies that historicism itself is not at stake here, but only its Rankean form. Despite these differences, it is obvious that already at the beginning of the twentieth century, a Nietzschean perception of time prevails over the Rankean romanticist one. This fits in with Hölscher's view concerning a discontinuity in the awareness of temporality around the First World War. However, it is not a rupture between a Koselleckian time of the modern and an embodied historicist time, as Hölscher's view implies; it is a break between a romanticist and a kairotic form of historical time.

Just like Hölscher, Assmann and Hartog also perceive a discontinuity between a time of the modern and an embodied historicist time. According to them, this break does not occur around the First World War but at the end of the century. All these views must be regarded as incorrect. In Germany it already happens at the end of the eighteenth century. However, their misunderstanding is comprehensible, because after the Second World War a new discontinuity occurs.

Koselleck's modernism

By rejecting romanticist historicism, Mann, Meinecke, Benjamin and Heidegger do not abandon historicism, in the broad, inclusive sense, as I comprehend it, following Mannheim. This is different with Koselleck. He is the first German who completely breaks with historicism and returns to the Enlightenment, comprehending Kant as the inventor of modern history.[22] With his famous statement that there is a tension between the past as space of experience and the future as the horizon of expectation, he accentuates the power (*Kraft*) of modern temporality. Time thus continuously accelerates, so that the space of experience is disappearing faster and faster, while the horizon of expectation keeps changing.[23] It is a time that Peter Osborne understands as "a form of historical time which valorizes the new as the product of a constantly self-negating dynamic".[24] Koselleck neglects the idea that time can be a burden; his time remains future-oriented and pushes the space of experience further and further away in a distant past. It creates a gap between the past and the future, which is characteristic of modern times. Progress shows itself, as Koselleck claims "*in den zeitlichen Brechungen ständig sich neu reproducierende Hiatus-Erfahrungen*" ("in the temporal refractions of constantly new reproducing hiatus experiences").[25] Aleida Assmann notes that the Enlightenment is important for Koselleck's vision on historiography, because by progress it gives a direct experience of time. And she explains: through progress, the past becomes different from the present, making it possible to discover a different, historical world. Events become unique, due to constantly changing times. As a result, the Enlightenment creates the individuality of historical changes and detects temporalization.

Modernist times disappear in England in the 1930s, with Butterfield and the economic crisis of those years, but they revive in Germany in the 1960s, with its *Wirtschaftswunder*. The German *Stunde Null* is meant to be an obliteration of the past, because its inhabitants want to forget. *Anfang* is more important than *Herkunft*.[26] Beginning has to do with a *tabula rasa*, origin with continuity and tradition.[27] Koselleck is the son of a time of the new beginning.[28] This explains why he highlights the modernizing aspects of it.[29] His "time of the modern", however, contains a strange paradox.

Fernando Esposito observes this by underlining that Koselleck's modern time is based on the idea that the traditional past and the utopian future distance themselves ever further from the present.[30] This happens, according to Esposito (and of course to Koselleck), between 1750 and 1850, in a period in which historicism and history also originate as a scientific discipline. This is the so-called *Sattelzeit*, from which stems the paradox of advancement into the future and attention to the past. In my view this paradox, created by Koselleck and taken over by Esposito, does not exist regarding historical time. In the period 1750–1850 the paradox disappears if we follow Brandom with his inferential conceived concepts. Then the "time of the modern" is empty, homogeneous, diachronic accelerating, future-oriented and originating in the Enlightenment. Since the Counter-Enlightenment we have an embodied time, which around 1820 results in a romanticist, embodied time of rise and fall, connected to continuing entities. Since 1830, a time of synchronicity of the non-synchronous develops, and since approximately 1880, a kairotic time, each with its own specific content.[31] Apart from this, the time of the modern evolves, which has its most pronounced form in the Whig-interpretation of history in England. Koselleck's and Esposito's paradox thus is the result of neglecting the separated developments of modernism and historicism in the eighteenth and nineteenth centuries, featured by a difference between an empty, accelerating and an embodied, historicist time.

Cracks in Koselleck's modernism

Esposito notes that Koselleck in the 1970s of the twentieth century utters criticism concerning modernism by the influence of Gadamer and the idea of synchronicity of the non-synchronous, which was popular at the Bielefelder University. Esposito connects this with the scepticism that arises in the 1960s, 1970s and 1980s of the twentieth century as a result of (1) decolonization, (2) the failure of the modernization in the former colonies, (3) the implosion of Marxism, (4) postmodernism and (5) the growing insight that the Holocaust is a pathological form of modernism.[32] He points out that this is the consequence of the paradoxical but still close *connection* between historicism and modernism.[33] I see it different. Scepticism with regard to modernism is the feature of a confused time perception since the 1960s of the twentieth century. Although doubts arise with regard to great stories about a rosy future, the past as an embodied time remains an obscure element in the modernist scepticism. The so-called connection between historicism and modernism does not fundamentally change modernism. Historicism and modernism still remain separated.

In my view, in the period 1950–1990 the so-called connection between historicism and (post)modernism is due to the dissatisfaction with the radical modernism, epitomized in the five points above, and the growing influence of the modernist social sciences. The scepticism of the 1950s and 1960s of the last century, of which Koselleck is a representative, stems from the forgetfulness of modernism in respect to historicism with its embodied and even burdensome time. The same applies to the comprehensive perspectivism of postmodernism in the 1980s and 1990s. They all maintain modernism, but only with a touch of historicism.

I prefer a historicism in which the problems of the present are seen as a result of the past, without which it is impossible to take the right decisions for the future. That is the correct remedy against a time of the modern. It also is an antidote against what Esposito calls *radical* historicism with its "reflexive modernization", in which the reaction on modern developments is more unintentional and reflexive than reflective.[34] Although this is in my view a very adequate analysis of society at the threshold of the twenty-first century and even though there is some Nietzschean flavour in its unintentional nature – which corresponds to my perception of historicism – I do not see radical historicism and reflexive modernization as a revival of historicism. Not every form of anti- or post-modernism is a renewal of historicism.[35] It is but a new, corrective form of modernism, showing how modernism needs historicist reflection. Esposito's repudiation of radical historicism is part of a deep, continuing stream of anti-(romanticist)-historicism, which lasts in Germany since Heidegger and Benjamin. Koselleck is also a representative of it. It is an anti-historicism opposing only its romanticist form, with Ranke as the main culprit. It misrepresents the more inclusive tripartite historicism with an embodied time, vindicated in this book.

The decline of modernism and the resurrection of an inclusive historicism

With her *Ist die Zeit aus den Fugen?*, Aleida Assmann gives a more adequate analysis of the decline of the time of the modern. Although she does not use terms for time as "empty" and "embodied", she exchanges Koselleck's empty time for an incarnated one, embodied by identity, culture, memory and even by a past that is not over.[36] She elaborates on it by taking stock of its advantages and disadvantages.

Assmann gives an overview of Germany's post-war struggle between historicism and modernism. She first praises Koselleck's insights about time and history. According to her, he even deserves the Nobel Prize in the Humanities for his known, aforementioned, dictum of space of experience and horizon of expectation.[37] Assmann also finds that Koselleck is right in noticing that time can be spoken about only in metaphors. The trope of the arrow enables time to be perceived as diachronic and dynamic.[38] She observes that Koselleck's past is over and closed, because he argues that the present must be freed from the past.[39] She admits that the acceleration of time, with its effects of musealization of the past and the shrinking of the present, has the advantage that it destroys continuities of traditional powers.[40] By that, the past is no longer a burden for the present.[41] Assmann refers to Schulin, associated to Koselleck's school, who considers tradition as not belonging to modern historiography.[42] However, Assmann concludes that Koselleck's and Schulin's observations about a past that is closed and over will be completely wiped out at the end of the twentieth century.

Assmann comes more close to a revitalization of historicism. She perceives a new phase in German modernism around the 1980s and 1990s of the twentieth century, calling it "the history of the late modern".[43] It is characterized by a slowing down of the accelerating time of the modern. She agrees with Lübbe that the dynamics of the modern are no longer linear but dialectical.[44] Progressive technics require the counterweight of the human measure and scepticism.[45] In doing so, she makes a first step in the direction of a resurrection of historicism. Moreover, she approves Marquard's statement that future needs provenance (*Zukunft braucht Herkunft*).[46]

But Assmann wants to go further than Lübbe and Marquardt. In her defence of cultural memory (*kulturelle Gedächtnis*), she creates a resurgence of historicism.[47] Cultural memory connects past, present and future, so that they are no longer closed and apart elements of time. She also creates embodied, collective identities (Ricoeur), allowing us to learn from the past (which reminds to Ranke).[48] Here Assmann returns to the political, romanticist historicism of Hegel and Ranke. However, she also has an eye for more societal and cultural forms of historicism. History is not only for specialists. She even "ontologizes" the past by claiming that man has to position himself in time, dealing with the past as an essential part of the human existence.[49] Assmann reaches complete cultural historicism in her treatment of Lorenz's "hot past" (*heissen Vergangenheit*) and Bevernage's "reversible past", in which both articulate that the past is not over. As trauma (Lorenz) and call for justice (Bevernage), it lives on in the present as well as in the future.[50] She thus combines romanticist and kairotic temporalities, abandoning completely Koselleck's accelerating and thus progressive time. Like others, she refers to the Indian Dipesh Chakrabarty, who also returns to two types of historicism, one of which is the heterogeneous temporality of Heidegger. Contrary to Assmann, Chakrabarty does not combine it with a romanticist type of historicism but with Marx's synchronicity of the non-synchronous.[51]

Assmann defends a time that is summarized in the metaphor of a time "out of joint". Implicitly Chakrabarty does the same. Both turn Habermas's negatively meant "*neue Unübersichtlichkeit*" ("new confusion" or "new obscurity") into something positive.[52] Both metaphors erase the boundaries between past, present and future, creating what Gumbrecht calls the "*breite Gegenwart*" (the enlarged present) and what I have subsumed under the header of "kairotic time".[53] It means that it is a return to historicism by articulating time in its romanticist, political (Ricoeur) as well as in its kairotic, cultural (Lorenz and Bevernage) aspects. Synchronicity of the non-synchronous remains a bit out of Assmann's view, but by agreeing with Chakrabarty, she is enclosing it anyway.

However, another interpretation of a time out of joint is also possible. Time can be understood as an agglomeration of the temporalities, produced by the three time regimes of historicism. So a "time out of joint" may involve the erasing of the boundaries between past, present and future but also *a rearranging of past, present and future in three different ways*, along the lines of the three historicist time regimes.

Looking at the title and content of Assmann's book (*Is Time Out of Joint?*) from my point of view, she gives the impression that a return to historicism is something that only happens in the twenty-first century.[54] Moreover, the subtitle of her book (*The Rise and Fall of the Modern Time Regime*) gives the wrong idea that her return concerns only its romanticist form. After all, I want to emphasize that it is not allowed to identify historicism only with its romanticist form and also that the three historicist regimes with embodied temporalities do not come into being at the end of the twentieth century, as suggested by Hartog, but already in the nineteenth century. Already then time is out of joint!

In summary, the three nineteenth-century time regimes are more important for contemporaneous historiography than the empty time order of the Enlightenment. At the end of the twentieth century, in the three main Western countries, all three historicist temporalities exist. That brings me to the last question of this book: how functional are these historicist temporalities for the future? Observing a historicist landscape with three different times, a wide horizon of possibilities opens up.

Notes

1 See also: Jansen, "Time, Narrative and Fiction", 5–11.
2 This section about Meinecke is partially derived from Krol, *Het Geweten van Duitsland*.
3 The eastern message of Wilhelm II in 1917 came too late. Stefan Meineke, *Friedrich Meinecke. Persönlichkeit und politisches Denken bis zum Ende des ersten Weltkrieges* (Berlin and New York: Walter de Gruyter,1995), 283.
4 Krol, *Het geweten van Duitsland*, 100.
5 Ibid., 185.
6 Ibid., 181–186.
7 See also Veronica Vasterling, "De rechte lijn en de lus. Heideggers onderzoek naar de tijd en de geschiedenis van het tijdbegrip", in: Grever and Jansen, *De ongrijpbare tijd*, 175–186.
8 Krol, *Het geweten van Duitsland*, 217–220.
9 Ibid., 188–189 and 196.
10 Walter Benjamin, *Über den Begriff der Geschichte* (1940), Thesis VI. English from: Walter Benjamin, Hannah Arendt and Harry Zohn, *Illuminations* (New York: Harcourt Brace Jovanovich, 1968), Thesis VI.
11 See Chakarabarty's shomoy-granthi!
12 "*So war für Robespierre das antike Rom eine mit Jetztzeit geladene Vergangenheit, die er aus dem Kontinuum der Geschichte heraussprengte*", Benjamin, *Über den Begriff der Geschichte*, These XIV.
13 Benjamin Aldes Wurgaft, "To the Planetarium – There Is Still Time!", *History and Theory* 53 (May 2014), 253–263, esp. 254.
14 Giacomo Marramao, "Messianism Without Delay: On the 'Post-Religious' Political Theology of Walter Benjamin", *Constellations: An Interdisciplinary Journal of Critical and Democratic Theory* 15, 3 (2008), 397–405, esp. 401.

15 Nitzan Lebovic, "The Last European", *History and Theory* 55, 3 (2016), 465–475, esp. 472.
16 Vanessa Schwarz, "Walter Benjamin for Historians", *American Historical Review* 106, 5 (2001), 1721–1743, esp. 1739 and Wurgaft, "To the Planetarium", 255.
17 Heidegger, *Being and Time*, 451–452; idem, *Sein und Zeit*, 400.
18 Ibid., 444; idem, *Sein und Zeit*, 391–392.
19 See the chapter about Nietzsche.
20 Heidegger, *Being and Time*, 448; idem, *Sein und Zeit*, 396.
21 Ibid., 455; idem, *Sein und Zeit*, 403.
22 Koselleck, *The Practice of Conceptual History*, 119.
23 Koselleck, *Futures Past*, 241–242.
24 A quote, I derive from: Esposito, "Transformationen geschichtlicher Zeitlichkeit nach dem Boom", 37.
25 Reinhart Koselleck and Christian Meier, "Art. Fortschritt", in: O. Brunner, W. Conze and R. Koselleck (eds.), *Geschichtliche Grundbegriffe. Historische Lexikon zur politisch-sozialen Sprache in Deutschland*, Bd. 2 (Stuttgart: Klett-Cotta, 1979), 351–424, esp. 392.
26 Assmann, *Ist die Zeit aus den Fugen?*, 154.
27 Ibid., 160.
28 See also: Esposito, "Transformationen geschichtlicher Zeitlichkeit nach dem Boom", 15.
29 Koselleck developed his central issues already in the 1950s, but they became more known in the 1970s of the last century. See: Lorenz, "Die letzte Fetisch des Stamms der Historiker", 77–80.
30 Esposito, "Transformationen geschichtlicher Zeitlichkeit nach dem Boom", 75.
31 See the end of Chapter 9.
32 Esposito, "Transformationen geschichtlicher Zeitlichkeit nach dem Boom", 54.
33 Ibid., 81.
34 Kyung-Sup Chang, "Reflexive Modernization" (December 4, 2017), *Wiley Online Library*: https://doi.org/10.1002/9781118430873.est0835
35 Esposito's idea to see it as a radical form of historicism, perceiving it at the same time as a second crisis of historicism, is an analysis based on the confusion of historicism and modernism, which has been scrutinized above.
36 Assmann, *Ist die Zeit aus den Fugen?*, esp. 288–326.
37 Ibid., 138.
38 Ibid., 143.
39 Ibid., 185–187.
40 Ibid., 205. Here we have Koselleck's so-called *Gegenwartsschrumpfung*. Reinhart Koselleck, "Zeitverkürzung und Beschleunigung. Eine Studie zur Säkularisation", in: idem, *Zeitschichten. Studien zur Historik* (Frankfurt a. M.: Suhrkamp, 2003), 177–202 and Hermann Lübbe, *Im Zug der Zeit. Verkürzter Aufenthalt in der Gegenwart* (Berlin: Springer Verlag, 1992).
41 Assmann, *Ist die Zeit aus den Fugen?*, 140–141.
42 Ibid., 180.
43 Ibid., 211.
44 Ibid., 226.
45 Ibid., 227–228.
46 Ibid., 228–238.
47 Ibid., 290.
48 Ibid., 288–296, esp. 293. In my view Assmann's "collective identities" are the same as Mandelbaum's "continuing entities".
49 "*Vergangenheit zu deuten und anzueignen ist für Menschen die sich in der Zeit positionieren müssen, eine existentielle Form der Daseinsbewältigung*". Assmann, *Ist die Zeit aus den Fugen?*, 242 and 303/4.
50 Ibid., 302–304 and 320.
51 Chakrabarty, *Provincializing Europe*, 253.
52 Jürgen Habermas, *Die neue Unübersichtlichkeit* (Frankfurt a. M.: Suhrkamp, 1985).

53 See Fernando Esposito and Hans Ulrich Gumbrecht, "Posthistoire Then. Ein Gespräch mit Hans Ulrich Gumbrecht über unsere breite Gegenwart", in: Esposito, *Zeitenwandel*, 255–277. See also the section "A preliminary definition of time" in my Introduction.
54 Let it be clear: Assmann does not think in terms of a return to historicism; I do. From that point of view my assessment of her book has been written.

12

EPILOGUE: THE BENEFITS OF HISTORICIST TIMES

Is this book an anti-Koselleck?

Although I criticize Koselleck, yet I can endorse many of his discoveries. His idea that historical time is not a given or an *a priori* fact but a historical phenomenon underlines that it is a human construction.[1] As such, historical time comes at a special moment, namely in the eighteenth century.[2] Then a discontinuity occurs, in which the physical times of Aristotle and Newton and the religious and prophetic times of Augustine *et alia* change into a secular, homogeneous time, in which the future becomes an important element. From these findings Koselleck's influential thesis emerges concerning a horizon of expectation that is increasingly moving away from the space of experience.[3] Herman Lübbe's "*Gegegenwartsschrumpfung*" (shrinking of the present) is based on it, as well as the relationship between an accelerating time and the phenomenon of stress.[4] This underlines Koselleck's perception of time as linear, upward going and homogeneous.

However, this also implies that without Koselleck's time of the modern, historicist times would not have been developed.[5] Looking at the historical time in its romantic form, we see that it remains homogeneous, despite its embodied and wavy character. In this way we must recognize that Koselleck creates the *conditions* of historicism. Yet, he also shows blindness to the historicist alternative itself. This already becomes clear at the beginning of his *Futures Past*.

Koselleck starts the mentioned book with an analysis of Albrecht Altdorfer's *Alexanderschlacht*, painted in 1529, showing the victory of Alexander the Great over the Persians at the river Issus in 333 BCE. He wonders why Altdorfer depicts the Greeks as the (then) present-day Germans and the Persians as contemporary Turks. The answer must be sought in the Ottoman siege of Vienna in 1529, marking the decline of the Holy Roman Empire. Koselleck considers Altdorfer's painting as part of an age-old prophetic time regime, connecting it to the foretelling dream of the demise of empires as presented in the Bible book of Daniel. In Koselleck's view, Altdorfer's prophetic time regime reveals a lack of modern historical consciousness, missing the experience of a distance in time between an event and its representation. He refers to Friedrich Schlegel's essay about the painting of Altdorfer from 1820, in which Schlegel praises it as "the greatest feat of the age of chivalry". Koselleck comprehends this as a distinction between Schlegel's own time and that of Altdorfer.[6] He comments:

> Stating my thesis simply, in these [German] countries there occurs a temporalization (*Verzeitlichung*) of history, at the end of which there is the peculiar form of acceleration, which characterizes modernity.[7]

I fully agree when it comes to a temporalization of history, which is the result of acceleration. Nevertheless, Schlegel's utterance is mainly nostalgic, a longing for more chivalric times than his own. Thus, he gives the past more importance than the future. As such it is a romanticist-historicist expression of time and not only an utterance of the "time of the modern". The perceptions of Koselleck and Schlegel make clear that different time regimes produce distinct views on the same event. Koselleck's time of progress has a lot of disadvantages, which I will discuss in the following. Still, in a oppositional relationship with historicist times, it can be very fruitful. This becomes especially clear with regard to the synchronicity of the non-synchronous. Therein the interaction between inevitable trends into the future and a burdensome past – applied carefully, like Chakrabarty does – is a better alternative than a simple time of the modern. Above all, a tripartite "time out of joint" offers the best alternative for the dominant time of progress, which is so common for us today.

Disadvantages of the empty time of progress

Koselleck is right in his observation that there is a transition from premodern into modern regimes of time. He is also right when he sees an acceleration in technology since the Industrial Revolution. Christopher Clark does the same, but he signals side effects, such as changes in travelling, punctuality, time wasting, shrinking of space and perception of time itself. He understands these side effects as processes "of acceleration, expansion, regeneration, narrowing, compression, distanciation, splitting, fracturing, emptying, annihilation, intensification and liquefaction."[8] Perhaps, apart from the first three processes, all these perceptions show negative connotations. Jérôme Baschet confirms this by pointing out that stress is its accompanying phenomenon.[9] Both Clark and Baschet refer to a burdensome temporality, for which Koselleck is blind.[10] The latter maintains a "Whig-interpretation" of time, without taking into account that technical improvements and globalization are accompanied by serious disadvantages, especially in the areas of ecology, pandemics, violence, misuse of means of communication and an uneven growth of income and wealth. Maybe in his time (the second half of the twentieth century), these facts do not weigh as heavily as they do now. It is important that Rosa notes that the acceleration of time goes hand in hand with the "solidification and hardening" of "deep structures". This clarifies all the more that the twenty-first century needs the ideas of an embodied historical time. It can function as a counterweight against the superficial time of progress by which scientists, physicians, politicians and even historians, like, for instance, Yuval Noah Harari in his *Homo Deus*, want to frame our current knowledge of the world.[11]

Therefore, I want to join Berber Bevernage, who also shows a form of historicism in the rejection of the empty, progressive time of modernism. He argues that it works on the assumption that the past is evil and evil is past. He thus endorses an embodied time, opposing a Manichaeism of time, in which past, present and future exclude one another.[12] Bevernage understands that the consequences of the past are still alive, although the past itself is gone. He affirms, without mentioning, Septimus Smith's experience in *Mrs. Dalloway*, that spectres of the past can be more real than the assumption that the past is over. This is confirmed by victims of the two World Wars, of the Holocaust, of Apartheid, of the dirty civil war in Argentina, of the dissolution of former Yugoslavia, of the atrocities of Rwanda and of other wounded nations. These great social-psychological traumas cannot be solved by a Truth Commission or the like.

The past is not yet over, which is also reflected in the self-sustaining growth that continues to haunt the present, a growth that experts see as a possible, autonomous decline for the present and the future. To put it differently: let's look at

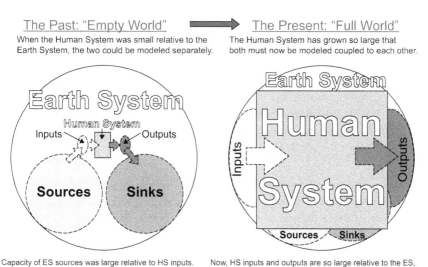

FIGURE 12.1 The change in the relationship between the human system and the earth system with regard to sources and sinks, respectively, to meet human needs and to get rid of their emissions[13]

the ecological footprint versus the capacity of the earth since 1960. Around 1980 the environmental burden is still equal to the earth's ability to provide humanity with the resources it requires and to absorb the emissions it produces.

This becomes clear when we compare the relation of the human and earth system before and after 1980. Before 1980 the human system is in balance with the earth system. The earth sources were more than enough to provide for the human system's needs and the sink space was big enough to absorb its output. Now the human inputs and outputs are so high that they deplete the earth system in sources and sinks. With a moderate effect of normal work, we need almost three planets the size of the earth to survive in 2050.

Thus the graph shows alarming data. To illustrate this, we need the embodied time of historicism. We have to take stock of the effects of exceeding the capacity of the earth. In *Limits of Growth. The 30-Year Update* in 2004, Donella Meadows, Jorgen Randers and Dennis Meadows summarize what this overshoot brings about:

1. Sea level has risen 10–20 cm since 1900. Most non-polar glaciers are retreating, and the extent and thickness of Arctic sea ice is decreasing in summer.
2. In 1998 more than 45 percent of the globe's people had to live on incomes averaging $2 a day or less. Meanwhile, the richest one-fifth of the world's population has 85 percent of the global GNP. And the gap between rich and poor is widening. (See hereafter).
3. In 2002, the Food and Agriculture Organization of the UN estimated that 75 percent of the world's oceanic fisheries were fished at or beyond capacity. The North Atlantic cod fishery, fished sustainably for hundreds of years, has collapsed, and the species may have been pushed to biological extinction.
4. The first global assessment of soil loss, based on studies of hundreds of experts, found that 38 percent, or nearly 1.4 billion acres, of currently used agricultural land has been degraded.
5. Fifty-four nations experienced declines in per capita GDP for more than a decade during the period 1990–2001.[14]

All these data exemplify what the empty time of progress hides behind its optimism. The aforementioned inventory runs only till 2004, but we should have an update of 2020 or later. I will show that point 2 has become even worse by presenting two analyses. First, the one of Branko Milanovic, the Croation lead economist of the World Bank's Research Department about global income growth, and second, the one of the French economist Thomas Piketty about globalization of capital. Especially the elephant graph of Milanovic is illustrative, showing the real growth of income for the entire world population, from the poor to the rich.[15]

Epilogue: the benefits of historicist times 229

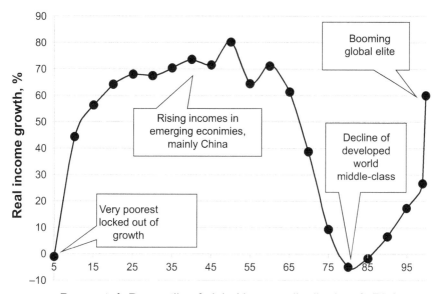

FIGURE 12.2 Global Income Growth 1988–2008[16]

Source: Milanovic, B., Lead Economist, World Bank Research Department, Global income inequality by the numbers

The elephant teaches how globalization has winners and losers. The winners are the upwardly mobile middle classes of China, India, Indonesia and the Arabic world. They occupy the long back line of the elephant. These middle classes see their inflation-adjusted incomes grow by 70 per cent or more. The world's elite, making more than €100,000 a year, is also better-off. Yet, the income of the world's poorest, as well as the one of the developed world's lower middle classes, displays a stagnation or even a drop. The consequences are dreadful. First, the increasing share of national income accrues to owners of capital. Second, there is a very high and rising concentration of incomes from capital. Third, people holding high-salary jobs also often have high capital income. Fourth, high-income individuals marry other high-income individuals; and fifth, the political power of the rich is on the increase.

There appears to be some flaws in Milanovic's findings. In a Report of the British Resolution Foundation, a middle-class support organization, the elephant turns into a crocodile. It argues that the Western middle classes are not as badly off as the elephant suggests.[17] Thus, a wealthy part of the world continues to believe in progress. Nevertheless, Piketty underscores for an important part of Milanovic's findings.[18] He argues that the contemporaneous international social and economic instability originates in the long term, increasing rate of return on capital, which has become larger than the rate of economic growth. The result is a concentration of wealth amongst a few: in 2020 approximately 25 persons own half world's entire wealth. Joseph Stigitz has shown this pattern for the United States in his *The Price of Inequality*.[19] Pandemics make all these developments worse.

Progress also has awful effects in politics. The declining middle classes in the West, Milanovic talks about, feel how their political influence is diminishing, despite their democratic rights. The global problems of migration reinforce their feelings of frustration and fear for the future. A substantial part of the European and American population expects a lot from national isolation and is blind to global benefits. It rejects a world in which new communication structures lead to increasing globalization, which in turn brings about new ideas about diversity in religion, race and gender. As a counter result, the declining middle and lower classes become "traditionalists", longing for a past, which the Germans call the *heile Welt*. They want a state which "heals the world" of all those global and intellectual novelties. The multi-cultural and open society is viewed as a consequence of political thinking, not as an inevitable reality. Populist politicians, like the Le Pens in France, the Brexiteers in Great-Britain, the Trumpeteers in the United States and the Wilders' and Baudets in the Netherlands, fish in this murky water. Every form of internationalism is declared a bogeyman by these populists. They reinforce tendencies that glorify the national past and oppose even benign forms of globalization, ignoring the problems of geopolitics. A long tradition of nationalistic education and little global historical consciousness hand them their opportunity.[20]

Most people in the West ignore the fact that the "developed" countries have created "underdevelopment" in the "Rest". Even if we consider secularization as a profitable result of the Enlightenment, it can produce disdain for non-secular societies. On their turn, Non-Western peoples reject secularized lifestyles. They may consider cultures permeated by secularization blasphemous and hedonistic. Western values often have been introduced into the non-Western world in a violent manner. Now this world itself produces war and terror, because of a desire for retaliation. By technical progress, there is more violence on both sides than it ever has been.

Because of its emptiness, a progressive temporality cannot be a useful tool to find the right direction from the past into the future. More appropriate to analyse the huge problems of our time is the embodied temporality in its threefold form.

Historicist times can be helpful

The *romanticist time* of rise and decline gives a better worldview than singular progressive linearity. The present ecological problems are predicting a severe downturn, more serious than people ever can imagine. With regard to less serious problems, there also are numerous warnings against progressive thinking. At the start of the twentieth century, Spengler's *Untergang des Abendlandes* and Toynbees's *Study of History* are full of the idea of ascent and descent. New studies about world history express the same romanticist undulating time. Amy Chua's

Day of Empire: How Hyperpowers Rise to Global Dominance – and Why They Fall provides already in its title the proof that romanticist time is still an option to perceive the world. The same is true for John Lukacs's *The End of the Twentieth Century and the End of the Modern Age* and for William H. McNeill's *Rise of the West. A History of the Human Community* and his study on *Arnold J. Toynbee*. They all are written under the aegis of the same romanticist temporality.[21] Aleida Assmann's *Ist die Zeit aus den Fugen?* has as its subtitle *Aufstieg und Fall des Zeitregimes der Moderne*. A return to the rise-and-fall paradigm of romanticist time cannot be demonstrated more explicitly.

The rise-and-fall paradigm has the advantage of bringing the values and ideas of all kinds of civilizations into perspective, breaking through the trend of absolutizing them. Astarte, Zeus and Jupiter once have dominated the beliefs of thousands of people, but they went down together with the political entities of their time. The same is true for ideologies such as communism, fascism and national-socialism. Even the rise of populism will be followed by a decline. On all these religions, ideologies and ideas, a quote can be applied of the dwarf in Nietzsche's *Thus Spoke Zarathustra*: "You throw yourself up high, but every stone that is thrown must fall".[22]

In this context it makes sense to refer to the journalist Robert Kaplan. In his *Monsoon, The Indian Ocean and the Future of American Power*, he wonders whether the Atlantic Civilization is not going the same way as once the civilization of the Mediterranean World.[23] Braudel and others show how this world is declining after the Renaissance and how the beginning of a new Atlantic civilization arises with the connection between the North-Italian cities and the cities in the Low Countries such as Bruges, Antwerp and later Amsterdam. Now, the United States has to deal with the expanding powers of China, India and the Islamic world in the South Chinese Sea and the Indian Ocean. Isn't this the decline of the Atlantic World and the rise of new civilizations, surrounded by other waters, as Robert Kaplan suggests? Kaplan refers to Janet Abu-Lughod's *Before European Hegemony*. In her book she sketches a world of civilizations around the Indian Ocean before 1250, of which the Mediterranean is only a part.[24] In that period Northern Europe is at the periphery of these main civilizations. Now that Europe has lost its world dominance, the future can meet us from the past, as it were, another example of a kairotic time.

The rise-and-fall paradigm of the romanticist time teaches us something about the world in which we currently live. Moreover, learning about the coming and going of civilizations around seas and oceans can be a good alternative for the history teaching from a nationalistic point of view, which is at this moment dominant in most of the European countries. The ascent and descent of cultures will tell the story of mankind as a whole.[25] As a matter of fact people in the West know very little about the histories of China, Japan, India and Indonesia as world powers on the rise. To me it is deplorable that there are daily reports in magazines and newspapers on these countries whereby many readers miss any historical background!

Although apt for the world of education, the paradigm of rise and fall is incapable of solving the great problems in today's world. If history is submitted to such an eternal law, then most values are relative and deemed to perish. It suggests that the values of every civilization are equal and exchangeable, which leads to a bad form of cultural relativism. There is a limit to cultural relativism and multi-culturalism. For example, can the hard-won rights of women be replaced by new forms of women's oppression? To solve the problems of a *globalizing* world, we must have a right relationship of modernist as well as historicist temporalities.

The time of *the synchronicity of the non-synchronous* shows the way how critical interference – not fusion – between modernism and historicism can be fruitful. In the chapters about Tocqueville and Marx, we have presented it as a historicist time with attention for modernization. Its historicism lies in the fact that it is embodied and often burdensome. Its modernism consists of an irresistible, almost self-sustaining trend into the future. If there is one trend now, following us from the past into the future, it is globalization. I regard this as something similar to the egalitarianism that Tocqueville encounters in the nineteenth century. We do not have to glorify globalization and Europeanization, but we must face them as irreversible, like Tocqueville does with egalitarianism.

Tocqueville sees occurrences hampering egalitarianism, and the same is true for globalization in our days. Despite its irreversible character, many events hinder its progress. Trade liberalization is stagnating and protectionism is on the rise.[26] Geopolitical pressure from both China and Russia is increasing. The same applies to international crime, problems with refugees and migration and last but not least the defence of democracy and the rule of law. This must be countered by close European and global cooperation. Any loss of national sovereignty is less an evil than continuing with unresolved issues.

Globalization, however, needs to be controlled too. It still needs national politics, because there are no international institutions with sufficient power that can rebalance the profits from capital and business to labour and society as a whole.[27] Thus, we need the state as a continuing entity and its embodied temporality of rise and fall to analyse our present condition, putting an end to the era of unbridled capitalism. It can impose restrictions on banks, establish regulations for data use and combat pollution by levying taxes on industries. The state must make the world of business aware that government adds value to capital by facilitating transport through infrastructure, technology through education and medical and pharmaceutical industries through health care.[28]

Despite this sound combination of international and national developments, not every form of synchronicity of the non-synchronous is useful. We can put question marks behind Braudel's approach, presenting developed countries as the future of the underdeveloped ones. Braudel is part of a long, mainly French tradition from Michelet to Le Play and others, which holds the opinion that the future is not an idea but a reality in another part of the world. This creates the disadvantage that, in our time, Europe or the West is the standard for the rest of the world. By intermingling the modernist present of the West with the "non-modern" future of non-Western regions, ethnocentrism comes up. Chakrabarty argues against these views by rejecting the modernization paradigm, which is a singular option. He calls the norms of capitalism and secularization "provincial".

However, he also discards a multi-culturalism which believes that countries, societies or cultures can remain outside the "metanarrative of progress". He mentions this "the raging Medusa of cultural relativism".[29] Provincializing Europe does not mean that Chakrabarty wants to dispose the Western standards entirely. India officially (not completely in reality) abolishes widow burning and the caste system. Chakrabarty accepts the "globalization of capital" which "inheres the Enlightenment universals".[30] Still, he also wants to preserve Indian traditions in a multitude of subaltern microhistories. As a result, he creates an alliance between the dominant metropolitan histories and the subaltern "peripheral" pasts.[31]

Chakrabarty's subaltern studies originate in nostalgia, and there is nothing wrong with that. Nevertheless, he keeps the world of progress and the one of tradition apart. According to Chakrabarty, Indians live in a "'constantly fragmentary' and 'irreducibly plural now'".[32] The Nobel Laureate physicist Raman and the Bengali word *shomoy-granthi* are examples of how a Nietzschean and a Heideggerian plural "now" manifests itself.[33] It is "a stretched present", in which the past must illuminate the problems that have to be solved in the future.[34]

Europe needs this disentanglement of nostalgia and progress as well. Nowadays there exists a hunger for a nationalist past with all kinds of traditions, mixed with a desire to maintain modernist, Western Enlightenment values. The *intermingling* of traditionalism and modernism often arises the bad odour of ethnocentrism. On the one hand, we need nostalgia as a source of inspiration for all kinds of art, from architecture, with its retro buildings to literature and films, based on stories from the past. On the other hand, liberal values are important in themselves. We must be aware of them, be proud of them and certainly protect them, but it is not right to mix them with traditionalism and nationalism. The same applies to our national states. As explained above, they still are important for our future. We cannot live without it for now. However, a too nationalistic approach of the state leads to a convulsive preservation of national sovereignty that impedes a healthy Europeanization and globalization. In the light of global geopolitics, this can lead to a Europe provincializing itself.

Modernism and traditionalism, internationalism and national sovereignty must remain in an irreducible plural now. Nostalgia and traditionalism need modernism to face the problems of the future. Modernist values like pride on liberal principles must be interrupted and critically questioned by historicist values like tolerance, empathy and curiosity. They must not be mixed but have to be juxtaposed in a dialectical way. Modernism without the opposition of historicism creates superficial thinking in terms of progress. Historicism, without a dialectical relation with modernism, remains stuck in traditionalism and blindness to the future, creating slackness and lethargy.

In what way can **kairotic time** support the other two time options? Microhistories with their kairotic temporality can illuminate the present human condition, because they touch us by empathy for deviant behaviour. I think of Carlo Ginzburg and his *The Cheese and the Worms*, in which the miller Menocchio, with his alternative worldview opposes the violence of the Inquisition.[35] Such a history displays the presence of intolerance with regard to unusual behaviour. It erases the differences between past and present, because in the present the same phenomena can be discovered, like the stance of the Hungarian government with regard to Soros and his Open Society Institute. Menocchio and the Inquisition are at the same time the stowaways in the continuing story of humankind and the abnormal passageways of things, happening in the past, but directly connected to the present. Their past-presence "leaks" into our present.[36]

Carnival in Romans by Le Roy Ladurie also is apt to play such a kairotic role. That book exactly fits in with the global problems we discussed before. The carnivals in Romans in 1579 and 1580 are time-knots in France's long fight of the common people against the rich. It is the ongoing struggle, taking place from the Middle Ages to the French Revolution, against the tax exemptions of the nobility, the clergy and the landowning bourgeoisie. Ladurie chooses the side of the commoners, because he believes that tax exemptions for the rich are unjust and immoral. Maybe, the since 1900 evolving Welfare State has been an exception in history, an exception with a little more equality. Piketty and Milanovic show that in the last twenty years, similar problems have arisen as in pre-revolutionary France. The old struggles of the then commoners "leak" into the contemporaneous problems of the citizens of the twenty-first century. The fight of commoners against wealthy, bad educated elites is an example of the eternal struggle for more justice and equality in society. The all-embracing idea of progress has made us blind to Nietzsche's eternal recurrence.

Studies like those of Ginzburg and Le Roy Ladurie are the subaltern histories of the Western world, showing time-knots in which the past is perceived in relation to their immediate meaning for the present and the future. That is what Benjamin means with his *Jetztzeit*. Thus, stories from the past must be given the presence that Nietzsche, Benjamin and Heidegger are talking about. Microhistories, such as *Carnival in Romans* and *The Cheese and the Worms*, perceived in the context of a kairotic time, form an essential part of the *historia rerum gestarum*.

Through a history of rise and fall, with analyses based on the synchronicity of the non-synchronous, we must discover contemporary tipping points to create a better future. That is why we argue for a new, historicist story, not based on progress or on a short-sighted "living in the present" but on a carefully analysed past and present. All three times can tell us about the human condition, enable us to understand the present and the future from the past and allow us to offer a realistic view of the future.[37]

Notes

1 Esposito, "Transformationen geschichtlicher Zeitlichkeit nach dem Boom", 13.
2 See for time as a collective human construction: Helga Nowotny, *Eigenzeit. Entstehung und Strukturierung eines Zeitgefühls* (Frankfurt a. M.: Suhrkamp, 1993).
3 Reinhart Koselleck, "Gibt es Beschleunigung in der Geschichte?", in: idem, *Zeitschichten. Studien zur Historik* (Frankfurt a. M., 2003), 150–176 and idem, "Zeitverkürzung und Beschleunigung. Eine Studie zur Säkularisation", 177–202; Rosa, *Beschleunigung*; Clark, *Time and Power*; Rainer Zoll, "Krise der Zeiterfahrung", in: idem, *Zerstörung und Wideraneignung von Zeit* (Frankfurt a. M.: Suhrkamp, 1988); Esposito, "Transformationen geschichtlicher Zeitlichkeit nach dem Boom", 16.
4 Lübbe, *Im Zug der Zeit. Verkürzter Aufenthalt in der Gegenwart*; For stress see: Lea Haller, Sabine Höhler and Heiko Stoff (eds.), "Stress", *Zeithistorische Forschungen/Studies in Contemporary History* 11 (2014).
5 Lucian Hölscher, "Von leeren und gefüllten Zeiten. Zum Wandel historische Zeitkonzepte seit dem 18. Jahrhundert", in: Esposito, "Transformationen geschichtlicher Zeitlichkeit nach dem Boom", 16.
6 Ibid., 9–11.
7 Koselleck, *Futures Past*, 11.
8 Clark, *Time and Power*, 9–10.
9 Baschet, *Défaire la tyrannie du présent*, 6.
10 In his "Gibt es beschleunigung in der Geschichte?", in: Koselleck, *Zeitschichten. Studien zur Historik* (Frankfurt a. M., 2003; original: 1976/1985), 150–176, Koselleck also points to some negative aspects of acceleration. However, they remain in the dark, especially by those who follow in his footsteps.
11 Noah Harari Yuval, *Homo Deus: A Brief History of Tomorrow* (New York: Harper Collins Publishers, 2016).
12 Berber Bevernage, "'The Past Is Evil/Evil Is Past', On Retrospective Politics, Philosophy of History and Temporal Manicheism", *History and Theory* 54, 3 (2015), 333–352, esp. 163.
13 Safa Motesharrei, Jorge Rivas, Eugenia Kalnay, Ghassem R. Asrar, Antonio J. Busalacchi, Robert F. Cahalan, Mark A. Cane, Rita R. Colwell, Kuishuang Feng and Rachel S. Franklin, "Modelling Sustainability: Population, Inequality, Consumption, and Bidirectional Coupling of the Earth and Human Systems", *National Science Review* 3, 4 (December 2016), 470–494, Figure 4. https://doi.org/10.1093/nsr/nww081. Note that the terms "empty" and "full" are used here contrary to the use of the same terms regarding the phenomenon of time.
14 Donella Meadows, Jorgen Randers and Dennis Meadows, *A Synopsis: Limits to Growth. The 30-Year Update* (White River Junction, VT: Chelsea Green, 2004). http://donellameadows.org/archives/a-synopsis-limits-to-growth-the-30-year-update/
15 Branko Milanovic, *Global Inequality: A New Approach for the Age of Globalization* (Cambridge, MA: Harvard University Press, 2016).
16 Real income growth at various percentiles of global income distribution, 1988–2008 (in 2005 PPPs) ©Branko Milanovic.
17 Maarten Schinkel, "Opeens twijfel bij dé grafiek over onvrede", *NRC/Handelsblad* (September 14, 2016), E5.
18 Thomas Piketty, *Capital in the Twenty-First Century* (Cambridge, MA: Belknap/Harvard University Press, 2014).
19 J. Stiglitz, *The Price of Inequality: How Todays Divided Society Endangers Our Future* (Old Saybrook, CT: Tentor Media Inc., 2012).
20 Timothy Snyder, *On Tyranny: Twenty Lessons From the Twentieth Century* (New York: Tim Duggan Books, 2017).
21 Amy Chua, *Day of Empire: How Hyperpowers Rise to Global Dominance – And Why They Fall* (New York: The Double Day Publishing Group, 2007); John Lukacs, *The End of the Twentieth Century and the End of the Modern Age* (New Haven and London: Yale

University Press, 1993); William H. McNeill's *Rise of the West: A History of the Human Community* (University of Chicago Press, rev. ed., 1992) and idem, *Arnold J. Toynbee: A Life* (Oxford: Oxford University Press, 1989).
22 *"Dich selber warfst du so hoch, aber jeder geworfene Stein muss – fallen!"* Nietzsche, "Also sprach Zarathustra", *Werke* II (Schlechta ed.), 681.
23 Robert Kaplan, *Monsoon: The Indian Ocean and the Future of American Power* (New York: Random House Publishing Group, 2010).
24 Janet-Abu-Lughod, *Before European Hegemony: The World System A.D. 1250–1350* (New York and Oxford: Oxford University Press, 1989).
25 Harry Jansen, "Wereldgeschiedenis vanuit Europees Perspectief", *Hermes. Tijdschrift van de Vlaamse leraren Geschiedenis* 22, 64 (2018), 24–31; and idem, "The Little Dog of the *Fondaco dei Tedeschi*. On Nations, Globalization and Periodization in the History Curriculum", *World History Connected* 9, 3, FORUM: The Question of Historical Perspective in World Historical Analysis. See: http://worldhistoryconnected.press.illinois.edu/9.3/index.html
26 Martin Wolf, "The Tide of Globalisation Is Turning. Trade Liberalisation Has Stalled and One Can See a Steady Rise in Protectionist Measures", *Financial Times* (September 6, 2016).
27 Dani Rodrik, "Populism and the Economics of Globalization", *Journal of the International Business Policy* (2018), https://drodrik.scholar.harvard.edu/files/dani-rodrik/files/populism_and_the_economics_of_globalization.pdf, Concluding Remarks.
28 Mariana Mazzucato, *The Entrepreneurial State: Debunking Public vs Private Myths* (London: Anthem Press, 2015).
29 Chakrabarty, *Provincializing Europe*, 83–90.
30 Ibid., 250.
31 Ibid., 42.
32 Ibid., 253.
33 Ibid., 112.
34 Ibid., 252.
35 Carlo Ginzburg, *The Cheese and the Worms: The Cosmos of a Sixteenth-Century Miller* (Baltimore: Johns Hopkins University Press, 20133).
36 Runia, "Presence", 16.
37 See for the rejection of an autonomous presentism: Baschet, *Défaire la tyrannie du présent*, 296.

BIBLIOGRAPHY

Abu-Lughod, Janet, *Before European Hegemony: The World System A.D. 1250–1350* (New York and Oxford: Oxford University Press, 1989).
Adhémar, Hélène, *Watteau, sa vie, son oeuvre. Catalogue des peintures et illustrations* (Paris, 1950).
Alfaix Assis, Arthur, *What Is History For? Johann Gustav Droysen and the Functions of Historiography* (New York: Berghahn Books, 20162).
Althusser, Louis, *Glossary*, "Dislocation" (transl. Ben Brewster, 1969). https://www.marxists.org/glossary/terms/althusser/index.htm
Althusser, Louis, *Politics and History* (transl. Ben Brewster; NLB, London: Verso, 1972).
Althusser, Louis, "Schets van het begrip historiese tijd", in: *Ter elfder ure* 31 (Geschiedenistheorie 1; Nijmegen: SUN, without year of ref.), 380–415.
Althusser, Louis and Etienne Balibar, *Das Kapital lesen I* (Reinbeck bei Hamburg: Rowohlt, 1972).
Althusser, Louis and Etienne Balibar, *Reading Capital* (transl. Ben Brewster; London: Verso, 1997).
Ankersmit, Frank, *Historical Representation* (Stanford: Stanford University Press, 2001).
Ankersmit, Frank, *Sublime Historical Experience* (Stanford: Stanford University Press, 2005).
Ankersmit, Frank, *Meaning, Truth and Reference in Historical Explanation* (Cornell: Leuven UP, 2012).
Ankersmit, Frank, "Koselleck on 'Histories' Versus 'History' or: Historical Ontology Versus Historical Epistemology". Lecture Ankersmit held at the conference of Outo Preto, August 2016.
Ankersmit, Frank, E. Domanska and H. Kellner (eds.), *Re-figuring Hayden White* (Stanford: Stanford University Press, 2009).
Aristotle (W. D. Ross ed.), *The Works of Aristotle II, Physics* (Oxford: Clarendon, 1947).
Arouet, F. M., *Oeuvres complètes de Voltaire*, tome XXXI "Commentaire sur l'Esprit des Lois. Section Esclavage" (1756).
Arouet, F. M., *The Works of Voltaire: A Contemporary Version: A Critique and Biography by John Morley*, 21 vols. (Trans. William F. Fleming, 1901), vol. XII. http://oll.libertyfund.org/titles/2132
Assmann, Aleida, *Ist die Zeit aus den Fugen? Aufstieg und Fall des Zeitregimes der Moderne* (München: Carl Hanser Verlag, 2013).

Bibliography

Assmann, Aleida, "Transformations of the Modern Time Regime", in: Lorenz and Bevernage, *Breaking up Time*, 39–56.

Auderset, Juri, Philip Müller and Andreas Behr, "Einleitung: Beschleunigung und plurale Temporalitäten = Introduction: Accélération et temporalités plurielles", *Traverse: Zeitschrift für Geschichte = Revue d'histoire* 23, 3 (2016).

Augustine, *Confessions*, Book 11 (transl. E.B. Pusey; Mount Pleasant, SC: Arcadia Press, 2017²).

Avineri, Shlomo, *Hegel's Theory of the Modern State* (Cambridge: Cambridge University Press, 1974²).

Balibar, Etienne, *The Philosophy of Marx* (London: Verso, 1995).

Balmuth, J., "Marx and the Philosophers", in: Freedman, *Marxist Social Thought*.

Baschet, Jérôme, *Défaire la tyrannie du présent. Temporalités émergentes et futurs inédits* (Paris: La Découverte, 2018).

Bechtold, Brigitte, "*More Than a Room* and *Three Guineas*: Understanding Virginia Woolf's Social Thought", *Journal of International Women's Studies* 1, 2 (2000).

Becker, Carl, *The Heavenly City of the Eighteenth-Century Philosophers* (New Haven: Yale University Press, 1932).

Beiser, Frederick, *Hegel* (New York and London: Routledge, 2005).

Beiser, Frederick, *The German Historicist Tradition* (Oxford: Oxford University Press, 2011).

Benjamin, Walter, "Theses on the Philosophy of History", in: Hannah Arendt and Harry Zohn (eds.), *Illuminations* (New York: Harcourt Brace Jovanovich, 1968).

Benjamin, Walter, *Über den Begriff der Geschichte* (Gérard Raulet hrsg.; Berlin: Suhrkamp, 2010).

Bentley, Michael, *Modern Historiography: An Introduction* (London and New York: Routledge, 2005).

Berding, Helmut, "Leopold von Ranke", in: Koslowski, *The Discovery of Historicity in German Idealism and Historism*, 41–58.

Bergson, Henri, *Matter and Memory* (London: Allen and Unwin, 1911).

Berlin, Isaiah, *Vico and Herder: Two Studies in the History of Ideas* (New York: Vintage Books, 1977).

Bevernage, Berber, "The Past Is Evil/Evil Is Past: On Retrospective Politics, Philosophy of History and Temporal Manicheism", *History and Theory* 54, 3 (2015), 333–352.

Blix, G., "Charting the 'Transitional Period': The Emergence of Modern Time in the Nineteenth Century", *History and Theory* 45, 1 (2006), 51–71.

Bloch, Ernst, *Philosophische Aufsätze zur objektiven Phantasie* (Frankfurt am Main: Suhrkamp Verlag, 1969).

Bloch, Ernst, "Nonsynchronism and the Obligation to Its Dialectics", *New German Critique* 11 (Spring 1977), 22–38.

Bloch, Ernst, *Heritage of Our Times* (Cambridge, UK: Polity Press, 1991).

Bloch, Ernst, "Non-contemporaneity and Obligation to Its Dialectic", in idem, *Heritage of Our Times*, 97–148.

Bloch, Ernst, "Ungleichzeitigkeit, nicht nur Rückständigkeit" in: idem, *Philosophische Aufsätze zur objektiven Phantasie*, 41–49.

Bloch, Marc, *Mélanges historiques* I (Paris: S.E.V.P.E.N., 1963).

Bloch, Marc, *The Historian's Craft* (Manchester: Manchester University Press, 2004).

Bowker, G. C., "Altogether Now: Synchronization, Speed and the Failure of Narrativity", *History and Theory* 53, 4 (December 2014), 563–576.

Brandom, Robert, *Making It Explicit: Reasoning, Representing and Discursive Commitment* (Cambridge, MA and London: Harvard University Press, 1998²).

Braudel, Fernand, *L'Écriture sur l'histoire* (Paris: Gallimard, 1969).
Braudel, Fernand, *The Mediterranean and the Mediterranean World in the Age of Philip II*. vol. I and II (transl. Siân Reynolds; Glasgow: Collins Sons and Harper and Row, 1972).
Braudel, Fernand, *Temps du Monde. Civilisation Matérielle, Économie et Capitalisme. XVe-XVIIIe Siècle*, tome 3 (Paris: Armand Collin, 1979).
Braudel, Fernand, *On History* (transl. Sarah Matthews; Chicago: The University of Chicago Press, 1980).
Braudel, Fernand, *Beschaving, Economie en Kapitalisme (15e–18e eeuw). De structuur van het dagelijks leven 1* (Amsterdam: uitgeverij Contact, 1988).
Brewer, A., "Adam Smith's Stages of History", in: *Discussion Paper* number 08/601 (March 2008).
Brunner, O., W. Conze and R. Koselleck, *Geschichtliche Grundbegriffe. Historische Lexikon zur politisch-sozialen Sprache in Deutschland*. Bd 2 (Stuttgart: Klett-Cotta, 1979).
Buiks, Peter, *Alexis de Tocqueville en de democratische revolutie* (Assen: Van Gorcum, 1979).
Burckhardt, Jacob, *The Civilization of the Renaissance in Italy* (London: Penguin Books, 1980).
Burges, Joel and Amy J. Elias, *Time: A Vocabulary of the Present* (New York: University Press, 2016).
Burke, Peter, *The Renaissance* (Houndmills, Basingstoke and New York: Palgrave, 19972).
Burke, Peter, "Introduction", in: Burckhardt, *The Civilization of the Renaissance in Italy*, 1–15.
Butterfield, Herbert, *The Whig Interpretation of History* (Harmondsworth: Penguin, 1973, 1st ed. 1931).
Carrithers, D., "The Enlightenment Science of Society", in: Fox, Porter and Wokler, *Inventing Human Science*.
Chakrabarty, Dipesh, *Provincializing Europe: Postcolonial Thought and Historical Difference* (Princeton and Oxford: Princeton University Press, 2008).
Chang, Kyung-Sup, "Reflexive Modernization", *Wiley Online Library* (December 4, 2017).
Chernus, Ira, "Frederick Jameson's Interpretation of Postmodernism". http://spot.colorado.edu/~chernus/NewspaperColumns/LongerEssays/JamesonPostmodernism.htm
Chua, Amy, *Day of Empire: How Hyperpowers Rise to Global Dominance – And Why They Fall* (New York: The Double Day Publishing Group, 2007).
Clark, Christopher, *Time and Power: Visions of History in German Politics, From the Thirty Years' War to the Third Reich* (Oxford: Princeton University Press, 2019).
Condorcet, Jean-Antoine-Nicolas de, *Esquisse d'un tableau des progrès de l'esprit humain* (Paris, 1795).
Conze, Werner (ed.), *Staat und Gesellschaft im deutschen Vormärz 1815–1848* (Stuttgart: Klett Verlag, 1978³).
Cronon, W., "Two Cheers for the Whig Interpretation of History", *Perspectives on History: The Newsmagazine of the American Historical Association* 50, 6 (September 2012).
Damamme, D., "Un Cas d'Expertise. L'Etrange Defaite de Marc Bloch", *Sociétés Contemporaines* 39, 3 (2000), 95–116.
Derrida, Jacques, *Specters of Marx: The State of the Debt, the Work of Mourning and the New International* (transl. Peggy Kamuf; New York and London: Routledge, 1994).
Descartes, René, *Principles of Philosophy*, part 4: the earth. (ed. Jonathan Bennett 2010–2015; 1st ed., Latin, 1644: French, 1647).
Dilthey, Wilhelm, *Gesammelte Schriften*, vol. II (Stuttgart: B.G. Teubner, 1957).
Dilthey, Wilhelm, "Pantheismus nach seinem geschichtlichen Zusammenhang mit den älteren Pantheistischen Systemen", in: idem, *Gesammelte Schriften*. vol. II.
Dries, Manuel (ed.), *Nietzsche on Time and History* (Berlin and New York: Walter de Gruyter, 2008).

Dries, Manuel, "Nietzsche's Critique of Staticism. Introduction to Nietzsche on Time and History", in: idem, *Nietzsche on Time and History*, 1–19.

Dries, Manuel, "Towards Adualism: Becoming and Nihilism in Nietzsche's Philosophy", in: idem, *Nietzsche on Time and History*, 113–145.

Droysen, J. G. *Historik* (ed. R. Hübner; München and Berlin, 1943).

Dudley, Will, *Hegel, Nietzsche and Philosophy: Thinking Freedom* (Cambridge: Cambridge University Press, 2002).

Dussen, Jan van der, *History as a Science: Collingwood's Philosophy of History* (unpublished ed.; Leiden, 1980).

Dyck, M. van, "Tijdmeting en tijdservaring in de Middeleeuwen", *Hermes*, 64, 22 (September 2018), 6–12.

Elm, Ralf, "Schenkung, Entzug, schöpferisches Fragen", in: Figal, *Hans-Georg Gadamer*, 151–176.

Engels, Friedrich, "Engels to J. Bloch" (September 21–22, 1890), in: Freedman, *Marxist Social Thought*, 130.

Engels, Friedrich, "Engels to H. Starkenburg" (January 25, 1894), in: Freedman, *Marxist Social Thought*, 133.

Engels, Friedrich, "Ludwig Feuerbach and the End of Classical German Philosophy", in: Freedman, *Marxist Social Thought*, 110–114.

Escudier, Alexandre, "Das Gefühl der Beschleunigung der Moderne Geschichte: Bausteine für eine Geschichte", *Esprit* (Juni 2008), 165–191.

Esposito, Fernando (ed.), *Zeitenwandel: Transformationen geschichtlicher Zeitlichkeit nach dem Boom* (Göttingen, Bristol: Vandenhoeck & Ruprecht, 2017).

Esposito, Fernando, "Transformationen geschichtlicher Zeitlichkeit nach dem Boom", in: idem, *Zeitenwandel*, 7–62.

Esposito, Fernando and Hans Ulrich Gumbrecht, "Posthistoire Then. Ein Gespräch mit Hans Ulrich Gumbrecht über unsere breite Gegenwart", in: Esposito, *Zeitenwandel*, 255–277.

Fèbvre, Lucien, *Combats pour l'histoire* (Paris: Colin, 1953).

Figal, G., *Hans-Georg Gadamer* (Berlin: Akademie Verlag, 2007).

Fleming, William F., *The Works of Voltaire: A Contemporary Version* (New York: Dingwall-Rock, 1927), vol. XIX, Pt. I.

Fox, Christopher, Roy Porter and Robert Wokler (eds.), *Inventing Human Science* (Berkeley: University of California Press, 1995).

Freedman, R. (ed.), *Marxist Social Thought* (New York: Harcourt, Brace & World Inc., 1967).

Friedrichs, C. R., "Capitalism, Mobility, and Class Formation in the Early Modern German City: A Cross Cultural Analysis", in: Ph. Abrams and E. A. Wrigley (eds.), *Towns in Societies, Essays in Economic History and Historical Sociology* (Cambridge: CUP, 1978).

Friedrichs, C. R., *Urban Society in an Age of War. Nördlingen 1580–1720* (Princeton, NJ: Princeton University Press, 1979).

Fritzsche, Peter, "The Ruins of Modernity", in: Lorenz and Bevernage, *Breaking up Time*, 57–68.

Furet, François, "Naissance d'un paradigme: Tocqueville et le voyage en Amérique (1825–1831)", *Annales, Économie, Civilisations* 39, 2 (1984), 225–239.

Gadamer, Hans-Georg, *Wahrheit und Methode. Grundzüge euner Hermeneutik, Gesammelte Werke I* (Tübingen: Erstausgabe, 1960).

Gadamer, Hans-Georg, "Concerning Empty and Full-filled Time", transl. R. P. O'Hara, in: E. G. Ballard and C. E. Scott (eds.), *Martin Heidegger in Europe and America* (The Hague: Martinus Nijhoff, 1973).

Gassett, Ortega y, "Die Aufgabe unserer Zeit" (1923), *Gesammelte Werke* (transl. Helene Weyl and Ulrich Weber, 4 vols.; Stuttgart: Deutsche Verlags-Anstalt, 1950).
Geppert, Alexander and Till Kössler (Hg), *Obsession der Gegenwart. Zeit im 20. Jahrhundert* (Göttingen, Bristol: Vandenhoeck & Ruprecht, 2015).
Geppert, Alexander and Till Kössler, "Zeit-Geschichte als Aufgabe", in: idem, *Obsession der Gegenwart*, 7–36.
Gibbon, Edward, *The History of the Decline and Fall of the Roman Empire*, vol. 1 (Dent and London: Everyman's Library, 1910).
Gierl, Martin, *Geschichte als präzisierte Wissenschaft: Johann, Christoph Gatterer und die Historiographie des 18. Jahrhunderts im ganzen Umfang* (Stuttgart: Frohmann-Holzboog Verlag, 2012).
Gilbert, Felix, *History: Politics or Culture. Reflections on Ranke and Burckhardt* (Princeton: Princeton University Press, 1990).
Ginzburg, Carlo, *The Cheese and the Worms: The Cosmos of a Sixteenth-Century Miller* (Baltimore: Johns Hopkins University Press, 2013^3).
Gordy, M., "Reading Althusser: Time and the Social Whole", *History and Theory* 22, 1 (February 1983), 1–21.
Gorman, Jonathan, "The Limits of Historiographical Choice in Temporal Distinctions", in: Lorenz and Bevernage, *Breaking up Time*, 155–175.
Habermas, Jürgen, *Die neue Unübersichtlichkeit* (Frankfurt am Main: Suhrkamp, 1985).
Halbwachs, Maurice, *The Collective Memory* (ed. and transl. Lewis A. Coser; Chicago: University of Chicago Press, 1992).
Hallam, H., *Constitutional History of England From the Ascension of Henry VII to the Death of George II*. www.gutenberg.org/files/39711/39711-h/39711-h.htm.
Haller, Lea, Sabine Höhler and Heiko Stoff (eds.), "Stress", *Zeithistorische Forschungen/Studies in Contemporary History* 11 (2014).
Hannoum, Abdelmajid, "What Is an Order of Time?", *History and Theory* 47, 3 (2008).
Harari, Yuval Noah, *Homo Deus: A Brief History of Tomorrow* (New York: Harper Collins Publishers, 2016).
Hartog, François, *Regimes of Historicity: Presentism and Experiences of Time* (New York: University of Columbia, 2017^3).
Hartog, François, "The Modern Régime of Historicity in the Face of Two World Wars", in: Lorenz and Bevernage, *Breaking up Time*, 124–133.
Harvey, David, *The Condition of Postmodernity: An Enquiry Into the Origins of Cultural Change* (Cambridge: Cambridge University Press, 1990^2), 284–307.
Hegel, Georg W. F., *Enzyklopedie der philosophischen Wissenschaften im Grundrisse*, vol. II (1817, 1st ed., and the G. Bolland ed.; Leiden, 1906).
Hegel, Georg W. F., *Political Writings* (ed. T. Knox; Oxford: Oxford University Press, 1964).
Hegel, Georg W. F., *Grundlinien der Philosophie des Rechts* (Frankfurt am Main: Suhrkamp Verlag, 1970).
Hegel, Georg W. F., *Vorlesungen über die Philosophie der Geschichte* (Frankfurt am Main: Suhrkamp Verlag, 1970).
Hegel, Georg W. F., *Phenomenology of Mind* (transl. J. B. Baillie [1910]; Mineola, NY: Dover Publications Inc., 2001).
Heidegger, Martin, *Sein und Zeit* (Tübingen: Max Niemeyer Verlag, 1927, 198616).
Heidegger, Martin, *Kant und das Problem der Metaphysik* (Frankfurt am Main: Klostermann, 19912).
Heidegger, Martin, *Zijn en Tijd* (Nijmegen: SUN, 1998).
Heidegger, Martin, *Being and Time* (transl. John Macquarrie and Edward Robinson; Oxford and Cambridge, MA: Blackwell, 2001).

Herder, Johann Gottfried, *Metakritik zur Kritik der reinen Vernunft* (Frankkfurt und Leipzig: Hartknoch, 1799). https://archive.org/details/einemetakritikz01herdgoog.
Herder, Johann Gottfried, *Reflections on the Philosophy of the History of Humankind* (ed. F. E. Manuel, selections from T. O. Churchill's translation of J. G. Herder's *Ideen zur Philosophie der Geschichte der Menschheit*; 2 vols., 1800–1803) (Chicago: University of Chicago Press, 1968).
Hermsen, Joke, *Kairos, een nieuwe bevlogenheid* (Amsterdam: de Arbeiderspers, 2015).
Himmelfarb, Gertrud, *The New History and the Old: Critical Essays and Reappraisals* (Cambridge, MA and London: Harvard University Press, 2004).
Hölderlin, Friedrich, *Hyperion and Selected Poems* (ed. Eric L. Santner; New York: Continuum, 1990).
Hölderlin, Friedrich, "Hyperion, or the Hermit in Greece", in: idem, *Hyperion and Selected Poems*.
Hölscher, Lucian, *Semantik der Leere. Grenzfragen der Geschichtswissenschaft* (Göttingen: Wallstein Verlag, 2009).
Hölscher, Lucian, "Time Gardens: Historical Concepts in Modern Historiography", *History and Theory* 53, 4 (December 2014), 577–591.
Hölscher, Lucian, "Mysteries of the Historical Order: Ruptures, Simultaneity and the Relationship of the Past, the Present and the Future", in: Lorenz and Bevernage, *Breaking up Time*, 134–154.
Hölscher, Lucian, "Von leeren und gefüllten Zeiten. Zum Wandel historische Zeitkonzepte seit dem 18. Jahrhundert", in: Geppert and Kössler, *Obsession der Gegenwart*, 37–70.
Homer, Sean, "Narratives of History, Narratives of Time", in: Caren Irr and Ian Buchanan (eds.), *On Jameson: From Postmodernism to Globalization* (New York: State University New York, 2006), 71–94.
Huizinga, Johan, *Verzamelde Werken*, vol. 1–9 (Haarlem: Tjeenk Willink, 1947).
Huizinga, Johan, "Het aesthetische bestanddeel van geschiedkundige voorstellingen", in: idem, *Verzamelde Werken*, vol. 7 (Haarlem, 1950), 3–28.
Huizinga, Johan, *Men and Ideas: History, the Middle Ages, the Renaissance* (New York: Meridian Books Inc., 1959).
Huizinga, Johan, *The Waning of the Middle Ages* (Mineola, NY: Dover Publications Inc., 1999).
Huizinga, Johan, "De Taak der Cultuurgeschiedenis", in: idem, *Verzamelde Werken*, vol. 7, 35–94.
Huizinga, Johan, "Een kleine samenspraak over de thema's der Romantiek", in: idem, *Verzamelde Werken*, vol. 4, 381–390.
Huizinga, Johan, "Erasmus", in: idem, *Verzamelde Werken*, vol. 6, 3–194.
Huizinga, Johan, "Herfsttij der Middeleeuwen", in: idem, *Verzamelde Werken*, vol. 3, 3–435.
Huizinga, Johan, "Het historisch museum", in: idem, *Verzamelde Werken*, vol. 2, 559–568.
Huizinga, Johan, "Het probleem der Renaissance", in idem, *Verzamelde Werken*, vol. 4, 3–194.
Huizinga, Johan, "In de schaduwen van morgen. Een diagnose van het geestelijk lijden van onzen tijd", in: idem, *Verzamelde Werken*, vol. 7, 313–428.
Huizinga, Johan, "Twee worstelaars met den Engel", in: idem, *Verzamelde Werken*, vol. 4, 441–496.
Humboldt, Wilhelm von, "Über die Aufgabe des Geschichtsschreibers", in: idem, *Gesammelte Schriften*, vol. IV (Hrsg. Albert Leitzmann, 1905, print 2015).
Humboldt, Wilhelm von, "On the Historian's Task", *History and Theory* 6 (1967), 57–71.

Hume, David, *History of England From the Invasion of Julius Caesar to the Revolution of 1689*, vol. I (6 vols.; London, 1754–1762).
Hutchings, Kimberley, *Time and World Politics: Thinking the Present* (Manchester: Manchester University Press, 2008).
Huyge, René, "L'Univers de Watteau", in: Adhémar, *Watteau, sa vie, son oeuvre*.
Israel, Jonathan, *Radical Enlightenment: Philosophy and the Making of Modernity* (Oxford: Oxford University Press, 2001).
Jameson, Frederick, *The Political Unconsciousness: Narrative as a Socially Symbolic Act* (Ithaca, NY: Cornell University Press, 2002³).
Jameson, Frederick, "The Ideological Analysis of Space", *Critical Exchange* 14 (Fall 1983), 1–15.
Jensen, Anthony K., "Geschichte or History? Nietzsche's Untimely Meditation in the Context of Nineteenth-Century Philological Studies", in: Dries, *Nietzsche on Time and History*, 213–230.
Jansen, Harry, "Duitsland, een geval apart" en "Krachtig, maar ook flexibel? – Politiekinstitutionele voorwaarden voor industrialisering", in: Hans Righart (ed.), *De Trage Revolutie. Over de wording van industriële samenlevingen* (Heerlen: Boom, Open Universiteit, 1991), 137–179.
Jansen, Harry, "Wrestling with the Angel: On Problems of Definition in Urban History", *Urban History* 23, 3 (1996), 277–299.
Jansen, Harry, *The Construction of an Urban Past: Narrative and System in Urban History* (Oxford and New York: Berg Publishers, 2001).
Jansen, Harry, "Braudels drie tijdlagen en de paradox van een dubbele en toch enkelvoudige tijd", *Tijdschrift voor Geschiedenis* 116, 4 (2003), 512–527.
Jansen, Harry, "Historische Ervaring en Tijd. Ankersmits *Sublime Historical Experience*", *Tijdschrift voor Geschiedenis* 121, 1 (2008), 72–85.
Jansen, Harry, *Triptiek van de tijd. Geschiedenis in Drievoud* (Nijmegen: Vantilt, 2010).
Jansen, Harry, "Is There a Future for History? On the Need for a Philosophy of History and Historiography", *Low Countries Historical Review* 127, 4 (2012), 121–129.
Jansen, Harry, "The Little Dog of the *Fondaco dei Tedeschi*. On Nations, Globalization and Periodization in the History Curriculum", *World History Connected* 9, 3 (2012), FORUM: The Question of Historical Perspective in World Historical Analysis.
Jansen, Harry, "Time, Narrative, and Fiction: The Uneasy Relationship Between Ricoeur and a Heterogeneous Temporality", *History and Theory* 54, 1 (February 2015), 1–24.
Jansen, Harry, "In Search of New Times: Temporality in the Enlightenment and Counter-Enlightenment", *History and Theory* 55, 1 (2016), 66–90.
Jansen, Harry, "Rethinking Burckhardt and Huizinga. On a Transformation of Temporal Images", *Storia della Storiografia* 70, 2 (2016), 95–112.
Jansen, Harry, "Wereldgeschiedenis vanuit Europees Perspectief", *Hermes. Tijdschrift van de Vlaamse leraren Geschiedenis* 22, 64 (2018), 24–31.
Jansen, Harry, "Research, Narrative and Representation: A Post-narrative Approach", *History and Theory* 58, 1 (2019), 67–88.
Jansen, Harry and Maria Grever (eds.), *De ongrijpbare tijd. Temporaliteit en de constructie van het verleden* (Hilversum: Verloren, 2001).
Johann, Gottfried Herder, *Sämtliche Werke*, vol. VIII (ed. B. Suphan; Berlin, 1877–1913).
Jordheim, Helge, "Against Periodization: Koselleck's Theory of Multiple Temporalities", *History and Theory* 51, 2 (2012), 151–171.
Jordheim, Helge, "Introduction: Multiple Times and the Work of Synchronization", *History and Theory* 53, 4 (2014), 498–518.
Jorgensen, L. and Newlands, S. (eds.), *Metaphysics and the Good: Themes From the Philosophy of Merrihew Adams* (Oxford: Oxford University Press, 2008).

Kant, Immanuel, *Kritik der reinen Vernunft* (Neu herausgegeben von Theodoor Valentiner; 11te Auflage; Der Philosophische Bibliothek Band. 37 (Leipzig: Verlag von Felix Meier, 1917).
Kant, Immanuel, *Critique of Pure Reason* (transl. Norman Kemp Smith; London: Macmillan and Co., 1929).
Kaplan, Robert, *Monsoon: The Indian Ocean and the Future of American Power* (New York: Random House Publishing Group, 2010).
Kaufmann, Walter, *Hegel, a Reinterpretation* (New York: Anchor Books, 1966).
Kellner, Hans, "Introduction", in: Ankersmit, Domanska and Kellner, *Re-figuring Hayden White*.
Kemble, J. M., *The Saxons in England* (London, 1849).
Kern, Stephen, *The Culture of Time and Space 1880–1918* (Cambridge, MA and London: Harvard University Press, 2003²).
Kevin Hill, R., "From Kantian Temporality to Nietzsche's Naturalism", in: Dries, *Nietzsche on Time and History*, 75–85.
Kleingeld, Pauline, "Kant, History, and the Idea of Moral Development", *History of Philosophy Quarterly* 16, 1 (1999).
Kojève, Alexandre, *Hegel, Kommentar zur Phänomenologie des Geistes* (Stuttgart: Suhrkamp Taschenbuch Wissenschaft 97, 1975).
Koselleck, Reinhart, *Vergangene Zukunft. Zur Semantik geschichtlicher Zeiten* (Frankfurt am Main: Suhrkamp, Taschenbuch Wissenschaft, 1989²).
Koselleck, Reinhart, *The Practice of Conceptual History: Timing History, Spacing Concepts* (Stanford: Stanford University Press, 2002).
Koselleck, Reinhart, *Zeitschichten. Studien zur Historik* (Frankfurt am Main: Suhrkamp, 2003; original: 1976/1985).
Koselleck, Reinhart, *Futures Past: On the Semantics of Historical Time* (New York: Columbia University Press, 2004).
Koselleck, Reinhart, "Concepts of Historical Time and Social History", in: idem, *The Practice of Conceptual History*, 115–130.
Koselleck, Reinhart, "The Eighteenth Century as the Beginning of Modernity", in: idem, *The Practice of Conceptual History*, 154–169.
Koselleck, Reinhart, "Geschichte, Geschichten und formale Zeitstrukturen", in: idem, *Vergangene Zukunft*, 130–143.
Koselleck, Reinhart, "Gibt es beschleunigung in der Geschichte?", in: idem, *Zeitschichten*, 150–176.
Koselleck, Reinhart, "Historia Magistra Vitae. The Dissolution of the Topos Into the Perspective of a Modernized Historical Process", in: idem, *Futures Past*, 26–42.
Koselleck, Reinhart, "History, Histories and Formal Time Structures", in: idem, *Futures Past*, 93–104.
Koselleck, Reinhart, "Modernity and the Planes of Historicity", in: idem, *Futures Past*, 9–25.
Koselleck, Reinhart, "'Space of Experience' and 'Horizon of Expectation'. Two Historical Categories", in: idem, *Futures Past*, 259–275.
Koselleck, Reinhart, "Time and History", in: idem, *The Practice of Conceptual History*, 100–114.
Koselleck, Reinhart, "Über die Geschichtsbedürftigkeit der Geschichtswissenschaft", in: idem, *Zeitschichten*, 298–316.
Koselleck, Reinhart, "Zeitverkürzung und Beschleunigung. Eine Studie zur Säkularisation", in: idem, *Zeitschichten*, 177–202.
Koselleck, Reinhart and Christian Meier, "Art, Fortschritt", in: Brunner, Conze and Koselleck, *Geschichtliche Grundbegriffe*, 351–424.

Koslowski, Peter, *The Discovery of Historicity in German Idealism and Historism* (Berlin, Heidelberg and New York: Springer, 2005).

Krieger, L., *The German Idea of Freedom: History of a Political Tradition* (Chicago and London: The University of Chicago Press, 1972²).

Krol, Reinbert A., *Het geweten van Duitsland. Friedrich Meinecke als pleitbezorger van het Duitse historisme* (Groningen, Dissertation, 2013).

Landwehr, Achim, "Die vielen, die anwesenden und abwesenden Zeiten", in: Esposito, *Zeitenwandel*, 227–253.

Lebovic, Nitzan, "The Last European: A Plea for a Politicized Benjamin. On Alexander Gelley, Benjamin's Passages: Dreaming, Awakening", *History and Theory* 55, 3 (2016), 465–475.

Leibniz, Gottfried Wilhelm, "Fifth Paper", in: *Samuel Clarke, A Collection of Papers*, which passed between the late learned Mr. Leibniz and Dr. Clarke, In the Years 1715 and 1716 (London, 1717), number 55. Published online: 2006. www.newtonproject.sussex.ac.uk/view/texts/normalized/THEM00234.

Leibniz, Gottfried Wilhelm, *The Principles of Philosophy Known as Monadology* (ed. J. Bennet), principle 22. www.earlymoderntexts.com/assets/pdfs/leibniz1714b.pdf

Le Roy, Ladurie, *Carnival in Romans* (New York: George Braziller, Inc., 1979).

Lessing, Gotthold Ephraim, *Laokoon oder über die Grenzen der Malerei und Poesie* (1776).

Lessing, Gotthold Ephraim, *Samtliche Werke*, vol. 2 (ed. by Karl Lachmann and Frank Muncker, Stuttgart, 1886–1924, Reprint: Berlin, 1979), 381–384.

Lorenz, Chris, "The Times They Are a-Changin. On Time, Space and Periodization in History", in: Mario Carretero, Stefan Berger and Maria Grever (eds.), *Palgrave Handbook of Research in Historical Culture and Education* (Houndmills: Palgrave, 2017), 109–133.

Lorenz, Chris, "Der letzte Fetisch des Stamms der Historiker. Zeit, Raum und Periodisierung in der Geschichtswissenschaft", in: Esposito, *Zeitenwandel*, 63–92.

Lorenz, Chris and Berber Bevernage (eds.), *Breaking up Time: Negotiating the Borders Between Present, Past and Future* (Göttingen: Vandenhoeck & Ruprecht, 2013).

Lorentz, Chris and Berber Bevernage, "Introduction", in: Lorenz and Bevernage, *Breaking up Time*, 7–35.

Lübbe, Hermann, *Im Zug der Zeit. Verkürzter Aufenthalt in der Gegenwart* (Berlin: Springer Verlag, 1992).

Lübbe, Hermann, *Zeiterfahrungen. Sieben Begriffe zur Beschreibung moderner Zivilisationsdynamik, Abhandlungen der geistes- und Sozialwissenschaftlichen Klasse 5, Akademie der Wissenschaften und der Literatur* (Mainz and Stuttgart: Steiner, 1996).

Lukács, Georg, *Der junge Hegel. Über die Beziehungen von Dialektik und Ökonomie,* 2 Bände (Frankfurt am Main: Suhrkamp Taschenbuch Wissenschaft, 1973).

Lukacs, John, *The end of the Twentieth Century and the End of the Modern Age* (New Haven and London: Yale University Press, 1993).

Lukacs, John, "Alexis the Tocqueville. A Bibliographical Essay". http://oll.libertyfund.org/pages/alexis-de-tocqueville-a-bibliographical-essay-by-john-lukacs#tocquevilleIIIv

Mandelbaum, Maurice, *The Anatomy of Historical Knowledge* (Baltimore and London: Johns Hopkins University Press, 1979).

Mann, Thomas, *Der Zauberberg*. Band 5/1–2. Teil (ed. Michael Neumann; Frankfurt am Main: S. Fischer, 2002).

Mannheim, Karl, "Das Konservative Denken I", in: *Soziologische Beiträge zum Werden des politisch-historischen Denkens in Deutschland* (Tübingen: Mohr, 1927).

Mannheim, Karl, *Essays on the Sociology of Knowledge* (ed. P. Kecskemeti; London: Routledge and Kegan Paul, 1952).

Marramao, G., "Messianism Without Delay: On the 'Post-Religious' Political Theology of Walter Benjamin", *Constellations: An Interdisciplinary Journal of Critical and Democratic Theory* 15, 3 (2008), 397–405.
Marshall, David L., "The Implications of Robert Brandom's Inferentialism for Intellectual History", *History and Theory* 52 (February 2013), 1–31.
Marx, Karl, *Capital*, vol. I (Moscou: Foreign Languages Publishing House, n.d.).
Marx, Karl, *Das Kapital* I (Ungekürzte Ausgabe nach der zweiten Auflage von 1872. Mit einem Geleitwort von Karl Korsch aus dem Jahre 1932).
Marx, Karl, "The Future Results of the British Rule in India", *The New-York Daily Tribune* (8 August 1853).
Marx, Karl, "Doktorsdissertation: Differenz der demokritischen und epikurischen Naturphilosphie nebst einem Anhänge", in: *Marx, Engels, Werke. Ergänzungsband I* (Berlin: Dietz Verlag, 1968), 257–373.
Marx, Karl, "Deutsche Ideologie I. Feuerbach", in: *Marx Engels Werke*, vol. 3 (Berlin: Dietz Verlag, 1969).
Marx, Karl, *Grundrisse: Foundations of the Political Economy* (1857–1861; transl. Martin Nicolaus; London: Penguin Books and New Left Review, 1973).
Marx, Karl, *The Eighteenth Brumaire of Louis Bonaparte* (New York: Cosimo Classics, 2008 [1852]).
Marx, Karl, "The Eighteenth Brumaire of Louis Bonaparte", in: Freedman, *Marxist Social Thought*, 188–211.
Marx, Karl and Friedrich Engels, *On Colonialism* (Moscow: Foreign Languages Publishing House, without year).
Marx, Karl and Friedrich Engels, *The German Ideology* (First ed. 1844; New York: International Publishers, 1970).
Marx, Karl and Friedrich Engels, "Manifesto of the Communist Party", in: *Marx/Engels Selected Works*, vol. 1 (Moscow: Progress Publishers, 1969, First ed.: February 1848, ed. Andy Blunden, 2004).
Mayer, Charles S., "Transformations of Territoriality 1600–2000", in: Gunilla Budde, Sebastian Conrad and Oliver Jansz (eds.), *Transnationale Geschichte. Themen, Tendenzen und Theorien* (Göttingen: Vandenhoeck & Ruprecht, 2006).
Mayer, J. P., *Alexis de Tocqueville, Analytiker des Massenzeitalters* (München: Beksche Verlagsbuchhandlung, 19723).
Mazzucato, Mariana, *The Entrepreneurial State: Debunking Public vs Private Myths* (London: Anthem Press, 2015).
McNeill, William H., *Arnold J. Toynbee: A Life* (Oxford: Oxford University Press, 1989).
McNeill, William H., *Rise of the West: A History of the Human Community* (Revised ed., Chicago: University of Chicago Press, 1992).
Meadows, Donella, Jorgen Randers and Dennis Meadows, *A Synopsis: Limits to Growth. The 30-Year Update* (White River Junction VT: Chelsea Green, 2004).
Megill, Allan, *Prophets of Extremity: Nietzsche, Heidegger, Foucault, Derrida* (Berkeley, Los Angeles and London: University of California Press, 1987).
Megill, Allan, "Historical Representation, Identity, Allegiance", in: S. Berger, L. Riksonas and A. Mycock (eds.), *Narrating the Nation: Representations in History, the Media and the Arts* (New York: Berghahn Books, 2013), 19–34.
Megill, Allan and Jaeyoon Park, "Misrepresenting Marx: A Lesson in Historical Method", *History and Theory* 56, 2 (June 2017), 288–306.
Meineke, Stefan, *Friedrich Meinecke. Persönlichkeit und politisches Denken bis zum Ende des ersten Weltkrieges* (Berlin and New York: Walter de Gruyter, 1995).
Michelet, Jules, *Introduction à l'histoire universelle* (1830).

Milanovic, Branco, *Global Inequality: A New Approach for the Age of Globalization* (Cambridge, MA: Harvard University Press, 2016).
Millar, John, *Observations Concerning the Distinction of Ranks in Society* (London: John Murray, 1773²).
Mille, Michelle, "Cenotaph for Newton". www.archdaily.com/544946/ad-classics-cenotaph-for-newton-etienne-louis-boullee
Miller, Nchama, "Hauntology and History in Jacques Derrida's *Spectres of Marx*". www.nodo50.org/cubasigloXXI/taller/miller_100304.pdf
Mink, Louis, "History and Fiction as Modes of Comprehension", *New Literary History* 1, 3 (1970), 541–558.
Mink, Louis, *Historical Understanding* (ed. Brian Fay, Eugene Golob and Richard Vann; Ithaca: Cornell University Press, 1987).
Mooij, J. J. A. *Tijd en geest. Een geschiedenis* (Kampen: Agora, 2001).
Müller, Adam H., *Elemente der Staatskunst. Sechsunddreissig Vorlesungen* (Leipzig: Handel Verlag, 1808, ed. 1936).
Murchadha, Felix O., *The Time of Revolution: Kairos and Chronos in Heidegger* (London: Bloomsburry Press, 2013).
Nietzsche, Friedrich, *The Antichrist* (1895, transl. H. L. Mencken, 1920).
Nietzsche, Friedrich, *Werke*, vol. I–V (ed. K. Schlechta; Frankfurt am Main, Berlin and Wien: Ullstein Buch, 19766).
Nietzsche, Friedrich, *Untimely Meditations*. Section 2. "On the Uses and Disadvantages of History for Life; Texts in the Philosophy of History" (Ed. Daniel Breazeale and Transl J. Hollingdale; Cambridge: Cambridge University Press, 1997).
Nietzsche, Friedrich, *On the Use and Abuse of History for Life* (Rev. ed. 2010, transl. Ian Johnstone; Nanaimo, BC, Canada: Vancouver Island University). https://records.viu.ca/~johnstoi/nietzsche/history.htm
Nietzsche, Friedrich, "Also Sprach Zarathustra. Ein Buch für Alle und Keinen", in: idem, *Werke*, vol. II (ed. Schlechta), 549–835.
Nietzsche, Friedrich, "Aus dem Nachlass der achtziger Jahre", in: idem, *Werke*, vol. IV (ed. Schlechta), 7–518.
Nietzsche, Friedrich, "Der Antichrist", in: idem, *Werke*, vol. III (ed. Schlechta), 598–714.
Nietzsche, Friedrich, "Die fröhliche Wissenschaft", in: idem, *Werke*, vol. II (ed. Schlechta), 281–535.
Nietzsche, Friedrich, "Die Geburt der Tragödie oder Griechentum und Pessimismus", in: idem, *Werke*, vol. I (ed. Schlechta), 21–134.
Nietzsche, Friedrich, "Ecce Homo. Wie man wird, was man ist", in: idem, *Werke*, vol. III (ed. Schlechta), 509–598.
Nietzsche, Friedrich, "Jenseits von Gut und Böse. Vorspiel einer Philosophie der Zukunft", in: idem, *Werke*, vol. III (ed. Schlechta), 9–206.
Nietzsche, Friedrich, "Menschliches, Allzumenschliches. Ein Buch für freie Geister", in: idem, *Werke*, vol. I (ed. Schlechta), 435–1008.
Nietzsche, Friedrich, "Unzeitgemässe Betrachtungen, Zweites Stück. Vom Nutzen und Nachteil der Historie für das Leben", in: idem, *Werke*, vol. I (ed. Schlechta), 209–285.
Nietzsche, Friedrich, "Zur Genealogie der Moral. Ein Streitschrift", in: idem, *Werke*, vol. III (ed. Schlechta), 207–346.
Nosàl, Martin, "The Gadamerian Approach to the Relation Between Experience and Language", *History and Theory* 54, 2 (2015), 195–208.
Nowotny, Helga, *Eigenzeit. Entstehung und Strukturierung eines Zeitgefühls* (Frankfurt am Main: Suhrkamp, 1993).

Ogle, Vanessa, *The Global Transformation of Time 1870–1950* (Cambridge, MA and London: Harvard University Press, 2015).
Orsucci, Andrea, "Nietzsche's Cultural Criticism and His Historical Methodology", in: Dries, *Nietzsche on Time and History*, 23–34.
Otabe, Tanehesa, "'Raphael Without Hands'. The Idea of the Inner Form and Its Transformations", *Journal of the Faculty of Letters. Aesthetics*, 34 (Tokyo: University of Tokyo, 2009), 55–63.
Parkinson, C. N., *Parkinson's Law: The Pursuit of Progress* (London: John Murray, 1958).
Piketty, Thomas, *Capital in the Twenty-First Century* (Cambridge, MA: Belknap/Harvard University Press, 2014).
Plato, "Timaeus", in: *Verzameld Werk*, vol. V, Dutch translation from: Xaveer de Win (Antwerpen: De Nederlandsche Boekhandel, Baarn: Ambo, 1978).
Proust, Marcel, *In Search of Lost Time* (transl. Andreas Mayor, Terence Kilmartin and D. J. Enright; New York: Modern Library, 1999), Vol. IV. *Time Regained*.
Ranke, Leopold von, *Die Grossen Mächte* (ed. Friedrich Meinecke, Insel-Verlag, Leipzig 1916, Erst Ausgabe, 1833), Kap. 7. Nach dem Texte der Historisch-politischen Zeitschrift 2. Band 1833.
Ranke, Leopold von, *Geschichten der romanischen und germanischen Völker von 1494 bis 1535* (Leipzig: Reimer, 1824).
Ranke, Leopold von, *Aus Werk und Nachlass*, 4 Bände, Band IV (ed. W. P. Fuchs; München: Oldenburg, 1965).
Ranke, Leopold von, *The Theory and Practice of History* (ed. Georg Iggers and Konrad von Moltke, transl. Wilma Iggers; London and New York: Routledge, 2011).
Ranke, Leopold von, "Abhandlungen und Versuche", in: idem, *Sämtliche Werke*, Band 24.
Ranke, Leopold von, *Englische Geschichte, vornehmlich im 16. und 17. Jh.*, *Sämtliche Werke*, Band 15 (Leipzig: Duncker und Humblot, 1870).
Ranke, Leopold von, *Sämtliche Werke*, 54 Bände. (herausgeb. Alfred Dove, Leipzig: Duncker und Humblot, 1867–1890).
Ranke, Leopold von, "Über die Verwandschaft und den Unterscheid der Historic und der Politik", in: idem, *Sämmtliche Werke*, Band 24.
Read, Jason, "The Althusser Effect: Philosophy, History and Temporality", *Borderlands e-Journal* 2, 4 (2005), Section 5, 6 and 7.
Reddy, William R., "The Eurasian Origins of Empty Time and Space", *History and Theory* 55, 3 (October 2016), 325–356.
Rée, J., *Heidegger* (London: Phoenix, 1998).
Rhys, E., *Hallam's Constitutional History*, vol. 1 (With an introduction of J. H. Morgan) (New York: Everyman's library, Knopf Publishing Group; The Project Gutenberg, 2012).
Richardson, John, "Nietzsche's Problem of the Past", in: Dries, *Nietzsche on Time and History*, 87–111.
Ricoeur, Paul, *Temps et Récit*, vol. 1, 2 and 3 (ed. Paris: Du Seuil, 1983, 1984, 1985).
Ricoeur, Paul, *Time and Narrative*, vol. 1, 2 and 3 (Chicago: University of Chicago, 1984, 1985, 1988).
Robin Small, *Time and Becoming in Nietzsche's Thought* (London and New York: Continuum, 2010).
Rodrik, Dani, "Populism and the Economics of Globalization", *Journal of the International Business Policy* (2018). https://drodrik.scholar.harvard.edu/files/dani-rodrik/files/populism_and_the_economics_of_globalization.pdf, Concluding Remarks.
Rosa, Hartmut, *Beschleunigung. Die Veränderiung der Zeitstruktur der Moderne* (Frankfurt am Main: Suhrkamp, 2005).

Rossi, P., *The Dark Abyss of Time: The History of the Earth and the History of Nations from Hooke to Vico* (Chicago and London: University of Chicago Press, 1987).

Rovelli, C., *Order of Time* (London: Penguin, 2018).

Ruehl, Martin A., "'An Uncanny Re-Awakening' Nietzsche's Renascence of the Renaissance Out of the Spirit of Jacob Burckhardt", in: Dries, *Nietzsche on Time and History*, 231–272.

Runia, Eelco, "Presence", *History and Theory* 45, 1 (2006), 1–29.

Runia, Eelco, *Moved by the Past: Discontinuity and Historical Mutation* (New York: Columbia University Press, 2014).

Safranski, Rüdiger, *Tijd. Hoe mens en tijd elkaar beïnvloeden* (Amsterdam and Antwerpen: Atlas Contact, 2016).

Sallis, John, "The Hermeneutics of the Art-work", in: Figal, *Hans-Georg Gadamer*, 45–58.

Salomon, A., "Tocqueville 1959", *Social Research* 26, 4 (Winter 1959), 449–470.

Savigny, Friedrich Carl von, *Vermischte Schriften*, vol. 1 (Berlin: Veit, 1850).

Schinkel, Maarten, "Opeens twijfel bij dé grafiek over onvrede", *NRC/Handelsblad* (September 14, 2016), E5.

Schlözer, A. L., *Weltgeschichte nach ihren Haupttheilen im Auszug und Zusammenhänge*, vol. I (Göttingen, 1792–1801²).

Schulin, Ernst, "Zeitgemässe Historie um 1870. Zu Nietzsche, Burckhardt und zum 'Historismus'", *Historische Zeitschrift* 281 (2005), 33–58.

Schwarz, Vanessa, "Walter Benjamin for Historians", *American Historical Review* 106, 5 (2001).

Shapiro, Gary, "Kairos and Chronos: Nietzsche and the Time of the Multitude", in: Keith Ansell Pearson (ed.), *Nietzsche and Political Thought* (London, New Delhi, New York and Sydney: Bloomsbury, 2013).

Small, Robin, *Time and Becoming in Nietzsche's Thought* (London and New York: Continuum International Publishing Group, 2010).

Smith, Adam, *The Wealth of Nations* (Toronto: Modern Library Paperback Edition, Random House, 2000), Introduction.

Smith, S., "Historical Meaningfulness in Shared Action", *History and Theory* 48, 1 (2009).

Snyder, Timothy, *On Tyranny: Twenty Lessons From the Twentieth Century* (New York: Tim Duggan Books, 2017).

Stern, Fritz, ed., *The Varieties of History: From Voltaire to the Present* (New York: Meridian Books, 1972).

Stiglitz, J., *The Price of Inequality: How Todays Divided Society Endangers Our Future* (Old Saybrook, CT: Tentor Media Inc., 2012).

Stuurman, Siep, "Tijd en ruimte in de verlichting. De uitvinding van de filosofische geschiedenis", in: Grever and Jansen, *De ongrijpbare tijd*, 79–96.

Terpstra, M., "Het geschiedenisbegrip bij Althusser", in: *Te elfder ure*, 31.

Tocqueville, Alexis de, *Drafts*, Yale, CVb, paquet 13 and CVh, paquet 3, cahier 3 (probably 1835).

Tocqueville, Alexis de, *Democracy in America*, vol. I and II. Electronic edition deposited and marked up by *ASGRP*, the *American Studies Programs* at the University of Virginia, June 1, 1997. (From the Henry Reeve Translation, revised and corrected, 1899) and www.marxists.org/reference/archive/de-tocqueville/democracy-america/ch44.htm (transl. Henry Reeve; London: Saunders and Otley, 1840. Source: Project Gutenberg, www.gutenberg.org; E-text: by David Reed, haradda@aol.com, February, 1997; HTML Mark-up: by Andy Blunden).

Tocqueville, Alexis de, *Memoir, Letters and Remains of Alexis de Tocqueville* (transl. from the French by the translator of Napoleon's Correspondence with King Joseph. With large additions. In Two Volumes (London, 1861)).

Tocqueville, Alexis de, *Mélanges, Fragments Historiques et Notes sur l'Ancien Régime, la Révolution et l'Empire, Voyages, Pensées Entièrements Inédits* (1865, 2010).
Tocqueville, Alexis de, *Souvenirs* (ed. Calman Lévy; Ancien Maison Michel Lévy Frères, 1893).
Tocqueville, Alexis de, *The Old Regime and the Revolution in France* (transl. John Bonner; Online Library of Liberty, 43. Translation, revised and corrected, 1899).
Tocqueville, Alexis de, *Ouevres Complètes* (Paris: Gallimard, 1964).
Tocqueville, Alexis de, *Correspondance d'Alexis de Tocqueville et de Gustave Beaumont, texte établi, annoté et préfacé par André Jardin* (Paris: Gallimard, 1967).
Tocqueville, Alexis de, *On Democracy, Revolution and Society. Selected Writings* (ed. J. Stone and St. Mennell; Chicago and London: Chicago University Press, 1980).
Tocqueville, Alexis de, *Selected Letters on Politics and Society* (ed. Roger Boesche, transl. by James Toupin and Roger Boesche; Berkeley, Los Angeles and London: University of California Press, 1985).
Tocqueville, Alexis de, *La Démocratie en Amerique* (Paris: Institut Coppet, 2012).
Tocqueville, Alexis de, "Letter to Eugène Stoffels, February 21, 1835, Paris", in: *Mélanges, Fragments Historiques et Notes*.
Vasterling, Veronica, "De rechte lijn en de lus", in: Maria Grever en Harry Jansen, *De ongrijpbare tijd* (Hilversum: Verloren, 2001), 175–187.
Vessey, David, "Gadamer's Hermeneutic Contribution to Time-Consiousness", *Indo-Pacific Journal of Phenomenology* 7, 2 (2007).
Vico, *The New Science of Giambattisto Vico*, Book I, Section III (transl. Thomas Bergin and Harold Fisch; Ithaca and London: Cornell University Press, 1948, first ed. 1744).
Wehler, Hans-Ulrich, *Deutsche Gesellschaftsgeschichte I, Vom Feudalismus des alten Reiches bis zur defensiven Modernisierung der Reformära 1700–1815* (München: C.H. Beck, 1987).
White, Hayden, "The Burden of History", *History and Theory* 5 (1966).
White, Hayden, *Metahistory: The Historical Imagination in Nineteenth-Century Europe* (Baltimore and London: Johns Hopkins University Press, 1975).
Wiener, P. P. (ed. vol. II), "'IV Enlightenment' and 'Counter-Enlightenment'", in: *Dictionary of the History of Ideas. Studies of Selected Pivotal Ideas*. http://xtf.lib.virginia.edu/xtf/view?docId=DicHist/uvaGenText/tei/DicHist2.xml
Wolf, Martin, "The Tide of Globalisation Is Turning. Trade Liberalisation Has Stalled and One Can See a Steady Rise in Protectionist Measures", *Financial Times* (September 6, 2016).
Wood, Allen, "Herder and Kant on History: Their Enlightenment Faith", in: Samuel Newlands and Larry M. Jorgensen (eds.), *Metaphysics and the Good: Themes from the Philosophy of Merrihew Adams* (Oxford: Oxford University Press, 2009).
Wood, Allen, *The Free Development of Each: Studies on Freedom, Right and Ethics in Classical German Philosophy* (Oxford: Oxford University Press, 2014).
Woolf, Virginia, *Orlando: A Biography* (Penguin Books, 1928).
Woolf, Virginia, *The Waves* (Hogarth Press, 1931).
Woolf, Virginia, *Between the Acts* (Hogarth Press, 1941).
Woolf, Virginia, *Mrs Dalloway* (Adelaide: The University of Adelaide, 2015). https://ebooks.adelaide.edu.au/w/woolf/virginia/w91md/
Wurgaft, Benjamin Aldes, "To the Planetarium – There Is Still Time!", *History and Theory* 53 (May 2014), 253–263.
Zammito, Jack, *Kant, Herder and the Birth of Anthropology* (Chicago and London: University of Chicago Press, 2002).
Zoll, Rainer, "Krise der Zeiterfahrung", in: idem, *Zerstörung und Wideraneignung von Zeit* (Frankfurt am Main: Suhrkamp, 1988).

INDEX

Note: Numbers in *italics* indicate a figure on the corresponding page.

acceleration 80
Alexanderschlacht (Albrecht) 225
Altdorfer, Albrecht 225
Althusser, Louis: essential section (coupe d'essence) 131–133, 143; on Hegel 80; heterogeneous time of 134; on the hierarchization of effects 135; on ideology 132; simultaneity of time of 131–132; topography and 146n56; on totality 136
amor fati 167
Ankersmit, Frank: on dialectic in historicism 61–62n40; on historical experience 23n89; on historicism 12, 23n91, 23n94, 23n98; on Huizinga and Nietzsche 180; Ranke and 13; on romanticist historicism 97; on the *Weltanschauung* of historicism 82
Annales school 196, 197, 201
Anti-Machiavel (Frederick II of Prussia) 40
antiquarian history 152, 165–166, 174–175
Arendt, Hannah 158–159
aristocracy: democracy and 108–109, 118–120; Hegel and 176–177; industrialization and 122
Aristotle: ancient time regimes and 14–17; change and 35; Hegel and 68–69; historical time and 225; the moment and 159; Newton and 27; synchronicity of the non-synchronous and 209
Arnold J. Toynbee (McNeill) 231

Assmann, Aleida: on creative destruction 2; critique of compensation theory 3; historicism of 221; on history of the late modern 221; on Koselleck 218; Koselleck and 220–221; on time out of joint 3, 196, 221
atomism 131; Hegel's critique of 75, 77–78; Marx and 128, 130–131; the state and 82; in Woolf 206–207
atoms 128, 131, 155, 167
Augenblick 157–158, 162, 173, 179–180, 183, 216
Augustine, Saint: on continuity of time 15, 16; Koselleck and 16; Plato and 24n112; time regimes and 14
Avineri, Shlomo 74, 76, 84n53

Babbage, Charles 127
Balibar, Etienne 80, 135
Baschet, Jérôme 24n119, 235n9, 236n37
becoming 153–155
Before European Hegemony (Abu-Lughod) 231
Beiser, Frederick: on Counter-Enlightenment 59n4; on Hegel 70–71; on historicism 84n49; on Ranke 91, 93, 99n49
Benjamin, Walter: anti-romanticism of 216; on the arcades 212n67; *Jetztzeit* of 216, 234
Bentley, Michael 51, 93, 204

Berlin, Isaiah 46, 50, 61n23, 61n25
Bernheim, Ernst 177
Bevernage, Berber 227
Beyond Good and Evil (Nietzsche) 167
Bildung (cultivation) 51, 55
Bildungsroman 205
Birth of Tragedy, The (Nietzsche) 164–165
Blix, Göran 104–105
Bloch, Ernst 139–140
Bloch, Marc 197
Boullée, Etienne-Louis 27–29
bourgeois society 137–138; synchronicity of the non-synchronous and 140
Brandom, Robert: on form and content 7; Gorman and 22n68; on Kant 7–8; Kant and 21n54; Koselleck and 22n64; modern time of 219
Braudel, Fernand: composite time of 197; on history and time 211n14; on the Mediterranean region as a whole 211n29; Ricoeur and 196, 199–201, 200, 211n26, 211n27; synchronicity of the non-synchronous and 4–5, 197–198, 232
Breaking up Time (Lorenz and Bevernage) x, 22n65
Buiks, Peter 106, 109, 118
Burckhardt, Jacob 186, 186–188, 215
burden: Assmann and 221; First World War and 196; genealogy and 161–162; historical time and 103; Koselleck and 218; memory and 165; Nietzsche and 151–153, 158–159; nobility and 125n64; the past as 188; in post-revolutionary France 104; Ricoeur and 200; the state and 72–73, 130; in Woolf 206
bureaucratization 115, 119, 122

calendars 19n2
Capital (Marx) 137
capitalism 130, 138–139, 198–199, 208–209, 232–233
Carnival in Romans (Ladurie) 201, 234
carnivals 201–203, 234
Cartesian Meditations (Husserl) 89
centralization 111, 115, 116, 119, 122
Chakrabarty, Dipesh: on globalization 208; heterogeneous time of 209; historicism and 12, 207–208; synchronicity of the non-synchronous and 144n5, 208, 233
Chateaubriand, François de 5, 103
Cheese and the Worms, The (Ginzburg) 234
chiasm 191n45
Chladenius, Johann Martin 2, 57
Christianity 16, 70
chronological time 33–34, 59, 206
Civilisation matérielle, économie et capitalisme (Braudel) 198, 198–199
Clark, Christopher 40, 226
Clarke, Samuel 47–48
climate change 52, 53, 90, 127
collective singular 33, 38, 42; continuing entities and 77; Counter-Enlightenment and 18; *Geschichte* and 2, 33–34; Hegel and 54, 90; historicism and 56–58; Marx and 128; multiplicity of time and 70; Ranke and 93; reason and 81; Ricoeur and 200; universal history and 38, 42
Collingwood, Robin 14, 17, 52, 60n13, 62n53
compensation theory 3, 144n9
Condorcet, Nicolas de 31–32, 41
Confessions (Augustine) 16, 17
conjectural history *see* philosophical history
conservatism 84n46, 95, 104
constitutional monarchy 73
Construction of an Urban Past, The (Jansen) 210n4
continuing entities: Braudel and 199; Counter-Enlightenment and 219; Hegel's estates as 77; Herder and 54; Koselleck and 97; Marx and 128; Nietzsche and 152; non-simultaneity of the simultaneous and 3; Ranke and 89; romanticism and 189; the Second World War and 215; the state as 232; temporal development of 18, 51–52
contradiction 72, 75, 81, 144n9, 157, 168n8
Counter-Enlightenment, the: embodied time of 59; the Enlightenment and 59n3; Hegel and 71, 75; Ranke and 93; romanticism and 80, 188
Coupe d'essence *see* essential section
crisis 6, 12
critical history 166
Critique of Judgment, The (Kant) 21n54, 70
Croce, Benedetto 61n28
Cronon, William 212n46
culture: the calendar and 19n2; Chakrabarty and 233; defined 8; Huizinga and 187; kairotic time and 189; Naumann and 215; romanticism and 231; super-personal 69; time regimes and 1
Culture of Time and Space, The (Kern) 126

Cunning of Reason, the 55, 74
customs 31, 78, 92, 116, 141–142, 160

Darwin, Charles 153, 176, 177
Darwinism 176–177
Day of Empire (Chua) 230–231
Decline and Fall of the Roman Empire (Gibbon) 41–42
Degrees of Ages (Pellerin) 88
democracy: aristocracy and 108–109, 119; equality and 107; habits and 110; industrialization and 119; inevitability of 106, 108
Democracy in America (Tocqueville) 105, 141–142, 188–189
Derrida, Jacques 141
Der Zauberberg (Mann) *see Magic Mountain, The* (Mann)
Descartes, René 30, 32, 34, 43n9, 75
Deutsche Katastrophe, Die (Meinecke) 215
Dilthey, Wilhelm 52
Dries, Manuel 153, 163–164, 168n8, 170n74
Droysen, Johann Gustav 57, 58, 199, 211n21

Ecce Homo (Nietzsche) 156
Eighteenth Brumaire of Louis Napoleon, The 129
Eine Metakritik zur Kritik der reinen Vernunft (Herder) 47, 60n9
Einfühlen (empathy) 52
embodied time: continuing entities and 90; Counter-Enlightenment and 59, 82, 91; defined 47; eternal recurrence and 163; in Hegel 56, 71, 73, 75, 79; in Hegel and Ranke 58; in Herder 51, 53; historicism and 5, 14; idealism and 92; philosophy of history and 94; pragmatism of 92–93; in Ranke 92; representative figures of 11; synchronicity of the non-synchronous and 4
Emilia Gaiotti (Lessing) 182–183
emplotment 19
empty time: Chakrabarty and 208; change and 36; chronological time and 18; Counter-Enlightenment and 47; the Enlightenment and 38, 59; Gadamer and 173; historical time and 82; Jordheim and 34, 55; Kant and 22n62; Koselleck and 12, 56; Marx and 128; mythology and 73; Nietzsche and 158, 163; non-simultaneity of the simultaneous and 199; origins of 20n13; progress and 228; romanticism and 95; Watteau and 28
Encyclopédie, the 33
End of the Twentieth Century and the End of the Modern Age, The (Lukacs, J.) 231
Enlightenment, the: Counter-Enlightenment and 59n3; empty time of 44n30; philosophical history of 37; pragmatism of 60n14; pre-Adamite time and 30; *res publica* and 7; time regimes and 7
Entschlossenheit (unlocking) 173
Entstehung des Historismus (Meinecke) 215
Enzyklopedie der philosophische Wissenschaften (Hegel) 68
equality 107, 115, 120, 122
Esposito, Fernando 2, 219, 223n35
esprit 45n66, 98n4
Esquisse (Condorcet) 31–32, 41
Essai sur les moeurs (Voltaire) 39–40
essential section 131–133, 143
estates 76–77
eternal recurrence 152, 156–157, 157, 161–163, 162, 163, 217, 234
eternity 16–17, 23n84, 24n112, 157
evolution 176–177

Fèbvre, Lucien 197
First World War, the: burdensome time of 196, 206, 214–215; discontinuity of time and 126, 203–204, 218; homogeneous time and 126; time of rise and fall and 214–215; time of the modern and 4, 218; Whig interpretation of history and 203–204
forces of production 128, 132, 134–135, 144n11
forecasting 125n83
forgetfulness 151, 155
Frederick II 40
Freeman, Edward 204
Friedrich, Caspar David 87
Fritzsche, Peter 38
future, the: decline and 227; democracy and 106, 108; equality and 119, 143; eternal recurrence and 162, 217; freedom and 121; genealogy and 152; in Hegel 71, 79; in Herder 90; historicism and 14; as history 113; homogeneous time and 95; as horizon of expectation 2; ideality of 17; kairotic time and 231; the moment and 161, 173; origin and 3; Paris Universal Exposition and 127; the past and 6, 72, 158, 208; the present and 18, 48, 164,

209; progress and 56; in Ranke 93; reality of 232; secular time and 225; synchronicity of the non-synchronous and 111, 131, 140, 142; time of the modern and 4, 58
Futures Past (Koselleck) 225

Gadamer, Hans-Georg 11, 60n11, 173, 179
Gatterer, Johann Christoph 33
Geertz, Clifford 186
Geist (spirit) 69, 80, 111, 155
genealogy 153, 160–161, 161, 162
Geneaology of Morals (Nietzsche) 161
German Historicist Tradition, The (Beiser) 59n4
German Ideology (Marx) 139
Geschichte und Gegenwart (Meinecke) 215
geschichtlichen Ursachen der Deutschen Revolution, Die (Meinecke) 215
Geyl, Peter x
Gibbon, Edward 41–42
globalization 208, 232
Goethe, Johann Wolfgang von 57
Gordy, Michael 80, 84n71, 132–133
Gorman, Jonathan 7–10, 17, 22n68
Green, John Richard 204

habits 31, 110–111, 115–116, 152, 159, 162
Halbwachs, Maurice 11
Half of Life (Hölderlin) 86
Hallam, Henry 203
Hartog, François x, 2, 5, 21n42
Haym, Rudolf 74
Heavenly City of the Eighteenth-Century Philosophers, The (Becker) 45n56
Hegel, Georg Wilhelm Friedrich: on aristocracy 176–177; Aristotle and 68–69; on *Bildung* 55; burdensome time of 188; the collective singular and 56; collective singular of 90; Collingwood and 60n13; conservatism and 74, 79, 83n33; Counter-Enlightenment and 54–55, 71; critique of the Enlightenment of 92; embodied time of 47, 79–80; on estates 75–77; on the externality of time 68; on the future 120–121; Herder and 94; historicism of 75, 83n32; homogeneous time of 80; Kant and 70; Lessing and 69; Marx and 129–130; on Napoleon 62n58; organicism of 69–70, 75; perception of time of 82; on the present 73; Ranke and 56–57, 72, 77, 89, 94, 143; on the Reformation 71; on representative government 77–78; romanticism of 74–77, 84n55, 97, 188; on the state 94; teleology and 95; on time as a burden 73; time of becoming of 67; on the time of philosophy 72; Tocqueville and 120–121; undulating history of 81; use of "phases" of 99n54; on *Weltgeist* 56
Hegel und seine Zeit (Haym) 74
Heidegger, Martin: on experience of the past 190n2; kairotic time of 209, 217; on Kant 36; on the moment 173; Nietzsche and 217; Ranke and 217; romanticism and 218
Herder, Johann Gottfried: on *Bildung* 51; Counter-Enlightenment and 46, 50–51; on culture 52; embodied time of 47, 53, 58; Hegel and 94; historicism of 54; idealism of 90–91; Jordheim and 51; Kant's influence on 60n9; Mandelbaum and 52; on nations 53, 90; Romanticism and 52; on time as endurance in change 45n49
heterogeneous time: Althusser on 131–132; of Braudel 198; of Chakrabarty 209; First World War and 126; of Nietzsche 143, 166–167; synchronicity of the non-synchronous and 221; of Tocqueville 122, 189
hierarchization of effects 135
Hill, Kevin 162
historical change 37
historical experience 23n89, 174, 180–181, 183–185, 187–188, 191n56
historical insight 184, 191n56
historical materialism 130, 133, 144n14
historical time: culture and 69; emptiness of 33–34; natural time and 33; social history and 6–7; spirit and 69
"Historical Time and Historical Society" 6
historicism: in Britain 196; defined 12, 208; embodied time of 5; epistemological form of 61n28; in France 195–196; the future and 14; in Germany 196; modernism and 107, 219; organicism and 13, 75; outside Europe 12; post-modernism and 220; pragmatism of 60n14; as principle of life 61n28; Ranke and 196; *Weltanschauung* and 12–13, 14
Histories of the Latin and Teutonic Nations 1494–1514 (Ranke) 91
historiography x, xi, 1, 9
history 2, 211n14
History of England (Hume) 39
history of time 23n80

Holden, Terence 5
Hölderlin, Friedrich 86, 97
Hölscher, Lucian: on empty time 20n13; on the First World War 126, 203; on historiography and geography 43n7; on Leibniz 48; on Newton 27
Homer, Sean 134
Homo Deus (Harari) 227
homogeneous time: Braudel and 197, 199; of the Enlightenment 28; the First World War and 126; in Germany 121; Hegel and 79, 132, 134; Koselleck and 225; Marx and 128, 135; Nietzsche and 159; Ricoeur and 203; romanticism and 18, 68; synchronicity of the non-synchronous and 3
Hooke, Robert 30
horizon in the Enlightenment 50
horizon of expectation (*Erwartungshorizont*): Assmann and 220; definition of historical time and 56; existence of the future and 17; the future as 2; Hartog and 5; influence of concept of 225; modern time and 42, 218; Ricoeur and 199–200
horizontality 81, 173, 180–181, 189, 215
Huizinga, Johan: burdensome time of 175; crisis and 11–12; critique of Darwinism of 176–177; critique of Nietzsche of 174–176; on the encounter between present and past 179; on experience of the past 180–181; kairotic time of 189; Ladurie and 202–203; on meaning of history 174; Nietzsche and 176–188; presence of the past and 174; on teleology 177; undulating time of 177–178
Human, All Too Human (Nietzsche) 160
Humboldt, Alexander von: critique of the Enlightenment of 92; embodied time of 58; idealism of 90–91; on nations 90; Ranke and 91
Hume, David 39
Husserl, Edmund 89
Huyge, René 30
Hyperion (Hölderlin) 86

idealism: burdensome time and 129–131; Counter-Enlightenment and 90; historical 58, 103; historical materialism and 122, 139; organicism and 70; of Ranke 92, 95–96
Idea of Universal History (Kant) 37
Idee der Staatsräson, Die (Meinecke) 215
identity 81

industrialization 111, 119
In Search of Lost Time (Proust) 164, 174, 195
intentionalism 169n54
interdetermination 110–111, 146n41, 163–164, 166
intrigue, undulating time and 200
intrigue/plot: conservatism and 184; Kairos and 174; manifestation of time and 5, 11; Mann's use of 214; romanticism and 195, 198–200
intuition: concept and 7; theological knowledge and 49; time as form of 34, 36, 52, 59, 118, 121, 163
Ist die Zeit aus den Fugen? (Assmann) 196, 220, 231

Jameson, Frederic: on experience of necessity 134–135, 136–137; on Hegelian idealism 145n31; on history 145n33; on modes of production 140; reductionism of 136
Jetztzeit 210, 216–217, 234
Jordheim, Helge: Herder and 51; natural and historical time and 33; on non-simultaneity of historical time 63n72; on non-synchronicity 62n49; pluri-temporality and 21n43; on synchronization 33, 34, 55; on time regimes 6

Kairos 18, 156, 167, 173–174, 182–185, 189, 215
kairotic time: burdensome time and 162; carnivals and 202; decline of Europe and 231; discontinuity of 189; *Entschlossenheit* and 173; historical insight and 184; micro-histories and 234; in Nietzsche 152, 182; Nietzsche on 173; representative figures of 188; Ricoeur and 4; romanticism and 186; synchronicity of the non-synchronous and 208
Kant, Immanuel: on the change of time 44n37; the Enlightenment and 22n62; Hegel and 70; on historical time 34–37; on ideality of time 44n38; influence on Herder of 60n9; judgements and 44n36; Nietzsche and 163; on the *nunc stans* 36; organicism of 70; on the particular and the general 21n54; on universal history 34
Kaplan, Robert 231
Kellner, Hans 10
Kemble, John Mitchell 204

Kleingeld, Pauline 37–38
Kojève, Alexandre 56
Koselleck, Reinhart: Assmann and 220–221; Augustine and 16; Brandom and 22n64; collective singular of 33, 38, 42; critique of modernism of 219; future-oriented time of 218–220; on historical investigation 58; on historical quality of time 60n16; on historical time x, 225; modernism of 218–220; natural time of 33; on the past 43n22, 97; on perspectivism 57; the present and 223n40; Ricoeur and 199–200; the Second World War and 196; on the synchronicity of the non-synchronous 20n13; on synchronization 56; time of the modern of 225; on universal history 43n29; Whig-interpretation of time of 226
Kronos 73, 74, 173

La Confession d'un enfant de siècle (Musset) 103
La Méditerranée et le Monde méditerranéen à l'époque de Philippe II (Braudel) 197
Lapeyrère, Isaac de La 30
Leibniz, Gottfried Wilhelm 47–48, 48
Le Roy Ladurie 197, 201, 202–203
Lessing, Gotthold Ephraim 69
Lessing, Theodor 174
Life of the Mind, The (Arendt) 158–159
London Crystal Palace Exhibition, the 127
Love in the Italian Theatre (Watteau) 30
Lübbe, Hermann 3, 144n9, 221, 225
Lundi Gras 201–202
Lutheran Reformation, the 71, 95

Magic Mountain, The (Mann) 195, 205, 214
Mandelbaum, Maurice 12, 13, 23n91, 52, 61n35, 98n8, 223n48
Mannheim, Karl: on conservatism 84n46; on historicism 12; on romantic conservatism 104; on romanticism 74–75; on the *Weltanschauung* of historicism 82
Mardi Gras 202
Marquardt, Odo 3, 221
Marx, Karl: atomism of 130–131; on bourgeois society 137–138; burdensome past of 141; burdensome time of 129, 188; on colonialism 128; on the development of forms 137; embodied time of 128, 130; Hegel and 129–130; heterogeneous time of 128–129; historical materialism of 130; on modernization 138; modernization and 135–136; on the Natural Individual 144n11; pluralism of 133–134; on the state 130; synchronicity of the non-synchronous and 131, 139–140; Tocqueville and 112; on totality 136
Meaning, Truth and Reference (Ankersmit) 11
Mediterranean 4, 197–198, 200–201, 231
Megill, Allan 11, 152, 169n50
Meinecke, Friedrich 61n28, 214–215, 215–216
Michelet, Jules 105, 126–127, 127
Middle Ages, the: Herder on 51; Huizinga on 183–187; Novalis on 87; the Renaissance and 178–179; Romanticism and 77–78; Schlözer on 32
Milanovic, Branko 228–229
Millar, John 31
Modern Historiography (Bentley) 93, 204
modernism: historicism and 69, 107, 107–108, 123n21, 190; of Koselleck 218, 219; progressive time of 227; synchronicity of the non-synchronous and 232–233; Tocqueville and 112
modernization: bureaucratization and 115; centralization and 115; equality and 122; habits and 116; inevitability of 108; noumenally experienced time and 138
modes of production 130, 132–140, 142, 145n38, 198–199
moeurs see habits
moment 158, 161, 173
Monadology (Leibniz) 48, 61n21
Montesquieu 45n56, 98n4
monumental history 165, 175–176, 206, 217
Mrs. Dalloway (Woolf): burdensome time of 206; historicist time of 205; kairotic time in 212n60; the past and 227; Ricoeur and 207; synchronicity of the non-synchronous and 195, 206; time of the modern of 206
Müller, Adam 78
Musset, Alfred de 103
"Mysteries of Historical Order" (Hölscher) 4

Napoleon Bonaparte, as world-historical figure 56, 58, 62n58, 71, 73
narrativism 4, 5
naturalism 152, 153, 177
natural selection 153
natural time 33, 34, 36, 37, 59, 103

Newton, Isaac 47–48
Niebuhr, Barthold 81
Nietzsche, Friedrich: on becoming 153–154, 155; becoming and 166; burdensome time of 152; on contradiction 157; on the Counter-Enlightenment 46; discontinuous time of 151; embodied time of 160; on the flow of time 17; on forgetfulness 151, 155; Heidegger and 217; heterogeneous time of 166; Huizinga and 176–188; on kairotic time 182–183; kairotic time of 152, 156–157, 179–180, 189; Kant and 163; Marx and 146n41; monumental history of 175–176; naturalism of 153; natural selection and 153; nihilism and 152; noumenal world of 143; synchronicity of the non-synchronous and 155; on teleology 161; undulating time of 177–178
nihilism 152, 168n8
non-simultaneity of the simultaneous/non-simultaneous 2, 18, 55, 199
Novalis 87
nunc stans 36, 44n46

Old Regime and the Revolution in France, The (Tocqueville) 122, 188
Order of Time (Rovelli) x
organicism: atomism and 131; Christianity and 70; Darwinism and 176–177; historicism and 13, 75; in Huizinga and Nietzsche 181–182; identity and 81; political significance of 67, 75, 95
overdetermination 135

Pappe, Helmut 46
Paris Universal Exposition *127*
past, the: burdensome time of 158, 160; as excluded from the present 227; experience of 179; the future and 6, 208; in *Mrs. Dalloway* 227; as personal 162; the present and 178–179; as space of experience 2, 97
phenomenological hermeneutics, of Ricoeur 5
Phenomenology of Mind (Hegel): Counter-Enlightenment and 54–55; historical time in 68; *Philosophy of Right* and 67; the present and 73; synchronization and 73
philosophical history: biblical history and 31; emptiness of 34; of the Enlightenment 37; historical narrative and 114

Philosophische Aufsätze zur objektiven Phantasie (Bloch), on heterogeneous time 139
Philosophy of Right (Hegel) 62n58; divine strategy and 72; organicism of 71, 75; *Phenomenology of Mind* and 67; the present and 73
Philosophy of World History (Hegel) 73, 79, 94
Piketty, Thomas 228–229, 234
Plato 24n112, 40, 50, 80, 130
plot *see* intrigue/plot
Pocock, John 22n61
political history 95
Politische Gespräche (Ranke) 94
post-modernism 2, 219, 220
post-narrativism 5
pragmatism 7–8, 60n14, 92, 93
pre-Adamite time 30, 38, 59
present, the: absence of past and future and 35; attention and 16; burdensome time of 159; change and 163; coexistence of past and future in 208; Counter-Enlightenment and 47, 74; crisis and 6, 12; Enlightenment time and 42; freedom and 72; the future and 127, 142, 164; future as history and 113; Hegel on 73; Heidegger on 173; Herder on 52; Hume on 39; institutions and 49; Marx on 139, 146n56; the moment and 167, 179; Nietzsche on 154–155; non-synchronicity and 140; now and 37; organicism and 54–55, 76; the past and 34, 158, 178–179, 180; Ranke on 60n14, 91, 93; the real as 17; romanticism and 75; time of the modern and 58; transition and 1
Presser, Jacques 110
Price of Inequality, The (Stiglitz) 230
Principles of Philosophy (Descartes) 30–31
profectus 2
progress: acceleration and 19n5; *Bildung* and 50–51; Chakrabarty on 232–234; in compensation theory 144n9; Condorcet on 41; Counter-Enlightenment and 56, 67; disadvantages of 226–227; empty form of 14; the Enlightenment and 1–4, 17–18, 218; equality and 108; eurocentric view of 127–128; expectation and 20n9; First World War and 196; Hegel on 54, 73, 79–82; Herder on 46–47; Huizinga on 176; Humboldt and 85n74; Kant's history of 37–38; Koselleck on 43n29, 60n15;

Nietzsche on 154, 159; nineteenth-century view of 6, 104–105; the past and 209; in the *Philosophy of Right* 71; Piketty on 229–230; revolution and 202–204; Ricoeur on 200; romanticism and 188; time regimes and 10; transition and 83n30; universal history and 30–34; Whig interpretation of history and 206
progressivism: Assmann on 221; burdensome time and 104; Butterfield and 204; democratization and 108; empty time and 34, 230; the Enlightenment and 199–200; ethnocentrism and 10; historicism and 227; of Koselleck 4, 196; Marx and 128–129; of Voltaire 40
progressus 2
Prophets of Extremity (Megill) 152
Provincializing Europe (Chakrabarty) 12, 139, 195, 199, 207–208, 208, 233

quietism 104, 105
Quine, Willard Van Orman 9, 22n68

Radical Enlightenment (Israel) 185
Raman, C. V. 209–210, 233
Ranke, Leopold von: Ankersmit and 13; on the appeal of history 50; continuing entities and 89; counter-enlightenment and 90, 93; critique of the Enlightenment of 92; embodied time of 92; the First World War and 196; Hegel and 56–57, 72, 77, 89, 94, 143; Heidegger and 217; historicism of 88–89; on historiography 9; Humboldt and 91; idealism of 92, 95; on ideas 98n11; on individual life 93; pragmatism of 60n14; realism of 91; romanticism of 96, 97; Savigny and 94; Seignobos and 196–197; on the state 94; on the task of history 91; teleology and 95; undulating history of 81, 96
reason: constitutional monarchy and 73; cunning of 74; history and 55; the Reformation and 71; romanticism and 81
Rée, Jonathan 173
reformation 62n58, 71, 95
regimes: of Antiquity and the Middle Ages 141; of historicism 214; of the nineteenth century 12, 18, 188, 195, 196; of the restoration 188; of time and temporality 10, 21n43, 190, 226
Regimes of Historicity (Hartog) 2, 5, 125n71

relations of production 128, 132, 135–137
Renaissance, the: Burckhardt and 187, 192n69; decline after 231; Nietzsche on 165, 185; Voltaire on 40; wavy time and 178, 179
representation: aspects and 22n77; defined 10; event and 226; Hegel on 74; Herder and 52; historical 57, 63n67; historical experience and 174; kairotic time and 189; the "now" and 36; political 77; time as 156; time experience and 5, 7; time regimes and 22n79
res publica 7
rhythm: of becoming 159; of Hegel's time 80; of Marx's time 132–134, 137; of Nietzsche's time 154–157, 170n71; of time regimes 6
Richardson, John 160, 161, 162, 164, 168n23, 169n53
Ricoeur, Paul: *Annales* school and 200–201; Braudel and 196, 199–201, 200, 211n26, 211n27; continuing entities and 89; experience of time and x; homogeneous time of 199; Koselleck and 199–200; on *Mrs. Dalloway* 207; on narrativism and temporality 4, 11; narrativism of 4–5; romanticism of 200–201; on time experience 16
Rise of the West (McNeill) 231
romanticism: *Annales* school and 196; Counter-Enlightenment and 80, 188; ecological problems and 230; Herder and 52; identity and 81; kairotic time and 186; reason and 81; undulating time of 96; *Weltschmerz* and 104
Rosa, Hartmut 2, 227
Rossi, Francesco de' 173
Runia, Eelco 49–50

Salomon, Albert 141
Savigny, Friedrich Carl von 92, 94
Schlegel, Karl Wilhelm Friedrich von 63n72, 70, 103, 226
Schlözer, August Ludwig von 31, 32
Scienza Nuova (Vico) 49
Second World War, the 196, 197, 214, 215, 216, 218
Sehepunkt 2
Seignobos, Charles 196–197, 197, 210n12
Short History of the English People (Green) 204
Siècle de Louis XIV (Voltaire) 40
Sittlichkeit (objectified morality) 74
Slave Market with the "Invisible" Bust of Voltaire (Dali) 116–117

Small, Robin 154
Smith, Adam 31
socialism 7, 141, 145n38, 162, 231
society: Althusser on 132–133, 135; Braudel on 199; class and 142–143; Enlightenment conception of 31; evolution and 177; the French Revolution and 11, 115–116, 118–120, 122; German 76; globalization and 232; Hegel on 71, 75; historicist conception of 13, 82; as individual 89; of Ladurie 201–202; Mandelbaum on 98n8; Marx on 127–130, 137–138; modes of production and 140; Nietzsche on 184; romanticist conception of 67; time of the modern and 27; Tocqueville on 105–112, 188–189, 195; Vico on 49
space of experience: Hartog and 5; historical time and 56; modern time and 42, 218; the past as 2, 97; the present and 17; Ricoeur and 199–200; shrinking of the present and 225
Spectres of Marx (Derrida) 141
Spinoza, Baruch 185–186
spirit 69, 80, 111, 155
Spirit of Christianity, The (Hegel) 70, 83n17
Stiglitz, Joseph 230
Strandszene in Wiek (Friedrich) 87, 96, 97n3
Study of History (Toynbee) 230
Sublime Historical Experience (Ankersmit) 97, 174
synchronicity of the non-synchronous: Aristotle and 209; in Braudel 5, 197–198, 232; in Chateaubriand 103; Dali's depiction of 116–117; in England 118–119; Enlightenment time and 18; in France 118–119; globalization and 208; in Hegel and Ranke 103; heterogeneous time and 209; historicism and modernism of 231; kairotic time and 208; in Marx 122; Marx and 131; in Michelet 127; modernization and 116; modes of production and 140, 142; non-simultaneity of the simultaneous and 18, 199; revolution and 111; spatial form of 117–118; succession of states and 142; time of the modern and 226; Tocqueville and 112; in the twentieth century 3
synchronization: the *Encyclopédie* and 33; the Enlightenment and 34, 59; Gatterer and 43n22; Hegel and 80; Herder and 53; historical change and 38; Jordheim and 55–57; progress and 51; universal history and 42

teleology 52–53, 95, 129, 143, 161, 176–177
Temps et Récit (Ricoeur) *see* Time and Narrative (Ricoeur)
Terpstra, Martin 146n56
The Mediterranean and the Mediterranean World in the Age of Philip II (Braudel) 4–5
"The Modern *Régime* of Historicity in the Face of Two World Wars" (Hartog) 4
thick description 186
This Too Is a Philosophy of History (Herder) 50–51
Thus Spoke Zarathustra (Nietzsche) 152, 157, 167, 231
time: as arrow 1; art and 68–69; becoming and 154–155; as burden 73, 94, 97, 104; change and 35; as condition 34; contradiction and 157; experience of x; historicist attitude towards 12; history and 211n14; mediating function of 35; progress and x–xi; rhythm and 154; spirit and 69; as transition 1; will and 158
Time and Narrative (Ricoeur) x, xi; discordant concordance in 195; historicist times in 4; homogeneous time of 199
time-knots 210
time nodes 156, 209
time of becoming 67, 146n41, 163, 164, 189
time of progress xi, 1–2
time of the modern: Brandom and 189; defined 2; the Enlightenment and 7, 22n63, 196; historicism and 208, 218–221, 225–226; Marx and 59; religious conceptions of time and 27; synchronicity of the non-synchronous and 226; time of the present and 3; time out of joint and 3; Woolf and 205–206
time out of joint xi, 3, 222, 226
time regimes: Aristotle and 14–15; assertions and 8; Augustine and 14; Christianity and 16; creation of xi; crisis and 11; culture and 1, 22n79; defined 6; early 14–18; in Germany 121; history of 23n80; multiple times and 21n42; of Nietzsche 167; as representations of time 10; romanticist 75, 79, 82, 96, 185; time out of joint and 221; of Tocqueville and Marx 126; tradition and 8, 15–18; the Whig-interpretation of history and 208–209

Tocqueville, Alexis de: on aristocratic society 109; burdensome time of 188; on causes of French Revolution 124n59; on centralization 116; on democracy 106, 109; embodied time of 114; on feudal times 125n64; on the future 121; on future as history 113; on general and accidental forces 111–112; Hegel and 120–121; historiography of 113; on industrialization and aristocracy 125n74; on interdetermination 111; on manners 142; Marx and 112; modernism of 105; on the past 6; on social determinism 124n48; socialism and 141; sociological aspects of 109–110; synchronicity of the non-synchronous and 112
tradition: Brandom on 8; Chakrabarty on 208–209, 233; conservatism and 95; defined 22n61; historiography and 221; horizontality and 180; modernism and 108; origin and 219; progress and 128; Tocqueville on 116
transition: ages of 103; burdensome time of 104–105; Chakrabarty on 209; Hegel and 80; Huizinga on 176, 178; incarnated time and 73, 83n30; inference and 22n71; Koselleck on 226; Marx on 133, 135; the moment and 158; synchronicity of the non-synchronous and 207; time as 1–2; Tocqueville on 114

Über die Begriff der Geschichte (Benjamin) 216
Übermensch (superman) 152, 167, 175, 178
undulating history 81
undulating time: continuing entities and 96–97; of Hegel 188; of Hölderlin 86; Huizinga and 215; intrigue and 200–201; kairotic time and 203; organicism and 70; Ricoeur and 211n27; romanticism and 81–82, 230; transition and 83n30
universal history 31–34, 38, 41, 43n29, 90, 98n12
Universal History (Schlözer) 32
Untergang des Abendlandes (Spengler) 230

Untimely Meditations (Nietzsche) 152, 163, 165
Use and Abuse of History for Life (Nietzsche) 165

Vico, Giambattista 48–49, 50
Volksgeist (spirit of the people) 80, 94, 99n45
Voltaire 27, 39–40
Vorlesungen über die Philosophie der Geschichte (Hegel) *see Philosophy of World History* (Hegel)

Waning of the Middle Ages, The (Huizinga) 181, 183–185
Watteau, Jean-Antoine 28–30
Wealth of Nations (Smith) 31
Weber, Max 23n91, 75, 84n50, 109, 123n30, 123n32
Weltanschauung 12–13, 14
Weltgeist (world-spirit) 56, 59, 62n58, 73
Welthistorische Persönlichkeit (World-historical figure) 56
Weltschmerz 104
Whig-historians 42, 204–205, 212n46
Whig Interpretation of History, The (Butterfield) 204–205
White, Hayden: on modernization 112; on practical philosophy 143; on Ranke 95; on Tocqueville 22n75, 62n42, 106, 109, 112–113, 124n43, 143
will 155, 158
will of the state 78
will points 152, 155–156, 167, 168n23, 170n74
will to truth, the 152, 160–161
Wood, Allen 46
Woolf, Virginia 195, 205–207, 210, 212n52, 212n56
world history 199; continuing entities and 89; Hegel on 99n54; Idea and 73; Michelet on 127; Ranke on 91, 95–96; rise and fall and 79; romanticism and 230

Zeitgeist 48
Zur Kritik der Hegelschen Rechtsphilosophie (Marx) 139